Politics and the Political Imagination in Later Stuart Britain

Politics and the Political Imagination in Later Stuart Britain

Essays Presented to Lois Green Schwoerer

edited by
Howard Nenner

 UNIVERSITY OF ROCHESTER PRESS

Copyright © 1997 Contributors

All Rights Reserved. Except as permitted under current legislation, no part of this work may be photocopied, stored in a retrieval system, published, performed in public, adapted, broadcast, transmitted, recorded or reproduced in any form or by any means, without the prior permission of the copyright owner.

First published 1997
1–878822–95–0

University of Rochester Press
668 Mt. Hope Avenue
Rochester, New York 14620, USA
and at P.O. Box 9, Woodbridge, Suffolk IP12 3DF, UK

Library of Congress Cataloging-in-Publication Data

Politics and the political imagination in later Stuart Britain :
  essays presented to Lois Green Schwoerer / edited by Howard Nenner.
    p.   cm.
  ISBN 1–878822–95–0 (alk. paper)
  1. Great Britain—Politics and government—1660–1688.
  2. Political science—Great Britain—History—17th century.
  3. Great Britain—History—Revolution of 1688.   I. Schwoerer, Lois G.
  II. Nenner, Howard.
  DA435.P65   1997
  941.06—dc21   97–40133
                                                               CIP

British Library Cataloguing-in-Publication Data

A catalogue record for this book is available from the British Library

This publication is printed on acid-free paper
Printed in the United States of America
Designed and Typeset by Cornerstone Composition Services

Contents

Notes on Contributors vii
Preface ix
Introduction   Howard Nenner 1

PART I. THE POLITICS OF VIOLENCE AND REVOLUTION

1. J. G. A. Pocock
   "Wicked and Turbulent Though It Was": The Restoration Era in Perspective 9
2. Howard Nenner
   The Trial of the Regicides: Retribution and Treason in 1660 21
3. Mark Goldie
   The Hilton Gang and the Purge of London in the 1680s 43
4. Melinda Zook
   Violence, Martyrdom, and Radical Politics: Rethinking the Glorious Revolution 75
5. Tim Harris
   Reluctant Revolutionaries? The Scots and the Revolution of 1688–89 . . . 97

PART II. THE PLAY OF POLITICAL IMAGINATION

6. Janelle Greenberg and Laura Marin
   Politics and Memory: Sharnborn's Case and the Role of the Norman Conquest in Stuart Political Thought 121
7. Hilda L. Smith
   "A General War amongst the Men but None amongst the Women": Political Differences between Margaret and William Cavendish 143
8. Linda Levy Peck
   Constructing a New Context for Hobbes Studies 161
9. Steven N. Zwicker
   Irony, Modernity, and Miscellany: Politics and Aesthetics in the Stuart Restoration 181

10. LOIS GREEN SCHWOERER
The Shape of Restoration England: A Response 197

Selected Publications of Lois Green Schwoerer 223
Index 225

Contributors

MARK GOLDIE is Lecturer in History at the University of Cambridge and Vice-Master of Churchill College. He studied at Sussex University and was a Research Fellow at Gonville and Caius College, Cambridge. He has published many articles on politics, religion, and ideas in seventeenth- and eighteenth-century Britain. He is co-editor with Tim Harris and Paul Seaward of *The Politics of Religion in Restoration England* (1990) and with J. H. Burns of *The Cambridge History of Political Thought, 1450–1700* (1991); he is editor of *John Locke: Two Treatises of Government* (1993) and *John Locke: Political Essays* (1997).

JANELLE GREENBERG is Associate Professor of History at the University of Pittsburgh. She is co-author with Corinne C. Weston of *Subjects and Sovereigns: The Grand Controversy over Legal Sovereignty in Stuart England* (1981). She has recently completed "'St. Edward's Ghost': The Radical Face of the Ancient Constitution in Stuart Political England," a book-length study of the ways in which Stuart radicals used medieval history and law to legitimate rebellion.

TIM HARRIS is Professor of History at Brown University. He is the author of *London Crowds in the Reign of Charles II: Propaganda and Politics from the Restoration until the Exclusion Crisis* (1987) and *Politics under the Later Stuarts: Party Conflict in a Divided Society, 1660–1715* (1993). He is the editor of *Popular Culture in England, c. 1500–1850* (1995) and co-editor with Paul Seaward and Mark Goldie of *The Politics of Religion in Restoration England* (1990). His study "British Revolutions: The Emergence of the Modern State, 1660–1707" is to be published by Penguin. He is also editing volume 2 of a projected five-volume edition of Roger Morrice's "Entring Book."

LAURA MARIN took an M.A. at Harvard University. She is an independent scholar working in Pittsburgh.

HOWARD NENNER is Roe/Straut Professor in the Humanities and Professor of History at Smith College. He is the author of *By Colour of Law: Legal Culture and Constitutional Politics in England, 1660–1689* (1977) and *The Right to be King: The Succession to the Crown of England, 1603–1714* (1995). His current project is a study of regicide in seventeenth-century English politics and political thought.

LINDA LEVY PECK is Professor of History at George Washington University and a member of the steering committee of the Center for the History of British Political Thought at the Folger Shakespeare Library. She is the author of *Northampton: Patronage and Policy at the Court of James I* (1982) and editor of *The Mental World of the Jacobean Court* (1991). Her *Court Patronage and Corruption in Early Stuart England* (1990) was awarded the annual John Ben Snow Prize by the North

American Conference on British Studies in 1991 for the best book in British history and the social sciences by a North American author. She is currently completing a book on Britain in the age of the baroque.

J. G. A. POCOCK is Harry C. Black Professor of History Emeritus at The Johns Hopkins University. Among his major publications are *The Ancient Constitution and the Feudal Law: A Study of English Historical Thought in the Seventeenth Century* (1957; reissued with a Retrospect, 1987) and *The Machiavellian Moment: Florentine Political Thought and the Atlantic Republican Tradition* (1975). He is currently completing the first two volumes of a projected four-volume study of "Barbarism and Religion: Civil History in Gibbon's *Decline and Fall*."

LOIS GREEN SCHWOERER is Elmer Louis Kayser Professor of History Emeritus at George Washington University and former president of the North American Conference on British Studies. She is a Fellow of the Royal Historical Society and, since 1982, a member of the steering committee of the Center for the History of British Political Thought at the Folger Shakespeare Library. Her publications (see "Selected Publications of Lois Green Schwoerer," 223) have garnered numerous awards. Among these were the award of the Berkshire Conference of Women Historians for *No Standing Armies!* for the best book published by a woman historian in 1975 and Honorable Mention in the John Ben Snow Foundation Prize competition for the best book in British studies published in 1981 and 1982 by a North American author, for *The Declaration of Rights, 1689*. Her current project, nearing completion, is "'The Ingenious Mr. Henry Care': A Restoration Polemicist. Print Culture, Politics, Law and Ideology, 1670–1688."

HILDA L. SMITH is Associate Professor of History at the University of Cincinnati, where she has also served as director of Women's Studies. She is the author of *Reason's Disciples: Seventeenth-Century English Feminists* (1982) and co-compiler with Susan Cardinale of *Women and the Literature of the Seventeenth Century: An Annotated Bibliography Based on Wing's Short Title Catalogue* (1990), selected as one of the best bibliographies in history for 1990 and 1991 by *Reference Quarterly*. She is editor of *Women Writers and the Early Modern British Tradition* (forthcoming from Cambridge University Press) and has recently completed a manuscript on the operation of the false universal in early modern thought.

MELINDA ZOOK is Assistant Professor of History at Purdue University. A specialist in late Stuart political culture, she has published articles in the *Journal of British Studies* and *Albion*. She is currently finishing a book-length manuscript on radical Whig politics and ideology.

STEVEN N. ZWICKER is Professor of English and co-director of the Literature and History Program at Washington University, St. Louis. He is the author of *Dryden's Political Poetry: The Typology of King and Nation* (1972), *Politics and Language in Dryden's Poetry: The Arts of Disguise* (1984), and *Lines of Authority: Politics and English Literary Culture, 1649–1689* (1993). He is co-editor with Kevin Sharpe of *Politics of Discourse: The Literature and History of Seventeenth-Century England* (1987). Among his forthcoming books is *Selected Poems of John Dryden* (Penguin).

Preface

This volume presented to Lois Green Schwoerer had its genesis in a symposium in April 1996 to commemorate Professor Schwoerer's retirement from the Elmer Louis Kayser Chair of History at George Washington University. The symposium, sponsored by the University and superbly organized by Edward Berkowitz, the chair of GW's Department of History, brought together a group of scholars to discuss the principal topics that have been central to Lois Schwoerer's interest during a distinguished scholarly career: politics, political thought, and the political role of women in later Stuart Britain.

It is fair to say, and obvious to all who know her, that Lois Schwoerer, having retired from teaching and the burdens of administration, has in no way taken leave of scholarship. Her research at her second home, the Folger Shakespeare Library, goes on, as does the stream of publications that has excited and informed the field of Stuart historical studies for more than two decades. It is also true that retirement has not diminished her interest in junior members of the profession, for whom she has been and continues to be both inspiration and friend.

Ed Berkowitz had the idea of collecting the essays into a presentation volume and asked me to be the editor. In assuming that role, I have been fortunate to have the cooperation of the individual authors, especially that of Mark Goldie and Tim Harris, both of whom were unable to participate in the symposium, yet who were pleased to be included and to submit chapters under the pressure of very tight deadlines. I am indebted to Chris Forgey for her research assistance, and to Sean Culhane, director of the University of Rochester Press, for his interest and understanding, and, most of all, for his encouragement. There are, however, no words with any approximation of adequacy to express my gratitude to Pamela White. Were it not for her comprehensive knowledge of seventeenth-century Britain and her meticulous copyediting in the most challenging circumstances, this volume might have fallen far short of the high editorial standard it deserves.

The essays that follow are divided into two parts, bracketed by the editor's brief introduction and the honoree's extended response. It is surely no surprise that Lois Schwoerer wanted to have, has had, and is plainly entitled to have—the last word.

Howard Nenner
Northampton, Massachusetts
July 1997

INTRODUCTION

Howard Nenner

I

For most of the twentieth century, the period of the Restoration through the Revolution has been a stepchild of Stuart historiography. During that time, when the Glorious Revolution was widely regarded as a footnote to the upheavals of the mid-seventeenth century, historians were much more concerned to explain the cataclysm of the Civil War and the anomaly of the Interregnum, those tumultuous times when Britain, if not the world, had been turned upside down. By contrast, it was generally accepted that what had transpired in 1688–89 was essentially conservative. At the end of the eighteenth century, Burke saw those events as "a revolution not made but prevented"; in the middle of the nineteenth century, Macaulay pronounced them "a revolution strictly defensive"; and early in our own century, Trevelyan applied the label "a sensible revolution."[1] In its historiographical essence it was the revolution that never was, a phenomenon which had been prophetically prefigured in a sermon by Gilbert Burnet in December 1688: "We have before us," he said, "a work that seems to our selves a dream, and that will appear to posterity a fiction."[2] It is no wonder, then, that scholars have found it more inviting to explore the breakdown of Caroline government and the rupture of political, constitutional, and religious orthodoxy that characterized the decades between 1640 and 1660. Whereas the quiet Revolution of 1688–89 was satisfying for its moderation, the clamorous Civil War was exciting for its excess. And because Whig historians had been so persuasive in their assumptions about the Elizabethan and Jacobean antecedents of the Civil War, scholars tended to look backward from the midcentury rather than forward.

Nonetheless, the Revolution, however muted, never surrendered its historiographical importance. Celebrated in the Whig canon for its sobriety and its sensible avoidance of violence, it also explained the seventeenth-century endgame in the progress from absolutism to constitutionalism: law, liberty, and religion, at repeated risk of succumbing to tyranny, had been defended and preserved. Whig historians saw the Revolution and its attendant settlement as restorative, and, in the same way that they understood the restoration of the monarchy three decades earlier, they located the success of the Revolution in the avoidance of bloodshed and innovation. They believed that the work of reestablishing the constitution, having been begun in the Parliaments of the 1620s, having grown more urgent in the 1640s, and having overcome religious fanaticism and military despotism in 1660, was, by 1689, effectively complete.

The Whig fashion in Stuart scholarship, focused for so long in the framework of a perceived struggle between absolutism and constitutionalism, began to lose ground in the period after World War II when the historiographical battleground shifted to the economic and social causes of the Civil War, specifically to the role of the gentry. Then, in the 1970s, in a striking assault on the Whig tradition, a new school of revisionists sought to demolish the "myth" of Jacobean and early Caroline opposition politics by demonstrating that prior to 1640, and particularly during the putatively turbulent 1620s, the kings' Parliaments were for the most part compliantly engaged in nothing more radical than doing the king's business. The results of that revisionism were that instead of looking to long-term explanations for the causes of the Civil War, the focus of Stuart specialists narrowed to the years immediately before the outbreak of war, while at the same time broadening in another direction to encompass the interrelationship of Charles I's three British kingdoms.[3]

The effect of these shifts was to place English affairs in a wider British context and to reject the model of an arbitrary government pitted against the rule of law. As to the broader view, Britain seen whole, it is certain that the major political episodes of the seventeenth century, notably the Civil War and the Glorious Revolution, are no longer susceptible of being understood without reference to "the problem of multiple kingdoms"—to Ireland and Scotland as well as to England.[4] And in the matter of the Revolution, it would be impossible to understand the full complexity of that event without calculating the larger European interests of the French and the Dutch. But it is ironic that in respect of the dichotomy of absolutism and constitutionalism, the historiographical wheel has seemingly come full circle. Recent work has again brought the issue of early Stuart absolutism into sharp relief,[5] an effect of which has been to underscore the conviction of most later Stuart historians that the specter of royal absolutism, at least after 1660, is not to be dismissed as a product of the Whig imagination. Charles II and James II were not only moving Britain back in the direction of Catholicism, they were effectively threatening to relocate legislative sovereignty exclusively in the king. There is also much to be said for the agents of opposition being interested in something more than restoring the ancient constitution and not being content to confine their opposition to the accepted channels of political discourse. From the work of the current generation of historians, notably that of Lois Schwoerer, it is clear that later Stuart politics needs to be reexamined and understood for what it was—often radical and more than occasionally violent. That, in large measure, is what the essays in this collection are about.

II

As absolutism revived after the failure of Exclusion, and then accelerated critically in the years of James II's reign, political opposition to royal policies took a distinctly radical turn. That radicalism bred violence at both ends of the political spectrum. Among the more radical Whigs there was a move toward extremism as Parliament was now foreclosed as an avenue of resistance to the encroachments of Catholicism. The result, discussed in Melinda Zook's essay, was an intensified climate of seditious rhetoric, assassination plots, and conspiracies for rebellion. Zook argues that Whig writers "created an ideology that legitimized violence as a political tool" (76), and that radical Whigs translated that discourse into agitation and insurrection. Extremist measures were not, however, confined to the Stuart opposition. Violent politics on the margins of the law was also a mark of royal policy, explored by Mark Goldie in his chapter on the Hilton gang, a team of government informers that in the 1680s conducted a vicious campaign of harassment and persecution of Dissenters in London. Like Zook's radical elite, Goldie's meaner sort of "men and women with murky pasts and grubby motives" (68) were not loath to act illegally or to put violence in the service of politics. The difference was that the Hiltons, at times acting brazenly outside the law, were the personal, even if unofficial, agents of the king. In the same vein of government-approved violence, my chapter on the trials of the regicides examines the return to England of an "absolute" king and brings into focus the nation's need to expiate its sins of rebellion and regicide in a ritual of blood. Those trials, dispensing royal vengeance and uneven justice, reveal one of the darker hues of the image of reconciliation so often depicted in the restoration of the throne. Then, looking beyond the boundaries of England and appealing for a multiple-kingdoms approach to 1688–89, Tim Harris demonstrates that the Revolution was not simply imported into Scotland. His analysis of the Scottish events of 1688–89 argues persuasively for a more radical understanding of the Revolution and its attendant settlement in that northern Stuart kingdom. As Harris has demonstrated in the activities of the Scots, and as Zook has written of the radical Whigs in the decade of the 1680s, these committed opponents of Stuart policies can scarcely be characterized as "reluctant revolutionaries."

In an essay on "Politics and Aesthetics in the Stuart Restoration," Steven Zwicker concludes that "it was the very form of politics in the rule of Charles II that structured its pleasures, its poetry, even its imagination" (193). That observation can easily be extended to the reign of James II. Certainly the role of the political imagination was no less important to the Revolution than it had been to the period of the Restoration. As an example, radical politics could claim a purchase on respectability when expressed in the language of the law, and especially when invoking ancient precedent. This is persuasively illustrated in the treatment by Janelle Greenberg and Laura Marin of *Sharnborn v. Warenne*, an eleventh-century case that resulted in the affirmation of a Saxon's post-Conquest right to hold land according to his pre-Conquest tenure. Greenberg and Marin, following Greenberg's earlier work on the radicalizing of the ancient constitution, show the ways in which seventeenth-century writers appropriated the case and invested it with radical and creative meaning to prove that William I and his successors ruled by compact and not by conquest.

Professor Zwicker, who as much as any of the contributors to this volume appreciates the imaginative power of language, doubts that the conventions of the ancient constitution and mixed monarchy were susceptible of sustained belief in the decades following the Restoration. John Pocock, equally impressed with the cynicism of the age, might agree; Greenberg and Marin likely would not. Yet in respect of those conventions, all would accept that by 1680 the advance of royal absolutism had significantly undermined most contemporaries' political confidence, if not their constitutional convictions. Certainly there can be no doubting the anxious concern about the growth of absolutism as a continuing theme of the later Stuart period. Nor is there any question of the assertive, and sometimes defensive, royalist insistence that a distinction be drawn between absolute monarchy and arbitrary rule. This is evident as early as 1660, when apologists for a king who could "do no wrong" were at the same time scrupulous in emphasizing that Charles II ruled "within the bounds of the law."[6] In his analysis of *Absalom and Achitophel*, Zwicker makes particular note of Dryden's defense of his king, carefully distinguishing between the celebration of patriarchalism and the charge of tyranny. Hilda Smith also strikes the chord of absolutism, particularly in her extended treatment of the duke of Newcastle's letter of advice to Charles II in anticipation of the king's restoration to his throne. Smith argues that Margaret Cavendish's political and social views diverged at a number of points from those of her husband, notably on the status of women and in the matter of freedom of conscience, but there is little to suggest significant differences between the couple on the positive value of prerogative rule. In the duke's Hobbesian view of the world and his desire for England to be restored to patriarchal order, there were no acceptable alternatives to a sovereign king.

The early twentieth-century view of the American jurist Oliver Wendell Holmes, Jr., that law is "not a brooding omnipresence in the sky, but the articulate voice of some sovereign"[7] can be read as an epitome of seventeenth-century English constitutional tension. Whether dealing with the immediacy of politics or the remove of political imagination, each of the essays in this collection treats people who struggled with the issues of sovereignty and the right of resistance. At one end of the constitutional balance were those who would have taken Holmes's epigram one critical step further and agreed with Filmer and Hobbes that law is the will of the sovereign. More to the point, they were persuaded that it was the king who was sovereign, not the law, not Parliament, and certainly not the people. John Dryden's defense of an absolute king, like that of many of his contemporaries, was born of that specific fear of a sovereign people.[8] At the other end of the balance were those who insisted that the king was obliged to rule according to the law and believed that should he violate that law, the people would have the right to resist. John Pocock speaks eloquently to this tension in his assertion of "the cynicism and not uncommon demoralization which afflicted the Restoration mind" (15). Pocock is especially concerned to describe how the cynicism of the age proceeded from an inability to explain the recent past of civil war, regicide, and republican rule, and from the insecurity of the present, to deal with phantom religious scapegoats and active secular plotters who threatened once again to destabilize an ordered society.

Law was not the only "brooding omnipresence" to hover over the era of the Restoration; the unsettling spirit of Thomas Hobbes appears to have been much in evidence as well. It is therefore fitting that Linda Levy Peck should attempt to discover more than the little that we know at present about the court career of the early Hobbes. Much has been written about the continental humanist influence on Hobbes, especially his contacts with French and Italian political theorists, but Peck breaks important new ground by resituating Hobbes's early political thought in an English as well as a wider European context. The implication of that finding is to provide further evidence of the continuity of English political ideas, especially of the English attraction to absolutist theory well before Charles II and James II made that theory a looming reality. It is hardly surprising, then, that Hobbes and Hobbesian thought appear in several guises in this volume's essays. Hilda Smith, for example, wrestles with the uncertainty of Hobbes's influence on the duchess of Newcastle, while Steven Zwicker speaks of Dryden's concern to distinguish patriarchal royalism from the taint of Hobbesian tyranny. And when John Pocock cites the 1683 Oxford book burning, in which half of the books destroyed were justifying resistance to monarchy while the other half were condemning it, he notes that Hobbes, whom he sees as a principal intellectual cause of Restoration insecurity, got much of the blame (12).

III

If none of the essays in the present volume appears to overstate the radicalism, the violence, the gathering absolutism, or the immoderate temper of the later Stuart age, and if we can subscribe comfortably to John Pocock's elaboration of the Restoration era as "wicked and turbulent," this is in substantial measure owing to the scholarship of Lois Schwoerer. We are more accepting of Restoration radicalism today because for nearly a quarter of a century Schwoerer has been persuasively arguing that point, especially in *The Declaration of Rights* (1981), her landmark study of the significance of the Revolution. Although the Revolution of 1688–89 might have been "sensible," she has insisted that we would be mistaken to celebrate it—or alternatively, to dismiss it—as having been essentially conservative. Whereas Macaulay confidently asserted the classic Whig view that "not a single flower of the crown was touched,"[9] Schwoerer, in a meticulous analysis of the declaration, concluded that the Revolution created a new kingship as well as offering up a new king. It may have been expedient for the members of the Convention to contend that their challenge to the dispensing and suspending powers, and their condemnation of a standing army without the consent of Parliament, were informed by settled law, but Schwoerer has shown how innovative and radical that contention was.

It might seem, therefore, to be a curious irony for John Pocock, in the essay that follows, to label Schwoerer a Whig historian, were it not that his stated intention is to invoke the "Whig commitment to the history of laws and constitutions" (11). By this description, Lois Schwoerer is very much a Whig. Her published work and her years of teaching testify as much. Through her scholarly output on the Revolution she has bid fair to making that subject her own. Certainly no one who in the last two decades has written on 1688–89 has failed—or can have afforded to fail—to take her work on board. The positions that she has staked out have increasingly come to be the starting point for any who would enter upon a study of that disorderly time. Not that those positions have won universal acceptance. Her assigning the success of the Revolution settlement to the role of the radical Whigs in the Convention has, for example, stimulated considerable controversy and debate. Yet in respect of the intellectual excitement that that controversy has generated, the outcome has been altogether to the good. One result is that some of the best in a new generation of historians have been drawn from the extensively charted ground of the Civil War to the "wicked and turbulent" terrain of the Restoration and Revolution. Schwoerer can take a large share of the credit for that result.

Schwoerer's interests, of course, have not been confined to the Revolution, but it is clear from her early work that she was already being drawn to the major constitutional issues of the Stuart era. In her first book, *No Standing Armies!* (1974), she explored the periodic eruptions of anti-army protest over the span of the seventeenth century, illustrating Parliament's defensive preference for the militia and underscoring the crises arising from opposition to an army under the government's control. From the early hostility to billeting and martial law expressed in the Petition of Right in 1628 to the standing army controversy of 1697–99, the subset of issues varied according to the changing political climate, yet the underlying theme and anticipation of a fearful slide into absolutism remained the same. However plausible the need might have been at any time for military security, the resort to a national army was always perceived as a threat to English liberties. The resulting tension created a precarious balance, and twice in the century that balance became so unstable as to tip the state into the dethroning of its king. In this regard, Schwoerer's treatment of the standing army controversy pointed to that persistent suspicion of absolutism. Although considering different issues, the essays that follow address this same overarching problem, the unresolved tension between a desire for monarchical stability and the apprehension of an emerging tyranny.

Schwoerer's interest in the parliamentary and polemical protests against standing armies set the stage for her later excursions into Stuart political radicalism. Taken as a whole, her work has developed as an integrated study of the ways in which that radicalism was molded and expressed in the England of the late seventeenth century. In the realm of political thought, she has made important contributions to the understanding of John Locke, Lockean ideas, and Whig resistance theory. Yet in none of her writings has she been seduced by disembodied abstractions. Her work is consistently grounded in the constitutional and political context of later Stuart England, and for that reason it has been successful in limning that complicated age. Schwoerer, as much as any working historian, has understood the political power of the printed word, not only in her extended treatment of its most conspicuous manifestation, the Declaration of Rights, but also in her studies of the role of the press and the uses of political propaganda, the shaping of images in political trials, and lately in her current project on the career of the Restoration controversialist Henry Care.[10] In a related vein, her careful explorations of the symbols and images of majesty and royal authority have demonstrated an archaeologist's appreciation of material remains as keys to a political culture. [11]

Perhaps most important, Lois Schwoerer has been, and continues to be, an indefatigable researcher who is never content to complete any study before she has exhausted all the known resources—and then some. This trait, well known to her colleagues and students, is what led her to the important discovery and subsequent publication of "A Jornall of the Convention at Westminster begun the 22 of January 1688/9," a manuscript record of the critical House of Commons debate on the abdication of the king and the vacancy of the throne. It may also be what led her in 1984, in a prize-winning essay, "Seventeenth-Century English Women Engraved in Stone?" to challenge Lawrence Stone's treatment of "the family, sex and marriage."[12] Observing that Stone seemed at the time to be little interested in women's history, she called him specifically to account for what she believed was his myopic neglect of sources that could have corrected his "masculine perspective."[13] This critical exercise, which served to stimulate Schwoerer's already considerable interest in the political role of Stuart women, moved her to closer examination of Mary II and the conviction that there was more to be said about the part played by women in general, and Mary in particular, in the era of the Revolution. It also resulted in her third major work, a book-length study of Lady Rachel Russell that affirms her argument that we act at our peril if we dismiss seventeenth-century aristocratic wives as mere appendages and echoes of their husbands.[14] A principal architect of Lord William Russell's inflated reputation as a Whig martyr, Lady Russell demonstrated the power of the political imagination in seventeenth-century discourse. By the authority of her impeccable scholarship, so, too, has Lois Schwoerer.

Notes

1. "Speech on the Army Estimates, 1790," in *The Works of Edmund Burke* (New York, 1937), 1:454; Lord Macaulay, *The History of England*, ed. C. H. Firth (London, 1913–15), 3:1306; G. M. Trevelyan, *The English Revolution, 1688–1689* (New York, 1965), 3.

2. Gilbert Burnet, *A Sermon Preached In the Chapel of St. James's Before His Highness the Prince of Orange the 23rd of December, 1688* (Edinburgh, 1689), 1.

3. See especially Conrad Russell, *The Causes of the English Civil War* (Oxford, 1990); Conrad Russell, *The Fall of the British Monarchies, 1637–1642* (Oxford, 1991).

4. Russell, *Causes of the English Civil War*, chap. 2.
5. See Glenn Burgess, *Absolute Monarchy and the Stuart Constitution* (New Haven, 1996).
6. See Nenner, chap. 2, 26–27.
7. See Holmes's dissenting opinion in *Southern Pacific Co. v. Jensen* (1917) as quoted in James Willard Hurst, *Justice Holmes on Legal History* (New York, 1964), 4.
8. See Zwicker, chap. 9, 184.
9. Macaulay, *History of England*, 3:1308.
10. Her book manuscript, in progress, is provisionally entitled "'The Ingenious Mr. Henry Care': A Restoration Polemicist. Print Culture, Politics, Law, and Ideology, 1670–1688."
11. For Schwoerer's published work, see "Selected Publications of Lois Green Schwoerer," 223–24.
12. Lawrence Stone, *The Family, Sex and Marriage in England, 1500–1800* (New York, 1977).
13. Lois G. Schwoerer, "Seventeenth-Century English Women Engraved in Stone?" *Albion* 16 (1984): 390.
14. In this regard see Smith, chap. 7.

Part I
The Politics of Violence and Revolution

"Wicked and Turbulent Though It Was":
The Restoration Era in Perspective

J. G. A. Pocock

"Wicked" and "turbulent" were the adjectives well chosen to describe the reign of Charles II by Sir William Blackstone, a great jurist and constitutionalist whom I am sure Lois Schwoerer admires no less for Jonathan Clark's discovery that he was a Tory. As Blackstone uses them, however, the two adjectives make a concessive clause: "wicked, sanguinary and turbulent though it was," he says, the reign produced some major achievements for the rule of law and the liberty of the subject, chief among them the Habeas Corpus Act.[1] This dictum, I think, is well suited to an occasion in honor of Lois Schwoerer, because—like Caroline Robbins before her—she is a leading historian who is at heart a constitutionalist and sees the rule of law and its achievement as important keys to what we have been doing in history, on those occasions, at least, when we have managed to do anything. To adopt this perspective is enough to get one called a Whig historian, and as was once said to me of Caroline Robbins, Lois Schwoerer is a Whig; but I am myself a former pupil of Herbert Butterfield and am in a position to testify that there is a difference between a Whig tendency to write complacently progressive histories and a Whig commitment to the history of laws and constitutions.[2] Whigs know, Butterfield knew, and Blackstone knew, that achievements in the rule of law, and government according to law, are hard to bring off and hard to sustain; sometimes, indeed, they are achieved by unworthy instruments in unlikely circumstances, and that was the point of Blackstone's observation concerning the reign of Charles II. It was not a scene of which, nor was it populated by characters of whom, much good might reasonably be expected; yet habeas corpus was achieved and did persist.

Lois Schwoerer has always insisted that we should look on the Revolution of 1688–89 in much the same way. At best, that amazing and unpredicted transaction was a spectacular display of reason of state rising above the restraints of common morality; daughters dethroned their father, even the sanitized version of *King Lear* was hard to perform for many years, and what William of Orange and John Churchill severally did is still enough to take your breath away if you think about it. At worst, the Revolution came close to uncoupling church and Crown and left both England and Scotland recurrently at the brink of civil war for the next sixty or so years. Yet Professor Schwoerer has staunchly and rightly insisted that the Declaration of Rights was a legislative achievement which established with finality that certain Crown practices had been and henceforth would be illegal, and that this is a moment of significance in a constitutional history we had better continue to regard as important. There was plenty of wickedness and turbulence still afoot, and yet these things were achieved. It is not Whiggish in the pejorative sense to say that they were achieved, only to write as if everything revolved around them. Sir William Blackstone knew the difference, and so does Lois Schwoerer; and even those who in the next century denounced the Revolution for trebling the influence of the Crown did not deny that it had set limits to its prerogative.

What was it, then, that made the era appear particularly wicked and turbulent, and how is this related to the history of the constitution—given, as I think unalterable, that there is such a thing? Any generation may find itself living in turbulent times and obliged to act accordingly, but (to adapt the old saying) to be wicked you have to work at it. Did the politicians of the Restoration and Revolution work at being wicked? As a firm believer in original sin, I am reluctant to believe that they were inherently wickeder than other people; but were they acting in a particularly wicked way? The incidence of judicial murder was unusually high for some years in the late seventies and early eighties, and there were moments, one from each side, when something like a limited reign of terror was going on; but reigns of terror as we know them are tyrannies of virtue, and these were launched by neither the saints nor their enemies in seventeenth-century England. Perhaps what we are inclined to find wicked about the political homicides of Charles II's reign was the outspoken and frequently brutal lack of principle with which they were conducted; the killing was both ideological and insincere, carried out by men who believed neither in the guilt of their victims nor in the moral grounds they themselves alleged. Our conventional image of the Restoration is an image of cynicism, coupled, of course, with one of picturesque but not elegant sexual misdoings in high society. This (the cynicism, not the fornication) is one of our principal reasons for thinking of the age as wicked; what are its sources?

If one thing is certain, it is that the image of cynicism was one that the public mind of the Restoration held of itself; self-accusations of the kind abound in the literature, and they are in a way self-justifying. People do not accuse themselves of cynicism unless they are rather drastically unsure of themselves, that is, of how far they believe what otherwise they know they ought to believe; unsure, as a further consequence, of the exact grounds on which they ought to believe it. Thomas Hobbes got much of the blame for this. In the great Oxford book burning of 1683, approximately half of the numerous propositions condemned justify resistance to monarchy, while the other half condemn resistance on Hobbesian grounds. We know, of course, that Hobbes was a cynic only in the philosophical sense. He believed very strongly in the need for a social and political morality, but he could not see his way to providing it with theological or metaphysical foundations as strong as the age wanted it to have. If he feared God—and it's not sure he didn't—he feared that God might not judge mankind for its misdeeds, but might leave it to endure their consequences, living in a perpetual exile without the terrible comforts of prophecy—and what kind of God was that? He told men not that they should get away with what they could, but that this was how they assuredly would behave and that God might not care very much about correcting their ways. If Hobbes's contemporaries denounced him for not fearing God, it was because they feared they did not fear God enough themselves, and more darkly feared that their failure to fear Him might be justified. Perhaps He did not care? Perhaps He was not there? There was a silence, and Hobbes was blamed for it.

Thus, Thomas Hobbes does have a role in this matter of Restoration wickedness. The Victorians, a sexually minded generation, took it to have been largely a matter of immorality in court circles and the London theaters and the vicinity of my Lord Rochester; they represented it as an explosion of libertinism—again more brutal than stylish—after the repressive rule of the Puritans. This has, of course, been challenged. The Puritans were not nearly such wowsers as the Evangelicals and Methodists the Victorians knew so well, and yet it can still be maintained that they had tried to commit the English to very high ideals and had failed in that purpose to the point where a reaction against godliness occurred. And yet there is more to it than a Rule of the Saints having been gratuitously attempted and having failed, and we need to identify that something more in order to understand Restoration cynicism. The noble but intrusive idealism of Puritans like Milton, the intense moral seriousness which George Fox noted among the ordinary people,[3] occurred in the context of a civil war which the serious and the high-minded had wanted no more than anybody else and did not want to think they had caused—as perhaps they had not. We can never overestimate the impact on the English of all classes of the Civil Wars, the regicide, and the deep uncertainties of the 1650s, a set of experiences which they had not desired, hated as they have hated nothing else in their history, and found incredibly difficult to explain to themselves. The tough minded, of course, saw that the effort to explain it was itself the heart of the problem. Thomas May, whose *History of the Parliament* is a neglected and underpraised analysis, made the point that it was probably a mistake to represent the First Civil War as a war of religion, since in the matter of Charles I's supposed popish leanings, the smoking gun could never be found (at least before they read his letters after Naseby), and a backlash of opinion occurred in the king's favor; whereas in the matter of his governing contrary to law, there were smoking guns wherever one looked.[4] A point to be made here is that precisely because nobody had wanted civil war, it was hard to explain how it had happened; and because of this, it was necessary to find both deep-seated causes to explain its origins and high principles, of whatever kind, to justify its continuance. Any rule by the saints, any attempt by high-minded republicans to transform the English people, has to be placed in this context, and it may be contended that a principal cause of Restoration cynicism is the simple fact that they had all failed in turn to explain what was happening. Each attempt was replaced in its turn by new needs to explain new emergencies, with the result not only that high ideals were seen as profoundly hypocritical, producing cynicism toward others, but that there was no satisfactory explanation by which the English could understand what they had been doing since 1640—thus making them deeply cynical toward themselves. Charles II, it was notorious, could not believe in the integrity of anyone's motives, which clearly meant that he did not believe in his own—as Ronald Hutton says, there was something missing at the heart of him[5]—and in the circumstances of the Restoration, a king who did not believe in himself, succeeding a father who had believed in himself far too much, was deeply disturbing to everyone's sense of his own integrity.

Here it is possible to fit Thomas Hobbes back into the picture. The relatively conservative "revisionist" readings of the Civil War that we now favor contain, it seems, this important truth: the wars happened in part (no explanation is total) because of a breakdown of consensus as to how the king could exercise that headship of the church, combined with that headship of the realm probably in Parliament, which the Tudors had made the necessary structure of the kingdom. In addition, there seemed to be irreconcilable differences as to how that headship was to be restored. A catastrophic breaking point was reached when leaders controlling armed force decided to liquidate the whole problem and the monarchy with it, but this revolutionary solution could not be sustained. Since we are all Enlightened liberals at heart, we are self-programmed to look for a solution in terms of religious pluralism and toleration, the separation of church and state; and we have to force ourselves to realize that this solution was simply not available, since it could be enforced only by a power so little legitimized that it must rely on revolutionary dictatorship and armed force. This being so, the most farseeing, and also in most cases the most conservative, were those who saw they were dealing with a country that could not be legitimately governed unless there was a national religious structure of some kind with a sovereign at its head who was part of it. Whether Oliver Cromwell's solution (a religion divided into sects, with a government in the role of constable to keep the peace among them) could ever have attained legitimacy we can only speculate; but it did not obtain legitimacy during his lifetime, and it had not begun to obtain legitimacy when Hobbes published *Leviathan* in 1651. That solution being absent, the most carefully thought out version of the essential formula was Anglican, the proposal to restore legitimacy by restoring the Tudor church-state. In the shattered conditions of the regicide and the Anglo-Scottish war of 1650–52, its most intelligent exponents were the exiles, Hyde, Nicholas, and Ormonde among the laity, companions of the refugee royal family, engaged on the apparently quixotic enterprise of insisting that the shattered and leaderless Church of England must some day be restored. Is not this, perhaps, a reason why it was necessary to present the Presbyterian Sir Hudibras as an absurd and debased Quixote ten years later?

These were the men who first reacted to Hobbes's *Leviathan* as an act of apostasy on the part of an old acquaintance from Great Tew;[6] and, of course, that is precisely what *Leviathan* was. In systematically rejecting any theological and philosophical foundation on which the Church of England could rest without subverting itself, Hobbes broke with that church and with the proposition that a king needed to be the head of a church as well as the sovereign over it; and the polemic against him for the next thirty years is overwhelmingly an Anglican polemic. In describing a regime in which men could worship as they chose so long as they did so as private beings, and the sovereign was not obliged to endorse any form of worship except as he chose to do so, Hobbes seemed to be endorsing the de facto regime in England to which he soon returned. We need to remember that Cromwell did not assume the role of Protector, constable, and dictator until 1653 at the earliest. Hobbes returned to an England at war, with Charles II in the role of king of Scots; but a military regime to be identified with no church and no Fifth Monarchy was liable to remain unlegitimized. And Hobbes's submission to the government of England as now established (if established is what it was) seemed less significant than the advice to the monarchy which he left behind him. Whatever Hobbes thought of Charles II's taking the Covenant, Hyde was fairly sure that the king was pushed toward Calvinism by his mother, who wanted to use it as an instrument to break up any Anglican restoration and bring about a Catholic regime in England.[7] In the light of what was to happen in the 1670s and 1680s, this was not at all a paranoid fantasy. Henrietta Maria did have something, though it needs to be established what, to do with the lazy Catholic leanings of her son Charles and the militant devotion of her son James. The Hobbesian solution could have turned out a Gallican Catholic one. When it came to complicity with popery, Charles II, unlike his father, left smoking guns scattered all over the place; and had James II been a lucid thinker, he might have looked more like a Leviathan and less like an elder son of the church than in fact he did.

Hobbes, then, helped open the issue of what a monarchy presiding over a plurality of confessions would be like. Would it be imperfectly legitimate because imperfectly sacralized, or would it be crypto-Catholic, exploiting religious diversity as a prelude to imposing its authority in a Gallican form? The less the monarchy aligned itself with the Church of England, the clearer it became that it must either remain unsacralized or adopt the only remaining mode of sacralizing itself as the head of a church; and given that there were ambiguities in the relationship of monarchy with either a Gallican or an Anglican church, one can understand how hard-thinking minds might come to prefer the former. John Dryden is one instance of a very powerful intelligence which took this route, but to many the very debate over these choices looked probabilistic, pragmatic, worldly, Machiavellian, Hobbist, or Jesuitical, and this is a point from which we can turn back to the cynicism and not uncommon demoralization which afflicted the Restoration mind. Not even the Anglican option was immune. We should allow its share of importance to the two-year interval between the return of the monarchy and the departure or expulsion of the Nonconformists, since at the beginning of that period it was unclear whether there even existed an Anglican hierarchy, still less whether it knew its own mind, and by the end of it there had taken place the great electoral backlash which created the Cavalier Parliament and the long eighteenth century of Anglican ascendancy—not all of whose activists were moved by a Clarendonian passion for piety and legitimacy. "Lewd young men" was Algernon Sidney's epithet for the new generation of Parliament members,[8] and we know enough about young reactionaries in politics to understand why their Church of England loyalties could look like the vindictiveness of a ruling class which had been badly frightened and now wanted its share of the loot that had been recaptured.

Vindictiveness, certainly, did much to create the wickedness and turbulence of Restoration politics; people were vindictive toward their opponents because they blamed them for the insecurity of the present and the Civil War memories of the very recent past. But the insecurity lay deeper than the vindictiveness. People behaved with cynicism and brutality because they were unsure of the principles on which they should act and were therefore unsure of their own motives, and the nastier forces of human nature rode triumphantly through the gap. The turbulence might come of sheer vindictiveness; it was the cynicism that made it wicked. As we all know, things came to such a pass that the English beheld that rhinoceros charging out of the past (in Jonathan Scott's memorable image[9]), the specter of a renewed civil war. Their fathers had told them what civil war had been like, how each individual had been compelled to choose sides in a conflict for which he could not see, but must invent, sufficient reason; and as a result the sons were convinced both that they had fewer principles than their fathers and that there were fewer principles which might justify the actions they might be required to take. Hence the savagery with which this generation destroyed either their scapegoats, as in the Popish Plot (most of whom they must have known were scapegoats), or their enemies, as after the Rye House Plot or the Monmouth Rising (most of whom were guilty as charged, but whom they would still bend the law to destroy). Melinda Zook's chapter takes us into a world of vengeful plotters a great deal more turbulent than they were wicked, though it may well be argued that Robert Ferguson and Roger L'Estrange were absolutely right about each other. Hence also, let us further suggest, the alacrity with which they submitted to any force or power which might render civil war an impossibility, whether the French money and French diplomacy which for a few years came close to controlling the politics of the normally chauvinistic English, or the planned betrayals, the Dutch army, and the altogether unprecedented monarchy of William III, which liquidated some of the problems of the Restoration monarchy and replaced them by others.[10] The incidence of judicial murder in English politics now declined sharply, though ambitious politicians continued to gamble with their lives for another thirty years. There was still plenty of wickedness, but rather less turbulence, or turbulence of a rather different kind; and if it is right to suggest that a main cause of wickedness and turbulence was the unlegitimated state of politics, perhaps the Revolution established new rules, and it was clearer what they were.

But what were they? What was the game, and what were its rules? Here we return to our starting point: Blackstone's insistence that important legal advances were made, and Lois Schwoerer's insistence that we continue to regard their importance as central. What we might do at this point is agree to take it as common ground that the English, later British, monarchy continued to be surrounded by consultative machinery and legal processes and that its subjects continued to regard this as qualifying them to be regarded as free; after which we can see that constitutional monarchy is important and has a history, while asking whether that history is the history of politics in the Restoration period. Blackstone was saying that it was not; a wicked and turbulent age produced the Habeas Corpus Act without ceasing to be wicked and turbulent, so that the history of the Habeas Corpus Act and government according to law was contingently related to the history of what made it wicked and turbulent. To a true Whig historian the history of constitutional monarchy, the history of the Crown seeking to expand its powers and the Parliament seeking to restrain them, is essentially, not contingently, situated among the other histories; and this is not just a matter of one's preferred values, but a matter of how the story is to be told in order to make sense of it.

Here we should go back to Thomas May, since whatever we think of his interpretation of Charles I's actions, he had the root of the matter in his mind's eye.[11] He saw that since the Elizabethan Supremacy a certain establishment of the Protestant religion had been an interest of state, that is, it had been so intimately bound up with the structure of English government that the sovereign's headship of the church and headship of the realm could not be separated. He thought (here we do not have to agree with him, though some do) that it was as Charles I had been tempted into actions incompatible with his headship of the church that he had been tempted into actions of arbitrary government incompatible with his unity with his Parliament. He thought that it was actions of the latter kind that had brought about the fateful separation of king from Parliament which was the occasion of civil war, and that the Parliament's case at the outbreak of that war should have been stated in terms of arbitrary government rather than of popery. After 1660 and before 1688, one may suggest, the relation between these two was the obverse of that May had diagnosed. The wickedness and turbulence of Restoration politics occurred because the Crown had not been properly restored to headship of the national church and was tempted to assume either a Hobbesian or a popish relationship with a plurality of churches. If Charles II left a trail of smoking guns, James II drew them up wheel to wheel on Hounslow Heath, until they deserted him on Salisbury Plain. It was his desertion of the church, followed too late by his return to it, which produced the invitation to William of Orange and brought about what would have been a civil war if the nature of military power had not changed drastically within a single generation. In the years preceding, acts of arbitrary government had very certainly occurred, sometimes because it is the nature of governments to perform them if not restrained from doing so; but considered as the occasions of civil war, they were performed by Charles II because his relations with his Parliament had reached the state of a bitter, wicked, and turbulent struggle for power. They were not merely arbitrary—meaning that the law could be invoked to revise them—but they appropriated legal procedures to deprive boroughs of their charters, with consequences very hard to calculate, and they were performed by James II because his policies toward the plurality of churches had become such as even his Parliament would not endorse. What he did was not significantly aimed at the taxable property of the subject, but he began dispossessing some subjects of fellowships, benefices, and offices they considered their freehold; he made use of the dispensing power in ways that, as Janelle Greenberg and Howard Nenner have told us, raised up the specter of a subversion of due process such that no man could be sure of his own. It therefore happened that judgments were made and statutes enacted which put an end to the dispensing power and some other measures of arbitrary government; and these, as Sir William Blackstone and Lois Schwoerer are at one in reminding us, are important measures in the history of constitutional government. What we may not want to do is situate them any longer, as they were so long situated, at the climax of a history beginning about 1603 in which the power of the Crown began increasing and the will of the Commons to resist its increase increased correspondingly, so that constitutional history became (as it still was for David Hume) the history of oscillation of power between the one and the other. It has been established that the history of constitutional government needs to be situated in the context of a history as well ecclesiastical as civil. But it outlives that history, and though the events of 1688 did not terminate that history of England, they may mark the beginnings of a Whig history which would do so. It was not long before it began to be noticed that the monarchy of William III was of a new kind and marked a new age in European history, one in which, though the prerogatives of formal powers of the Crown had been defined with some finality, its influence or informal powers had increased, were increasing, and, as many thought, ought to be diminished. As Englishmen, Scotsmen, and Americans lived out this new history during the eighteenth century, they rewrote that of the seventeenth and tried to make a single history of them. But that—the counter-history of the long eighteenth century—seems to be a history following directly from that which Professor Schwoerer has made her own.

Notes

1. William Blackstone, *Commentaries on the Laws of England*, 4 vols. (Oxford, 1765–69, facsimile Chicago, 1979), 4:431.

2. Herbert Butterfield, *The Whig Interpretation of History* (London, 1932); Herbert Butterfield, *The Englishman and his History* (Cambridge, 1944).

3. For popular or non-elite godliness see Brian Manning, *The English People and the English Revolution, 1640–1649* (London, 1976); Paul S. Seaver, *Wallington's World: A Puritan Artisan in Seventeenth-Century London* (Stanford, 1985).

4. Thomas May, *The History of the Parliament of England which began November the third, MDCXL. With a short and necessary view of some precedent years* (London, 1647), bk. 1, pp. 115–18.

5. Ronald Hutton, *Charles the Second: King of England, Scotland, and Ireland* (Oxford, 1989), 458 (the last words of the book).

6. Thomas Hobbes, *Leviathan*, ed. Richard Tuck (Cambridge, 1991), ix-xi, xxiii-xxv.

7. Edward Hyde, earl of Clarendon, *The History of the Rebellion and Civil Wars in England*, 6 vols. (Oxford, 1731), 5:344, 6:443–46.

8. Jonathan Scott, *Algernon Sidney and the English Republic, 1623–1677* (Cambridge, 1988), 165.

9. Jonathan Scott, *Algernon Sidney and the Restoration Crisis, 1677–1683* (Cambridge, 1991), xiii-xiv.

10. In the current climate of denationalization, some historians are tempted to deny that there was any English history that made things happen in the 1680s, and declare that the course of events was utterly controlled by the French court, the calculations of William of Orange, and the decisions of the Amsterdam regents. See Dale Hoak, "The Anglo-Dutch Revolution of 1688–89," in *The World of William and Mary: Anglo-Dutch Perspectives on the Revolution of 1688–89*, ed. Dale Hoak and Mordechai Feingold (Stanford, 1996), 1–26. To say that a milieu did not make everything happen does not mean that it made nothing happen. See also Scott, *Restoration Crisis*, 39 n.47, where the "European" context is specifically said to exclude the "national." Were there no nations or states in seventeenth-century Europe, and if there were, did their presence make no difference?

11. May, *History of Parliament*, bk. 1, pp. 2–3, 6, 11–12.

The Trial of the Regicides: Retribution and Treason in 1660

Howard Nenner

I

In the sixteen years between the death in 1587 of Mary, queen of Scots, and the accession of James I in 1603, the Scottish king was obliged to steer a difficult political course. He could not be expected to condone the condemnation of his mother, but neither could he be seen to object too strenuously to her execution. If he had protested too much, he might well have forfeited English favor and destroyed his expectation of succeeding to his cousin Elizabeth's throne. A half century later Charles II faced a somewhat similar problem, yet he at first addressed it in a strikingly different way. Charles, too, needed to react to the "murder" of a parent while at the same time fashioning his response to the dictates of political necessity. Like his grandfather, the uncrowned Charles II kept his political eye fixed on the prize of the English throne and was prepared to overlook anything necessary to preserve it, but unlike that of England's first Stuart king, Charles's taste for forgiveness did not extend initially to those who were responsible for his father's death.

By the autumn of 1649, Charles II was already experimenting with a model of pardon and indemnity that could appeal to the nation and allow him possession of the throne. Passing lightly over the rebellion of the past seven years, characterizing it merely as "matters relating to the late unhappy wars and distractions,"[1] he forswore extensive retribution against his subjects, excepting only those who had condemned and executed the late king. In his Declaration from Jersey, Charles stated that he was resolved "to be a severe avenger of his [father's] innocent blood . . . [and] will endeavour to pursue and bring to their due punishment those bloody traitors, who were either actors or contrivers of that unparalleled and inhuman murder."[2] The next year, to satisfy the Scots, he proposed another plan of oblivion, which added "the chief obstructors of the work of Reformation" to those excepted from his mercy while repeating his intention to hold fast to the punishment of his father's murderers.[3]

In the early years of his exile, Charles Stuart was to demonstrate both conviction and an unwavering sense of purpose in avenging the death of the late king. For a short time it even seemed that in respect of his vengeance there was no reason to suspect him of ambiguity or equivocation. None of this, however, was to last. By 1654, when Charles, from his court in Paris, was promising a considerable reward to anyone who kills "a certain mechanic fellow, by name

Oliver Cromwell," he was at the same time extending a conditional pardon to all except three named miscreants, only one of whom, John Bradshaw, had been involved in either the trial or execution of Charles I.[4] Charles's vengeance, like most of his principles, was negotiable, and the nearer he came to a restoration of the crown the more he was prepared to negotiate whatever was necessary for his return. In September 1659, after the rising led by Sir George Booth had failed to topple the republican government, Charles offered to pardon all but seven of the regicides. And some eight months later, when restoration was in sight, it was suggested by General Monck that the number excepted be reduced to five and by the Commons in the Convention that it be seven. Finally, with the new king's assent, the number at risk was settled in the Act of Indemnity and Oblivion at forty-nine.[5]

By April 1660, at the time of his Breda declaration, Charles was ready to disavow any interest in retribution. He assured the mayor, aldermen, and Common Council of London of "how far we are from the desire of revenge," and he asked Monck to communicate to the Council of State and the officers of the armies under Monck's command that it was the king's "wish that the memory of what is past, may be buried to the world."[6] Consistent with that wish, Charles declared from Breda that he would issue a free and general pardon to all, "excepting only such persons as shall hereafter be excepted by parliament" and emphasizing that his pardon would extend to any crime that had been "committed against us, or our royal father."[7] Once on the throne he repeated those intentions, proclaiming his wish to pardon all save "notorious offenders who are in danger, or like to be excepted by the Parliament."[8] Nor did Charles waver in this resolve. He remained intent upon upholding an image of royal conciliation, displaying "the clemency . . . which is most agreeable to my nature" and reserving "severity" for "such cases where the malice is notorious and the publique peace exceedingly concerned."[9]

In this regard, then, Charles had moved in eleven years from unalterable vengeance to near-total forgiveness. That about-face may well have been consistent with Charles's personal taste for clemency, but it showed a consciousness of political reality and an awareness as well of the need for political conciliation. That consciousness was not misplaced.[10] In determining who would be excluded from the king's mercy, the two houses of Parliament had, as expected, entered into negotiations based less upon the measure of guilt than upon a complex of long-standing animosities and loyalties both personal and political. As Ronald Hutton has observed, the fact that of the more than sixty who were being considered, relatively few were excepted from the final Act of Indemnity was attributable in the end "to the tendency of the two Houses to reject each other's victims."[11] Still, Charles had to exhort the Convention to remain narrowly focused on the task at hand, the national rather than any individual agenda. Despite assurances from the Commons in early May that it was making "good progress," six weeks later the king was obliged to press the House to move more quickly so that false rumors of his insincerity in regard to pardon and indemnity might be dispelled.¹² Later he urged the Lords not to delay any further the passage of the bill, which had taken inexcusably long to come up from the House of Commons. In particular he informed the peers that it was never his intention to except any but the regicides from his mercy. Suggesting that there would be ways of dealing with other offenders of admittedly "dangerous and obstinate principles," he implored the Lords "to depart from all particular animosities and revenge, or memory of past provocations . . . [and to] pass this act without other exceptions than of those who were immediately guilty of that murder of my father."¹³

The king's willingness to be generous was understandably limited by his insistence that the regicides at risk surrender themselves as a condition of his forgiveness. Those who had gone into hiding or fled the realm to avoid the king's justice could expect to have no claim on his mercy.¹⁴ Otherwise, it was left to Parliament to take whatever measures were deemed either necessary or desirable to satisfy the nation's appetite for vengeance and the kingdom's need to expiate its sin. As a result, although those to be punished would ultimately be few, it was certain from the start that those same few would nonetheless be made to suffer the full burden of retribution for the crimes of rebellion and republicanism as well as for the sin of regicide. Representing the Commons in its initial response to the king's Declaration of Breda, the speaker, Sir Harbottle Grimstone, immediately established what was to be the tone of the Restoration settlement. Referring to the execution of Charles I, he reported first that the Commons "cannot think of that horrid act committed against the precious life of our late Sovereign, but with such a detestation and abhorrency, as we want words to express it." He then moved quickly to distance all but a few from complicity in the events of the former king's death. "The nation itself as well as the Parliaments, were most innocent of it," he insisted, "it having been only the contrivance and act of some few ambitious and bloody persons, and such others, as by their influence were misled."¹⁵ Indemnity and oblivion were to be the general order of the day, but once again, as it had been in January 1649, the stage was being set for a purgative political trial and a national demonstration of bloodletting.

In furtherance of the goal of singling out a small group to carry the weight of a nation's collective guilt, the statute detailing those to be excepted from the king's pardon went far beyond a mere exclusion. Not only were the forty-nine named individuals exposed to the king's justice, they were effectively condemned in language suggestive of an act of attainder. The act, passed on 29 August 1660, stipulated, "All which persons for their execrable treason in sentencing to death, or signing the instrument for the horrid murder, or being instrumental in taking away the pretious life of our late sovereign Lord Charles the first of glorious memory are left to be proceeded against as traitors to his late Majesty according to the lawes of England and are out of this present Act wholly excepted and foreprized."¹⁶ That statutory condemnation was immediately seconded. On the occasion of Charles's assenting to the act, Speaker Grimstone echoed and reinforced the national intention to "expel the poison of sin and rebellion." In his speech to the king, Grimstone underscored the implicit truth that those named had already been attainted and damned by Parliament. In "looking over a long, black, prodigious, dismal roll and catalogue of malefactors," he said, "we there meet not with men, but monsters, guilty of blood, precious blood, precious royal blood, never to be remembered without tears."[17] The ritual of trials, judgments, and public executions was all that remained for vengeance to be exacted and the king's justice to be done.

It was clear from the start that justice would be swift as well as certain. In a preliminary meeting of the judges and several others who were to frame the indictment of treason upon which the trials would be conducted, it was agreed that the proceedings should move forward without delay (CC, 298).[18] The prisoners, who were then being held in the Tower, were all to be arraigned on the same day, the trials were to begin on the following day, and the same jurors were to be used in as many of the trials as possible (CC, 298–99). The Middlesex Grand Jury was convened at Hicks Hall on 9 October. It received the indictment after hearing the presiding judge's speech and immediately returned a true bill. On the tenth, the court adjourned to the Sessions House in the Old Bailey, where the prisoners were arraigned. They had been brought from the Tower under heavy guard, a regiment of the trained band being employed not merely to escort the prisoners to Newgate, but "to keep them from the fury of the people."[19] By one spectator's account, "the presse of the people . . . were so numerous in the streets that all the way as they came to Newgate, you could hear nothing for deriding shouts, nor hardly see them for the crowd of the multitude."[20] That night Samuel Pepys recorded in his diary that "they all seem to be dismayed and will all be condemned without question."[21]

The first of twenty-nine trials began on 11 October. By the nineteenth, the court's work was done. Within nine days the trials were concluded, the verdicts delivered, and judgments rendered. All defendants had been found guilty of having compassed and imagined the death of the late king and had been convicted of high treason. And already by the nineteenth, sentences had been carried out against ten of them. Pepys attended several of the executions, commenting on the twentieth, what "a bloody week this and the last have been." He reported of the hanging, drawing, and quartering of Thomas Harrison, who on the thirteenth at Charing Cross was the first to die, that the spectacle was greeted with "great shouts of joy." Pepys considered that a circle had been closed: "Thus it was my chance to see the King [Charles I] beheaded at White-hall and to see the first blood shed in revenge for the blood of the King at Charing-cross."[22]

II

The Christian ritual of cleansing sin by blood, as old as Christ's own sacrifice, was firmly established in the nation's political culture. Shakespeare's history plays had sounded that theme across the entire landscape of England's fifteenth-century dynastic wars. His *Henry IV*, in particular, agonizes endlessly about the legitimacy of his right to the throne and vows to expiate the sin of murdering Richard II by undertaking a crusade "to the Holy Land, / To wash this blood off from my guilty hand."[23] In the next generation the ritual is repeated as Prince Hal, King Henry's initially feckless son, undertakes to redeem himself in his father's eyes by killing Hotspur: "I will wear a garment all of blood, / And stain my favors in a bloody mask, / Which, washed away, shall scour my shame with it."[24] Shakespeare's Hal does win redemption, not merely by making good on his oath, but by becoming, as Henry V, a warrior-king and the hero of Agincourt. Still, the glory of fifteenth-century victory in blood on foreign fields would not be enough to atone for England's sin of rebellion and regicide at home—as the Wars of the Roses would attest. "What subject," asks Shakespeare's Bishop of Carlisle in *Richard II*, "can give sentence on his king," can depose one king and crown another, and not bring down "disorder, horror, fear, and mutiny" upon the land? Carlisle's terrible prophecy, to be realized in the wars of Lancaster and York, was ominous and clear: "The blood of English shall manure the ground, / And future ages groan for this foul act."[25]

In the seventeenth century the theme of cleansing by blood would recur not once but twice. First, in clear echoes of the blood sacrament, Charles I was brought before the bar of the High Court of Justice to be informed of the charges against him, first among which was that "the innocent blood that had been spilt in [the Civil Wars] . . . is fixed upon you as the principal author of it."[26] He would in consequence be made to pay with his own blood for shedding that of his subjects in civil war. The cycle, however, did not end there. Within months of Charles's death, a prophecy was advanced that once again England would be called upon to redeem itself in blood for the deposition and murder of its rightful king. Robert Brown, a royalist priest, predicted in the year of the regicide that the late king's life would prove to be the nation's greatest "temporall happiness, and his death the first act of that tragicall woe which is to be presented upon the theater of this kingdome."[27] And in 1660 the blood ritual would indeed be repeated. In July, when the Lords were debating the Bill of Indemnity, the earl of Bristol warned in hauntingly familiar language that England would be abhorred by all nations "if the infamy of our Sovereigns murther should not be thoroughly washed away by justice in the bloud of the guilty."[28] And Chief Baron Bridgeman, at the end of his opening address to the grand jury, drove that same point home. "To conclude, you are now to enquire of blood, of royal blood, of sacred blood, blood like that of the saints under the altar, crying Quosque Domine? How long, Lord, &c. This blood cries for vengeance, and it will not be appeased without a bloody sacrifice" (CC, 303). As Robert Brown had foreseen, Bridgeman was heralding the last act of the "theater of this kingdom"; and as Pepys had sensed and recorded, redemption by blood had come full circle.

Notwithstanding this chorus of condemnation, regicide, as distinct from the murder of a lesser being, was not a separate, identifiable crime. In English law it never had been. The regicides would be condemned in the sight of God for the *sin* of taking away the life of their sovereign, but the *crime* of high treason for which they were tried and convicted had been committed before Charles I was ever brought to the scaffold. Even if the king had been acquitted by the High Court of Justice and his life spared, the accused would have been no less guilty. The defendants' treason lay not in killing the king; rather, according to the fourteenth-century statute 25 Edward III (1352), it was located solely in their "compassing and imagining" his death (CC, 299).[29] This was made explicit in the meeting and discussions preliminary to the drafting of the indictment and was spelled out fully in the indictment submitted to the grand jury on 9 October. It was agreed that evidence would be adduced to prove that the compassing had already taken place on 29 January 1649, the day that the High Court of Justice rendered its judgment on the late king. The "actual murder" of Charles I the following day would only be "made use of as one of the overt-acts, to prove the compassing of his death."[30] The murder was clearly the most important of the overt acts in proving the treason, and as such it was to be "precisely laid in the indictment,"[31] but still it was only one overt act among several upon which evidence would be sought at the trials.[32]

It should be noted that the English had a history of murdering their kings, namely, Edward II, Richard II, Henry VI, and, most recently, Edward V,[33] but no one had ever before been tried at law for those crimes. These kings' immediate successors, having profited from the murders, obviously had no reason to prosecute. The "judicial" murder of Charles I, however, was a different matter. It presented a unique opportunity for official retribution, yet retribution that was to be limited and controlled. The preliminary agreement made it plain that the court to be constituted in 1660 to try the regicides, although clearly willing—and likely eager—to exact vengeance for what it regarded as Charles I's murder, would not be prepared to go beyond the bounds of the known law in order to do so. As the trials began, the lord chief baron made it plain that the prisoners were being brought to the bar of justice for having violated an imperial crown, one that differed from other crowns in that "it was not to be touched in the person"; but this was not to suggest that a righteous Charles II would abuse his prerogative by visiting summary punishment on those who had slain the former king. "We do not speak any thing of the absolute power of the king," Bridgeman said, "for you see he cannot judge concerning the death of his father, but by laws" (CC, 324). Bridgeman would return to that theme several times during the trials, most conspicuously, perhaps, in his speech prior to rendering judgment against John Cook and Hugh Peters. "The law," he maintained, "hath taken care that the people shall have justice and right; the king's person ought not to be touched; the king himself is pleased to judge by the law; you see he doth by law question the death of his father; he doth not judge it himself, but the law judges it . . . This I speak, not that the king should or ought to govern but by the fundamental laws of the land; they that keep within the bounds of the law are happy" (CC, 365). Bridgeman's purpose throughout the proceedings was to keep firmly fixed on the joint principles of absolute monarchy and the rule of law. First, because the king was absolute, he was in his person beyond the reach of any temporal judgment or punishment. Second, because the king was committed to rule by law, his subjects' lives and property were secure.

It was for that reason that the court was to be sensitive to requirements of law and legal procedure, even when it would be interpreting those requirements as strictly as possible. It would focus principally on the compassing of the king's death and not on the death itself, the former being the operative crime of treason. Words alone would not be counted against any defendant, although "if a man be indicted for compassing the king's death, these words may be laid as an overt-act" (CC, 299).[34] Similarly, there would need to be two witnesses against each defendant, although the judges determined from the beginning that those witnesses did not need to testify to the same overt act.[35] Comparably strict scruples were in evidence on lesser matters as well. Notwithstanding the judges' wish to move the trials along as speedily as possible, in the selection of a jury all defendants were to be afforded the full number of peremptory challenges allowable by law and an unlimited number of challenges for cause; any defendant, upon request, was to have pen, ink, and paper made available to him; and prisoners were to have their irons removed when testifying at the bar "so that they be not in any torture while they make their defence, be their crime never so great."[36]

Nonetheless, the magnitude of the offense was to be underscored by the court at every turn. In explicating the law to the grand jury, Bridgeman made certain that the jurors understood the critical differences between treason and other crimes. He noted specifically that whereas in other crimes there needed to be "an actual effect," high treason required only that there be *intent*. Because the king's "life was so precious," it was to be protected, even as against the private designs of men who would think to destroy it—albeit some overt act would have to be proved in furtherance of those designs. "Treason it is in the wicked imagination, though not treason apparent; but," he continued, "when this poison swells out of the heart, and breaks forth into action, in that case it is high-treason." Bridgeman's focus then shifted expansively to those actions that might qualify as overt acts within the meaning of the law. In effect they were "any thing," he said, "which shows what the imagination is"; and although words alone might not be treasonous, he concluded that "in many cases [they] are evidences of this imagination; they are evidence of the heart." In this regard the chief baron was deliberately locating the treason of most defendants in actions that they had taken before the king's trial, actions concluded significantly before Charles I was condemned and executed. Specifically, he was establishing the ground upon which any who had been party early on to consultations leading to the king's trial were thereby guilty of an overt act proving the compassing of his death (CC, 300).

In this opening statement to the Middlesex Grand Jury, Bridgeman was not only attempting to define treason and actions tending to prove that treason, he was also anticipating a defense to be put forward by most of the prisoners as soon as their trials began. He understood correctly that the defendants would seek refuge in the authority of what they would refer to as "parliament," that they would assert that the purged House of Commons in 1649 was the only authority functioning in January 1649, and that those who were commissioned by the Commons to sit on the High Court of Justice to try the king were, in obedience to that authority, saved harmless in their willingness to serve. To meet that defense, Bridgeman undertook to restate and underscore the constitutional doctrine of divine right. "I must deliver to you for plain and true law," he said, "that no authority, no single person, no community of persons, not the people collectively, or representatively, have any coercive power over the King of England." To which he added, so as to make what was already plain even more certain, that a monarch *jure divino* is "immediate under God" and is possessed of an "imperial crown" that "is not subject to any human tribunal, or judicature, whatsoever" (CC, 301).[37] As a matter of constitutional law, Bridgeman's pretrial pronouncement was thoroughly consistent with the maxim "The king can do no wrong," not because kings hedged by divinity were incapable of doing wrong, but rather because there was no forum in existence invested with the jurisdiction to try them. This was the constitutional underpinning of the trials and a theme to which Bridgeman would return when the proceedings were done.

While he was meticulously undermining any defense based on the authority of a renegade rump of the Commons, Bridgeman was making it equally clear that his invocation of absolute monarchy was not to be misconstrued as an argument for absolute government. "God forbid . . . It is one thing to have an absolute monarchy, another thing to have that government absolutely without laws" (CC, 301). Implicitly recalling Charles I's final political testament, in which the doomed king had proclaimed that he spoke "for the true liberty of all my subjects, which consists not in the power of Government, but in living under such Laws, such a Government, as may give themselves the best assurance of their lives, and property of their goods,"[38] Bridgeman asserted that the kings of England ruled and were bound by the laws that they made. In unmistakable echoes of Charles's testament, he advanced a nearly identical interpretation of England's absolute monarchy. It is, he maintained, "so far from infringing the peoples rights, that the people, as to their properties, liberties, and lives, have as great a privilege as the king. It is not the sharing of government that is for the liberty and benefit of the people; but it is how they may have their lives, and liberties, and estates, safely secured under government" (CC, 302). The chief baron's purpose, therefore, was threefold: he was denying categorically that subjects had either the moral or legal right to sit in judgment on an absolute king; he was preparing the way to punish those who had pretended that right; and he was declaring that an absolute king who could do no wrong, but who ruled according to law, would proceed against the regicides on the ground of that law.

III

On 9 October the grand jury, having received the indictment and heard Bridgeman's speech, returned a true bill against the thirty-two men presented. Of that number, twenty-nine were arraigned. Two pleaded guilty,[39] twenty-seven pleaded not guilty and were tried over the course of the next nine days, and three others, having fled abroad, were later apprehended in Holland, tried, and executed.[40] From the court's first encounter with the prisoners at their arraignments on the tenth, it was clear that the defendants could expect nothing other than swift and certain justice. Unlike the impatient and temporary toleration the High Court of Justice showed toward Charles I's refusal to plead to the charges against him in 1649, this court refused to countenance any dilatory tactics whatsoever. Bridgeman informed the defendants that they had but three choices: they could say not guilty and proceed to trial; they could enter a plea of guilty and proceed to judgment; or they could choose to stand mute, in which case their silence would, according to law, be taken as equivalent to a confession (CC, 304). In advance of entering a plea, six of the defendants asked for counsel, claiming unfamiliarity with the law and insufficient time to prepare for their trials.[41] Their requests were peremptorily rejected and immediately swept aside. Similarly, no man was allowed to quarrel with the indictment, although several tried. Henry Marten objected that not he, but someone named Henry *Martin*, was excepted from the Act of Indemnity and Oblivion (CC, 305); two other defendants offered to plead guilty to some particulars of the indictment, but not to all of them;[42] and Daniel Axtell protested that as the proceedings against Charles I had been "in pursuance of an Act of Parliament, I conceive no inferior court ought to judge of it." These objections, too, were rejected out of hand.

Thomas Harrison, a Fifth Monarchy man and one of Cromwell's major generals, was the first of the regicides to be tried. Harrison had been a party to the initial discussions about bringing the king to trial, he had sat on the High Court of Justice, he had been present on the day that judgment was pronounced against the king and had stood up to signify his assent to the sentence of death, and he had signed the warrant for Charles's execution. Therefore, almost every major issue to be raised in the prosecution and defense of the remaining twenty-eight defendants was available to be treated in the proceedings against him. At the start of his trial, Harrison acquiesced uncomplainingly in matters of procedure. He availed himself of the full number of thirty-five peremptory jury challenges and accepted that he might challenge none further except for cause (CC, 309–10); he offered no objection to Solicitor General Finch's opening statement denying any time limitation on prosecutions for treason;[43] and when his request to raise an early objection to the jurisdiction of the court was denied, he accepted that he would have to wait until the evidence against him was heard. "I would go the best way," he said to Bridgeman, "and would not willingly displease you,"[44] whereupon six witnesses were called to testify to the overt acts constituting proof of Harrison's alleged treason (CC, 312–13).

From the earliest discussions preparatory to framing the indictment all the way through the trials, the law of treason to be applied was stated and repeated with unmistakable clarity. Harrison and the others were being called to account for having compassed and imagined the death of the king. Their crime, like none other, was one of intent. It did not matter in law that the intent had actually been carried out, that the king in 1649 had been brought to trial, convicted, and executed. These were held to be overt acts only, proofs of the crime of compassing and imagining Charles I's death. The operative point in law was that the treason consisted in "the thoughts of the heart," not in the overt acts which were "but evidence of it" (CC, 310).[45] The rationale for making high treason such a broadly defined crime was grounded in the unique status of "kings, who are God's vice-gerents upon earth, [and who] have thus far a kind of resemblance of the divine majesty, that their subjects stand accountable to them for the very thoughts of their hearts" (CC, 310). By this reckoning of the law, anything that pointed to a defendant's design would be sufficient to prove the treason.[46] It was unnecessary to establish that Harrison or any other defendant had signed the death warrant or had called explicitly for the king to be executed. No one act was critical for the imputation of guilt. "The consultations, the assuming power to try and condemn the king, the assault upon him, and the fatal blow that was given him, are but so many demonstrations, and open acts, proving the first treasonable design of the heart" (CC, 312). Any one of these was enough. Even if Charles had been acquitted of the charges against him, those who had so much as presumed to try him would have been no less guilty of treason (CC, 315); even if the king's trial had never taken place, those who had taken the first step in consulting about trying him were already traitors in the contemplation of law (CC, 302, 319).

There was never any question of Harrison's having sat on the High Court of Justice or of his having participated in passing capital judgment on Charles I. Harrison, in fact, had trumpeted his participation in Charles's condemnation and was prepared to wear that involvement as a mark of honor. He remained unmoved by Finch's assertion that the regicides' "impudence should make them more odious than their treason" (CC, 311). In beginning the case against him, Finch referred to the acts of the prisoners as having been open and notorious, "not done in a corner" (CC, 310), and Sir Edward Turner (the duke of York's attorney) later embellished the point by contrasting the killers of earlier kings with the defendants in the present case. "The actors in those [earlier] murthers were modest to these," said Turner. "They did it in private, these in the face of the sun, and the people" (CC, 312). Yet rather than shrink from those characterizations, Harrison seized the opportunity to repeat them and to have them stand as a partial defense for what he and his fellow regicides had done. Defiantly he agreed that it "was not a thing done in a corner," but rather "done upon the stage, in the sight of the sun" (CC, 315, 319). To Harrison's mind the fact of Charles I's having been tried and judged openly, not in some secret place, was its purchase on both moral and legal justification. It was also what Cromwell had meant years earlier when he vowed that the king's head would be cut off with the crown still on it.

Harrison's principal defense, like that of his codefendants, was that in 1649 the High Court of Justice had been invested with the authority necessary to try and to condemn the king. Harrison divided that defense into two parts. He contended in the first instance that the present court was without jurisdiction, that it did not have the standing to challenge what Parliament had done eleven years before. "Whatever was done by their commands or their authority," he said, "is not questionable by your Lordships, as being . . . a power inferior to that of an High-Court of Parliament." This court, having been established by an ad hoc commission of oyer and terminer, could neither contradict nor negate the higher authority of Parliament, a court of demonstrably superior jurisdiction. Interestingly, Bridgeman agreed with Harrison's larger premise that the present court's authority was limited. It did not extend so far as to contemplate a right of judicial review. Although "the judges have power after laws are made to go upon the interpretation of them," he said, they were "not to judge of those things that the Parliament do" (CC, 318).[47] But what a true Parliament might do was not what a purged House of Commons had done without benefit of either the Lords or the king.

Harrison contended that at the time of the king's trial, the House of Commons was the "supreme authority" in the land, and following on this premise he concluded that he, like all men, was obliged to submit to that authority. "Otherwise we are in a most miserable condition, bound to obey them that are in authority, and yet to be punished if obeyed. We are not to judge what is lawful, or what is unlawful" (CC, 316). Here, then, was an already familiar inversion of traditional political theory, an argument that adapted a long line of homilies on obedience and the principle of divine right monarchy to the support of de facto authority. The power of the magistrate, wherever it resided, was ordained of God and therefore not to be questioned. It was to be accepted and obeyed. That argument had been invoked to good effect in 1649 to justify an engagement to the Commonwealth, and it would be revived successfully in 1689 to support the new oath of allegiance to William and Mary; but in the climate of the newly restored monarchy, it had absolutely no chance of acceptance.

It was one thing to rehearse discredited arguments for de facto authority. These the court could sweep aside on the ground that "no authority upon earth can give authority for murthering the king" (CC, 318). It was a somewhat different matter to assert that a rump of one house of Parliament might pretend to the authority of the whole. Constitutionally, this might have been even more indefensible than a plea for obedience to de facto authority, but at a minimum it raised the issue of coordination. It reopened the question whether king, Lords, and Commons were of equal status, and in this instance whether the Lords and Commons in Parliament might act legally in the absence of the king. Finch, of course, denied that they could. Moreover, he said, what had been pretended in 1649 was not even that. He spoke contemptuously of the Rump as "this wretched little company which was left a Parliament" (CC, 311), to which Bridgeman added in a similar vein that it was "a thing never known or seen under the sun, that the Commons, nay a few Commons alone, should take upon them, and call themselves the Parliament of England" (CC, 317).[48] Harrison, however, was unchastened and unapologetic—and refused to yield. He responded that "if it was done by one Estate of parliament, it is not to be questioned" (CC, 317).

John Jones, Adrian Scroop, Thomas Scot, Gregory Clement, and John Carew were next to be tried. All were brought to the bar on Friday, 12 October, to be treated as a group. Yet despite the court's eagerness to proceed as swiftly as possible, the defendants' cases had to be separated because they could not agree on challenges to individual jurors (CC, 320, 326).[49] Scroop, who was tried first, had participated in all of the proceedings against Charles I. He was involved in the consultations that led to the High Court of Justice, he sat as a member of that court, he assented to the judgment passed, and he signed the death warrant (CC, 321).[50] Not that it was necessary to prove all of these overt acts. Any one of them was sufficient to testify "the treason of his heart, which was compassing and imagining the death of the king," a point to be made repeatedly here and throughout all of the trials. Yet in laying the case against Scroop, Finch also remarked that the defendant's treason consisted in "that corrupt and wicked heart of his, by which he first thought such a thought against his sovereign" (CC, 320). If nothing further, Finch had underscored that a man's thoughts alone might be treason, requiring only that by some overt act those thoughts could later be proved.

Like Harrison before and others who would follow, Scroop sought refuge in his having acted pursuant to the authority of Parliament, which he pleaded "was then accounted the supreme authority of the nation." Once again that plea was summarily dismissed. Bridgeman paused only to remind Scroop that "when there was but 46 sate, whereas there was above 240 excluded," the "parliament" being conjured was not even so much as a proper House of Commons (CC, 324). That issue had already been decided. As to new matter of legal consequence, Scroop was the first of several defendants to allege that he had been innocent of malice. In accepting the command of the Commons to sit on the High Court of Justice, he asserted, he had made an error of judgment and not of will. Here, too, the plea was brushed aside, the lord chief baron invoking a rule of constructive malice. In cases of high treason such as this one, he said, the law would operate to supply the malice. Scroop's excuse that he had acted out of "ignorance or misguided conscience" might mitigate his crime in the eyes of God, but it could not serve as a defense in law (CC, 324–25).[51]

Carew and Scot, the two prisoners remaining to be tried on the twelfth, also attempted the defense of having been subject in 1649 to Parliament's authority. But after having listened at some length to both Harrison and Scroop on the same subject, the court was of no mind to hear any more. Carew was cut short by Justice Foster with the reproof that "it is your course to blow the trumpet of sedition," while Scot was advised by Bridgeman that by claiming the authority of Parliament for presuming to judge the king, he was aggravating rather than extenuating the fact of his treason (CC, 328, 332). Carew and Scot also shared Harrison's defiantly unapologetic stance. Neither denied any of the testimony introduced against him. Carew protested that in addition to his obedience to Parliament, he had been bowing as well to the will of the Lord (CC, 327),[52] and Scot accepted by implication that he had "so gloried in the act [of condemning his king] that he desired it might be writ upon his tomb" (CC, 330–31). Scot did, however, challenge the introduction of words he had allegedly spoken in the Commons, claiming that it was a breach of the recognized privilege of free speech, but his objection was dismissed, counsel replying summarily that "there is no privilege of parliament for treason" (CC, 331). Accordingly, Scot and Carew were convicted of treason and on the same day, 12 October, were sentenced along with Jones, Clement, and Scroop. In passing sentence Bridgeman not only reminded the defendants of Charles I's many virtues, but took the opportunity to warn of the dangers of fanaticism. Men in the thrall of "spiritual pride," he said, "may over-run themselves by their own holiness" (CC, 336).

In respect of the national desire to punish those who had sat in judgment of Charles I, these first six defendants, all willing members of the regicide court, were comparatively easy marks. Harrison and Scot in particular were tempting targets for retribution since both remained so egregiously unrepentant. The next group of prisoners, however, presented a more difficult legal challenge. John Cook, Hugh Peters, Daniel Axtell, and Francis Hacker, all brought to the bar for trial on Saturday the thirteenth, were in a significantly different category. None of them had sat on the High Court of Justice, and none therefore could be charged with having tried the king, assented to the judgment against him, or signed the warrant for his execution. At the king's trial Cook had conducted the prosecution, Axtell was commander of the guard, and Hacker, a member of the guard, was a commander of halberdiers. Peters, a notoriously fiery preacher, although present at the trial, occupied no official position, nor did he have any designated function to perform.

Finch acknowledged at the opening of the case against Cook that this defendant's situation was different from those who had been tried over the two previous days: "they sat as judges to sentence the king, and he, my Lord, stood as a wicked instrument of that matter at the bar." From Finch's opening statement it was evident that he would attempt to prove that Cook's treason consisted principally in his having drafted the charge against the king and having asked the regicide court to find Charles guilty (CC, 337). Not surprisingly, this trial would be the longest, both because the case against him was more legally complex than those of the others who had been and remained to be tried, and because Finch found in Cook a worthy legal adversary. Although there could be little doubt about the outcome, Cook parried the accusations against him with ingenuity and skill.[53] The judges on the court could not help but take notice of that skill, even if, as Sir Edward Turner chose to do, they were inclined to characterize it as "cunning" or, as Bridgeman preferred, to hold it as a mark against him. "Other men may be impudent and ignorant," said Bridgeman, "but you that were a learned lawyer, your being of council doth aggravate the thing" (CC, 348, 350).

Cook's defense centered on his role as counsel in the king's trial, specifically the argument that he was doing only what was required of him. To hold him guilty of treason for pleading against the martyred king would be equivalent to making it a felony for a lawyer to prosecute an alleged felon who, in analogous circumstances, had been falsely accused. It is not the lawyer who accuses; he merely pleads. Cook argued that it was for "the counsellor . . . to make the best of his client's case, then to leave it to the court." He had done only what he was obliged to do; he had acted in a "ministerial" capacity, not one that was "judicial" or "magisterial." Cook contended in this regard that he was acting entirely without the malice set forth in the indictment and necessitated by law for the crime of treason. "I did nothing but what I was required to do, to set down such and such words, I did not invent nor contrive them . . . [W]hat I then spoke it was for my fee; it may be called *avaritia*, but not *malitia*" (CC, 343–44). For that reason he insisted that the charge of treason against him ought to fail. It was a plausible defense, but not one that was likely to impress the court, especially a court that had already demonstrated its willingness to read constructive malice into the actions of other defendants. The court was also prepared to hold Cook to a higher legal standard. Wadham Windham agreed that "a counsellor carrying himself within the compass of his profession is not answerable; but if he will exceed his bounds, his profession is so far from sheltering him, that, as it has been opened, it is very much an aggravation" (CC, 348). Nor did it seem necessary to elaborate the charge of professional excess. Simply stating it was enough. The court fully accepted Finch's pronouncement that "no man hath, or can have, a lawful calling to pursue the life of his king" (CC, 347).

Cook's defense, that he was acting only in a professional capacity at the king's trial, was developed further in his argument that he had not in fact called for the king's death. He asserted that all he had done was to ask for "justice" in the case and would have the present court believe that when he pressed for judgment, "I meant judgment for his [the king's] acquittal" (CC, 339). Although straining credibility beyond the point of reason,[54] Cook might have hoped for some support from evidence of a conversation he had had with James Nutley in 1649 several days before the king's trial began. Nutley, a young law student at the time, testified that Cook had appeared exceedingly troubled by the assignment that he was about to undertake. He said that Cook had expressed the hope that the Parliament did not intend to take away the king's life. It was, Cook had protested, "a very base business, but they put it upon me; I cannot avoid it, you see they put it upon me" (CC, 338–39).[55] This, too, fell on unsympathetic ears. Bridgeman allowed that Cook might well have expressed the hope, or even the belief, that the king would not be killed, but it would not suffice to excuse his crime. Accepting the "pretended authority" of the so-called High Court of Justice was enough to convict him of his treason. Then, in an expression of contempt reminiscent of Algernon Sidney's famous epigram, Bridgeman observed that "First, it was not a court: Secondly, no court whatsoever could have any power over a king in a coercive way, as to his person" (CC, 349, 352).[56]

Cook returned several times to his argument that he was not a party to the condemnation of the king: he was not a witness against Charles, nor was he judge, jury, or executioner. Yet as many times as he attempted that defense, he was reminded that he was nonetheless an instrument complicit in the dread result of the king's death, and as such he was as guilty as any of those who had sat as members of the court (CC, 344, 346). Moreover, as a lawyer "of great understanding, and of good parts," he knew "very well there are no accessories in treason, but he that acts any part in so wicked a conspiracy . . . stands responsible for the utmost consequences of it" (CC, 346). It was of no moment that he had, as he averred, merely written the words of accusation against the king, not by choice, but as he had been commanded to do. Words, despite Cook's assertion to the contrary, were ruled by Bridgeman to be acceptable proof of treason. Still, as Bridgeman further reminded him, Cook had not been indicted for words, yet those words which were "evidences of the compassing and imagining of the king's death" would be used to testify to the imagination of his heart (CC, 342–43, 348, 350).

It was similarly unavailing for Cook to attempt refuge in Henry VII's De Facto Act. Asserting that he had been obliged to obey the authority of the Rump of the Long Parliament since it was the only authority in existence at the time, Cook likened the circumstances of 1649 to those that had obtained in the insecure political climate of the late fifteenth century. In 1495, Henry VII's legislation had attempted to secure the allegiance of his potentially dissident subjects by assuring them that they could not be punished for supporting the king then in being. By that act in support of de facto authority, Cook now claimed that he, too, ought to be saved harmless. Unsurprisingly, the lord chief baron rejected that argument as well. However murky the actual intention of Henry VII's statute, Bridgeman accepted that it was designed "to preserve the king *de facto*"; so much more would it be "to preserve the king *de jure*." For that reason, he was able to distinguish it from the present case. Cook, he said, was attempting to invoke the act against a king and in support of "an anti-monarchical government"—clearly never the intention of Henry VII or his Parliament (CC, 352).

Like Cook, both Daniel Axtell and Francis Hacker had acted in ministerial capacities during the king's trial. Because they were soldiers in the exercise of their duties, they might have expected—or at least hoped for—more sympathetic treatment from Parliament and the court, yet both were named as exceptions from the Act of Indemnity and Oblivion. Axtell, commander of the guard in Westminster Hall during the trial, was alleged to have directed his soldiers to shoot the unnamed person [Lady Fairfax] who had disrupted the High Court's proceedings by crying out that it was a lie that the court was acting on the authority of the Commons of England. Axtell was further charged with having commanded his guard several times during the trial to shout, "Justice, Justice" and having similarly encouraged them to shout, "Execution, Execution" on the day that Charles was sentenced to die (CC, 365). Hacker's unfortunate distinction was that he had assumed charge of bringing the king to Westminster Hall every day of the trial, and, much more to his misfortune, he had signed the order appointing the executioner and had supervised the execution itself. It was further alleged that he had been on the scaffold on the day of the king's death and that he had held the axe in his hand, none of which Hacker denied (CC, 378, 380).

Axtell proved to be as vigorous in his defense as Cook had been, although he had pleaded ignorance in matters of law and requested counsel to assist him. Appreciating that his request would be denied, he reminded the court that it was a judge's responsibility to act as "mediator" between the prisoner and the king. As to the substance of the treason with which he was charged, he denied explicitly that he was within the compass of 25 Edward III. He asserted that he had acted under the authority of the "Parliament of England," he sought the protection of the 1495 De Facto Act, and he argued that he was not a private person but a soldier, an "inferior officer" whose duty it was to carry out the orders of his superiors. "I was," he said, "no counsellor, no contriver, I was no parliament man, none of the judges, none that sentenced, signed, none that had any hand in the execution" (CC, 369–70); but he had no more success in these pleas than had Cook. Nor did it serve him to insist that his words alone could not establish his treason and to protest that if he were guilty of treason, so, too, were the Commons in Parliament that had established the High Court of Justice and so, too, were all the people who had elected them (CC, 370–71, 376). Again Bridgeman's response was to deny that there could ever be any excuse for treason, and again in Hacker's trial as well in Axtell's, he returned to his particular gloss on the principle of passive obedience. "No man by his commission can warrant the doing of an act which is treason: You must take notice of the authority, whether it be good or no . . . [A]ll unjust commands are invalid. If our superiors should command us to undue and irregular things . . . we are in each case to make use of our passive, not active obedience" (CC, 372, 381). In other words, Bridgeman was agreeing that no man had a warrant to resist superior authority, but neither was he privileged to obey an illegal command. He must refuse to comply and yet be willing to accept the penalty for that refusal. As a constitutional position it was consistent with the seeming paradox that a king who could do no wrong was also capable of acting illegally. "The King of England," as Bridgeman had declared earlier, "is one of those princes who hath an Imperial Crown . . . It is not to do what he will; no, but it is that he shall not be punished in his own person if he doth that which in itself is unlawful."[57]

Hugh Peters, although not treated by the court as sui generis, was clearly different from all the others excepted from the Act of Indemnity and brought to justice. Not only had Peters not taken any part in the formal proceedings against the king, but unlike Axtell and Hacker, he had had no official role or function at Charles's trial. Nonetheless, Peters had been particularly outspoken in his objection to monarchy and had been heard on many earlier occasions to call for the deposing and destruction of the king. A parade of witnesses testified generally to Peters's contempt of monarchy, to his having characterized it as "a dangerous, chargeable, and useless office," and specifically to his call for Charles's death as a tyrant (CC, 354–59). One witness recounted Peters's having preached to Parliament for several hours at St. Margaret's, Westminster, thundering against tyranny and exhorting the members on the authority of Scripture "to bring the king to condign, speedy, and capital punishment" (CC, 358). None of these acts had been done at the king's trial, all having occurred in advance of the ordinance establishing the High Court of Justice. That distinguishing circumstance, however, made little difference to a Parliament that had excepted Peters from the Act of Indemnity and Oblivion, or to a court that was now ready to condemn him. Bridgeman made it plain that Peters's having called for and encouraged Charles I's trial was enough; it was an overt act that had tended to the compassing and imagining of the king's death. Nor was Peters to be allowed any pretended privilege of the pulpit. Just as Cook's being a lawyer and Axtell's and Hacker's being soldiers were insufficient to shield them in their offices from the reach of the law, Peters was not to be protected in his function as a divine. "The pulpit," said Bridgeman, "ought not to be a place where men with impunity may speak any thing, what they list, of sedition and treason" (CC, 361–62).[58]

IV

By the time the regicide trials were completed, twenty-seven men had been brought to the bar, all of whom were found guilty and convicted of treason, yet of that number only the ten whose trials have been discussed here were ever executed. The reasons for what amounted to official clemency, or perhaps laxity, were various. In some cases it was because the defendants had given themselves up voluntarily, in others because they were persuasive in their confessions of contrition.[59] It may also have been that by that time the taste for ritual vengeance had been satisfied. Certainly Charles II was reluctant to go further. Some time later, when the issue was again raised in the Privy Council, he noted to Clarendon that he had had enough. "I must confess," he wrote, "that I am weary of hanging except on new offences; let it sleep."[60] As it happened, most of the remaining defendants distinguished themselves by confessing their guilt while at the same time protesting in extenuation of their crime that they had been misled by their ignorance of the law and had acted without malice. "My Lord," William Heveningham said, "in 1648 we were under a force, under the tyranny of an army; they were our masters; for a malicious and traitorous heart I had not." Gilbert Millington put it more succinctly: "I was awed by the present power then in being" (CC, 396, 390).[61] In these later cases the court was not entirely unsympathetic, although Bridgeman was careful to instruct the jury that it was to consider only whether in fact the defendants were guilty of treason. As to the possibility and effect of there being mitigating circumstances of ignorance and contrition, these were not for the jury, but rather for king and Parliament to consider before any sentence of execution would be carried out. The lord chief baron made it plain to both the defendants and the jury that "we can do nothing in point of mercy, but judgment . . . That which concerns mercy is referred to another place" (CC, 391–92, 397).

The trials of the regicides ended on the same note on which they had begun. The defendants were reminded that their crimes of high treason consisted in their compassing and imagining the death of the king and that any overt act tending to that terrible result was proof of the culpable evil of their hearts. It had not been necessary to prove that a given defendant had consulted about bringing Charles I to trial, had sat as a member or other functionary of the High Court of Justice, had assented to the judgment against the king, had signed the warrant of execution, and had been on the scaffold on the day of the king's death. Any one of these overt acts was sufficient for a finding of treason. In his speech preliminary to pronouncing judgment, Bridgeman made the point that "in law and in conscience" all were "guilty of it, in that you prepared the ways and means to it, in that you brought his head to the block, though you did not cut it off" (CC, 399). There could be no justification in law, temporal or divine, for what had been done. A king who in law could do no wrong might not be above the law, but he was clearly beyond its reach. Repeating for emphasis what he had said before the trials began, Bridgeman returned to the "fundamental laws" and his injunction "that no power, no person, no community or body of men (not the people, either collectively or representatively,) have any coercive power over the person of the king" (CC, 399). The king of England, possessed of an imperial crown, was accountable only to God. Although care had been taken to limit the national appetite for retribution, and the trials had been scrupulously fair, there could never have been any doubt of the outcome. Having allowed "the execrable murther of the blessed king" (CC, 300), the nation was obliged to make some demonstration of its contrition and shame.

Notes

1. "Charles's Declaration from Jersey, 31 October 1649," in *A Complete Collection of State Trials and Proceedings for High Treason and Other Crimes and Misdemeanors from the Earliest Period to the Year 1783*, ed. T. B. Howell, 21 vols. (London, 1811–26), 5:961 (hereafter cited as *State Trials*). In the same vein, see also Charles's letter to the House of Lords in April 1660, accompanying his four-point Declaration of Breda, in which he speaks euphemistically of "composing the confounding distempers and distractions of the kingdom." *His Maiestie's Gracious Letter To The House of Peers, From Breda, April 4/14. 1660* (London, 1660), 2.

2. *State Trials*, 960.

3. See "A Declaration by the King's Majesty to his Subjects of the Kingdom of Scotland, England, and Ireland" (Edinburgh, 1650), in ibid., 966.

4. The other two were William Lenthall and Sir Arthur Hazelrig. "Instrument issued by Charles II, at his court at Paris, 3 May 1654," in *A Collection of the State Papers of John Thurloe . . .* , 7 vols. (London, 1742), 2:248 (hereafter cited as *Thurloe State Papers*).

5. *The Statutes of the Realm*, 12 vols. (London, 1810–28, reprint London, 1963), 5:231–32; see, too, Ronald Hutton, *The Restoration: A Religious and Political History of England and Wales, 1658–1667* (Oxford, 1987), 132. Hutton puts the number at thirty-three.

6. *State Trials*, 947, 955.

7. Ibid., 952.

8. *By the King. A Proclamation Concerning His Majesties gracious Pardon, In pursuance of His Majesties former Declaration*, 15 June 1660 (London, 1660).

9. *His Majesties Gracious Speech To Both Houses of Parliament, On the 29th day of August, 1660. At the Passing of the Act for Free Pardon, Indemnity and Oblivion, And several other Acts* (London, 1660), 4. See also Steven N. Zwicker, *Politics and Language in Dryden's Poetry: The Arts of Disguise* (Princeton, 1984), 9.

10. See, for example, Charles's letter to the House of Commons accompanying his Breda Declaration, in which he explicitly recognized that the Commons would want to provide security for many "who, in these calamitous times, either wilfully or weakly have transgressed those bounds which were prescribed," and then went on to assure the Commons that "we have left to you to provide for their security and indemnity, and in such a way, as you shall think just and reasonable." *State Trials*, 951.

11. Hutton, *The Restoration*, 133. *The House of Lords Order, Die Veneris, 18 Maii, 1660* (Edinburgh, 1660), named sixty-six alleged to have sat in judgment on Charles II. A. W. McIntosh puts the number at sixty-nine. A. W. McIntosh, "The Numbers of the English Regicides," *History* 67 (1982): 195.

12. *Declaration of the House of Commons, May 8. 1660* (London, 1660); *His Maiesties Gracious Message to the House of Commons, June 18. 1660* (London, 1660), in *A Collection Of His Majestie's Gracious Letters, Speeches, Messages, and Declarations Since April 4/14.1660* (London, 1660), 41–42.

13. *His Majesties Gracious Speech To The House of Peers, The 27th of July, 1660. Concerning the speedy passing of the Bill of Indempnity & Oblivion* (London, 1660), 2, 4–5; McIntosh, "Numbers of the English Regicides," 208, quoting *Lords Journals*, 11:108. Returning to his promise to deal appropriately with other offenders, those especially who "continue to manifest their sedition and dislike of government, either in action or words," Charles, at the passing of the Act of Indemnity and Oblivion, called upon Parliament to "be so jealous of the publick peace, and of my particular honor, that you will cause exemplary justice to be done upon those who are guilty of seditious speeches or writings, as well as those who break out into seditious actions." *His Majesties Gracious Speech . . . 29th day of August 1660*, 4–5.

14. *By the King. A Proclamation To summon the Persons therein named, who sate, gave Judgment, and assisted in that horrid and detestable Murder of His Majesties Royal Father of blessed memory, to appear and render themselves within Fourteen days, under pain of being excepted from Pardon*, 6 June 1660 (London, 1660); *State Trials*, 959.

15. *State Trials*, 957–58.

16. *Statutes of the Realm*, 232.

17. *The Speech Which the Speaker of the House of Commons Made unto the King In the House of Lords, at His Passing of the Bills therein mentioned, The 29. of August in the Year of our Lord 1660* (London, 1660), 7.

18. Those who consulted in that preliminary meeting were Orlando Bridgeman, chief baron of the Exchequer; Justices Foster and Hyde, judges of the Common Pleas; Justice Mallet, judge of the King's Bench; Sir Geoffrey Palmer, attorney general; Sir Heneage Finch, solicitor general; Sir Edward Turner, attorney to the duke of York; and two barristers, Wadham Windham and John Kelyng. *A Complete Collection of State-Trials, And Proceedings For High-Treason, And Other Crimes and Misdemeanours; From the Reign of King George I*, 2nd ed., 6 vols. (London, 1730), 2:298 (hereafter cited as CC; page references to this work will be incorporated into my text where possible); *State Trials*, 971.

19. *The Arraignment, Tryal, and Condemnation of Thomas Harrison Late Major General, and one of the pretended Judges that sign'd the Warrant for the murder of King Charles the first, of ever blessed memory, and appointed the place for that fatal Execution to be at White-Hall Gate* (1660), 2.

20. *The Manner of the Arraignment of Those Twenty eight Persons who were appointed to be tried at the Sessions-House in the Old-Bayly on Wednesday the tenth day of October 1660 by a speciall Commission of Oyer and Terminer from His Sacred Majesty* (London, 1660), 4.

21. *The Diary of Samuel Pepys*, ed. Robert Latham and William Matthews, 11 vols. (Berkeley and Los Angeles, 1970–83), 1:263.

22. Ibid., 265, 270. Pepys, as a boy of 15, had by his own embarrassed admission witnessed and approved the execution of Charles I in 1649. Ibid., 280.

23. William Shakespeare, *Richard II*, act 5, sc. 6, lines 49–50.

24. William Shakespeare, *Henry IV, Part 1*, act 3, sc. 2, lines 135–38.

25. Shakespeare, *Richard II*, act 4, sc. 1, lines 121, 142, 137–38.

26. Roger Lockyer, ed., *The Trial of Charles I* (London, 1974), 81.

27. [Robert Brown], *The Subjects Sorrow; or, Lamentations Upon the Death of Britaines Iosiah, King Charles, Most Unjustly and cruelly put to Death by His owne People, before His Royall Palace White-Hall, January the 30. 1648. Expressed in a Sermon upon Lam. 4. 20.* (London, 1649).

28. *The Earle of Bristoll His Speech In the House of Lords, The xx. Day of July 1660. upon the Bill of Indempnity* (London, 1660), 2.

29. "Compassing" and "imagining" are "synonymous terms; the word compass signifying the purpose or design of the mind or will, and not, as in common speech, the carrying such design to effect." William Blackstone, *Commentaries on the Laws of England*, 4 vols. (Oxford, 1765–69; facsimile Chicago, 1979), 4:78.

30. A technical problem arose over the dating of Charles's execution. There having been two kings in being on 30 January 1649, it was uncertain whether to refer to the overt act of execution and the other events of that day as having occurred during the reign of the first Charles or the second. It was decided to do neither and simply to speak of that day as January 30th. Ibid.

31. "Resolutions of the Judges Upon the Case of the Regicides" (from *Kelyng's Reports*), *State Trials*, 974. In designating those responsible for the actual execution, it was clear that only one unknown person, i.e., the hangman, did the act itself. It was therefore to be laid in the indictment "that Quidam Ignotus, with a visor on his face, did the act . . . and the other persons be laid to be present, aiding and assisting thereunto." CC, 299.

32. At the trial of John Carew, Chief Baron Bridgeman corrected Carew when the latter said that he had been indicted for treason and murder. Bridgeman explained "that it is treason only, but it carries the other in with it, murther." CC, 327.

33. Richard III was the last king before Charles I to have died of other than natural causes, but as he was slain in battle, he was not considered to have been murdered.

34. *State Trials*, 983.

35. It was not until the end of the century that by statute (7 Will. 3, c. 3) both witnesses had to attest to the same overt act.

36. "Resolutions of the Judges upon the Case," (from *Kelyng's Reports*), *State Trials*, 974.

37. "For the person of the king, he is the supreme head, he is not punishable by any coercive power; the laws provide for that. The king can do no wrong; it is a rule of law, it is in our law books very frequent . . . If he can do no wrong, he cannot be punish'd for any wrong." CC, 302.

38. Lockyer, *Trial of Charles I*, 151.

39. George Fleetwood and Sir Hardress Waller, after first pleading not guilty, changed their pleas to guilty, thereby avoiding the necessity of being tried. *State Trials* (*Kelyng's Reports*), 982.

40. John Barkstead, Miles Corbet, and John Okey.

41. Hardress Waller, Thomas Harrison, Robert Tichborne, Robert Lilburn, John Cook, and Daniel Axtell.

42. Hardress Waller and Gilbert Millington.

43. Finch dismissed as "strange" and "very new" Sir Edward Coke's "conceit" that 25 Edw. 3 had contemplated "a time limited for the party to be accused." If that were true, there would now, more than twelve years after the treason at issue, be "no time nor place left for punishment." *State Trials*, 1012–13.

44. Ibid., 1017.

45. See, too, Bridgeman's charge to the jury in Harrison's trial wherein he instructed the jury that "because the compassing and imagining the death of the king is secret in the heart, and no man knows it but God Almighty, I say, that the imagination is treason; yet it is not such as the law can lay hold of, unless it appears by some overt-act." CC, 319.

46. Kelyng, who had done a gloss on the law of high treason in advance of the trials, pointed out that "if any one do any thing by which he sheweth his liking and approbation to the traitorous design, this in him is High Treason." *State Trials*, 983.

47. Bridgeman made a similar point in the trial of Thomas Scot. When Scot alleged that the court had no authority to call into question the act of the Commons establishing the High Court of Justice, Bridgeman replied that "it is no derogation to parliaments, that what is a statute should be adjudged by the common laws." CC, 332.

48. Harrison had requested that counsel be assigned to assist him in framing his defense. The request was denied on the ground that "council cannot put into form that which is not matter pleadable itself." Later a similar request by Adrian Scroop was also denied. Ibid., 316, 318, 323.

49. In the end, Gregory Clement did not have to be tried. When his turn came he waived his earlier plea and confessed his guilt. Ibid., 334.

50. Scroop confessed ultimately to all the charges against him except that he stood up to signify his assent to the judgment. Ibid., 321, 323.

51. See, too, the trial of John Jones. Jones also claimed the absence of malice as a defense.

52. In response Bridgeman offered the cynical observation that "they [the people] know too well the old saying, In Nomine Domini, in the name of the Lord, all mischiefs have been done," CC, 329.

53. In anticipation of what would become law by the end of the century, Cook argued in vain that the requirement of two witnesses to the overt acts proving treason ought to be two witnesses to the *same* overt act. Ibid., 351.

54. Bridgeman observed that "to say that the demanding of justice is not treason, though injustice do follow, is a very weak gloss upon a wicked action." Ibid., 346.

55. Testimony by another witness, however, was that at about the same time as Cook's conversations with Nutley, he was heard to say that the king "must die, and monarchy must die with him." Ibid., 342.

56. In a letter to his father in 1660, Sidney took the position that "First, the King could be tried by noe court; secondly, that noe man could be tried by that court." Blencowe, *Sidney Papers*, 236–39, quoted in Jonathan Scott, *Algernon Sidney and the English Republic, 1623–1677* (Cambridge, 1988), 92.

57. His remarks at the conclusion of the trials of John Cook and Hugh Peters. CC, 365.

58. Cook, having returned to the bar to receive judgment along with Peters, repeated his claim of privilege. Bridgeman responded that "the profession of a lawyer will not excuse them, or any of them, from treason, and this has been over-ruled, and is over-ruled again." Ibid., 364.

59. In the case of William Hulet, the man who was accused of being either the executioner or one of the two men disguised on the scaffold, it may have been because the evidence against him was weak and contradictory. Although in the end the jury did convict him, the report of his trial indicates that it was "after a more than ordinary time of consultation." Hulet continued through to judgment to protest his innocence. Ibid., 386, 399.

60. Maurice Ashley, *Charles II: The Man and the Statesman* (London, 1971), 112.

61. Others pleading ignorance and the absence of malice were Isaac Pennington, Henry Marten, Robert Tichborne, Owen Roe, Robert Lilburn, Henry Smith, John Downes, Simon Meyne, Peter Temple, and Thomas Wayte. Ibid., 387–96 passim.

THE HILTON GANG AND THE PURGE OF LONDON IN THE 1680S

Mark Goldie

I

John Hilton, "Captain" Hilton, as he spuriously called himself, was an odious thug. He was a bully, a liar, a drunk, a blackmailer, and a rapacious fraudster. Yet from 1682 until 1686 he was able to terrorize London with the connivance of some of the highest figures in the land. True to the best traditions of urban gangsterism, he had a vicious younger brother, George. They and their henchmen were informers, operating within, on the margins of, and outside the pale of the law. Their victims were Protestant Dissenters: the Presbyterians, Congregationalists, Baptists, and Quakers who, contrary to the laws for Anglican uniformity, worshiped in illegal conventicles. The gang infiltrated their meetings, laid informations against them, secured justices' warrants, gave evidence in court, and when fines were not paid, broke down their doors and shop hatches and seized and sold their goods. All the while they loudly trumpeted their services to religious orthodoxy and the king's government. Their own assessment of their worth was echoed by no less a person than the archbishop of Canterbury, William Sancroft. The pious primate's response, when George Whitehead, the Quaker grocer who eventually secured the Hiltons' downfall, remonstrated with him, was "to excuse them," for "there must be some crooked timber used in building a ship."[1]

We know little about the Hiltons before the 1680s and nothing about their fate after their downfall.[2] This is apt, for they were called into being by the circumstances of that decade and dismissed from history when religious toleration arrived in James II's reign. But in their heyday they were probably the most audacious and organized team of informers in English history. Informers were usually furtive, small-time operators, acting in ones and twos; the Hiltons led a gang of more than forty people. They monopolized London's informing trade. They did not shirk from prosecuting eminent men, and they secured convictions worth tens of thousands of pounds. John Hilton swaggered about town disporting himself as a gentleman, fashionably bedecked in a blue velvet cape, the best periwig, and a white beaver hat.[3] In the height of his hubris, he expected to be knighted by Charles II for cleansing London of its Puritan and Whig vermin.[4] It is surely unique for an informer to publish a newspaper advertising his exploits: from July 1682 to February 1683, in thirty weekly or biweekly issues, *The Conventicle Courant* cataloged "the daily troubles, dangers and abuses that loyal gentlemen meet with, by putting the laws in execution against unlawful and seditious meetings."[5]

Historians have characterized the English state in the 1680s as treading a path toward absolutism. There is much to be said for this view. No parliament met during Charles II's last four years; the Crown's fiscal and military resources were unusually secure; and the Whigs and Dissenters who had brought the Restoration monarchy to a crisis were repressed with singular viciousness in show trials and mass arrests. Yet it is salutary to test abstract claims about what "the state" or "the Crown" was undertaking by considering precisely who was doing what to whom, with what effect, and under what constraints. John Hilton acted by the king's personal, if verbal, commission, and his career provides a case study by which to gauge the amplitude of state power in the later Stuart age. The business of forcing people to worship in ways that were obnoxious to their consciences was an arduous one and called for unparalleled energy in mobilizing the law's resources. In the early 1680s Dissenters feared that nothing less than their total destruction was intended. But visions of a purified and unitary Anglican society were apt to break upon the rocks of stubborn Nonconformity. The outcome offers a classic instance of the gap between enactment and enforcement, between legislative intention and executive achievement. John Hilton's efforts were heroic, the misery he caused unprecedented, but the picture that emerges is scarcely one of a state whose machinery of enforcement could be made to turn smoothly in one direction only. The framework of law and the structure of authority remained sufficiently cross-grained and ambiguous that even at the apogee of Stuart power, neither the Crown nor the political elite was able to act with unequivocal single-mindedness.

II

We first need to note that informing was an institutionalized feature of early modern legal practice, long predating its notoriety in the context of Restoration religion. It was especially prevalent in the enforcement of economic regulations. Justices were glad of news about grain hoarding or weights and measures abuses, and the law provided informers with a fee.[6] But informing was rarely popular, and it sailed beyond the law when informers engaged in private compounding. Compounding had a public and legal form: it was an out-of-court settlement by which an agreed sum was paid to law officers in lieu of the full penalty, an arrangement that suited both parties, since it saved the effort, expense, and uncertainty of court proceedings. A justice could lawfully license an informer to compound with his victims, but this was a short step from an informer compounding on his own account, which was unlawful. Private compounding was a close neighbor of simple blackmail and extortion; the victim was threatened with having an information laid unless he or she paid the informer not to go to law. In consequence of the degradation of the practice of informing, the whole business occasionally met with a crisis, and there were several Elizabethan and Jacobean statutes expressly limiting what informers could do. The Hilton gang caused another crisis for informing, but the practice was too ingrained to be abandoned by a society that lacked the infrastructure of modern policing.[7]

The detection of crime and the near monopoly of indictments by professional state functionaries were largely creations of the nineteenth century. At the close of the twentieth, however, it is no longer obvious that this was an irreversible characteristic of the transition to modernity. There is today increasingly a privatized market in law enforcement services, an expansion of private policing, a burgeoning of vigilantism and informer phone lines, and a brisk trade in modern compounding—plea-bargaining. Paradoxically, the pattern of early modern law enforcement now seems less alien than it did during the era of universal state provision. Histories of crime written a generation ago, which traced the rise of benign professional competence and the demise of corrupt amateurism, may now seem tendentiously Whiggish.[8]

What remains alien is that the Hilton gang's targets were religious Dissenters. They were the agents of the final attempt in English history to coerce people into a single, uniform, national church. The Second Conventicle Act of 1670 was the most notorious statute for religious conformity in the Clarendon Code. It allowed for summary indictment before a single justice on the evidence of two witnesses. It allocated one-third of the fine to the informer, the other two-thirds going to the Crown and the poor relief fund.[9] There had been informers against Dissenters in the 1660s, but this act multiplied them. They were especially active in the act's immediate aftermath and again after 1675 during the earl of Danby's "Church party" administration. A sign of their flourishing was the flurry of pamphlets that denounced them. An informer, it was said, was "the church's chief scavenger," "a pettifogging caterpillar," "a mischievous vermin."[10] That the act also made provision for the prosecution of constables and justices for failing to enforce uniformity was indicative of the frustration felt by zealots at the blind eye turned to Dissenters by many officials. It bespeaks a tension between avid informers and indifferent officers.

Historians of Restoration Dissent have documented instances of informers at work.[11] The general picture is of piecemeal harassment often undertaken by people apparently more pathetic than vicious, an image enhanced by the Dissenters' penchant for recording the miserable fates that, by the hand of Providence, often befell informers.[12] The most thorough recent analysis relates to Devon, where in the early 1670s syndicates of informers operated across many parishes, and where the most notorious of them, John Beare, achieved the rank of magistrate (rising, it was said, from being the head of the informers to the tail of the justices).[13] John Hilton, like most informers, was criminal, needy, and finally broken and impoverished, but nobody matched him in twenty-five years of the Dissenters' travail.

III

The Hiltons came from Westmorland, were probably brought up as Catholics of minor gentry status, and were cronies of Sir Richard Sandford, Cavalier baronet of Howgill Castle. John, according to a Quaker report, lived "a lewd dissolute life," troubled his neighbors with vexatious lawsuits, and absconded owing drinking debts. The brothers may have become soldiers, though neither held the title of captain that both claimed. John came to London early in the 1670s. He persuaded an innkeeper's daughter, who was "not much above" twelve years old, to marry him with big talk of his northern estate. With a forged warrant of attorney, he secured a large sum from his father-in-law. When the forgery was discovered, he was jailed. His later enemies, in an effort to identify the psychological roots of his hatred of Dissent, put it down to reprisal for his humiliation at the hands of a Dissenting innkeeper. After that, Hilton himself ran an alehouse in Fetter Lane, selling up when he turned to the informing business. In 1675 George Hilton and Sir Richard Sandford, who was visiting the brothers, got into a fight with two assailants outside a tavern in Fleet Street over a demand for payment of John's gambling debts. Sandford was killed and his assailants hanged for murder, though it was put about that Sandford died in a fair fight. The Hiltons were also reported to have engaged in counterfeit coining, taking care to work in Dutch currency in order to avoid the gallows.[14]

In May 1682 George Hilton sought an audience with the king and duke of York at Windsor. The king

> intimating his displeasure that the laws against Dissenters were not more vigorously put in execution, the said captain did freely and voluntarily offer his services to his majesty to that end, wherewith his majesty and royal highness seemed so well satisfied (and being well satisfied with his loyalty and conformity to the Church of England) as expressly to command him to suppress and disturb them.[15]

Thus fortified, the brothers' campaign began immediately. They took out warrants against thirty-four meetinghouses in their first two weeks of operation and during the early months took out about twenty a week, often blank warrants into which they inserted names. They disturbed meetings all over the City and Westminster, from Wapping to the Strand, Southwark to the Barbican. They repeatedly harassed the same meetings, such as the Quakers at Devonshire House, the Presbyterians at Wine Office Court off Fleet Street, the Independents at Swallow Street in Westminster, and the Baptists in Gravel Lane, Stepney. This was work for Sundays; weekdays were occupied in distraining goods for nonpayment of fines. Sometimes they secured imprisonments, but their main concern was to damage livelihoods. A shoemaker lost eighty-one pairs of shoes, a cheeseman a cheddar worth £7. Fines for attending conventicles were modest, but for preaching they were savage, and the law allowed the imposition of the latter fine upon the hearers. Thus, Anne Bellamy paid five shillings for herself and £9 15s. as her portion of the preacher's fine.[16]

John Hilton claimed he was "forced to have fifty or more persons every Sunday and some other days for his assistance."[17] We know the names of more than forty gang members.[18] They acted as spies, litigants, bailiffs, and bouncers, in twos, threes, and fours, and in differing combinations, such that the trail of the overwhelming number of London prosecutions for Dissent during four years leads inexorably to the Hilton brothers. The gang lived in all parts of London. John Brown of Bermondsey handled Southwark prosecutions; John Sharples was a mason in St. Martin-in-the-Fields; Christopher and Elizabeth Smith and Martha Fogg lived in Shoreditch; Arthur Clayton was a cordwainer in Aldgate.[19] A handful crop up as the leading figures: Gabriel Shadd, Christopher Smith, John and Hester Collingwood, and Eleanor Shafto. Shadd and Smith specialized in forcible distraint. Their habit was to appear with several assistants at a victim's house in the evening and make a night of it. On 10 October 1683 they broke into a carpenter's shop and demanded £20; they stayed all night "making themselves very merry" on brandy and rum and in the morning took away several cartloads of timber. Smith broke in upon Ephraim Sylvester and his dying father and ransacked the house; the old man died a few hours later.[20]

At least fifteen of the gang members were women.[21] George Whitehead protested that "many of them [are] impudent women, who swear for their profit . . . their husbands being prisoners for debt."[22] Eleanor Shafto and Frances Sculthorpe were illiterate and witnessed with their marks. Shafto was also called Mrs. Hilton, for she was John Hilton's mistress, he having abandoned the innkeeper's daughter. She and Hester Collingwood regularly invented testimonies against people they knew to be Dissenters; if they could not sustain a case, they contrived not to withdraw their evidence before having put their victims to legal costs. Collingwood was said to "dictate" to the lord mayor. On one occasion when she reported a conventicle, the constables brought back two culprits, but she "bawled out" to the justices that there were a great many more, so more constables were sent off. On another occasion she charged a Quaker couple with barratry after an exchange of angry words in the street. Another of the gang, Elizabeth Smith, followed people around London streets for an hour at a time hoping to trace a conventicle.[23]

Despite the combative energy of Hilton's women, one of his own themes was the unnatural practice of female preaching among the Quakers. A "she-holder-forth" in Westminster was fined £20 for preaching. Even more unnatural was the violence of female Presbyterians and Independents. When the gang turned up to distrain upon the Independent minister Stephen Lobb, they "found the doors barricaded, the windows fast shut, and five or six Amazonian religious sisters upon their defence . . . each armed with a spit, fire fork, or some suchlike weapon." But the women were defeated, prosecuted for obstruction, and fined £5 each. Hilton reported that a constable called Townrow, when trying to arrest a Presbyterian preacher, was stopped by "women making most hideous outcries, [who] with their feminine weapons forced him to the ground, rending and tearing him like so many wolves, or mad beasts, to the great hazard of his life." In Red Cross Street Hilton broke up Mr. Cockin's "Protestant nunnery." Hilton also deployed sexual innuendo; of a young preacher he remarked upon "the sisterhood's zealous opinion of his sufficient parts."[24]

Gradually the Hiltons cut a swathe through London's conventicles. In 1683 prosecutions for Dissent reached unprecedented levels. In January 1684 the Hiltons reported to the king that they had broken and dissolved forty or more meetinghouses "and also driven from their dwellings, made conform or put into prison forty or more teachers." In November 1682, after six months' work, they reckoned they had levied £17,000 in fines. After two years they put the total at £40,000. But they complained that despite "continual importunities," cases were falling because magistrates were neglecting to process "the records in time." For instance, they noted the failure of the justices sitting at St. Martin's to authorize the serving of a set of warrants for distraint, which cost "the king, the poor, and the informer" several thousand pounds. The Hiltons estimated that up to three-quarters of the amounts nominally secured in fines went unlevied by virtue of obstruction and the sheer legal and personal effort needed to pursue all distraints. There is little reason to doubt their estimates of sums nominally levied, but every reason to suspect their own claims to have made little money personally. George Hilton said he was out of pocket, having gained only £70 while defraying £600 in expenses.[25]

How the Hiltons, new entrants to the informing trade, managed immediately to stage such a major operation free of interlopers is a mystery. They may have used their royal commission to gather up old hands into a cohesive ring, offering economies of scale and the shelter of authority. But their followers seem absent from the records beforehand; they apparently stepped from nowhere into the vacuum left by the collapse of the Whigs' domination of London. What is striking is that imposition of religious conformity depended upon the opportunism of a freelance syndicate. In a society where the machinery of enforcement was not professionalized, it was possible for an alehouse-keeper to go to the king and come away with executive authority over a major element of royal policy. As Cynthia Herrup has remarked, this was a legal system in which "the direct participation of aggrieved parties added determination to the detective process, although it also gave rein to social prejudice and private malice."[26] And, of course, to religious and political zeal.

IV

From the spring of 1681, three London newspapers had thundered against Whiggery and Dissent: Sir Roger L'Estrange's *Observator*, Edward Rawlins's *Heraclitus Ridens*, and Nathaniel Thompson's *True Domestic Intelligence*. Hilton's *Conventicle Courant* belongs in their company, "being elevated and perverted by the drollery and sophistry of *Heraclitus* and the *Observator*."[27] Its first issue began with a jeremiad cribbed from its mentors. The prophecies of Jeremiah foretell "modern history" since "forty-one" (1641), portending that "an evil shall break forth" from a people that "hath a revolting and rebellious heart." During the Puritan tyranny of the 1640s, "the Lord's flock was carried captive, were sequestered, imprisoned, or exiled." The evil ones of those times were still present in our "backsliding Israel," for "can . . . the leopard change his spots?" But help was at hand. There was "balm in Gilead," for the "noble-spirited" would "venture their lives and fortunes, for the delivering us from this threatened destruction." Such high-flown rhetoric did not come naturally to Hilton's pen, and he quickly turned to the prosaic task of reportage from the streets, leaving L'Estrange to descant on the gang as "servants of the king and the laws" and "necessary supporters of public order."[28]

The connection with Nat Thompson was probably closer than their shared slogans. Like Hilton, he was a Catholic masquerading as a loyal Anglican. A list of conventicles that Thompson published in 1683 (today a valuable source for the topography of London Dissent) constitutes Hilton's hit list.[29] The only advertisement carried in Hilton's *Courant* was placed by Thompson. Thompson published from Fetter Lane, where John Hilton had his alehouse. Thompson may have put Hilton up to the idea of turning informer. The two were further connected through Elizabeth Cellier, the notorious "popish midwife." Thompson's news-sheet had given credence to Cellier's allegations about the Meal Tub Plot, a supposed Presbyterian plot against the Crown, the revelation of which was designed to draw the sting of the Popish Plot.[30] Hilton was seen resorting to Cellier's lodgings.[31]

It is significant that the Hiltons' campaign began in the summer of 1682 and not a year or more earlier. The king's sudden dissolution of the Oxford Parliament in March 1681 is generally taken to mark the beginning of the Tory Reaction. And so it was. But Tories had to move cautiously until they had crushed the Whigs in the City of London, and that was a hard-fought battle.[32] Until it was achieved, Dissent remained free; so unhampered were London's Dissenters that in 1681 new meetinghouses were being built, and a dozen of the merchant company halls were available to them for regular worship. After the execution in July 1681 of Stephen College, the victim of the first of the show trials, George Jeffreys (who later presided over the Bloody Assizes against the Monmouth rebels and became lord chancellor) was appointed chairman of the Middlesex justices, with the express purpose of moving against the Dissenters. There was a wave of prosecutions of Presbyterian ministers in the autumn,[33] but no further progress could be made while the City's judicial system was in the hands of Whig aldermen (who constituted the justices with power to issue warrants and summarily convict) and the "ignoramus juries" packed by the Whig sheriffs Cornish, Bethel, and Goodenough. At the beginning of 1682 Jeffreys moved to revoke the City's charter. That was finally surrendered in 1683, after which the City was governed by royal commission. The crucial breakthrough came in June 1682, when two Tories, Dudley North and Peter Rich, were nominated as sheriffs and forcibly installed after a viciously disputed election. The Whig leaders, including Pilkington, Shute, Player, Bethel, and Cornish, were convicted of riot in February 1683. By the time Sir William Pritchard was installed as lord mayor in October 1682, he could be confident of London juries. He lectured the grand jury on the need to suppress the conventicles that "distil the poisonous principles of schism and rebellion." Now, said Jeffreys, "the king of England is at last the king of London."[34]

George Hilton's timing in appearing at Windsor in May 1682 was impeccable, for he was precisely what Jeffreys and Secretary of State Sir Leoline Jenkins needed at that moment. The Hiltons became their instrument, and sometimes they had recourse to them for protection and for cash to cover expenses.[35] The Hiltons' campaign began therefore on the cusp of Tory victory in London politics. A Whig ballad, *A Word of Advice to the Two New Sheriffs*, makes clear the connection between the Hiltons and the Tory City grandees, denouncing City leaders who orchestrated informers against godly Protestants instead of against papists and whores:

> Thus preaching seems a crime, and whoring none,
> Poor Mr. Hilton, Oh! let him alone,
> He's a harmless youth and out of pity,
> Disturbs the meeting houses in the City.

One surviving copy of this ballad has a handwritten asterisk against Hilton's name and the note, "Informer General."[36]

It becomes apparent that the early stages of the Hiltons' campaign provided an important adjunct to the Tory coup, for they set about purging Whig office-holders in London's parishes. The early issues of the *Courant* were only indirectly concerned with Dissenters; the primary focus of attention was the political loyalties of parish constables. The constable was a linchpin in the structure of local government. He was the justice's parish servant, but he was a peacekeeper rooted in the parish community and often elected by it; he was an artisan or shopkeeper whose only social pretension was that he paid the poor rate; sometimes he was not literate. Although he acted as an agent of the state, he did not belong to a governing class set apart.[37] The enforcement of law was no more possible without the constable's cooperation than it was without the magistrate's. He stood at a crucial pressure point, subject to executive orders from above, but sympathetic to the values of his neighbors. As Keith Wrightson has written, "ensnared at the point where national legislative prescription and local customary norms intersected were the wretched village officers, the much tried, sorely abused, essential work-horses of seventeenth-century administration."[38] In the same way that other offices and institutions fell prey to political purging from the late 1670s onwards, so, too, the office of constable became (at least in London) increasingly dependent on visible loyalty to the dominant political mood. This did not necessarily mean sackings, but it did mean cowing the recalcitrant into cooperation—or making their job so unpleasant as to provoke resignations.

This was exactly the pressure that Hilton now exerted upon the London constables. He secured warrants in order to challenge Whig constables to do their legal duty. When they demurred, he publicly named them in his *Courant* and announced that he would prosecute them for dereliction of duty. Sometimes he printed their addresses, a scarcely veiled invitation to Tory thugs to pay them a visit. His first victim was Charles Dudley, a "caneman" in Fleet Street, who had got up a crowd to shout "Informer." (Sometimes Hilton made a mistake: he apologized for naming one Mr. Paulfrey, who was a "true churchman and a good kingsman," for it was his Whig neighbor whom he had meant to identify.) Pressure bent the will of some. Hilton sneered at a fishmonger in Thames Street who "did faintly set his hand to the plough, for the eradicating these malignant weeds in God's garden, to save him from the lash of a pecuniary mulct." Likewise, a shoemaker was soon made "as pliable as wax." He found the loyalty of a Mr. Picket hard to judge at first, but a second warrant "will give us occasion to have a more candid opinion of him." Hilton hit out at other officials, too. A man who helped preacher Lobb held the post of crier in one of the law courts, but he "will be eased of that job." Hilton stage-managed a regime of intimidation less visible but more pervasive than the show trials of Whig magnates. He cleaned up the small fry when the large fish were caught. In January 1683 he prosecuted for riot a Whig constable called Richard Holmes, who had formerly been a servant of Sir William Waller, a Baptist and leading Whig activist in Parliament who had fled to Holland.[39]

The constables found out several ways of evading the execution of warrants. Some declared their simple refusal to do "the informers' drudgery"; some questioned the authenticity of warrants; some promised to act and failed to do so; some gave the intended victims warning of their approach; and some found business that took them out of town on Sundays. Constable John Gilbert locked away a warrant in his shop till. Constable John Ward of Coleman Street, the heartland of London Puritanism since the 1640s,[40] boasted "of his ingenuity in juggling, that he could evade the performing of his duty, be kind to his brethren, and absolve himself from any penalty, by his non-serving his warrant." Some constables were plainly Dissenters themselves, and Hilton caught them worshipping at meetings. Mr. Kadgel, tallow-chandler in Honey Lane, had a "zealous love of the brotherhood and sisterhood [that] supersedes all obligations of duty." Charles Dudley was caught worshiping with an unexecuted warrant in his pocket. He was fined twice, for conventicling and for not executing the warrant against the conventicle.[41]

Another of the constables who obstructed Hilton soon acquired notoriety as a Whig conspirator and then betrayer. Josiah Keeling, a Baptist oilman of East Smithfield, was determined to "save the [City] charter and deliver the nation." He took part in the audacious arrest of the Tory lord mayor in April 1683 and was recruited as a member of the assassination squad that was to have killed Charles II at the Rye House later that year. He got cold feet, revealed the plot, and set in train savage reprisals against Whigs and Dissenters.[42]

On 15 August 1682 all the City constables were summoned at Hilton's behest by the lord mayor, Sir John Moore, to give an account of what they had done with their warrants over the previous three months. John and George Hilton and Gabriel Shadd were present. John announced that he had issued warrants to 110 constables since 16 May and that he now knew where they all stood. Duly "those that had done their duty, were commended . . . and those that had not, were pricked down, in order to be convicted for neglect of their duty." Some made their excuses and agreed to be better instructed by the Hiltons in future. Others denounced Hilton and "bid my Lord Mayor to take account of whence Mr Hilton was." The mayor replied, "he was very well satisfied what he was." In September George Hilton took the stubborn cases further, presenting a list of names, including Charles Dudley's, to the Privy Council. Secretary Jenkins ordered King's Bench to hear their cases.[43]

The reluctance of many constables to act on the Hiltons' warrants did not stem only from principled sympathy for Dissent. They were concerned for cohesiveness and consensus in their parishes. Thomas Ellwood denounced informers for forcing constables to act "too officiously against their honest neighbours." Another critic wrote that the Hiltons' crime was "to compel one neighbour . . . to prosecute another."[44] Constable Halkins, a basket maker in Newgate Street, was "unwilling to go so far to disturb his peaceable neighbours." It was common practice for goods distrained from a Dissenter to be purchased by nearby friends. Preacher Plant's shop in Fore Street, Cripplegate, was stripped of £40 worth of goods, but they were bought back by a neighbor. In December 1683 Justice Sir William Smith dismissed a case brought against a Quaker, John Vaughan, because of his "quiet conversation among your neighbours." As Edward Pearse, a tireless recorder of the Dissenters' travail, commented, the parish officer must now either be fined or lose the love of his neighbor, for "the informer is now *pro tempore* his superior officer."[45]

As several historians have stressed, the judicial schemes of enthusiasts were mediated and moderated by the need to avoid destabilizing neighborly social relations. Hilton, as a socially unanchored zealot prepared to devote himself full-time to a cause, was uninhibited by such considerations. The constables, by contrast, held "an office which was amateur and communal in both its qualifications and duties."[46] Small communities had often destroyed informers by ostracism. In 1662 a small-time informer in Southwark had complained that he had "lost his trade" because "living . . . amongst the most numerous factious people . . . [he had] consequently ruined himself by being marked out by them as a Saul or persecutor."[47] But the Hiltons, by transcending parish boundaries, by operating on an unprecedented scale, and by relying on elite backing, were able to tip the balance of social forces in favor of the ruthless enforcer.

John Hilton's role in the Tory crackdown in the City reached its apogee when he challenged not only the constables, but the great aldermen too. By October 1682 he was applying his techniques to Whig justices. Dissent and Whiggery were interconnected at the highest levels in City politics; seven of the nine aldermen sitting between 1680 and 1683 were Dissenters. Hilton "demanded" warrants from the Whig aldermen Sir Thomas Gold, Sir Robert Clayton, Sir Patience Ward, and Henry Cornish, but all refused to comply. Cornish persistently refused to sign a warrant of distraint against Benjamin Antrobus, a Quaker linen-draper. But Whig judicial power had been broken, and Hilton triumphantly observed that Dissenters were now deciding not to appeal against convictions, knowing that "packing juries, suborning witnesses, etc." was no longer possible, "the loss of which privilege is much bewailed and (peradventure) was the only basis that supported all the insolences of the whole herd of the factious."[48] In January 1684 Hilton claimed to have cases worth £10,000 pending against Whig aldermen. He had become "a bugbear to the Justices of the Peace."[49]

But he overreached himself when he took on Sir Robert Clayton. Clayton was a fabulously wealthy financier, John Evelyn's "prince of citizens," who had been lord mayor in 1679–80 and M.P. for the City in the Exclusion Parliaments, and had introduced the Exclusion Bill into the Oxford Parliament. He belonged to the committee of twelve who organized resistance to the surrender of the City's charter. In November 1682 he stood trial before Lord Chief Justice Francis North, charged by John Hilton under the Conventicle Act for "denying him a warrant to disturb a meeting." But Clayton had prepared his ground by investigating Hilton's past; when Hilton was shown to be a convicted forger, the case collapsed, and Hilton was rabbled by a Whig crowd in court. Hilton had trodden where even the king dared not go; Clayton was the only senior City Whig to survive the 1680s unscathed. Remarkably, Hilton came out of this debacle untouched. Despite its being "commonly said" in December that he was "very obnoxious to the law in matters of perjury, forgery or felony," he sailed inexorably on the Tory political tide.[50]

If some constables resisted Hilton, others relished his invitations. When need arose, the Hiltons fetched constables and churchwardens out of Sunday worship in order to take action against conventiclers. Overseers of the poor could be enthusiasts, too. They were struggling to hold down the poor rate, and the Dissenters' enforced contribution to the parish chest of one-third of their fines was welcome. The Quaker Thomas Ellwood reported that he knew a parish that had not set a poor rate upon "a declared expectation of monies likely to come in by fines and forfeitures . . . by which they hope and propose to ease the parish of that charge." In 1682 the coffers of St. Dunstan-in-the-West were boosted by a fine levied on Richard Baxter. In September 1683 Timothy Emerson, oilman in St. Martin's, was distrained of £30 worth of goods by a team that included four constables, one churchwarden, and seven overseers of the poor. When a batch of distrained goods went unaccounted for, John Hilton was quick to tell the victim that he had given the goods "out of charity to poor people."[51] Hilton recorded the gathering of crowds favorable to his cause. In November 1682 the windows of Lobb's meetinghouse were smashed; in December Mead's meeting in Stepney was wrecked when constables went to disrupt it.[52]

It is manifestly the case that attitudes to religious uniformity cut vertically through all social layers; persecution was not simply visited on the lower sort by the elite. There were justices and constables on both sides. Whig constables included a cheesemonger, fishmonger, and shoemaker; among Tories an apothecary, a barber, and a victualer. Social snobbery could operate in two directions. Hilton called Dissenters "vermin." But his enemies poured equal scorn on his own social pretensions. It was "all the mode, nowadays, for the very scum of mankind, to take upon them as persons of quality." Hilton's gentlemanly estate, they pointed out, amounted to a garret in Whitefriars.[53]

V

Such success as Hilton met with depended on the support of friends in high places. "John Hilton, His Majesty's Informer" constantly claimed the king's immediate authority, as if he were a commissioner empowered to cut through the ordinary encumbrances of the social and legal order. From its third issue, *The Conventicle Courant* carried the subtitle "setting forth the proceedings for suppressing unlawful meetings—By the King's Command." Hilton purloined a vicarious divine right by claiming that since God had given a "sublime commission" to his "vicegerent" the king to preserve "the true primitive, apostolic church," that divine commission would falter if "secondary agents be wanting." More prosaically, he told a constable who doubted his credentials to go and see the king at Windsor. And periodically the Hiltons addressed themselves to the Privy Council.[54]

Yet the *Courant*'s regal masthead did not save it from the attentions of the government's press agent, Robert Stephens, whose more usual business was the suppression of Whig newspapers. At the end of December 1682 Hilton was greatly affronted when Stephens turned up with "an order to suppress the publishing this paper." He was lucky it survived several weeks longer, for Thompson's *Intelligencer* had been closed down in October and its author fined and pilloried; his popery was too evident for the government's comfort. Whig papers were also suppressed in a general crackdown.[55] In the early weeks of 1683, L'Estrange's *Observator* and Hilton's *Courant* were the only newspapers (aside from the official *Gazette*) available for sale in London. The *Courant* suddenly disappeared in mid-February, almost certainly because it had been suppressed, although it is true that Hilton was running out of literary steam and could claim to have succeeded in his initial task of cowing the constables and shutting up meetinghouses. By the same token, the Hiltons had, from the government's point of view, served their turn in the final assault on Whig London. When they petitioned the Crown in July 1683 for recompense, the Treasury lords ordered £500 to be paid, but the Hiltons "never received a farthing." Similarly, in January 1684 they moaned to the king that "they had not had their expected encouragement" and asked for some stronger empowerment.[56]

Even to their political masters, the Hiltons were at best a "necessary evil,"⁵⁷ to be privately and verbally encouraged, but not too publicly countenanced.

Hilton's regal claims cut no ice with the Dissenters. Royal authority lay with Whig constables, too. When Hilton's agent told constable Shaw, a "brazier," that "he was upon the king's business," Shaw retorted, "You dare to stand with your hat on before the king's representative." When Shadd rampaged around a carpenter's shop "saying that he was the king's servant and what he did was for the king," a Quaker commented, "Thus they cloak their base unworthy, dishonourable and unlawful actions on the king."⁵⁸ The king's authority was negotiable currency, and Charles II's reputation remained, rhetorically at least, undented in Dissenter eyes. A belief commonplace among Restoration defenders of toleration was still upheld: that the king had promised freedom for tender consciences in his Declaration of Breda of 1660 and in his Indulgence of 1672, and that he had been frustrated by others. It was the forces of Toryism and the church hierarchy that were blamed, a party and not the Crown. The Hiltons said they were "the king's informers"; their enemies said they were "the Tory informers."⁵⁹

Hilton's real supporters were the Tory magistrates in the City. His most "eminent friend and encourager" was Sir Thomas Jenner, who was appointed recorder of London when the charter was quashed in 1683. He was prosecuting counsel in several state trials, including those of Alderman Cornish and the republican Algernon Sidney.⁶⁰ Jenner signed countless warrants for the Hilton gang. Whitehead accused Jenner of concealing the identity of informants and of "altering records and warrants, both as to persons, days, and places." When Hester Collingwood dragged a Quaker off to a justice whom she found unwilling to act, she could be sure of better luck with Jenner. Jenner bullied constables: when Charles II died he altered a warrant by inserting the new king's name; a constable queried it, but he ordered him to see that it was "speedily executed at your peril." Jenner bullied juries: when two witnesses repented of laying an information against an ironmonger, saying they were drawn into it "by the subtlety" of Hilton's agents "and some bad women of his," Jenner "endeavoured all he could to sustain the evidence." The Quakers prepared a substantial dossier of sufferings attributable to Jenner between 1683 and 1685.⁶¹

There were other friends besides Jenner. Warrants were secured from Sir Dudley North, Sir John Moore, Sir William Pritchard, Sir Henry Tulse, Sir James Smith, Sir George Waterman, Sir Jonathan Raymond, Sir Thomas Beckford, and Sir Thomas Orby. When the Hiltons drew up a defense in 1684, they cited as witnesses on their behalf the loyal justices Sir Richard Deerham, Sir Clement Armiger, and Sir James Butler. Armiger passed the names of Quakers to Shadd. Sir Thomas Orby sent Hilton lists of warrants executed in Westminster. On 7 October 1682 Hilton accompanied justices Bridgeman and Dewy to Lord Chief Justice North to obtain a legal opinion. They asked, Was a preemptive information that a conventicle would be held at a future date a good enough information in law? Yes, thought North. Might a conviction be made without the victim being summonsed? North was less sure, but asked Sir Edmund Saunders, who said yes. This meant that convictions could be secured without the victims' knowledge; Hilton's men turning up forcibly to distrain goods would be the first they would know of it.[62]

Hilton's support among the church hierarchy is harder to document. Pamphlets against informers accused parish clergy of working with them.[63] Although the evidence is scanty, one link with Archbishop Sancroft is visible. This is through Dr. Thomas Pinfold, who was a character witness on Hilton's behalf in the Clayton case. Pinfold was an ecclesiastical lawyer, chancellor of Peterborough diocese, and a crony of Sancroft's; in 1686 he was knighted and made king's advocate on the Ecclesiastical Commission, where he was said to stand servilely at Lord Chancellor Jeffrey's elbow. A Whig ballad of 1687 linked Hilton to "Pinfold, that spiritual dragoon, who made / By soul-money a pretty thriving trade." There were rumors that Pinfold was to be prosecuted for peculation of moneys from Dissenters and papists. In 1692 he was accused of conniving eight or ten years previously with the vicar of St. Botolph's, Aldgate, Richard Hollingworth, at taking bribes not to cite Dissenters in the church courts: "you received a constant contribution from such of them as you preserved from Doctors Commons."[64]

With the Tory tide flowing fast, in a London deafened by the hectorings of L'Estrange and Nat Thompson, and with the judicial underpinnings offered by Jenkins, Jeffreys, Jenner, and Pinfold, Hilton could afford a remarkable degree of audacity. He used the *Conventicle Courant* to blacken the names of Whig justices. He prosecuted London's most socially elevated conventicles. On 6 February 1683 he invaded the Pinners Hall lecture, the Presbyterians' chief public platform, which had been established under Charles II's Indulgence of 1672. Some fifteen hundred people, including the "wives of citizens of no small account," were present to hear an "old seducer . . . run over . . . his schismatical stuff." Hilton denounced the earl of Clare, whose chapel in the Old Play House in Westminster he raided, and prosecuted the countess's chaplain. He convicted the Dissenter Sir John Shorter, who had stood for mayor in 1681, and pronounced that he was now disqualified from ever being mayor; Shorter was immediately sacked as alderman.[65] Hilton was not constrained by ties of social deference.

None of the well-known Dissenting preachers were left alone. The Presbyterians' aged and redoubtable leader Richard Baxter was prosecuted in October 1682. "I was (being newly risen from extremity of pain) suddenly surprised in my house by a poor violent informer and many constables and officers, who rushed in and apprehended me and served on me one warrant to seize on my person for coming within five miles of a corporation, and five more warrants to distrain for £190, for five sermons." Baxter had no forewarning of this and learned later from the justice who signed the warrants "that the two Hiltons solicited him for them." Dr. Thomas Coxe made oath that Baxter "could not go to prison without danger of death," and the king allowed him house arrest "that I might die at home." This cut no ice with Hilton, whose spies reported that Baxter was up and well enough to go under his own steam to "the necessity house in the yard." Baxter's books and sickbed were seized and sold, but friends bought them back. The gang threatened more warrants, so Baxter took "secret lodgings distant in a stranger's house."[66]

Hilton's victims included the Presbyterians Matthew Sylvester, Baxter's literary executor; Vincent Alsop, whose harassment steadily drove him away from hopes of accommodation with Anglicanism;[67] and Thomas Doolittle, who ran the best-known Dissenter academy in London and whose "incendiary" pupils shouted for Whig candidates in the 1682 shrieval election. One of Hilton's—and the Tory press's—favorite targets was the Independent Stephen Lobb, who was apt to disappear through a trapdoor beneath his barricaded pulpit. Nat Thompson printed a spoof seditious sermon which ended, "Enter informers, and exit teacher at a trap-door." Another ballad imagined the sudden interruption of a Dissenter's rant against the "scarlet whore" of the Church of England:

> But heark!—who'r they without that force the door
> With such importunate officious pow'r?
> Th'Informer comes they cry, th'Informer comes,
> 'Tis Captain Hilton and his Myrmidons!

Down through the trapdoor goes the preacher.[68]

The venerable founder of the Quakers, George Fox, was seized by Shadd, "who was so full of impertinent talk, that the justice grew angry" and ordered Fox's release. William Penn had two brushes with Hilton, just before traveling to and after returning from his new colony in America. On a Sunday in August 1682, he began to preach in Gracechurch Street when a constable, with Hilton as his minder, ordered him to cease. But the constable was so affected by the sermon that he was "as it were disarmed" and so "could not discharge his office." Hilton slunk away. On his return from America, Penn was successfully convicted before Jenner in January 1685 for conventicling in St. Margaret's, Westminster. The witnesses were Eleanor Shafto ("Mrs. Hilton") and Hester Collingwood. Penn remarked on the irony of his position, "One day I was received well at Court as proprietor and governor of a province of the crown, and the next taken up at a meeting by Hilton and Collingwood."[69]

We earlier saw that Hilton was foolhardy in challenging the plutocrat alderman Sir Robert Clayton. He similarly overreached himself on the one occasion that he played for the highest of judicial stakes. In September 1684 Thomas Rosewall, a Presbyterian minister in Rotherhithe, was dragged from his bed, taken before Jeffreys, and charged with treason for words spoken in a sermon. The case came to trial in November, with Jenner and Roger North counsel for the Crown. Rosewall was alleged to have said, "We have had two wicked kings together, who have permitted Popery to enter in under their noses." The witnesses were Eleanor Shafto, Elizabeth Smith, and Hester Collingwood. The trial offers a series of illuminating vignettes. When Smith and Shafto won the trusting friendship of one of Rosewall's hearers, they were instructed to wear soft-soled shoes so that they, like the four hundred others making their way to the meeting through labyrinthine alleyways, would not attract attention. When Rosewall first came before Jeffreys, he addressed him in Latin and Greek in order to disabuse him of his notions about ignorant canting fanatics. When cross-questioned in court, the informers were able to debate scriptural texts. Rosewall skillfully blackened the informers by bringing forward witnesses who showed that the gang regularly tried to bribe and blackmail Dissenters, and he rattled Jenner by imputations of systematic compounding. Rosewall's defense was widely admired; it made a deep impression on the young Presbyterian journalist John Dunton, and even the leading courtier the earl of Sunderland conceded that it was a fine performance. But Jeffreys summed up with a characteristic harangue against "seminaries of sedition," and the jury brought in a guilty verdict within half an hour.

One of Rosewall's witnesses, Sir John Talbot, who had once employed Shafto in his household, went to the king and denounced the Crown witnesses: Smith was a blackmailer and Shafto "a naughty filthy woman," Hilton's "whore." If Rosewall were executed, London would be totally at the mercy of a gang of grasping perjurers. The king was persuaded. Rosewall was given a lenient sentence, later canceled by royal pardon. The chastened law officers patched up the informers' reputations as best they could. Rosewall had no doubt as to who had put the Hilton gang up to prosecuting him. "I am well assured the Recorder of London [Jenner] hath been the bloody contriver of all this from first to last."

That an "over-credulous jury . . . infamous evidence and . . . the Lord Chief Justice's law" might have sent a man to the gallows merely for preaching was "very hard," wrote a Whig commentator. The "great justice and mercy in the king . . . extremely satisfies" the Dissenters, and, Dunton noted, Rosewall "came off with a great deal of reputation."[70] A wave of relief spread through London, giving rise to premature hopes that the persecuting fever would abate. A quarter of a century later Lord Harcourt, speaking for the defense at the impeachment of the Tory clergyman Dr. Henry Sacheverell, paralleled the Whig trial of Sacheverell for words in a sermon with Rosewall's trial by Tories. The great state trial of Sacheverell produced another parallel. The Presbyterian meetinghouse in Fetter Lane, so often a target for Hilton, was destroyed by a Sacheverellite mob on 1 March 1710.[71]

VI

Repeatedly, even in the worst of times, Hilton met with resilient and inventive countermeasures from the Dissenters. Craig Horle has shown how the image that the Quakers projected of martyred passivity in the face of persecution is belied by their legal resourcefulness.[72] Quakers had no qualms about muckraking in order to expose informers. There were also non-Quaker hands at work in organizing retaliation. Hilton complained of a Stoke Newington caucus, calling it "the Sanhedrim of Newington" and "the convocation of the scattered churches at Newington." This referred to the Independent conventicle that had been served for a generation by "Cromwell's pope," John Owen, until his death in 1681, and which was now presided over by Sir John Hartopp. Hartopp, a leading Whig who sat for Leicester in the three Exclusion Parliaments, was the son-in-law of the Cromwellian major general Fleetwood and was nearly assassinated in 1681 by a trigger-happy Tory keen to kill "all fanatics." The Stoke Newington caucus also included old Charles Fleetwood himself and the wealthy Jamaica merchant William Coward. It is evident from Hilton's sneering asides that Hartopp's circle was giving spirit to Whig constables and advising them on legal tactics. The Hiltons broke up Hartopp's conventicle several times and levied massive distraints.[73]

We earlier encountered the constables' everyday evasions. But their countermeasures were more concerted. Their cross-questioning of Hilton's servants' credentials and frog-marching them to a justice to get confirmation became a regular technique "according to the Whiggish way." Whig justices colluded by contriving to avoid being at home on Sundays. In September 1682 the Hiltons were hauled off to the homes of several Whig justices—Clayton, Ward, Lawrence—until eventually Frederick was found at home. Frederick begrudgingly said that the constable must do his duty, but a good deal of delay had been effected. The following week constable Robert Bates, a locksmith in Lothbury, dragged Hilton's man off to five justices in turn. Sir Patience Ward was at home, but "indisposition of body was pretended by Sir Patience's servants." This tactic easily became a way of making Hilton's men run the gauntlet of hostile streets. The constables carried George Hilton and his henchmen "up and down the City to show him, and with whoops and halloos to incense the rabble, cried Informer, Informer"—"to the great hazard of their lives."[74]

The most elementary countermeasure was physical violence. Jenner protested on the Hiltons' behalf that "they could not walk the streets in safety, but they had stones thrown at them." The cry of "Informer, Informer" quickly brought out an angry crowd. One Sunday in August 1682, the cry went up, "[There is] the great rogue that belongeth to Hilton; let us stone him to death." In November, three hundred people gathered in Spitalfields Square, and refuge had to be taken "out of danger of being massacred." When the goods of Nathaniel Partridge, who had once been chaplain to General Fleetwood, were seized, it "caused such a rabble that two files of musketeers were forced to be sent for from Whitehall to preserve quietness."[75]

Sometimes violence was encouraged by the noncompliance of justices. On 25 June 1682 John Hilton, on his way to make some arrests, "was followed by a rude multitude" who threw dirt and stones. In Basinghall Street he would have been "murdered" had not a man pulled him into a house. He eventually took twenty prisoners to the Guildhall, but neither Frederick nor Clayton "would be spoken with," which "so animated the rabble" that they liberated the prisoners. Hilton needed musketeers to conduct him to the riverside, but no boatman would take him, for the mob threatened to sink them. He took refuge with "a truly loyal" victualer by Bow Church and the crowd was "for pulling the house down, to have the informer out." In September Hilton lost his sword, wig, and cravat in a melee.

Hilton recognized that the Quakers were committed to pacifism, but observed that Presbyterians were ready to protect Quakers. When Christopher Smith was beaten up at the Devonshire House Quaker meeting, he conceded that it was the Presbyterians' and not the Quakers' doing. The violence of Dissenters who were not Quakers, especially when sometimes they mistakenly attacked innocent bystanders thinking them informers, was grist for Hilton's sneer about those who "ought to bear the cross patiently, [but do] crucify." Certainly Dissenter rhetoric about the passive suffering of Israel in Egypt obscures the readiness of Presbyterian apprentices to take to the streets.[76]

The printing press offered oppositional tactics, too. Dissenters put pressure on street hawkers not to sell the *Conventicle Courant*.[77] They published attacks against it: *A Letter to Hilton, the Grand Informer*, *A Second Letter*, and *The English Guzman; or, Captain Hilton's Memoirs* (1683), numbers 1 and 2.[78] The last of these looked like developing into a regular riposte, and may help explain why the government became anxious to suppress the *Courant* itself. Hilton's "Holy War" also drew fire in general attacks on informers, including *The Informer's Looking Glass* (1682) and *The Informer's Doom* (1683), early productions from the printing press of the Presbyterian John Dunton. The gang were denounced as "viperous vermin," as papists "doing the Jesuits' drudgery, persecuting alamode de France," men who in Queen Mary's time would have been among "bloody Bonner's catchpoles," who in Spain would have served the Inquisition. In them "the words loyal and gentlemen are grown common prostitutes."[79] In 1683 Dunton reprinted *The Arraignment of Mr. Persecution* by the Leveller Richard Overton, first published nearly forty years before.

A verse tract, *The Informer's Lecture to his Sons* (1682), took a different tack. It expressed the Puritan moralist's distaste for the victory of formal church membership as the badge of public Christianity, instead of the conduct of an upright and spiritual life. It protested that nobody cared to rid the nation of whoring, drinking, swearing, and Sabbath breaking. In the prevailing climate, "Praying and preaching!, this is worse by far, / Than all the crying sins of Sodom are." In England now, "The fault is greater, and the dangers more, / To teach five sisters, than to bed a score."[80] John Hilton was perhaps responsible for an antidote to this tract, *The English Jeroboam* (1683), which depicts a pompously busybodying shopkeeper-constable, earnest in the moral policing of the parish, strict in the enforcement of laws against swearing and drinking, but "strangely startled at the appearing of an informer . . . presenting a conventicle warrant." Upon taking office these men swore to uphold the laws that defended the church and so to destroy conventicles, "yet so treacherous are their memories, that they forget it, and alas . . . are found members of such meetings." This tract poked fun at the Puritan tradition of a godly parish magistracy.[81]

The attacks on Hilton went beyond general abuse, for the Dissenters took considerable trouble to investigate the Hiltons' background. *The English Guzman* was a ruthless catalog of the Hiltons' insalubrious past of fraud, forgery, coining, underage sex, adultery, and the "title of Protestant . . . as falsely assumed as that of captain." The account was based partly on a report sent from Westmorland to the Quaker leader George Fox,[82] but also on the search of legal records undertaken for Sir Robert Clayton. To this was added the splendid humiliation of printing a letter from Hilton to his mother announcing his imminent knighthood. Hilton's main agent, Shadd, was exposed, too. In 1675 he had been convicted of stealing £300 worth of tobacco, jailed, and burnt in the hand, and in 1678 he was again jailed, at Coventry, as a papist. *The English Guzman* closed with an invitation to read more in the next issue: "Enough for a penny till next." Given that by the beginning of 1683 these papers had "much weakened" Hilton's credit and made his "perjury, forgery, and felony" common knowledge, the surprise is that his career continued so long afterwards.[83]

More subtle measures against the Hiltons lay in the intricacies and ambiguities of the law. Constables were warned that they were open to actions for trespass and false imprisonment if their warrants were unsound. In December 1682 Lobb took out a warrant for the arrest of Shadd for stealing his cloak, pulled from him as he fled arrest. In 1682 one White, a worshiper at Samuel Annesley's Presbyterian conventicle, prosecuted Justice Balch for false imprisonment. Charges of trespass were brought against distrainers. Some constables were encouraged by having their fines paid for them. Mr. Harris, tallow-chandler in Little Wood Street, was distrained for not acting on his warrants, but "no doubt, he will expect to be reimbursed by the fraternity, that he is so kind to."[84]

For several years the Quakers had gathered legal opinions on the interpretation of the Conventicle Act. They were encapsulated in Thomas Ellwood's *Caution to Constables* (1683). This was plainly prompted by Hilton's attack on the constables, for it offered advice on how they might stand their ground and "not be so scared" of informers. Justices, it urged, should not give credit to informers of notorious character. Warrants should not be issued on informations that amounted only to a future presumption of a meeting for worship. Informers should prove that they were present throughout a meeting and that the meeting was demonstrably a "seditious" conventicle under "colour and pretence" of religion. Constables were only required to inform justices of a conventicle, not to go armed with musketeers and forcibly arrest people, and still less to pass names to informers. Constables might choose which justice to report to. Defendants must be summoned to a justice, and witnesses publicly confront them; secret convictions were a scandal against natural justice. Constables could only be fined if shown to have "wilfully and wittingly" forsaken their duty; "absence, illness, urgency of business, ignorance, [and] misunderstanding" might exonerate them. Officers should not break doors or windows in order to distrain, nor strive unduly to find purchasers for distrained goods when none were forthcoming, nor sell below market price. Ellwood finally urged that the Conventicle Act "doth not forbid women to preach and teach," because in that part of the act the prohibition is restricted "to the male sex, by using the masculine gender only," whereas another clause refers to "him or her." This was, no doubt, an optimistic interpretation of a drafting slip.[85]

There appear to have been three serious cases brought against the Hiltons. In December 1683 the Dissenters, who now had a defense fund, succeeded in temporarily imprisoning George Hilton and others in the Marshalsea for debt. In January Jenner bailed him. The case came to court in April 1684, but when it emerged that the Dissenters had bribed a man to whom Hilton owed £5 to bring the case, it fell at the order of Sir James Butler. This verdict, Hilton hoped, "will have that influence on the Dissenters as utterly to discourage them from buying any more of his or his servants' debts." Even so, the Hiltons claimed that several thousand pounds' worth of prosecutions fell because of this distraction.[86]

In January 1684 Roger Morrice reported that the two Hiltons were in Newgate, "charged to have cheated the crown of £500 or £1100 in money that they had levied upon conventicles and converted to their own use." In December 1685 a far more serious charge brought John Hilton into custody again. Jenner himself was constrained to sign a warrant for his arrest, "being charged on oath before me of compounding several warrants under my hand and seal." Hilton went into hiding and was still at large in January.[87] "Defrauding the king [and] the poor of their respective third parts" was not to be tolerated.[88] That Hilton was compounding was not a new discovery. He was accused of it early in 1683, when he took thirty shillings in private settlement from two people in Drury Lane. The Hiltons of course claimed that everything they levied was handed over to legal officers as the law required. It does seem that they had acted cautiously for some time, for they were aware that the Dissenters were attempting to lure them into compounding.[89] Quite apart from the Crown's fiscal interest, it angered overseers of the poor if moneys were diverted into informers' pockets.

The Hiltons still did not desist. It is at least a tribute to the consistency of their politics that after the accession of James II in February 1685, they ignored the king's crablike shifts toward easing the Dissenters' condition. On 10 March 1686 the king published a general pardon that suspended proceedings against Dissenters. Christopher Smith spent the day breaking down doors in Edmonton. On the twenty-eighth, George Hilton, with Eleanor Shafto and John Brown as witnesses, prosecuted the Stoke Newington circle once more, claiming that it was the sixth time they had caught their preacher. In April the gang was as active as ever, although the Edmonton case was overturned under the king's pardon.[90] Constables, nervous of where they stood after the pardon, were told by Justice William Cleeve to carry on; he would "stand by them." But the pardon began to turn the tide. Christopher Smith was beaten when suppressing a meeting at Devonshire House, and when the culprits were charged with riot, they got off lightly. The mayor was persuaded to moderation now that the gang had, by the pardon, "lost their plea as being the king's officers and king's witnesses and put on by the king." The Dissenters were now "upon more equal terms."[91]

VII

It was the Quaker George Whitehead who finally destroyed the Hilton gang. He was one of their victims. In 1682 he was prosecuted before Sir Clement Armiger on the evidence of John Hilton and Gabriel Shadd. In 1683 his goods were distrained; he lost bedding, chairs, looking glasses, currants, and sugar from his shop. In 1684 he was again prosecuted, for riot, informed against by Hester Collingwood.[92] Since 1682 he had been helping George Fox gather the ample evidence against the gang that today can be found in the papers of the Meeting for Sufferings.

Whitehead made a habit of boldly seeking audiences with the king, and despite keeping his hat on and addressing his monarch with "thee" and "thou" in the Quaker way, he was successful at winning respites for oppressed Friends. Whitehead was convinced of James's commitment to toleration and claimed that at the outset of the reign he had a premonition "that the Lord would be good to his people, and they should have ease, even under that king's reign." Within weeks of James's accession he secured an audience, cataloging the number of Quakers in jail and protesting against the informers. Several hundred Quakers were released, but in May Whitehead complained again, specifically about Sir Thomas Jenner, whom he identified as the informers' protector. When over a year later the general pardon was seen not to be properly effective, he petitioned James yet again against Jenner's "mercenary and merciless informers." He asked the king for commissioners to investigate the "false swearing, clandestine convictions, excessive and outrageous distress and havoc, which they made, and cause to be made, upon the goods and estates of our Friends, shopkeepers, tradesmen, manufacturers, and many industrious families deep sufferers thereby, tending wholly to dissolve and ruin them."[93]

James complied, and on 4 and 14 June 1686 the Treasury solicitors, Richard Graham and Philip Burton, took evidence at Clifford's Inn.[94] Whitehead gathered information on some fifty cases, charging the informers with perjury and violent seizure of goods. Witnesses and informers were summoned to appear, and in a hot and overcrowded room he held forth hour after hour, getting through only a quarter of his cases on the first day. We know the names of the victims whose cases he investigated. The Friends Library has his case notes, endorsed with numbers.[95] Number four was a case in which one Henry Kindon of Basinghall Street had five warrants served against him on the same day, all signed by Jenner. Number six was a case that showed the hold that Hilton's agents had over minor gang members; the excuse of two perjured witnesses was that they were Hester Collingwood's "witnesses and what she said, they must and should swear."[96]

The Hiltons themselves were summoned to appear. John Hilton turned up drunk, shouting that "he cared not a fart for the king's commissioners." Whitehead dryly responded that "such drunken informers esteemed themselves eminent servants to the king and church." The Hiltons, "bitterly enraged," took steps to forestall Whitehead's inquiry. They had him arrested and taken before the lord mayor on the day before the second hearing was due. Whitehead told the mayor that there was no case against him, but only after being detained until ten at night was he released. After the second hearing the Treasury solicitors cut short the proceedings, saying they had enough evidence to make their report. When Whitehead went to see them, he found their draft report to be thoroughly inadequate, recommending merely that there were perhaps less severe ways of punishing Dissenters. The whole inquiry was indeed distasteful work for Graham and Burton, who were Tory instruments, themselves avid receivers of fines, traders in pardons of Monmouth rebels, and eager for a conviction in the Rosewall trial. Burnet thought them "fitter men to have served in a court of Inquisition than a legal government," and Roger Morrice compared them to Henry VII's infamous agents Empson and Dudley. In due course the king sacked them. They confessed to Whitehead that they had been prevailed upon, "sent to out of London, from some great person, or persons of the Church, and much requested to do or report nothing that might disable the informers, or put them by from their service, they being of so great service . . . to the Church." Unfortunately, those churchmen were not named.[97]

The indomitable Whitehead made sure the inquiry's findings were properly reported to the king. In July several of the Hiltons' accomplices were charged with perjury at the quarter sessions. It was "the Newington gentlemen" (Hartopp's caucus) who then brought charges of subornation and perjury against John Hilton and John Brown. In October the matter was "so full proved that the jury could not but find them guilty." Hilton was undaunted. He "made a long harangue to the court setting forth that he was a captain, a person of condition, of good quality." His plea to be excused the pillory was granted; he was fined five hundred marks and imprisoned until it was paid. He was incapable of seeing which way the new political wind was blowing; with Brown, his mistress, and others, he petitioned Secretary of State Sunderland for the sacking of several London justices as "favourers of fanatics," to which Lord Chancellor Jeffreys (now singing a new tune) responded that the Hiltons were "rogues and rascals." The last public figures prepared to put in a word for them were Sir Richard Holloway, a judge who had presided at several of the Whig show trials, who insisted they "were loyal persons, and had done the crown very good service," and Sir Robert Wright, a colleague of Jeffreys in the Bloody Assizes, who complained that it was "well known that the informers had been prosecuted with great impetuousness and severity by conventiclers." Morrice reported that "the hierarchy seem to think that it is much to their disserve that the informers are some of them convicted of perjury." By January 1687 the justices had little choice but to suspend prosecutions of Dissenters for lack of informers.

Some of the gang "stood in the pillory," some "were forced to escape and fly, and others turned to beggary" and came "to miserable ends." How many were formally charged is not clear. We know that John Hilton, Shafto, Brown, Clayton, Anne Smith, and Charles Austin were found guilty of perjury and that Shadd died in jail. Clayton and Smith stood in the pillory for two hours "and were very much pelted . . . with dirt, etc." Eleanor Shafto was convicted and "whipped . . . at the cart's tail." Hester Collingwood, Christopher Smith, and Charles Baker were reported to be in penury. George Hilton managed to get himself a job as "servant to a great person" (perhaps Jenner), but lacking a decent suit of clothes to present himself to his new master, he turned up at, of all places, Whitehead's house to beg some money ("I gave him something, being willing to render good against evil"). Whitehead was "comforted . . . now these wretches were fain to come and beg of us."[98]

VIII

When in April 1687 James II issued his Declaration of Indulgence formalizing toleration for Dissenters, the past deeds of the Hilton gang became useful ammunition for his Whig propagandists. A poem besmirched the Church of England:

> What's now become of our informing crew,
> The Browns, the Hiltons? O loyal men and true!
> Once pillars of our church—true church by law—
> Far more were bugbear'd to her out of awe
> Than all our sermon-readers e'er could draw;
> Those useful sparks, implements orthodox.

In 1688 Henry Care used stories about these "infamous wretches" in his tolerationist newspaper *Public Occurrences*. He recorded with relish that the "Generalissimo of the Arabian troops called informers" now lived incognito and that his brother had recently been beaten up.[99]

The Hiltons disappeared without trace, but after the Revolution they haunted the Tory grandees who had given them succor. During the general election of 1690, a Whig pamphlet exhorted London's citizens not to vote for the old persecutors. It named Sir George Waterman, Sir James Edwards, Sir James Smith, Sir Robert Jeffries, Sir Jonathan Raymond, and Sir Thomas Beckford and said that they had "made it their practice to grant five or six warrants apiece upon a weekday" to John Hilton, "a villain who had been guilty of forgery and coining," and to Gabriel Shadd, a papist felon, and that they had encouraged Hilton to prosecute Sir Robert Clayton "for discountenancing their villainous undertakings." One diarist thought that the Convention Parliament was dissolved in order to preclude an attack on those Tories "who had any hand in King Charles II's and King James II's reigns in persecuting, fining, punishing and imprisoning the separatists."[100]

Many Whigs were furious that those who engaged in state terror in the early 1680s got off scot-free, and they sought ways of weakening King William III's pragmatic indemnity. Pressure mounted on Tories believed to have lined their pockets. Rival syndicates competed to secure a commission to "discover and recover from divers persons who formerly levied sums upon Dissenters . . . and did not pay the same into the Exchequer." The Crown was concerned that this would cause "vexation and disturbance" to mayors, sheriffs, justices, and other public servants and that unsupervised compositions might occur. Nonetheless a commission was issued, and for a time Tories were harassed. But before long the commissioners were encouraged to pursue recusancy fines from a less politically embarrassing prey—Roman Catholics.[101]

One Tory victim was Sir Dudley North, who was harassed to and beyond the grave by the "malice and revenge" of "the fanatics," who claimed that more than £100 was owing to the Exchequer. His loyal brother Roger devoted several pages in his *Life* of Dudley to vindicating him. True, "he had a full share" in the informing trade, as perforce a justice must at that time, but "it is certain that he took very little pleasure in this office" and positive that all monies were meticulously accounted for. The case against North lapsed.[102] The Hiltons' chief patron, however, was successfully ruined. Jenner had few friends; he had collaborated with James II until the end, sitting as a member of the Ecclesiastical Commission. He fled with the king in December 1688 and was captured at Faversham and kept in the Tower for a year. In November 1692 his son was arrested for distributing Jacobite propaganda, and the government decided to destroy the father. He was accused of levying £3,000 worth of fines on Dissenters in the 1680s without having turned the money into the Exchequer. The charge was hard to substantiate, and Jenner was allowed to plead James II's pardon, but he was a broken man, "despised and neglected to the last degrees of infamy, till the hour of his death, which nobody thought worth recording."[103] John Locke had the likes of Jenner in mind when he composed his *Third Letter for Toleration* (1692). He wrote sarcastically of "the watchful charity of others in this age [who] hath found out ways to encourage informers."[104]

Yet it cannot be said that England's governors resolved to do without informing. Certain categories of informing were restricted by an act of 1692, but in many cases rewards to encourage private indictments were increased. An act of 1700 offered £100 to informers who secured the conviction of Catholic priests, and both a Game Act of 1722 and the Gin Act of 1736 allowed them half of the fines incurred. Late in the eighteenth century, itinerant informers made a living out of turnpike prosecutions, bringing in their train the usual grievances of perjury and compounding.[105] Moreover, the Hiltons' chameleon admixture of law enforcement and criminality was a persistent phenomenon, exemplified most famously in the career of "the thief-taker general," Jonathan Wild. The thief-taker, Ruth Paley has written, "straddled the margins of the conventional and criminal worlds and formed, in effect, a sort of entrepreneurial police force, dependent on fees and rewards."[106]

The Hilton gang did very little damage to informing, for it was their targets rather than the practice itself that provoked general disapproval. In the 1690s the burgeoning Societies for the Reformation of Manners made extensive use of informers, whom Roy Porter has called "vigilante smut hounds."[107] In 1691 between 150 and 200 informers were active in London rooting out blasphemy, Sabbath breaking, and prostitution. Blank warrants were used; constables were sacked for failing to execute warrants; and there were rumors of peculation, private compositions, and vexatious suits. Astonishingly, the new informers' public defender was John Dunton, the Presbyterian journalist who had published tracts against Hilton, had witnessed Rosewall's trial, and had married the daughter of one of Hilton's victims, Samuel Annesley. In his *Athenian Mercury*, a popular magazine that answered readers' questions, Dunton dealt with the query, "Whether an informer is not as much a rogue now for informing against those vices that the law now takes hold on as he was for informing against the Dissenters formerly?" Dunton roundly pronounced it a foolish question, for informing was honorable when directed against abominable vice and odious only when done "for lucre, malice and faction" against innocent worshipers. Some senior Londoners did try to discourage the Reformation of Manners movement by damning informing. There can be little doubt that it was to guard against unfortunate historical parallels that the societies of religious young men "for promoting the execution of the laws made against profaneness and debauchery" drew up elaborate constitutions to prevent "indiscreet zeal" and inadvertent illegality. Careful accounting put the finances aboveboard, and weekly meetings for prayer and "sober conversation" swathed informing in the cloak of a godly confraternity, a secular monasticism of the pure life. This was the Revolution's answer to the Hilton gang: it proclaimed a society that preferred moral to ecclesiastical uniformity, but which was no less vigorous and interventionist in its social discipline.[108]

The realization of any political, religious, or moral program in early modern England could scarcely be achieved without informers; this is as evident from Thomas Cromwell's postbag in the 1530s and William Pitt's in the 1790s[109] as it is from Sir Leoline Jenkins's in the 1680s. The enforcement of law depended upon the cooperation of ordinary householders who took up the office of constable. The galvanizing of such officers often required the zeal of other amateurs, informers acting as freelance law enforcers with roving commissions, unlettered in the law but with easy access to magistrates and courts. The extent of their power over people's lives depended in turn upon the legal and political resourcefulness of their victims. Even when the machinery of state was tightly in the grip of a single-minded Tory elite, the law remained a contested resource manipulable by all parties. The history of religious persecution under Charles II is less a history of statutes than of contingent decisions about enforcement. It took a herculean effort by a Tory zealot substantially to close the yawning gap between enactment and enforcement. The Hiltons' audacity is breathtaking: they crossed every social boundary in pursuit of their prey. Their campaign was the best that could be done by the Tory elite to purge the metropolis of Dissenters. It produced four years of misery, but it was fatally flawed by its dependence upon men and women with murky pasts and grubby motives; by the fact that the law provided an arena for contestation rather than a simple instrument of elite coercion; and by the tension that existed between vexatious zeal and communal solidarity. James II's abandonment of Toryism and religious intolerance was the Hiltons' downfall, yet even during their ascendancy they often faltered or were caught out. Archbishop Sancroft learned that it was difficult to build the Anglican Zion with crooked timber.

Notes

For commenting on a draft of this essay I am grateful to Justin Champion, Tim Harris, Christine MacLeod, Steven Pincus, and Amanda Vickery. I am indebted to Sara Pennell for undertaking some of the preliminary research. Versions of this paper were given in Cambridge, London, Norwich, Oxford, and Sheffield. An abridged version appears in *History Today* (October 1997). Readers unfamiliar with the period may note that "Dissenters" and "Nonconformists" are synonymous terms (I have preferred the former), and so are "magistrates" and "justices" when referring to justices of the peace. All works cited were published in London unless otherwise stated.

1. George Whitehead, *Christian Progress* (1725), 500; William Crouch, *Posthuma Christiana* (1712), 104–5.

2. The Hiltons have hitherto only fleetingly surfaced in modern histories. C. Horle, *The Quakers and the English Legal System, 1660–1688* (Philadelphia, 1988) provided vital clues. T. Harris, *London Crowds in the Reign of Charles II* (Cambridge, 1987) offered an appropriate framework. An account of the suppression of Dissent is given in A. G. Smith, "London and the Crown, 1681–1685," Ph.D. diss., Wisconsin, 1967, chap. 11. For a parallel case study of the impact of religious division on a London urban community see M. Goldie and J. Spurr, "Politics and the Restoration Parish: Edward Fowler and the Struggle for St. Giles Cripplegate," *English Historical Review* 103 (1994): 572–96.

3. *The English Guzman; or, Captain Hilton's Memoirs* (1683), no. 2. Canada was opened up to provide Europeans with beaver hats.

4. *English Guzman*, no. 1; *A Letter to Hilton, the Grand Informer* (1682), 2.

5. *The Conventicle Courant* (hereafter cited as CC) began on 14 July 1682, became weekly from no. 4 (14 August), went biweekly with no. 19 (22 November), reverted to weekly with no. 25 (1 January 1683), and ceased publication after no. 30 (14 February). The fullest set is in the Bodleian Library: Nichols Newspapers, vols. 4–5 (which lacks no. 18). The paper is a single sheet folio, except no. 1, which has two sheets. The colophon usually reads, "London, printed by the assigns of John Hilton, Gent." It is briefly noted in J. Sutherland, *The Restoration Newspaper and its Development* (Cambridge, 1986), 175–76.

6. See, for example, J. A. Sharpe, *Crime in Seventeenth-Century England* (Cambridge, 1983), 47–48, for an Essex case of someone who "progressed from quasi-professional informer to county weights and measures inspector."

7. See M. W. Beresford, "The Common Informer, the Penal Statutes, and Economic Regulation," *Economic History Review* 10 (1957): 221–38; G. R. Elton, "Informing for Profit," in his *Star Chamber Stories* (1958); M. G. Davies, *The Enforcement of English Apprenticeship* (Cambridge, 1956), chaps. 2–3; R. B. Shoemaker, *Prosecution and Punishment: Petty Crime and the Law in London and Rural Middlesex, c.1660–1725* (Cambridge, 1991), passim; M. J. Ingram, "Communities and Courts: Law and Disorder in Early Seventeenth-Century Wiltshire," in *Crime in England, 1550–1800*, ed. J. S. Cockburn (1977), 122–23; Sharpe, *Crime in Seventeenth-Century England*, 46–48.

8. L. Johnston, *The Rebirth of Private Policing* (1992); D. Hay and F. Snyder, eds., *Policing and Prosecution in Britain, 1750–1850* (Oxford, 1989).

9. See A. Fletcher, "The Enforcement of the Conventicle Acts, 1664–1679," in *Persecution and Toleration*, ed. W. J. Sheils, Studies in Church History, 21 (Oxford, 1984).

10. *The Character of an Informer* (1675), 1, 3. See also John Hicks, *A True and Faithful Narrative of the Unjust and Illegal Sufferings* (1671); *Don Quixot Redivivus encountring a barns-door* (1673); Owen Stockton, *A Rebuke to the Informers* (1675); *The Devouring Informers of Bristol* (1680); *A Word of Advice* and *The Present Distress* in *The Works of John Owen*, ed. W. H. Goold (1850–53), 21:445–56, 473–80.

11. See T. Ellwood, *The History of the Life of Thomas Ellwood*, 6th ed. (Manchester, 1855), 193–205; J. Gough, *A History of the People Called Quakers* (Dublin, 1789); W. Sewell, *The History of the Quakers*, 2 vols. (1834); W. C. Braithwaite, *The Second Period of Quakerism* (1921); A. W. Braithwaite, "Early Friends and Informers," *Journal of the Friends Historical Society* 51 (1966): 107–14; Horle, *Quakers and the English Legal System*, especially 122–25, 131–36, 194–208; G. R. Cragg, *Puritanism in the Period of the Great Persecution, 1660–1688* (Cambridge, 1957); C. E. Whiting, *Studies in English Puritanism* (1968), 156–57, 162, 387, 435–41; M. R. Watts, *The Dissenters* (Oxford, 1978), 244–47; C. Hill, *A Turbulent, Seditious, and Factious People: John Bunyan and his Church* (Oxford, 1988), 247–49, 317; N. H. Keeble, *The Literary Culture of Nonconformity in Late Seventeenth-Century England* (Leicester, 1987), 55, 74; G. L. Turner, "Williamson's Spy Book," *Transactions of the Congregational Historical Society* 5 (1912): 242–58, 301–17, 345–56.

12. Especially Edward Pearse, *The Conformist's Fourth Plea* (1683), which includes "some account of the infamous lives and lamentable deaths of some informers."

13. P. Jackson, "Nonconformists and Society in Devon, 1660–1689," Ph.D. diss., Exeter, 1986, chap. 7.

14. *English Guzman*, no. 1; H. E. Rollins, ed., *The Pepys Ballads*, 8 vols. (Cambridge, Mass., 1929–32), 3:16–21; *The Bloody Murtherers Executed* (1675); John Tonge, *God's Revenge Against Murther* (1680). Sandford's father was a Cavalier M.P. in the Long Parliament; his son was Whig M.P. for Westmorland, Morpeth, and Appleby, 1695–1724.

15. British Library, Stowe MS. 305, fol. 7; *Calendar of State Papers, Domestic* (1682), 314.

16. Original Record of Sufferings, Friends Library, London, fol. 827; J. C. Jeaffreson, ed., *Middlesex County Records*, 4 vols. (1892), 4:246–47, 308.

17. *Cal.S.P.Dom.* (1682), 520–21. "Forty, or thereabouts, being wholly employed in that affair": BL, Stowe MS. 305, fol. 7.

18. Forty names are listed in Whitehead, *Christian Progress*, 596 (except that Martha Hagg is a mistake for Martha Fogg, and Francis Scoltrop for Frances Sculthorpe). Other gang members not listed in Whitehead include Ann Clayton, John Collingwood, and Mary Fairey.

19. Great Book of Sufferings, Friends Library, 5:475–76, 480; *Middlesex County Records*, 4:308; *Cal.S.P.Dom.* (1683), 221.

20. First Day's Meetings, Friends Library, 1682–83:150; Original Record of Sufferings, fols. 43, 195, 360, 825; Great Book of Sufferings, 5:357–58; Horle, *Quakers and the English Legal System*, 131–32.

21. Several husband-and-wife teams were involved: Charles and Mary Austin, Gabriel and Dorothy Shadd, Christopher and Elizabeth Smith, John and Anne Smith, Arthur and Ann Clayton, John and Hester Collingwood.

22. Whitehead, *Christian Progress*, 584.

23. Great Book of Sufferings, 5:456; Original Record of Sufferings, fols. 47, 133, 246, 508, 552, 829; Whitehead, *Christian Progress*, 560, 585; T. B. Howell, ed., *A Complete Collection of State Trials and Proceedings for High Treason and Other Crimes and Misdemeanors from the Earliest Period to the Year 1783*, 21 vols. (1811–26), 10:221.

24. CC, nos. 3, 6, 16, 17.

25. CC, passim; BL, Stowe MS. 305, fols. 7–8; *Cal.S.P.Dom.* (1682), 314, 520–21; Ibid. (1683–84), 229.

26. C. Herrup, *The Common Peace* (Cambridge, 1987), 68.

27. *The Informer's Looking Glass* (1682), 1.

28. CC, no. 1; Roger L'Estrange, *The Observator*, no. 203, 11 September 1682. For the theological case for intolerance see M. Goldie, "The Theory of Religious Intolerance in Restoration England," in O. P. Grell, J. I. Israel, and N. Tyacke, eds., *From Persecution to Toleration* (Oxford, 1991).

29. "London Conventicles in 1683," in *Congregational Historical Society Transactions* 3 (1907–8): 364–66; W. T. Whitley, "Thompson's List of Conventicles in 1683," Ibid. 4 (1909–10), 49–53; CC, no. 26. When Edmund Calamy collected information in the 1690s on the fates of the Puritan ministers, he made use of CC. A. G. Matthews, ed., *Calamy Revised* (Oxford, 1934), xlvi, 384.

30. *The Fetter Lane Loyalist* (1681) is a print showing Thompson kneeling to offer his services to Cellier and popery. See G. M. Peerbohms, *Nathaniel Thompson, Tory Printer* (Nijmegen, 1983), 29, 31–32, 68; L. Rostenberg, "Nathaniel Thompson, Catholic Printer and Publisher of the Restoration," *The Library* 10 (1955): 186–202; Sutherland, *Restoration Newspaper and its Development*, 55–56, 74, 193–97.

31. *Letter to Hilton*, 1. See also, against Thompson, *Trincalo Sainted; or . . . the Jesuit Implement* (1682).

32. See G. S. De Krey, "London Radicals and Revolutionary Politics, 1675–1683," in T. Harris, P. Seaward, and M. Goldie, eds., *The Politics of Religion in Restoration England* (Oxford, 1990); J. Levin, *The Charter Controversy in the City of London, 1660–1688* (1969); Smith, "London and the Crown"; R. R. Sharpe, *London and the Kingdom*, 3 vols. (1894–95), vol. 2; J. Scott, *Algernon Sidney and the Restoration Crisis* (Cambridge, 1991), 169, 172–73, 272–73.

33. They were secured by an informer called William Shermar who reported to Secretary of State Jenkins and Sir Richard Deerham. *Cal.S.P.Dom.* (1680–81), 592, 613; Ibid. (1682), 8, 29, 93.

34. H. Bowler, *London Sessions Records, 1605–1685* (1934), 363; S. Schofield, *Jeffreys of the Bloody Assizes* (1937), 56–58, 62.

35. *Cal.S.P.Dom.* (1680–81), 252, 613; Ibid. (1682), 8, 29, 520–21, 614; Ibid. (1683–84), 204, 228–29.

36. *A Word of Advice* (1682); Cambridge University Library classmark Sel.3.232(8).

37. H. B. Simpson, "The Office of Constable," *English Historical Review* 10 (1895): 623–41; J. R. Kent, *The English Village Constable, 1580–1642* (Oxford, 1986), chaps. 7–8; K. Wrightson, "Two Concepts of Order: Justices, Constables, and Jurymen in Seventeenth-Century England," in *An Ungovernable People*, ed. J. Brewer and J. Styles (1980), 21–46; J. Boulton, *Neighbourhood and Society: A London Suburb in the Seventeenth Century* (Cambridge, 1987), 140, 262–68, 139–46; J. M. Beattie, "London Juries in the 1690s," in J. S. Cockburn and T. A. Green, eds., *Twelve Good Men and True* (Princeton, 1988), 248–50; J. A. Sharpe, "Crime and Delinquency in an Essex Parish," in *Crime in England*, ed. Cockburn; Sharpe, *Crime in Seventeenth-Century England*, 34–36, 173–76.; J. Samaha, *Law and Order in Historical Perspective* (New York, 1974), 84–88.

38. Wrightson, "Two Concepts of Order," 21–22.

39. CC, nos. 1, 2, 7, 17. For attempts in the localities to discipline constables see T. C. Curtis, "Quarter Sessions Appearances and their Background," in *Crime in England*, ed. Cockburn, 144–45; A. M. Coleby, *Central Government and the Localities: Hampshire, 1649–1689* (Cambridge, 1987), 203.

40. V. Pearl, *London and the Outbreak of the Puritan Revolution* (1961), passim.

41. CC, nos. 2, 3, 4, 9, 10, 12; *Cal.S.P.Dom.* (1682), 446, 474–75. A ballad pursued the same theme: "Thus officer, (tho gravely sworn) cologues, / Calls Hilton fool, and all th'Informers rogues. / Though he hath warrants with him, that's all one, / In spite of laws, he executeth none." *The Hypocritical Christian; or, the Conventicling Citizen Displayed* (1682), reprinted in Nathaniel Thompson, *A Collection of Loyal Poems* (1685), 331.

42. G. S. De Krey, "London Radicals and Revolutionary Politics, 1675–1683," in *Politics of Religion*, ed. Harris, Seaward, and Goldie, 149–55; R. Ashcraft, *Revolutionary Politics and Locke's "Two Treatises of Government"* (Princeton, 1986), 365, 367, 370, 383.

43. CC, nos. 5, 6, 10.

44. Thomas Ellwood, *A Caution to Constables* (1683), 1, 2, 4; *Letter to Hilton*, 1–2.

45. CC, nos. 9, 17; First Day's Meetings, 186; Edward Pearse, *The Conformist's Third Plea* (1682), 6; *Letter to Hilton*, 2.

46. Herrup, *Common Peace*, 68. See I. Archer, *The Pursuit of Stability: Social Relations in Elizabethan London* (Cambridge, 1991), chap. 3; Harris, *London Crowds*, 72–73; Boulton, *Neighbourhood and Society*, passim; Kent, *English Village Constable*, chaps. 7–8; Wrightson, "Two Concepts of Order"; K. Wrightson and D. Levine, *Poverty and Piety in an English Village* (New York, 1979), 139, 104–5. Recent literature stresses community rather than anonymity in early modern London, but it is worth noting that Dissenting ministers fled to London in search of anonymity when the pressure of harassment in rural communities became too great: Hilton was especially pleased to catch "rustic preachers."

47. Boulton, *Neighbourhood and Society*, 232.

48. CC, nos. 13, 14, 15, 16; Roger Morrice, Entring Book, Dr. Williams's Library, London, P, 346.

49. *Cal.S.P.Dom.* (1683–84), 229; *Informer's Looking Glass*, 1.

50. Narcissus Luttrell, *A Brief Historical Relation of State Affairs* . . . , 6 vols. (Oxford, 1857), 1:241; *Cal.S.P.Dom.* (1682), 553; Morrice, Entring Book, P, 346; B. D. Henning, ed., *The House of Commons, 1660–1690*, 3 vols. (1983), 2:85–86; F. T. Melton, *Sir Robert Clayton and the Origins of English Deposit Banking* (Cambridge, 1986).

51. Original Record of Sufferings, fols. 247, 355; Ellwood, *Caution to Constables*, 14; Matthews, ed., *Calamy Revised*, 39; BL, Stowe MS. 305, fol. 7.

52. CC, nos. 21, 23.

53. *Letter to Hilton*, 1.

54. CC, nos. 1, 5, 6.

55. CC, no. 24; Peerbohms, *Nathaniel Thompson*, 59, 76–77, 81.

56. BL, Stowe MS. 305, fol. 8; *Cal.S.P.Dom* (1683–84), 204, 229.

57. Pearse, *Conformist's Fourth Plea*, 108.

58. CC, no. 8; Original Record of Sufferings, fol. 360.

59. *Informer's Looking Glass*, 2; Whitehead, *Christian Progress*, 570; Pearse, *Third Plea*, 14–16; L'Estrange, *Observator*, no. 180.

60. Whitehead, *Christian Progress*, 550; E. Foss, *The Judges of England*, 9 vols. (1848–64), 7:243–45.

61. Original Record of Sufferings, fols. 154, 562, 779, 826, 832; Crouch, *Posthuma Christiana*, 99–100; Horle, *Quakers and the English Legal System*, 124, 136, 138–39, 158 n, 202, 258, 273.

62. CC, nos. 7, 13, 15; BL, Stowe MS. 305, fols. 7–8; First Day's Meetings, 153. Saunders appears in Horle's list of lawyers who advised the Quakers, but he was scarcely favorable to them. Horle, *Quakers and the English Legal System*, 195–96, 290.

63. See particularly Ellwood, *Life*, 194ff.

64. CC, no. 20; Morrice, Entring Book, Q, 61; P, 564, 566; G. deF. Lord, ed., *Poems on Affairs of State*, 7 vols. (New Haven, 1963–75), 4:105; F. Maseres, ed., *Three Tracts Published . . . Under the Name of General Ludlow* (1812), 146; *Calendar of Treasury Books*, 9 (1689–92), 1829; *Cal.S.P.Dom.* (1691–92), 499; Historical Manuscripts Commission, *Downshire*, 1:195, 202; *Cal.S.P.Dom.* (1691–92), 499; *The History of King James's Ecclesiastical Commission* (1711), 19. Hollingworth was charged in 1686 with conducting clandestine marriages.

65. CC, nos. 2, 4, 5, 12, 28, 30; J. J. Baddeley, *The Aldermen of Cripplegate Ward, 1276–1900* (1900), 79. In 1687, in very different circumstances, Shorter became mayor at James II's behest.

66. *The Autobiography of Richard Baxter*, ed. N. H. Keeble (1974), 250–52; CC, nos. 14, 15; Morrice, Entring Book, P, 339.

67. R. A. Beddard, "Vincent Alsop and the Emancipation of Restoration Dissent," *Journal of Ecclesiastical History* 24 (1973): 161–84.

68. CC, nos. 1, 2, 7, 9, 11, 21, 25, 30; *A Lecture Held Forth at a Conventicle* (printed by N.T., c.1682); *Upon the Suppressing of Conventicles* (1685). Lobb later gained notoriety for his enthusiasm for James II's toleration policy.

69. Sewell, *History of the Quakers*, 2:304; William Penn, "Fragment of an Autobiography," quoted in B. Dobree, *William Penn* (1932), 323, and cf. 168–69; T. Clarkson, *Memoirs of the Private*

and *Public Life of William Penn*, 2 vols. (1813), 1:295–96; S. M. Janney, *Life of William Penn* (Philadelphia, 1852), 182–83. 261–62; *Middlesex County Records*, 4:265–66.

70. *The Arraignment and Tryal of the Late Revd Mr Thomas Rosewall for High Treason* (1718), 44, 54, 56, 58–59, 61–63, 175; *State Trials*, 10:150, 159, 162, 165–75, 191, 217–24, 229–32, 239; Luttrell, *Brief Historical Relation*, 1:317–18, 320–22, 328; *Cal.S.P.Dom.* (1684), 171, 180, 184, 187, 222–24, 226, 290, 297; Morrice, Entring Book, P, 441, 450; John Dunton, *Life and Errors of John Dunton* (1705), 461–62; G. W. Keeton, *Lord Chancellor Jeffreys and the Stuart Cause* (1965), 223–25; Schofield, *Jeffreys of the Bloody Assizes*, 128–32.

71. *Arraignment and Tryal of . . . Rosewall*, 88; G. Holmes, *The Trial of Dr Sacheverell* (1973), 165.

72. Horle, *Quakers and the English Legal System*.

73. CC, nos. 10, 12; Morrice, Entring Book, P, 570, Q 34; BL, Add. MSS 38856, fol. 98; Henning, ed., *House of Commons*, 2:503; D. Neal, *The History of the Puritans*, rev. ed., 3 vols. (1837), 3:264; *DNB*, s.v. Fleetwood, Coward; Mark Knights, *Politics and Opinion in Crisis, 1678–1681* (Cambridge, 1994), 196, 288. In the 1690s the hymnologist Isaac Watts lived in Hartopp's household as tutor to his son.

74. CC, nos. 4, 8, 9, 10; *Cal.S.P.Dom.* (1682), 446.

75. CC, nos. 5, 19; *State Trials*, 10:218; Anne Emily Garnier, Lady Newdigate-Newdegate, *Cavalier and Puritan in the Days of the Stuarts* (1901), 98.

76. CC, nos. 1, 7; Original Record of Sufferings, fol. 742; Smith, "London and the Crown," 262–63. From 1681 to 1685 a company of militiamen was stationed at the Guildhall at night and weekends.

77. CC, no. 3.

78. Published respectively on 19 and 28 August 1682 and 27 January and 1 February 1683. "Guzman" refers either to the commander of the Spanish Armada or to the Spanish ruler Olivares.

79. *English Guzman*, no. 1; *Informer's Looking Glass*, 2; *Letter to Hilton*, 1–2.

80. *The Informer's Lecture* (1682), 5.

81. *The English Jeroboam: or, the Protestant Reforming Magistrate* (1683), sig. Bv and passim. On moral reformers seeking to become constables, see W. Hunt, *The Puritan Moment* (Cambridge, Mass., 1983), chap. 6; Kent, *English Village Constable*, 257ff, 295; Sharpe, *Crime in Seventeenth-Century England*, 175.

82. Book of Cases, Friends Library, 1:114–15.

83. *English Guzman*, nos. 1, 2; *Letter to Hilton*, 2; Morrice, Entring Book, P, 350, 353.

84. CC, nos. 23, 24, 25; *The Opinion of the Barons of the Exchequer* (1682).

85. Ellwood, *Caution to Constables*, 3, 5, 16, and passim; Ellwood, *Life*, 220. See also *Second Letter to Hilton*; Book of Cases, 1:47–49, 115–17; BL, Stowe MS. 305, fol. 7.

86. BL, Stowe MS. 305, fols. 7–8; *Cal.S.P.Dom.* (1683–84), 228–29.

87. Morrice, Entring Book, P, 416; Book of Cases, 1:166; Sewell, *History of the Quakers*, 2:316.

88. *English Guzman*, no. 2; Horle, *Quakers and the English Legal System*, 124.

89. BL, Stowe MS. 305, fols. 7–8; *English Guzman*, no. 2.

90. Original Record of Sufferings, fol. 196; BL, Add. MSS 38856, fol. 98; *Middlesex County Records*, 4:303–4.

91. Original Record of Sufferings, fols. 15, 26, 44, 196, 742–43; Great Book of Sufferings, 5:475–76, 479–80.

92. CC, no. 5; Whitehead, *Christian Progress*, 519–21, 541–42, 560, 562.

93. Whitehead, *Christian Progress*, 569–70, 577–79, 583–85, 618; Richard Hawkins, *A Brief Narrative of the Life and Death of . . . Gilbert Latey* (1707), 111–18; cf. a similar petition, perhaps by Penn: *To the King and Both Houses of Parliament*, in *Somers Tracts. A Collection of Scarce and Valuable Tracts . . .* , 2nd ed., ed. Sir Walter Scott, 13 vols. (1809–15), 9:28–31.

94. For the following account see Whitehead, *Christian Progress*, 591–609; and Hawkins, *Brief Narrative of . . . Gilbert Latey*, 118–20.

95. There are draft lists of cases in Original Record of Sufferings, fols. 42, 44.

96. Ibid., fols. 508, 519.

97. Whitehead, *Christian Progress*, 601–4; Morrice, Entring Book, Q, 57. On Burton and Graham see S. B. Baxter, *The Development of the Treasury, 1660–1702* (1957), 232, 242–43, 245–46; *Arraignment and Tryal of . . . Rosewall*, 47–48, 57.

98. Morrice, Entring Book, P, 563, 564, 570, 574, 623, 638, 656; Q, 9, 34, 118; Whitehead, *Christian Progress*, 607–9; Original Record of Sufferings, fol. 62; Great Book of Sufferings, 5:397, 474, 496; Luttrell, *Brief Historical Relation*, 1:387; *Arraignment and Tryal of . . . Rosewall*, 68. Morrice thought the hierarchy made a vain attempt to find "new tools." Entring Book, Q, 9.

99. *Poems on Affairs of State*, 4:105; Henry Care, *Public Occurrences*, nos. 6, 7, 10. Lois Schwoerer is preparing a study of Henry Care. For another aspect of the fate of the persecutors, see M. Goldie, "James II and the Dissenters' Revenge: The Commission of Enquiry of 1688," *Historical Research* 66 (1993): 53–88.

100. *Advice to the Citizens of London* [1690]; Robert Kirk, London Diary, Edinburgh University Library, MS Laing III.545, fol. 98.

101. *Calendar of Treasury Books*, 9 (1689–92), 1796–97, 1829; 10:61; *Cal.S.P.Dom.* (1691–92), 499. The commission was issued to Peter Stepkin and Thomas Baker, who in February 1693 were placed under a new receiver general of recusancy fines, John Richards. For their anti-Catholic campaign see P. A. Hopkins, "The Commission for Superstitious Lands of the 1690s," *Recusant History* 15 (1980): 265–82.

102. Roger North, *The Lives of the Norths*, 2 vols. (1890), 2:188–92. North's biographer accepts rather readily his brother's retrospective exculpation: R. Grassby, *The English Gentleman in Trade: The Life and Works of Sir Dudley North, 1641–1691* (Oxford, 1994), 204.

103. Henning, ed., *House of Commons*, 2:646–47; Foss, *Judges of England*, 7:243–45; *History of King James's Ecclesiastical Commission*, 74.

104. John Locke, *A Third Letter for Toleration* (1692), 294. In the first *Letter Concerning Toleration* (1689), Locke remarked, "Dissenting Christians" cannot "with any right be deprived of their worldly goods, by the predominating faction of a court-church." Locke, *Letter Concerning Toleration*, ed. J. Tully (Indianapolis, 1983), 43.

105. 4 & 5 W. & M., c. 18; 11 Will. 3, c. 4; 8 Geo. 1, c. 19; J. H. Baker, "Criminal Courts and Procedure at Common Law, 1550–1800," in *Crime in England*, ed. Cockburn, 20–21; Hay and Snyder, eds., *Policing and Prosecution in Britain*, 356 and passim; D. Hay et al., *Albion's Fatal Tree: Crime and Society in Eighteenth-Century England* (1975), passim; J. M. Beattie, *Crime and the Courts in England, 1600–1800* (Oxford, 1986), 50–55, 134–35; J. Styles, "'Our Traitorous Money Makers': The Yorkshire Coiners and the Law, 1760–83," in *An Ungovernable People*, ed. Brewer and Styles, 217–19.

106. R. Paley, "The Thief-Taker in London, c.1745–54," in Hay and Snyder, eds., *Policing and Prosecution*, 302. On Wild and "the origins of modern organized gangsterdom," see Gerald Howson, *Thief-Taker General: The Rise and Fall of Jonathan Wild* (1970).

107. R. Porter, *English Society in the Eighteenth Century* (1982), 293.

108. *The Athenian Mercury*, 4 and 18 August 1691; Edinburgh University Library, MS Laing III.394, fols. 49–50, 63ff, 82–85, 92–93, 135–36, 139–141, 263–65, 278–79, 224–25, 359–68, 409–13, 417–18, 436, 447ff. For a similar defense see Edward Stephens, *Phineas; or, The Common Duty of All Men* (1695), 9–10. For attacks see *The Modern Fanatical Reformer* (1693); Ned Ward, *The London Spy*, ed. P. Hyland (East Lansing, 1993), 277–79. There is an extensive literature on the Reformation of Manners movement, but see especially A. G. Craig, "The Movement for the Reformation of Manners, 1688–1715," Ph.D. diss., Edinburgh, 1980, 31–39, 44–47, 59, 91–95, 121–22, 131; Shoemaker, *Prosecution and Punishment*, 241–43; T. Claydon, *William III and the Godly Revolution* (Cambridge, 1996). On Dunton see G. D. McEwen, *The Oracle of the Coffee House: John Dunton's "Athenian Mercury"* (San Marino, Cal., 1972).

109. G. R. Elton, *Policy and Police* (Cambridge, 1972), passim; E. P. Thompson, *The Making of the English Working Class* (1963), 532.

Violence, Martyrdom, and Radical Politics: Rethinking the Glorious Revolution

Melinda Zook

> I am perfectly lost in wonder when I think of this Revolution. To us, that knew it, it looks like a dream, but to posterity it must certainly seem like a romance . . . that all the politics of the several years last past should be unravelled in three months.
>
> *A Dialogue between Dick and Tom* (1689)

By 13 February 1689 the Revolution was over. In less than four months the rightful king of England, James II, had been removed, replaced by the dual monarchy of William and Mary. A Protestant succession had been achieved. Little wonder that it might all have seemed like a "dream" to the anonymous Whig scribbler of *A Dialogue between Dick and Tom*. Yet this pamphleteer was also well aware "that all the politics of the several years last past" had had something to do with the momentous events of that winter. This essay is about rethinking the Glorious Revolution in terms of several of the political episodes that "unraveled" in the decade before it. It is my contention that the political culture capable of producing revolution in 1688 was the work of Whigs and Dissenters over the previous decade, especially the most daring and extremist among them, whom I call radical Whigs. These individuals were the real revolutionaries of the late Stuart era, though many of them were already dead by 1688.[1]

The controversy over the royal succession traditionally known as the Exclusion Crisis, which began in the late 1670s, generated the need for like-minded individuals to organize and propagate their positions. All Whigs prior to 1685 were Exclusionists, demanding the exclusion of the heir presumptive to the throne, the Catholic James, duke of York. But not all Whigs were "radicals." What distinguished radical Whigs from other Whig Exclusionists was their willingness to use and to justify violence to obtain their ends. Between 1679 and 1685, their goal was to bar the duke of York from the throne. After 1685 their aim was to remove King James II from his throne. For these men and some women, the 1680s were one long Exclusion Crisis.[2]

The activities of Whig radicals were highly dangerous. They wrote about, discussed, plotted, and carried out violent political tactics. Many suffered violent ends. The 1680s can be characterized by one Whig debacle after another, as well as by an escalating cycle of violence between the court and Whig radicals.

As a result, radical numbers were constantly diminishing. The discovery of the Rye House conspiracy in 1683 resulted in the loss of much of the radical aristocratic leadership. The defeat of the duke of Monmouth's army two years later completed that loss and seriously diluted the numbers of rank and file. If we add to the death toll the series of imprisonments, whippings, deportations, public humiliations, and the devastating fines that many radicals incurred, the true cost of revolutionary politics rises even higher.

This cycle of violence preceding the Revolution shaped another aspect of radical politics in the 1680s that is often overlooked—cults of martyrdom. The blood of Whig brethren was not spilled for naught. Radicals learned early on how to profit from their losses; dying speeches, both authentic and fabricated, became some of the most powerful weapons in the Whig propaganda arsenal. The fallen often became more useful to the cause once dead than they had been alive. Whig scribblers not only created an ideology that legitimized violence as a political tool and sanctified rebellion, their work turned rebels and conspirators into Protestant sufferers and martyrs.

These individuals, then, were hardly "reluctant revolutionaries."[3] Placing Whig radicals at the heart of the revolutionary process in the 1680s and reexamining that decade as one long Exclusion movement, we realize that 1688 was far less glorious and bloodless and far more violent and bloody than its reputation as a "sensible revolution" would allow.[4] Traditionally we have been comforted by the notion that political liberalism, enshrined in Locke's *Two Treatises*, blossomed at just such an enlightened moment. But if we rethink the Revolution in terms of the politicking and spectacles that came before it—the clubbing, the plotting, the radical manifestos and treatises, the scaffold dramas and dying speeches—England's Revolution begins to look a bit more like modern revolutions elsewhere in the West and not so smooth, clean, peaceful, or particular.

The work of Tim Harris, Mark Knights, and other Restoration scholars has demonstrated the very divisive and contentious nature of politics in this period, particularly in London in the 1670s and 1680s.[5] London's political culture was not divided by class, popular and elite, but rather by party, Whig and Tory. These cultures divided vertically; London harbored a divided elite as well as a divided mob.[6] In 1678 and 1679, amid the Popish Plot and Exclusion Crisis, the cultural initiative resided with the Whigs. They organized street processions, mass petition signing, political clubs, and political feasts. Their plays dominated the stage, their newsletters and weeklies dominated the news market, and their partisans dominated London civic politics. But already by 1681 Whigs and Dissenters faced a far stiffer and more organized challenge from the court and its proponents, Anglican churchmen, and Tories. It was within this atmosphere of adversity, particularly following the dissolution of the last Exclusion Parliament in 1681, that Whig politics truly began to radicalize. With peaceful solutions to their demand for a Protestant succession cut off, Whig radicals began to formulate and hone an ideology which deemed violence an acceptable political weapon. They first planned to attain their ends by violent means in 1682 and 1683.

The Whig conspiracy known as the Rye House Plot was first hatched by the earl of Shaftesbury and other Whig firebrands after the abortive Oxford Parliament in 1681, but it was not until the summer of 1682 that plans for a general insurrection were seriously considered by other prominent Whigs. They included William, Lord Russell; the duke of Monmouth and his supporters Lord Grey of Werk and Sir Thomas Armstrong; and the parliamentary leader and former chair of the Green Ribbon Club John Trenchard of Somerset.[7] A lower circle of conspirators included the lawyers John Ayloffe, Robert West, Aaron Smith, Edward Norton, John Wildman, Nathaniel Wade, and the Goodenough brothers, Richard and Francis; the soldiers Richard Rumbold, Thomas Walcot, and John Rumsey; and the Whig hack and Independent preacher Robert Ferguson.

Throughout the autumn of 1682, Shaftesbury urged his fellow conspirators to act. He told Lord Howard of Escrick that he had "several thousands of men that were all in readiness to rise when he did but hold up his hand."[8] In fact, there was little evidence that this was the case. The other Whig lords hesitated. Lord Russell advocated patience, pointing out that there were no provisions for arms and ammunition, nor even a declaration of their intentions and grievances. "Patience," Shaftesbury angrily responded, "will be our destruction."[9] Aware that the government was preparing new charges against him, Shaftesbury went into hiding in October 1682 and finally in frustration and fear left England for the last time the following month, seeking refuge in Amsterdam. He took Robert Ferguson with him. Before he departed Shaftesbury reportedly said of his fellow conspirators that "they were too few to do the work, and too many to conceal it."[10] His words proved prophetic.

At first the departure of Shaftesbury and Ferguson was greeted with relief by the other Whig conspirators. But according to Lord Grey, it soon became apparent that it was "impossible for us to act, they [Shaftesbury and Ferguson] having managed the greater part of our City affairs and knew all those considerable gentlemen."[11] Ferguson was sent for in order to "explain Shaftesbury's connections with the City."[12] He returned shortly after Shaftesbury's death at the end of January 1683, and the meeting and planning of the higher and lower conspirators resumed.

In the winter and spring months of 1683, both circles of conspirators often spoke of the need to compose a declaration of their reasons for overtaking the government. None of the declarations exist today, and there is only the briefest information about those planned by the higher cabal. Of those declarations discussed or actually written by the lower level of conspirators, there is more information. Although these men presented their grievances and demands in a conservative language, the rhetoric of restoring lost liberties, what they proposed would have fundamentally altered the church and state in England. Taken together, they comprised a radical Whig reform program.

Their most frequent demand was for liberty of conscience for Nonconformists.[13] As Thomas Walcot admitted shortly before his execution in July 1683, he entered the plot to "stand for liberty of conscience and to assert and preserve the people's liberties now in hazard."[14] The desire of religious toleration for Protestants so often asserted in Whig propaganda was a reaction to the sufferings caused by the enforcement of the penal laws against Dissent and what the Whigs believed to be the coming of popery. "The King had a visible enough design to introduce popery and arbitrary government and overwhelm the light of the Scripture," John Ayloffe told his fellow plotters. Aaron Smith agreed; he told his clerk that "the King and his cursed Council were papists in their hearts, that they were resolved to destroy all old English liberty and totally extirpate the Gospel and that it was high time to arm themselves against such horrid designs and regain their lost rights and privileges."[15]

Frustrated by the frequent dissolution of Parliament, the lower cabal of plotters also demanded the establishment of annual parliaments which could only be dissolved after all petitions and other business were addressed. They were also nervous about the threat posed by standing armies, which were created and maintained by the Crown. Hence, several of their declarations called for the militias to be placed in the hands of Parliament. Other declarations demanded that all bills which twice passed both houses of Parliament be made law without the king's consent and that all sheriffs be popularly elected.[16]

Members of the lower cabal also discussed how they would secure London and reform English society. After the assassination of the royal brothers at Rye House mill, they hoped to terrorize the opposition into submission and appease the populace into compliance. These plans included murdering the former Tory lord mayor Sir John Moore; "if the people did not pull him to pieces, his skin should be fleeced off and stuft and hung up in Guild-hall as one who betrayed the rights and privileges of the City." The same fate was designated for the present royalist lord mayor and Tory sheriffs of London. The wealthy City Whig Thomas Papillon was to be declared one of the new sheriffs, and the Whig alderman and former sheriff Henry Cornish, the new lord mayor. If they refused these new offices, they, too, would be executed.[17]

Most of the judges "should be killed or brought to trial for their arbitrary judgements and their skins stuft and hung up at Westminster hall." The Oxford judge who had sentenced the Protestant joiner Stephen College to death was to be hanged from the same post as had College. Several of the king's chief ministers of state should be "taken off," including Lords Halifax, Hyde, and Rochester.[18] Ferguson wanted the presses at Whitehall seized. He also believed that "nothing was to be expected from the rich old citizens [of London] and therefore a half dozen of them must be taken out of their houses and hanged on sign-posts and their houses given as plunder to the mobile." This, Ferguson argued, would certainly frighten the rest.[19]

Still further, it was decided that the people should be "eased of the chimney money" and that no taxes be imposed in the future except a moderate excise and land tax. The lower echelon of conspirators also discussed the general "uselessness" of the bishops and deans and decided they should be "wholly laid aside." Some of the revenues allocated for the universities were to be confiscated and used to ease the people's burden from taxation. Several colleges were to be converted into schools for the teaching of mechanical arts.[20] The conspirators also discussed making England a free port and naturalizing all aliens as a "means to engage foreigners on our side." Finally, they resolved that Princess Anne, the duke of York's second daughter, should be "preserved" and married to "an honest country gentlemen to raise a breed for keeping out foreign princes to the crown."[21]

Though wild and extravagant, the plans of these barristers, soldiers, and tradesmen resonated with certain consistent themes. They wanted to retake control of London, place their candidates back into positions of power, and punish the Tory opposition. They even wanted two of their own partisans, City Whigs Sir Patience Ward and Sir Robert Clayton, both of whom had served as lord mayor, to apologize publicly for not doing enough during their terms of office to prevent the ascension of royalist candidates. If Ward and Clayton refused to do so, they were to be "knocked on the head." The conspirators' designs to retake London also displayed a degree of populism, pragmatism, and anticlericalism. A large part of their populism was probably motivated by their need to secure the support of the "meaner people." Their plans to keep the excise and the land tax but remove the chimney tax, which was especially unpopular with the lower orders, suggest a desire to please the common people without offering any compensation to the wealthy. In fact, the lower echelon of conspirators never once discussed measures to ensure the support of the landed and merchant classes. They may have felt some degree of support within these groups from the beginning; they may also simply have been willing to terrorize any opposition into submission.

Their feelings that the bishops were useless, and that the colleges would better serve the "public use" if they taught vocational skills or their revenues were used to "ease the people from taxes," betrayed a strong anticlericalism and a sort of hard-boiled utilitarianism. Their attitudes toward the universities and the clergy were not surprising. Oxford was a royalist stronghold. Charles II had moved Parliament there in 1681 because he could count on the loyalty of the scholars and students. Likewise, the clergy had ardently supported the court and preached against the tenets of the Whigs and Dissenters. Confiscating church lands and transforming the universities would not only avenge past wrongs, but would forever cripple two royalist centers of power.

These plans discussed by the lower circle of Rye House conspirators amounted to a revolution complete with the kinds of atrocities modern historians usually associate with the French Revolution. How much the Whig lords who met regularly with Ferguson and Rumsey knew of these plans is impossible to know. They may have passively approved or they may have found them absolutely abhorrent. Yet they themselves were not unwilling to use violence to obtain the exclusion of the "popish successor." Only their endless delays, as Shaftesbury had predicted, made for their destruction.

The Whig plotters were betrayed by one of their own in the spring of 1683. Aware that their designs had been exposed, several of the lower echelon of conspirators met one last time. Nathaniel Wade proposed that they immediately muster what men they could and lead a rising "here or in the west to die like men [rather] than be hanged like dogs." But Colonel Rumsey declared that their situation was hopeless. "The hearts of the people are down and our great men are good for nothing."[22] Feeling confused and dejected, they finally decided that each man should "shift for himself." But Robert Ferguson did not share their fears and somber mood. He "laughed at us all and gave us his parting complement, Gentlemen, you are all strangers to this kind of exercise; I have been used to flight and I will never be out of a plot so long as I live, and yet I hope to meet some of you at Dunbar before Michaelmas."[23]

The discovery of the Rye House Plot, with the trials and executions that followed, prompted a new phase in the radical Whig Exclusion movement. On the one hand, the plot's discovery was devastating to the movement, effectively removing all radical activity to the continent. The leadership was decimated. Lord Shaftesbury died in exile in January 1683; the earl of Essex committed suicide in July 1683; a few days later Lord Russell was beheaded, and Algernon Sidney followed him to the scaffold in December. A second tier of potential Whig leaders—John Trenchard, Lord Delamere and his son, Henry Booth, John Hampden the younger, and others—were imprisoned, fined, tried, or otherwise humiliated. All that remained of the leadership were the Lord Grey, who managed to escape to Holland shortly after his arrest, taking his would-be jailer and mistress with him, and, of course, "Absalom," the duke of Monmouth, who lost his father's favor and was soon roaming about the continent as well.

Yet the effects of the plot's disclosure were not all negative. After all, the great Whig patrons and leaders had done little for the Exclusion movement in practical terms. They had not dared to print their own political principles; others had done so for them and could continue to do so. Though Colonel Rumsey had flatly declared that the lords "were good for nothing," in many ways they turned out to be more useful to the cause without their heads than with them. The deaths of Essex, Russell, and Sidney gave the Protestant cause its most powerful martyrs. Whig scribblers now accused the government of an actual murder and cover-up in the case of Essex and of judicial murder for the deaths of Russell and Sidney. Russell's and Sidney's dying speeches became powerful propaganda weapons.

Hence, it is not entirely surprising that reports from around the country in the months following the first Rye House trials describe local Whigs and Dissenters as ever "bold and venomous," "insolent and proud," and "bold and presumptuous."[24] A new round of propaganda wars had begun, and Whig scribblers were hard at work declaring the plot a royalist fraud and canonizing the new martyrs for the cause. A London newsletter from July 1683 reported that though proof of the plot was clear, "yet the factious party have the face to make a sham of almost every branch of it. They have this day published a sly Relation of Rouse's Case and wild stories of Lords Russell and Essex insomuch that the King has ordered a Declaration of the conspiracy to be forthwith published."[25]

The "wild stories" concerning the earl of Essex proved to be the most damaging. Essex had been arrested and charged with high treason shortly after the discovery of the Rye House Plot. He was imprisoned in the Tower, and on the morning of 13 July 1683 his servant found him lying in a pool of blood with a razor beside him. Essex's throat was cut from ear to ear; the gash had severed his windpipe, nearly decapitating him. A coroner's inquest was held the next day and returned a verdict of self-murder.[26] Despite the verdict, many believed that a dark deed had ended the Whig grandee's life, that lies were being perpetuated in order to cover it up and ensure guilty verdicts in the remaining Rye House trials.

Whig newsletters, ballads, and handwritten papers positing a murder theory circulated almost immediately. George Speke of White Lackington in Ilminster had such a paper in September 1683. He offered it to a neighbor in order to convince him that "the earl's throat was not cut by himself but by some other." When his neighbor refused it, Speke "called him a cursed Tory and struck him in the face with a stick."[27] George Speke's son, Hugh, and his friend and fellow Green Ribbon brother Laurence Braddon were the first to bring the murder charge to the national stage. Braddon, a Whig lawyer, began his own investigation into Essex's death. He was interviewing witnesses and collecting evidence when the government moved to arrest him. Letters of introduction by Hugh Speke were found in Braddon's possession, and Speke was jailed and tried with Braddon for high misdemeanor.[28] Braddon used their trial to prove his case, but an unimpressed jury found them both guilty, and they remained in prison until the Glorious Revolution.

Braddon's and Speke's trial made a lot of noise. A transcript of the trial was published, only increasing suspicions about Essex's death.[29] The Essex murder theory was asserted in Whig polemics such as Henry Danvers's *Murder Will Out*.[30] The most sophisticated of these was Robert Ferguson's *Enquiry into and Detection of the Barbarous Murder of the Late Earl of Essex*, first published in Holland in 1684. Ferguson ascribed Essex's murder to part of the ongoing worldwide Catholic conspiracy. Those who had fired London in 1666 and murdered Sir Edmund Berry Godfrey in 1678 and then the "Protestant Joiner" Stephen College in 1681 could now add to their list the slaughter of "virtuous and religious," "heroic and generous" Essex. The "Vatican, Louvre and St. James [the duke of York's residence]" had conspired to ruin Essex because he had sought to expose the Popish Plot, defend the Protestant religion, and fight against the introduction of popery and slavery.[31] For Ferguson, Essex's murder was proof that violence had first been perpetrated by a popishly infected government and that the Rye House plotters were merely defending themselves and the nation's liberties. "If we hear of our neighbor's throat getting cut, should not we look to our own?" Ferguson concluded his tract by laying the murder of Essex at the feet of the duke of York and by calling on all "English peers and gentlemen" to awaken and avenge Essex's death.[32]

The charge of murder against the duke of York, crowned James II in February 1685, had tremendous propaganda value, as Ferguson well understood. It was a charge not easily answered or forgotten, and it haunted James's reign. Yeoman farmers and London gentlemen echoed the charge in the first year of his rule. Papers lying on country roads blamed the murders of "Justis Godfrey and Grate Essex" on the new king.[33] The Declaration accompanying Monmouth's invasion in June 1685 accused James of Essex's murder. In 1687, writing from Amsterdam, Ferguson reminded his readers once again of the barbarous murder of Essex, claiming he had "convincing proofs of it." When asked by a fellow Whig what those proofs could be, Ferguson replied, "Take no thought of that, it doth not concern you or me whether it be true or false. The report is spread and will have all the effects as true and so serve our end."[34]

Whig aims were also served by the trial and execution of William, Lord Russell. In the post-Revolution era, the much-remembered Russell became the darling of the Whig radicals. While Shaftesbury, the crafty schemer whose long political career had taken numerous shifts and turns, was quietly forgotten by the Whigs, the images of Russell and Sidney, the fallen liberators, loomed large. Russell was styled a victim of royalist wrath; his only crime had been his steadfast defense of the nation's religion and liberties. Whig propaganda asserted time and again that Russell's trial had been a "travesty of justice and his execution judicial 'murder.'" As Russell himself put it in his dying speech, "For to kill with forms and subtleties of law is the worst sort of murder."[35]

Russell said little on the scaffold, instead assuring his martyrdom with the paper he handed to the sheriff. His dying speech magically transformed the Whig lord from a political agitator and conspirator into a Protestant hero and patriotic liberator. He had had some help crafting it. Russell was far from eloquent during his trial, but his dying speech was a masterpiece of propaganda, blending together the tropes of Protestant martyrdom and radical Whig polemic.[36] It began in the formulaic discourse of martyrdom, assuring his readers that he would soon "partake of that fullness of joy which is in His presence." It went on to plead with all Protestants to give up their "unhappy differences" and consider "the common enemy," popery. This was standard Whig rhetoric, to which Russell added, in typical martyr fashion, his prophecy that the worst was yet to come: "Popery is breaking in upon this nation"; the Smithfield fires lurk but around the corner. "Blessed be God," Russell declared, "I fall by the axe and not by the fiery trial." Naturally, Russell asserted that he died wholly innocent of the charges brought against him, which he saw as the court's revenge for his zealous promotion of the Exclusion bill. His blood was innocent, a sacrifice to "satiate some people's revenge."[37]

Three different editions of Russell's speech were published in 1683 alone.[38] Tory propagandists even produced their own fraudulent edition of Russell's speech wherein he properly confessed his crimes.[39] Still, this was not enough; the speech had to be answered point by point. L'Estrange rushed his contribution into print; he blamed Russell's misguided principles on his chaplain, the Reverend Samuel Johnson.[40] But neither L'Estrange's tract nor the more sophisticated Tory assault by Bartholomew Shower could squash Russell's growing legacy.[41] Whigs countered Tory polemics with their own broadsides and pamphlets, vindicating Russell's speech, fashioning his martyrdom.[42] His dying speech was reprinted in Edinburgh and Dublin, sent in cartons to the countryside, and reprinted during the Glorious Revolution.[43] By the time of the Revolution Russell had become a powerful and evocative symbol for the Whig cause. In the Whig martyrologies published and republished in the post-Revolution era, their author, John Tutchin, reserved his highest praise for Lord Russell. He was simply "the finest gentleman England ever bred."[44] Death had glamorized Russell and made him useful to the cause.

Colonel Algernon Sidney's trial in November and execution on 7 December 1683 were the last dramatic episodes of the Rye House conspiracy investigation and trials, which had begun some six months earlier. Whereas Russell had appeared cowed and inarticulate during his trial, Sidney gave a strong and eloquent defense of himself. The case against him was weak. There was only one witness to his treason. Lacking a second witness, the government introduced the colonel's own unpublished papers, found in his study, which they argued proved that Sidney sought to "persuade the people of England that it was lawful to raise rebellion."[45] Those papers were published posthumously in 1698 as Sidney's *Discourses concerning Government*.

Sidney's "papers," extracts of which were read during his trial and summarized in his dying speech, became his most significant contribution to the radical Whig cause after his martyrdom. Though Sidney denied his authorship, the "papers" were obviously his answer to Filmer's *Patriarcha*. The portions of his "papers," pulled out by the attorney general, Sir Robert Sawyer, to prove Sidney's treason asserted three propositions: that "the power of the king was derived from the people upon trust"; that "the king has no authority to dissolve parliament"; and that since the king had dissolved parliaments and thus "invaded" the people's rights, "he hath broken his trust." Therefore, the people "might assume that original power they had conferred" upon him.[46]

Sawyer also instructed the jury to "show your abhorrence of these republican principles," raising the bogey of the Civil Wars and Protectorate.[47] It was "forty-one all over again." This was a powerful talisman, and Sidney found himself condemned as much for his past politics as his present. Sidney recognized this tactic. He denied his "papers" and labeled Cromwell "a tyrant."[48] But the jury, well chosen by Tory sheriffs, came back with a guilty verdict.

Sidney prepared a powerful dying speech wherein he fully embraced his republican principles and his past. He used the occasion publicly to declare his political thinking, glossing four main points from his "papers": first, that governments were man-made; second, that "magistrates were set up for the good of the nation"; third, that magistrates derived their "right and power" from the laws of the nation and were bound by those laws; finally, that each nation's laws "have the force of a contract between the magistrate and people." Should that contract be violated, the "whole fabric" of government was dissolved. Only in the final paragraph of his dying speech did Sidney sound anything like a martyr. But Sidney was not the patient sufferer; instead he was the angry prophet, calling upon God to "suffer not idolatry [popery] to be established in this land . . . Defend thy cause and defend those that defend it. Stir up such as are faint; direct those that are willing; confirm those that waver." Defiant to the end, Sidney thanked God that he died "for that Old Cause in which I was from my youth engaged."[49]

Unfortunately for the Whigs, Sidney's trial and dying speech, both of which were published, were not nearly as useful propaganda tools as Russell's had been.[50] They were far too blackened by the dark strokes of republicanism and its association with the chaos of the Civil Wars. Though the same principles had been espoused by numerous radical Whigs, including Robert Ferguson, the taint of republicanism so willingly embraced by Sidney in his dying speech made it hard for Whigs to defend their hero's final moments. Whigs did come to his defense, but their responses to Tory attacks on Sidney's dying speech were tempered and lukewarm.[51] Even a sympathetic account of Sidney's execution and burial written for Dissenters in New England reported that his speech was "stufft with expressions savoring of Republican principles."[52] The radical Whig martyrologies of the post-Revolution era produced by veterans of the 1680s did praise and vindicate Sidney's principles. Still, though the "brave old man" was great, Russell was greater still.[53]

With the deaths of Shaftesbury, Essex, Russell, and Sidney, the mantle of radical Whig leadership was passed to the Protestant duke, Monmouth. Monmouth himself was at first slow to take on this role. Though continually in touch with Whigs both in Europe and at home, Monmouth spent much of 1684 skating, dancing, and dining with the prince and princess of Orange at The Hague. He did not become serious about returning home and championing the Protestant cause (as well as his own) until after Charles II's death in February 1685 and the ascension to the throne of his uncle and enemy, the duke of York.

In the spring of 1685 Monmouth, galvanized by a small but committed group of radical Whig and Dissenting refugees in Holland, launched the next assault on the Stuart government. Among the men who set sail with Monmouth were many former Rye House plotters, including Lord Grey, Nathaniel Wade, the Goodenough brothers, and Robert Ferguson. Ferguson, in fact, was responsible for the Declaration that accompanied Monmouth's bid for the throne, the only surviving manifesto of radical Whig proposals from the pre-Revolution era.

Monmouth's Declaration was printed in English, Flemish, and French and distributed in both Holland and England.[54] Clearly Ferguson had not forgotten the demands of the Rye House plotters. The Declaration called for liberty of conscience, annual parliaments, the removal of the king's right to dissolve parliaments, and the placement of the militias under the control of the people's representatives. The ideology behind Monmouth's Declaration was similarly based on the very principles the Rye House conspirators had claimed to follow: the essential and sacred bond between prince and people had been encroached upon and destroyed. The people were set at liberty and had the right to defend themselves and erect a new political settlement.

Monmouth and his followers hoped to attract the West Country gentry families who had so warmly welcomed the Protestant duke during his western progress in 1680. His Declaration was meant to appeal to their sense of honor and devotion to Protestantism. Their ancient rights were invaded; the Protestant religion was in peril. As Monmouth's banner summed it up, his mission was "For God and Privileges."[55] These old and honorable families were supposed to come to the duke's aid and lend his cause, among other things, legitimacy.

Yet it was not the gentry whom Monmouth's cause attracted. The risks that he was asking them to take were far too great, and they were cowed by the arrests, trials, and scaffold dramas that had followed the discovery of the Rye House Plot.[56] His cause appealed instead to the artisans, tradesmen, cloth-workers, and yeoman farmers of Somerset, Devon, and Dorset.[57] For these men and women, a great many of whom were Dissenters, Monmouth's Declaration, with its promise of liberty of conscience, was good news for the godly. The Independent congregation at Axminster rejoiced to learn of Monmouth's "declarations to restore liberty to the people of God for the worship of God, to preserve the rights and privileges of the nation."[58] Ferguson's use of antipapist rhetoric in the Declaration was also powerfully appealing. Joshua Lock's father, a tobacconist, testified that his son would never have "run over to Monmouth" had he not seen the Declaration. An Anabaptist named Lark reported that he had joined Monmouth after reading the Declaration. A soldier, Captain Walberton, was "ensnared" by the Declaration and was captured with a copy of it in his pocket. Samuel Storey of London knew parts of the Declaration by heart and warned Anglicans fearful of joining Monmouth that though "we Dissenters shall be the first brought to the stake but depend upon it you will follow."[59]

The power and the appeal of Monmouth's Declaration was vividly demonstrated by the fact that much of its content was echoed three years later in the prince of Orange's *Declaration of Reasons* which accompanied his successful invasion of England.[60] Both Monmouth's and Prince William's declarations maintained that James had violated his coronation oath; both called for a free and legal Parliament to settle the matter of the succession and redress the kingdom's manifold grievances; both contained long lists of the current administration's crimes, including the appointment of papists to high offices and the illegal usurpation of the City charters; and both proclaimed that their main concern was the restoration of England's constitution and the subject's invaded liberties. Ironically, Ferguson twice styled Monmouth's cause "glorious"—a word that never appeared in William's Declaration, yet one that became synonymous with his revolution.

The failure of Monmouth's Rebellion in western England and the earl of Argyll's invasion of Scotland fed the increasingly vicious cycle between the promoters of a Protestant succession and the Stuart government, a cycle of Whig violence and Whig defeat. In the aftermath of the Rye House trials of 1683, Whig activists and Dissenters could still boldly voice and print their opinions, create larger-than-life martyrs out of their fallen heroes, and place all hope in the romantic Protestant duke, Monmouth. But the wake of the 1685 rebellions left radicals in complete disarray with little to salvage from their defeat. True, the rebellions did produce a great pantheon of new Protestant martyrs, heroes, and heroines, from the handsome Dissenting Hewling brothers, hanged and quartered in the west, to the Londoner Elizabeth Gaunt, burned at the stake. Yet most of the stories of Protestant suffering associated with the Bloody Assizes were not widely known prior to 1689; it was only with the Glorious Revolution that rebel dying speeches and heroic last deeds became a part of Whig mythology.[61]

The rebellions and their aftermath left radicals and Dissenters little to glorify, nothing to celebrate, and nowhere to place their hopes. James II had come into "his own" with a vengeance. The new king and his lord chief justice, George Jeffreys, were certainly not averse to spilling the blood or ruining the lives and fortunes of their enemies. In 1685 and 1686 they did just that with a number of beheadings, hangings, quarterings, deportations, whippings, pilloryings, humiliating confessions, extraordinary fines, and close imprisonments. Their campaign further truncated the radical Whig network and snuffed out its remaining leaders.

Monmouth, "the people's darling," cut a poor figure in his last moments. Found munching peas in a farmer's field a few days after the defeat of his ragtag army at Sedgemoor, he was hauled back to London "starving and exhausted, filthy and friendless."[62] He was no Russell or Sidney. Parliament had already passed an act of attainder against his life, so there was no need for the formality of a trial before his execution. From the Tower Monmouth scribbled, in a childlike hand, pathetic letters to James and the queen, begging for mercy, offering to convert to Catholicism, willing to name his former friends to the king. James did grant his nephew an interview, at which Monmouth supposedly threw himself at the king's feet.[63] But it was to no avail. The king was disgusted by Monmouth's behavior, and he had not forgotten the thrust of Monmouth's notorious manifesto "to make me a murderer and poisoner of my dear brother, besides all the other villainies you charge me with in your declaration."[64] Monmouth blamed his misdeeds on the "knaves and villains" who had misled him, particularly Robert Ferguson, and maintained that he had never read the Declaration. The taking of the title of king, he asserted, had been forced upon him.[65]

Monmouth's execution at Tower Hill on 15 July was a sad and morbid spectacle. To the prattling pleas of the accompanying bishops Monmouth now refused to confess any misdeeds, including the sin of rebellion. He made no speech; "he had come to die," as he told the bishops. Further, he was mindful of Russell's botched beheading and told the executioner not to "serve me as you did my Lord Russell."⁶⁶ But instead Monmouth's death was more horrible still; it took the executioner five strokes finally to sever the duke's head. Thus "Absalom," the great Protestant hope, died a "shameful death" and was more "pitied than lamented," according to Aphra Behn.⁶⁷ He left no dying speech. In his last days he left little material out of which legends could be created. Even the fanciful pens of the Whig martyrologists in the post-Revolution era had to struggle to make a great martyr out of Monmouth: "'Twas thought at first better to draw a veil before that unfortunate prince and say nothing at all of him."⁶⁸

Though Monmouth had forgotten the cause his manifesto had so boldly declared, many of his followers had not, and they died reasserting basic Whig ideology. Such was the case of Colonel Richard Rumbold, whose dying speech reminded the public of the principles of the Exclusion movement. Rumbold, a former Rye House plotter, had escaped to Holland in 1683 and joined the earl of Argyll's invasion of Scotland, launched shortly before and in sympathy with Monmouth's adventure. Rumbold was hanged, drawn, and quartered in Edinburgh on 26 June 1685.⁶⁹ On the scaffold Rumbold declared that he died in the cause of the nation's "just rights and liberties, against popery and slavery." He proclaimed that the political powers he had fought were illegitimate. According to the "ancient laws and liberties of these nations," the king and the people are "contracted to one another. And who will deny me that this was not the Just Constituted Government of our Nation? How absurd it is then for Men of Sense to maintain, That though the one Party of this Contract breakth all Conditions, the other should be obliged to perform their Part? No, this Error is contrary to the Law of God, the Law of Nations and the Law of Reason." Rumbold's last speech was radical Whig ideology plain and simple. The contract upon which England's government was built had been violated. The current government was illegitimate; hence, resistance to it was both lawful and necessary.

Elizabeth Gaunt, the London Baptist who was burned alive for harboring a Monmouth rebel, made an equally powerful and provocative speech. Her dying speech was published in both English and Dutch in October 1685. It struck an extraordinarily defiant note. Gaunt told the crowd that she was honored to be the first to suffer by fire in this reign. She died, as the Marian martyrs had before her, not because of any criminal offense, but because of her faith. She quoted Scripture, which commanded one to "hide the outcasts and betray not him that wanderth," and ended by laying her blood at the door of the "furious judge and unrighteous jury." Her message was clear. She had acted on the authority of a superior guide, Scripture, and was condemned by corrupted, unlawful powers.⁷⁰

The gruesome exhibition of Elizabeth Gaunt's burning, the beheading of the ancient Alice Lisle, and Judge Jeffreys's notorious campaign of vengeance, known to history as the Bloody Assizes, left vivid impressions on contemporaries and deep-rooted scars. In the west the conducting of more than two hundred executions in six towns in less than a month's time could not have been anything but horrific. The full punishment for high treason was carried out. Rebels were hanged until unconscious, disemboweled, beheaded, and quartered. Their remains were then boiled in brine, covered in black tar, and set up on poles and trees and lampposts. Green Ribbon brothers, London Whig lawyers, Rye House plotters, and Nonconformist ministers were among those who received this treatment.[71] Residents and visitors in the west found the sight of the exhibited body parts frightening and the smell nauseating. Only after a progress through the west the following year did James II himself, disturbed by what he saw, order the heads and quarters to be removed and buried.[72]

But the business of retribution was not yet over. The capture after Sedgemoor of several Rye House conspirators, who turned king's evidence in order to save themselves, permitted the king to settle some old scores and complete some unfinished business. With the confessions of Nathaniel Wade and Lord Grey of Werk and the testimony of Richard Goodenough, James was able to pursue several of his former enemies. He proceeded against the former Whig sheriff Henry Cornish in October 1685. Cornish's real crime was the packing of juries in 1680 and 1681, thus allowing Whigs and Dissenters to escape justice. But on the perjured evidence of Richard Goodenough and John Rumsey, who wrongly accused Cornish of participation in the Rye House conspiracy, he was hanged and quartered.[73] Charles Bateman, the late earl of Shaftesbury's surgeon, met the same fate in December.[74]

John Hampden the younger was next. The government was able to try him for high treason for his role in the Rye House conspiracy since it now had two witnesses, Lords Howard and Grey. Hampden pleaded guilty and confessed. He received a death sentence nonetheless. Yet James was more interested in embarrassing and discrediting young Hampden, the second son of the Great Patriot, and commuted his sentence to a fine of £6,000. As Hampden later let it be known, he had "lost his goods, his estate, his wife, and reputation" at the hands of James and Jeffreys. He never recovered from the psychological blow of his humiliation, and though he styled himself a great martyr after the Revolution and became an active member of William and Mary's government, he was rumored to be quite mad at times. He committed suicide in 1696.[75]

James's government also pursued those individuals who had told tall tales during his brother's reign. In May 1685 Titus Oates, the initiator of the Popish Plot stories, was tried for perjury, condemned, fined, pilloried, and whipped from Aldgate to Newgate and from Newgate to Tyburn.[76] The Reverend Samuel Johnson suffered a similar fate. For his antipapist tract addressed to the Protestant soldiers serving in James II's army encamped outside London, he was convicted of high misdemeanor, sentenced to pay five hundred marks, stand in the pillory for three days, and be flogged from Newgate to Tyburn.[77]

James II's reign of terror ended when in 1687 he shifted and began to court with favors and offices his former enemies, Whigs and Dissenters.[78] He hoped to gain their support in his move toward liberty of conscience for Catholics and Nonconformists. His reach extended even to the many hardened rebels skulking about Holland, to whom pardons were liberally granted.[79] The promise of religious toleration was highly attractive to those who had been persecuted for their faith, and an increasing number began to reconcile with his government. In fact, so many of the king's former enemies were willing to live in peace with his administration that James II's courtship of Whigs and Dissenters in 1687 and 1688 was even more damaging to Whig politics and solidarity than the failed rebellions of 1685 and their aftermath had been. His policy of reconciliation and liberty of conscience in the last two years of his reign was more effective than the brutality and oppression of his first two years. Yet James carried his policies too high, too far, too fast. He alienated those he needed far more than he gained favor from those he did not. James's pro-Dissent policies and the increasing prominence of Catholics at court and within the government, universities, and army frightened Tory elites and the Anglican establishment. When the prince of Orange landed at Torbay on 5 November 1688, James found that his new friends were few and fickle. With very few exceptions they failed to support him. When yet another Protestant deliverer appeared, Whig and Dissenting lords, gentlemen, lawyers, soldiers, publishers, and preachers hastened to his side. From Cheshire, Henry Booth, Lord Delamere, whose strident Whig politics had landed him in prison twice under Charles II and again under James, galvanized his tenants to arm themselves and follow him to meet the prince. "I am of the opinion," he declared, "that when the nation is delivered, it must be by force or by miracle; it would be too great a presumption to expect the latter and therefore our deliverance must be by force."[80] The Protestant cause was not forgotten, nor the blood of Whig radicals spilled for naught. In 1688 the ideology that permitted resistance and the culture that disseminated it triumphed. The cycle of violence and defeat, terror and oppression, was broken.

Radical Whigs played numerous and important roles in the Revolution. Refugees like Robert Ferguson sailed with William to Torbay; others like Lord Delamere joined William's army; still others like John Hampden the younger were elected to the Convention which met in January to settle the future of the country. The most significant contribution of the radicals, however, had already been accomplished. Their insistence over the previous decade on the right of the people to restore the constitution provided the English with a justification for their actions in 1688–89. The removal of a king was not an easy operation. For a decade Tory opinion-makers had been hawking ideas of divinely anointed kings and passively obedient subjects, not exactly the stuff of revolution. But radical words and deeds gave the Revolution its discourse, wherein violence was justifiable.

Robert Ferguson spelled out those ideas once again in the winter of 1688 in *A Brief Justification of the Prince of Orange's Descent*, which was probably the most influential tract published during the Revolution. It not only promoted and defended William's claim to the throne, it also gave members of the Convention, who met in January 1689 to solve the current crisis, an interpretative framework. It provided them with both a verbal and a historical context in which to place, discuss, and explain the final months of 1688.

In his *Brief Justification*, Ferguson set forth a contractarian theory of government which he claimed was the basis of England's ancient constitution. As with Monmouth's Declaration, Ferguson began this tract by stating that government "derives its ordination and institution from God." Yet God does not meddle with "our civil concerns." The people "at the first election of and submission to government . . . prescribe and define what shall be the measures and boundaries of public good, and unto what rules and standard the magistrate shall be restrained." The articles of the agreement between the ruler and the people become the "fundamentals of the respective constitutions of nations." All legal governments have their origins in such "compacts, stipulations, compromises, and agreements."[81]

Ferguson's rulers were not divinely ordained, but chosen by the people: "One person becomes advanced from the common level to the title and authority of a sovereign, and all others are by their own consent reduced and brought down to the condition of subjects." Subjects owe their allegiance first to the constitution and only secondly to the sovereign. With the Rye House martyrs in mind, he asserted that "they neither are nor can be traitors who endeavor to preserve and maintain the constitution." Should the ruler invade the fundamental laws of the constitution, the people are restored "to their state and condition of primitive freedom" (9–10).

Applying the principles of civil government set forth in the first part of his text, Ferguson justified the revolutionary events of 1688 in the second half of the *Brief Justification*. His argument was predictable, but it contained a bit of a twist. Through his subversion of the constitution and invasion of the people's rights and liberties, James II had "unqualified himself" from his position as king. It was the "duty of every Protestant and Englishman" to take up arms against him. Yet in the end force had not been necessary. Perhaps it was a "sense of his own guilt" which "chased him from his throne out the nation." But it was more likely his "fear of a free parliament," called for in the prince of Orange's Declaration. In this respect James II did the nation a "kindness" by "retiring across the sea" (9, 21–22).

Ferguson's forfeiture theory, the assertion that resistance to James was not necessary since he himself had forfeited the throne, was crucial. This was the interpretation of the Revolution later adopted by the Convention, which sought to neutralize the more radical implications of the events of 1688. Its members agreed that James had simply vacated the throne and that there had been no active resistance on the part of the people. Ferguson also used the word "abdicate" throughout *A Brief Justification* and pointed to historical examples of kings who "abdicate themselves" (18). The members of the Convention took the same tack, proclaiming in the Declaration of Rights that James had abdicated himself when he left England.

According to Ferguson, once the throne became "empty and vacant," political power devolved to the people's representatives in Parliament, whose ancient right it was to settle the royal succession. He did not deny the right of the people to choose any form of government they wished, but he recommended monarchy, arguing that kingship was essential to the constitution: "it is woven into our laws." Since the "disposal" of the crown had fallen to the people, they were also free to choose the next successor (23–24,34,32). Ferguson recommended that Parliament endow the prince of Orange with "sovereign and legal power" while allowing his wife, the princess of Orange, to be "named with him in all leases, patents and grants." This formula, which placed both William and Mary on the throne while investing administrative power in William alone, was the one adopted by the Convention. By choosing William, the "nation hath in its whole political body exercised the power belonging to it" and restored "the government upon its primitive and original foundation" (36–37).

Ferguson's *Brief Justification* was a significant contribution to English political thought. Though it was a radical defense of the Revolution which both justified the use of force and asserted the concept of devolution of power to the people, many of its ideas were consistent with the thinking of the Convention, and it may well have influenced the Revolution settlement. We will never know who among the members of the Convention read Ferguson's pamphlet. Many were radical Whigs themselves and knew Ferguson. But it was not for the converted that Ferguson preached. He sought to persuade the more timid members of the Convention, providing them with an escape from the radical implications of resistance: kings could abdicate their crowns and vacate their thrones all by themselves. With all its compromises, *A Brief Justification* was the true manifesto of the Revolution.

The conspiratorial politics of the Whig radicals came to an end with the coronation of William and Mary, but the politics they had propagated continued to have a lasting influence on English political culture and ideology in the 1690s and early 1700s. In the 1680s they had made the manipulation of the royal succession a viable and acceptable alternative to a Catholic monarchy. They had justified the use of violence and attempted to use force to accomplish their ends. The Glorious Revolution was not theirs alone. But their ideas, tropes, and slogans were central to it, incorporated into the prince of Orange's Declaration of Reasons, debated at the Convention, and inscribed in the Declaration of Rights. It is no wonder that the scribbler of *A Dialogue between Dick and Tom* was at a loss when he contemplated the events of the winter of 1688–89. They were like a "dream," and to the coming ages they became "a romance"—so much so that it is easy to forget that the road to that Revolution was not nearly so bloodless, glorious, or tame.

Notes

1. This essay is based on my book manuscript, "Revolution Culture: Conspiratorial Politics and Radical Whig Ideology in Late Stuart England," which examines the activities and ideas of a network of Whig radicals in the 1680s.

2. I have tracked the activities of approximately one hundred Whig radicals. They came from all social castes from aristocrats to artisans, and while most were Dissenters, there were several practicing Anglicans as well.

3. W. A. Speck, *Reluctant Revolutionaries: Englishmen and the Revolution of 1688* (Oxford, 1988).

4. John Morrill, "The Sensible Revolution," in his *The Nature of the English Revolution* (London, 1993), 419–53.

5. Tim Harris, *London Crowds in the Reign of Charles II: Propaganda and Politics from the Restoration until the Exclusion Crisis* (Cambridge, 1987); Mark Knights, *Politics and Opinion in Crisis, 1678–81* (Cambridge, 1994).

6. Tim Harris, "The Problem of 'Popular Political Culture' in Seventeenth-Century London," *History of European Ideas* 10 (1989): 51.

7. Lord Ford Grey, *The Secret History of the Rye House Plot and of Monmouth's Rebellion* (1754), 3–18.

8. Howard's testimony at the trial of John Hampden the younger, in *A Complete Collection of State Trials and Proceedings for High Treason and Other Crimes and Misdemeanors from the Earliest Period to the Year 1783*, ed. T. B. Howell, 21 vols. (London, 1811–26), 9:1066 (hereafter cited as *State Trials*). Nathaniel Wade also reported that Shaftesbury "imagined to himself that he had thousands at his devotion in an hour's warning." British Library, Harl. MSS 6845, fol. 266.

9. Grey, *Secret History of the Rye House Plot*, 20, 26.

10. K. H. D. Haley, *The First Earl of Shaftesbury* (Oxford, 1968), 708–12; *State Trials*, 9:364.

11. Grey, *Secret History of the Rye House Plot*, 41.

12. John Dalrymple, *Memoirs of Great Britain and Ireland...*, 2 vols. (Edinburgh, 1771–73), 1:25. It is not certain who exactly sent for Ferguson. In his confession Grey made it sound as if the higher cabal of conspirators had done so, but Robert West reported that a group of the lower level of conspirators agreed that Ferguson should be sent for and claims he wrote "a canting letter to Mr. Ferguson, inviting him over for his health." West's Confession, BL, Add. MSS 38847, fols. 95, 96.

13. West's Confession, fols. 96, 102; Colonel Rumsey's Information, *State Trials*, 9:379; Zachary Bourne's Information, *State Trials*, 9:416.

14. Certificate by Samuel Smith, ordinary of Newgate, *Calendar of State Papers, Domestic* (July-September 1683), 154.

15. The Information of Nathaniel Hartshorne, in ibid., 12; The Information of Samuel Starkey on Oath, in ibid., 42.

16. West's Confession, fol. 96; Bourne's Information, *State Trials*, 9:416; West's Information, *State Trials*, 9:405; Rumsey's Information, *State Trials*, 9:379.

17. The Further Examination of Robert West, *State Trials*, 9:420.

18. *State Trials*, 9:394, 422; West's Confession, fols. 103–4.

19. *State Trials*, 9:419, 417. Also see Robert Ferguson, *The History of All Mobs, Tumults and Insurrections in Great Britain* (1715), 43, wherein Ferguson reiterated these plans.

20. *State Trials*, 9:420–21; West's Confession, fol. 104. On popular resentment to the chimney tax see Lydia Marshall, "The Levying of the Hearth Tax, 1662–1688," *English Historical Review* 51 (1936): 628–46.

21. West's Confession, fol. 104; *State Trials*, 9:421–22.

22. Further Examination of Robert West, *State Trials*, 9:409.

23. West's Confession, fol. 119; *State Trials*, 9:409.

24. *Cal.S.P.Dom.* (July-September 1683), 307, 330 (London, 19 August 1683; Windsor, August 1683); *Cal.S.P.Dom.* (October 1683–April 1684), 89 (Kingston, 14 November 1683).

25. *Cal.S.P.Dom.* (July-September 1683), 215–16. The writer was referring to a Whig polemic

defending John Rouse, who was convicted of treason for the Rye House Plot and executed on 20 July 1683.

26. *An Account of How the Earl of Essex Killed Himself in the Tower of London* (1683); Michael MacDonald, "The Strange Death of the Earl of Essex, 1683," *History Today* 41 (1991): 13–18.

27. The Information on Oath of Henry Warr of Ilminster, *Cal.S.P.Dom.* (July-September 1683), 430.

28. In August 1683 Speke wrote Braddon letters of introduction to persons of quality, including Sir Richard Atkyns. Speke claimed he was drinking at the time he wrote the letters and "knew not well what I writ." The letters were plainly incriminating, informing Atkyns that "we hope we can bring the earl of Essex's murder on the stage, before they can any of those [Rye House plotters] in the Tower to a trial." *State Trials*, 9:1196, 1162.

29. *The Trial of Laurence Braddon and Hugh Speke, gent. upon an information of high misdemeanor* (1684).

30. Henry Danvers, *Murder Will Out; or, A Clear and Full Discovery that the Earl of Essex did not Murder Himself, but was murdered by others* (1684).

31. Robert Ferguson, *An Enquiry into, and Detection of the Barbarous Murther* (1689), 5–12.

32. Ibid., 1, 75.

33. John Cordy Jeaffreson, ed., *Middlesex County Records*, 4 vols. (London, 1886, reprint London, 1975); 4:268, 292; *Cal.S.P.Dom.* (February-December 1685), 61.

34. Nathaniel Salmon, *The Lives of the English Bishops* (1733), 212. Ferguson's tract repeating the murder charge was *A Representation of the Threatning Dangers, impending over Protestants in Great Britain* (1687).

35. Lois Schwoerer, "William, Lord Russell: The Making of a Martyr, 1683–1983," *Journal of British Studies* 24 (1985): 50; "The Paper Delivered to the Sheriffs by my Lord Russell," *State Trials*, 9:694.

36. Contemporaries believed that either Gilbert Burnet or Russell's chaplain, Samuel Johnson, had written his dying speech. George Agar Ellis, ed., *The Ellis Correspondence, 1686–1688*, 2 vols. (London, 1831), 1:190–91; Dalrymple, *Memoirs of Great Britain and Ireland*, 1:49.

37. "The Paper Delivered to the Sheriffs by my Lord Russell," *State Trials*, 9:689–94.

38. *The Last Speech and Behavior of William, Lord Russell, upon the scaffold in Lincoln-Inn Fields* (reprint Edinburgh, 1683); *The Last Speech and Carriage of Lord Russell upon the Scaffold* (reprint Edinburgh, 1683); *The Speech of the Late Lord Russel, to the Sheriffs together with the Paper Delivered by him to them at the Place of Execution* (London, printed for J. Darby, by direction of Lady Russell, 1683).

39. *The Speech and Confession of William, Lord Russell, Who was Executed for High-Treason against His Majesty* (1683). The fraud, of course, did not go undetected or unanswered; see *Animadversions on the last Speech and Confession of the late W. Lord Russell* (1683); *Animadversions upon a Paper entitled, The Speech of the late Lord Russell* (1683).

40. Roger L'Estrange, *Considerations upon a Printed Sheet Entitled, The Speech of the late Lord Russell to the Sheriffs* (1683), 10–15.

41. Bartholomew Shower, *An Antidote against Poison* (1683).

42. *A Vindication of the Lord Russell's Speech and Innocence* (1683); *A Vindication of the Lord Russell's Speech and Paper . . . from the foul imputations of falsehood* (1683); *The Last Legacy or Affectionate and Pious Exhortations of the late W. Lord Russell to his Lady and Children* (1683).

43. Schwoerer, "William, Lord Russell," 55.

44. [John Tutchin], *The Western Martyrology* (1705), 31–35.

45. *State Trials*, 9:838.

46. *State Trials*, 9:866, 840.

47. *State Trials*, 9:854, 840.

48. "Cromwell . . . was a tyrant and a violent one (you need not wonder I call him tyrant, I did so every day of his life and acted against him too) . . . " *State Trials*, 9:866.

49. Sidney's dying speech published in George Meadley, *Memoirs of Algernon Sidney* (London, 1813), 390–98.

50. Two editions of both the trial and the dying speech were published: *An Exact Account of the Trial of Algernon Sidney, esq., who was tryed at the King's Bench-Bar* (1683); *The Arraignment, Trial & Condemnation of Algernon Sidney, Esq., for High-Treason* (1684); *A Very Copy of a Paper Delivered to the Sheriffs upon the Scaffold on Tower Hill . . . by A. Sidney* (1683); *Colonel Algernon Sidney's Speech, delivered to the Sheriff on the Scaffold* (1683).

51. See, for example, S. Ward's halfhearted defense of Sidney, *The Animadversions and Reflections upon Col. Sydney's Paper Answered* (1684).

52. "Account of Transactions in Europe, 1683," probably written for Nonconformist minister Increase Mather, in *The Mather Papers*, Collections of the Massachusetts Historical Society, 4th ser. (Boston, 1846), 3:636.

53. [Tutchin], *Western Martyrology*, 67.

54. *The Declaration of James Duke of Monmouth, and the Noblemen, Gentlemen and others, now in Arms for Defense and Vindication of the Protestant Religion and the Laws, Rights, and Privileges of England from the Invasion made upon them and for delivering the Kingdom from the Usurpation and Tyranny of James Duke of York* (1685).

55. BL, Add. MSS 41817, fol. 151.

56. Many potential supporters of Monmouth were imprisoned prior to his landing as part of an official dragnet that included those who kept correspondence with the rebels and all Nonconformist ministers. *Cal.S.P.Dom.* (February-December 1685), 232, 260–63.

57. Robin Clifton, *The Last Popular Rebellion: The Western Rising of 1685* (New York, 1984), 245–76; Peter Earle, *Monmouth's Rebels: The Road to Sedgemoor, 1685* (New York, 1977), 196–97.

58. *Ecclesiastica; or, A Book of Remembrance* (Barnstaple, 1874), 80.

59. BL, Add. MSS 41819, fol. 15; BL, Lansdowne MSS 1152A, fol. 238; BL, Add. 41808, f. 265; Historical Manuscripts Commission, *Stopford-Sackville*, 1:26.

60. *Declaration of His Highness William Henry, Prince of Orange, of the Reasons Inducing Him to appear in Armes in the Kingdom of England for Preserving of the Protestant Religion and for Restoring the Laws and Liberties of England, Scotland, and Ireland* (1688).

61. Melinda Zook, "'The Bloody Assizes': Whig Martyrdom and Memory after the Glorious Revolution," *Albion* 27 (1995): 373–96.

62. [Tutchin], *Western Martyrology*, 154; Clifton, *Last Popular Rebellion*, 227.

63. Earle, *Monmouth's Rebels*, 163–64; Clifton, *Last Popular Rebellion*, 222–28.

64. John Bramston, *Autobiography* (London, 1845), 187–88.

65. "An Account of the Actions and Behavior of the Duke of Monmouth from the time he was taken to his execution," in George Rose, *Observations on the Historical Works of Charles James Fox* (London, 1809), app. 8, lxv-lxvii.

66. "An Account of what passed at the Execution of the late Duke of Monmouth, on Wednesday, the 15th of July, 1685, on Tower-hill," reprinted from *Somers Tracts* in E. H. Plumptre, *The Life of Thomas Ken, D.D.*, 2 vols. (London, 1888) 1:218–23.

67. Aphra Behn, *Love Letters Between a Noblemen and His Sister*, intro. Maureen Duffy (New York, 1987), 460.

68. [Tutchin], *Western Martyrology*, 154.

69. Richard Rumbold, *The Last Words of Richard Rumbold* (London, 1685). Rumbold's speech was particularly famous; see Douglas Adair, "Rumbold's Dying Speech, 1685, and Jefferson's Last Words on Democracy, 1826," *William and Mary Quarterly* 9 (1952): 520–31.

70. *Mrs [Elizabeth] Gaunt's Last Speech who was burnt at London, October 23, 1685* (1685); [Tutchin], *The Western Martyrology*, 136–37.

71. Examples include John Ayloffe and Richard Nelthorpe, who were both members of the Green Ribbon Club, lawyers, and Rye House conspirators. Ayloffe was executed for his part in Argyll's rebellion, Nelthorpe, for Monmouth's. John Hicks and William Disney were Dissenting preachers. Hicks was captured at Alice Lisle's house and executed; Disney was executed for printing Monmouth's declaration. Colonel Abraham Holmes was an old Cromwellian soldier who had participated in the Rye House conspiracy. He lost his son and his arm at Sedgemoor; he was hanged and quartered at Lyme.

72. Clifton, *Last Popular Rebellion*, 240; Earle, *Monmouth's Rebels*, 175–77; Zook, "'The Bloody Assizes,'" 382–83.

73. *The Trials of Henry Cornish for conspiring the death of the King . . . and Elizabeth Gaunt . . . for harboring and maintaining Rebels* (1685).

74. "The Trial of Charles Bateman, Surgeon, at the Old Bailey for High Treason," in *State Trials*, 11:468–80; Richard L. Greaves, *Secrets of the Kingdom: British Radicals from the Popish Plot to the Revolution of 1688–1689* (Stanford, 1992), 250.

75. *State Trials*, 1:479–95; HMC, *Hastings* 4:309; H. C. Foxcroft, *The Life and Letters of George Savile, Bart., First Marquis of Halifax*, 2 vols. (London, 1898), 2:93.

76. *A True Narrative of the Sentence of Titus Oates for Perjury* (1685); *The Proceedings upon the Second Trial of Titus Oates* (1685).

77. *State Trials*, 10:1336–54; *Cal.S.P.Dom.* (January 1686–May 1687), 143, 313; *Journals of the House of Commons*, 10:193–94.

78. See John Miller, "The King and the Dissenters (April 1687 to June 1688)," chap.12 in *James II: A Study in Kingship* (Hove, Sussex, 1978), 165–87; Mark Goldie, "John Locke's Circle and James II," *Historical Journal* 35 (1992): 557–86; Mark Goldie, "James II and the Dissenter's Revenge: The Commission of Enquiry of 1688," *Bulletin of Historical Research* 66 (1993): 53–88; J. R. Jones, "James II's Whig Collaborators," *Historical Journal* 3 (1960): 65–73; J. R. Jones, "James II's Revolution: Royal Policies, 1686–92," in *The Anglo-Dutch Moment: Essays on the Glorious Revolution and its World Impact*, ed. Jonathan I. Israel (Cambridge, 1991), 41–71.

79. Among those within the network who received pardons were John Speke, Edward Norton, John Trenchard, Joseph Tily, and Samuel Barnardiston the younger. Robert Peyton and Slingsby Bethel applied for pardons but were denied. BL, Add. MSS 41819, fols. 51, 183, 45, 97, 166, 135; BL, Add. MSS 41813, fol. 96.

80. Henry Booth, Lord Delamere, *Lord Delamere's Speech* (1688).

81. Robert Ferguson, *A Brief Justification* (London, 1689), 5–6, 8. Subsequent quotations from this work will refer to page numbers in this edition, and citations will be included parenthetically in the text.

Reluctant Revolutionaries? The Scots and the Revolution of 1688–89

Tim Harris

I

One of the most exciting developments in early Stuart historiography in recent years has been the pursuit of a three-kingdoms approach to the problems of the first half of the seventeenth century.[1] It is a trend that Restoration historians have, on the whole, been reluctant to follow. In his recent biography of Charles II, Ronald Hutton paid due attention to developments in the Merry Monarch's other realms,[2] while Richard Greaves had much to say about Scotland and Ireland in his trilogy on the Restoration radicals.[3] Yet there has been no effort as yet to replicate for the period up to the Glorious Revolution of 1688–89 the type of close analysis of the interaction among the three kingdoms of the Britannic archipelago that has been shown to be so fruitful in helping to explain the origins and nature of the midcentury revolution. Indeed, it remains far from clear whether there is much of a British story to tell for the Restoration; Mark Goldie, for example, has lately drawn attention to the divergent tendencies pushing the kingdoms of Scotland and England further apart in the period between 1660 and 1707.[4] When trying to understand the problems that developed in England during the reigns of Charles II and James II and the reasons for the eventual demise of the restored polity, many would hold that it makes more sense to look to Holland and France rather than to the north of Hadrian's Wall or across the Irish Sea.

Whatever one's feelings about the pros and cons of British history (and far from all early Stuart historians have been converts), the Glorious Revolution surely remains an obvious candidate for a three-kingdoms treatment.[5] After all, removing James II from his English throne inevitably had implications for Scotland and Ireland, where he was also king. Further than this, however, one might suggest that the explanation for why James's regime collapsed in the first place needs to be sought at the British, or pan-archipelagic, level. For example, James quite consciously used Scotland as a testing ground for what he wanted to do in England;[6] by looking north of the border, the English could see what was in store for them under their popish king. Developments in Ireland similarly convinced the English that James was hell-bent on destroying the Protestant religion and the liberties and properties of his subjects in all the dominions under his rule. Indeed, some contemporaries believed that it was the buildup of a Catholic army in Ireland under the earl of Tyrconnell, and the decision in the autumn of 1688 to deploy some of these troops in England in defense of James's regime, that explain why William of Orange's risky venture in invading England "met with such easy and speedy Success."[7] What James did in Scotland and Ireland, in other words, goes a long way toward explaining why he lost the support of both the political elite and the mass of the population in England. The three-kingdoms approach is also valuable for the comparative perspective it provides. Much light can be shed on that old chestnut of English history, "How revolutionary was the Revolution of 1688?" if we compare what the English set out to do and were able to achieve with what transpired, say, in Scotland.

If we are to take a pan-archipelagic perspective, however, we must do justice to Scotland and Ireland in their own right and not marginalize those aspects of the Scottish and Irish pasts that appear unimportant from an Anglo-imperialist point of view. British history has to be more than an attempt to explain developments in England by bringing in the Scots and Irish where relevant. Problems of balance are most likely to develop when there is a stronger historiographical tradition for a particular time period for one kingdom than there is for the others. This perhaps explains why historians have been so reluctant to pursue a three-kingdoms approach for the period leading up to and including the Revolution of 1688–89; there has simply not been the same body of scholarship on Restoration Scotland or Ireland as there has been on England. There is a particularly serious gap in the Scottish historiography.[8] We have no major published works on the 1680s, no major study of the reign of James VII (as James II was in his northern kingdom), and no analysis of the Scottish Claim of Right and Articles of Grievance of 1689 comparable to Lois Schwoerer's sophisticated examination of the English Declaration of Rights.[9] Those interested in the period must rely on surveys covering a broader time period, which while often excellent at the more general level, are typically rather brief on the 1680s, or else much older studies, which though still of value are somewhat dated. The reason for this neglect may in part be that Scottish historians have convinced themselves there is not much of a Scottish story to tell; rather, they tend to look to England for an explanation of the events that culminated in the overthrow of a king of Scotland and the working out of a revolutionary settlement north of the border. For example, Ian Cowan has argued that "the antecedents to the Glorious Revolution in England found few if any parallels in Scotland, despite the similarity of the policies pursued by James VII in his northern kingdom." The Scots were "reluctant revolutionaries."[10] "There were no indications of any readiness on the part of the Scots by themselves to initiate a revolution," Gordon Donaldson wrote in his influential survey; "the Revolution was made in England and imported into Scotland."[11] Or, as Rosalind Mitchison has maintained, "Discontent in Scotland remained passive . . . in striking contrast to the events precipitating the Great Rebellion, the Revolution of 1688–9 was solely made in England."[12]

All of these conclusions are questionable. The purpose of this essay, therefore, is to begin the process of opening up the possibilities for a multiple-kingdoms approach to the Revolutions of 1688–89 by focusing on the case of Scotland, setting that kingdom's own history against the backdrop of what we know transpired in England in order to produce fresh insights and suggest new ways of thinking about what remains a neglected area of Scottish historical inquiry. A closer examination of developments in Scotland from 1685, it will be argued, reveals striking parallels to the way those in England reacted to the initiatives of the Catholic king precisely because the policies pursued by James VII in his northern kingdom were so similar to those he pursued in the south. Furthermore, it seems doubtful whether we should see the Scots as more reluctant revolutionaries than the English. While some Scots were reluctant, there were others, of varying social backgrounds, who were keen to see the downfall of James VII and who took an active part in trying to restructure the political and religious system north of the border. Moreover, it is seriously misleading to conclude that the Revolution was essentially imported into Scotland from England. Whereas those who made the Revolution in England sought to preserve the existing establishment in church and state against what they saw as the illegal transgressions by the Crown in the 1680s, and particularly under James II (though they certainly introduced some additional safeguards for the rule of law and the security of the Protestant religion at the same time), the Revolution in Scotland amounted to a conscious effort to undo the Restoration settlement in church and state. Why this should have been the case was related to particular historical developments north of the border; in this sense the Scottish Revolution was very much one made in Scotland, shaped by issues deeply rooted in the Scottish past that were of a distinctively Scottish nature.

II

Let us start by looking at the reaction to the policy of catholicization under James, first reminding ourselves briefly of what happened in England in order to provide a suitable comparative point of departure. It is now recognized that there was a marked loyalist reaction in the final years of Charles II's reign. People rallied behind the Crown in defense of the existing government in church and state as by law established, against what was perceived to be a threat to both posed by radical Whigs and Nonconformists. Many people, of all social ranks and throughout England, welcomed James's accession in 1685, but they did so in the belief that he would "Preserve the Government both in Church and State as it is now by Law established," as he promised in a declaration issued immediately upon his accession to the throne.[13] When James used his prerogative powers to undermine the existing establishment in church and state by encouraging Catholics to worship openly, appointing Catholics to military and civil offices under the Crown in violation of the Test Acts, and breaking the legally established Anglican monopoly of worship and education, he met with opposition from his former Tory and Anglican allies, who took a stance in defense of the rule of law. Thus, James's Parliament of 1685, an overwhelmingly Tory-Anglican body, objected to his employment of Catholics within the army and had to be prorogued to forestall further opposition. There were riots in London, Bristol, and other provincial towns in the spring of 1686 against the public celebration of the Mass, and local Tory magistrates typically refused to suppress such disturbances. Anglican clergy spoke out in condemnation of James's policies and had to be silenced by a specially established Ecclesiastical Commission. And there was widespread opposition from the clergy and the Anglican gentry to James's attempts to establish religious toleration through the use of the suspending power. In short, over the course of his reign James alienated the very people who had supported his right to the succession against the efforts of the Whigs and Nonconformists to exclude him. Before William of Orange even set foot on English soil, James's regime had begun to collapse from within.[14]

What transpired in Scotland was very similar. James's accession in his northern kingdom was popular among most groups. There were celebrations when he was proclaimed in February[15] and loyal addresses;[16] the Scottish Parliament, which began its first session on 23 April 1685, proved so determined to show its commitment to the new king that it granted an extremely generous financial settlement, affirmed that the kings of Scotland possessed "sacred, supreme, absolute Power and authority," and passed a number of savage measures against the Presbyterians, including an act which made it a capital offense merely to be present at a field conventicle.[17] The earl of Argyll's rebellion in May generated considerably less popular support than the similarly ill-fated venture by the duke of Monmouth in England that summer; hoping to recruit an army of twenty thousand foot, the earl barely managed to enlist one-tenth that number, and by early June his rebel army had dwindled to a mere fifteen hundred, a poor comparison to the eight thousand men who had joined the rebellion of 1679 in Scotland.[18] Yet if the loyalty of the majority of Scots in 1685 is not to be questioned, it was a loyalty based on an understanding that James would, as he promised in his letter to the Scottish Parliament, "defend and protect" their "Religion as established by Law" and their "Rights and propertys."[19]

When it became clear that James was not going to keep his promise, the Scots reacted in ways remarkably similar to the English. There was an immediate attempt in Scotland to bring Catholics into the military and civil administration. Argyll's rebellion gave James the excuse to appoint the Catholic earl of Dumbarton commander of all forces in Scotland in May 1685, while another Catholic, the duke of Gordon, was made lord lieutenant of the north in command of the Highland forces. In the autumn of 1685 the lord chancellor, James Drummond, earl of Perth, converted to Catholicism, and although Perth offered to step down, James refused to accept his resignation. A few months later, Perth's brother, John Drummond, earl of Melfort and James's secretary of state for Scotland, also converted. In November 1685 James directed a letter to his

Scottish Council granting dispensations to twenty-six Catholic landlords to serve as commissioners to collect the taxes voted by Parliament the previous spring.[20] When Perth returned to Edinburgh from London in late December 1685, he began to encourage the open celebration of Mass in the Scottish capital, and issued an order for a Catholic chapel to be built at Holyrood Palace.[21] An act of the Scottish Reformation Parliament of 1560, confirmed at the accession of James VI in 1567, had declared the Mass idolatrous; attendance was a high crime punishable by death at the third offense.[22] Yet Perth confidently encouraged the king to believe that his powers were such that he could do what he wanted to help the Catholics in Scotland, regardless of the law. "Scotland is not as England," he wrote to James VII on 29 December; "Measures need not be too nicely keept with this people, nor are wee to be suffered to imagine that your Majesty is not so far above your laws as that you cannot dispence with them." Only the western fanatics would prove "uneasie" about the measures taken, Perth assured James, and even this uneasiness would vanish with time.[23]

Perth had seriously misread the situation. The conversions to Catholicism in high places provoked a storm of antipopish sermons by clergy of the established church, so much so that the bishop of Edinburgh had to warn his clergy in October to forbear personal reflections in their sermons and not "be so panical for Popery." Despite such warnings, Episcopalian clergy continued their pulpit campaign. The following spring the bishop had to rebuke one of his clergy, George Shiell, for having "preached rudely against Popery" and saying that "he would believe the moon to be made of green cheese as soon believe Transubstantiation." Shiell defended himself by stating that he thought "a ridiculous religion might be treated in ridicule."[24] The most notorious attack on popery at this time was delivered by James Canaries, minister of Selkirk, at the East-Church of St. Giles in Edinburgh on 14 February 1686. Canaries had preached a strongly loyalist sermon the previous 29 May, the published version of which he had dedicated to the earl of Perth. Now he turned against the chancellor, condemning the recent conversions to Catholicism among eminent persons and warning about the political dangers of a religion that gave the pope the power to depose kings. For Canaries, popery was intolerable not only because it was a nonsensical religion, but because it was "of disloyal Principles, and vastly prejudicial to the Rights of Princes."[25] He was to be suspended from his ministry for preaching and publishing such a seditious sermon.

The open indulgence of Catholicism and the conversions to the Roman faith by those in the highest level of government not only alarmed the Episcopalian clergy, but also caused concern to the inhabitants of the Scottish capital. A riot broke out in Edinburgh on Sunday 31 January 1686, when large numbers of tradesmen, apprentices, and college students gathered in the middle of the afternoon to protest against the public celebration of Mass. They first marched on Holyrood Palace, where the earl of Perth was attending Mass, and broke "the alter [sic] and crucifixes, and candles, and all the things in the chappel, and . . . the windowes of the house" before going on to attack the houses of several Catholics in the city. The city guards eventually managed to restore order and make a number of arrests. When the magistrates tried to have a baxter's apprentice publicly whipped the next day for his participation in the riots, however, a crowd of youths came to his rescue; having saved their accomplice, they then went on a search for local papists, storming their houses, rifling their goods, and breaking open their doors and windows. The troops sent in to dispel the crowd opened fire, killing three people. Two of the ringleaders of the riots were subsequently sentenced to death, as was one of the soldiers who had taken the apprentices' side, saying "he would not fight in that quarrel against the Protestants, for he was sworn to that religion."[26]

James met considerable opposition to his policies in the second session of his Scottish Parliament when it reconvened at the end of April 1686. James asked Parliament to repeal the penal laws against Catholics and grant them "the Protection . . . and . . . Security under Our government which others of Our Subjects have."[27] He had every reason to feel confident; this was the same body that had offered such a forthright demonstration of loyalty the previous year, while government control over the composition of the Lords of the Articles, the select committee that steered legislation through the House, normally ensured that the Crown's legislative initiatives met with success. The Lords of the Articles eventually did agree by a narrow margin of eighteen to fourteen to a draft bill in favor of Catholic toleration, but it contained so many restrictions that in essence it amounted to a defeat for the king, and his high commissioner refused to accept it. The bill proposed that Catholics should be given liberty to worship only in their private houses, "all publick Worship being hereby excluded," and that they should continue to be barred from all public offices, civil and military. The preamble to the bill contained a reminder that "the Estates of Parliament" were "firmly resolved to adhere to the true Protestant Religion by Law established within this Kingdom." There was opposition within Parliament even to this limited measure, especially from the Episcopalian interest. The archbishop of St. Andrews and the bishop of Edinburgh, it is true, backed the king's plans for Catholic toleration, but the other four bishops who sat on the Committee of Articles voted against the proposed bill. Most of the rest of the bishops present in Parliament also objected to any form of Catholic relief, believing it would be a violation of the test oath they had taken under the terms of the act of 1681 to consent to any alteration of the laws protecting the present legal establishment in the church. Leading lay Episcopalians such as the earl of Mar, governor of Stirling Castle, and the laird of Gosford, colonel of a regiment of dragoons, also played a prominent role in the campaign against compliance with the king's wishes in the House.[28]

Frustrated in his efforts to secure toleration through Parliament, James fell back on his prerogative. In February 1687 he issued his first Scottish Declaration of Indulgence, suspending all the penal laws against his Roman Catholic subjects by dint of his "Prerogative Royal, and Absolute Power." The concessions to the Presbyterians were somewhat more grudging, and he had to issue another indulgence in June lifting the restrictions contained in the first before the Presbyterians were willing to take advantage of the freedom now afforded them.[29] As with England, there was much opposition to the policy of indulgence in Scotland. There were even grumblings within the Privy Council, which James had recently extensively purged to try to secure a pliant body. The duke of Hamilton and his two sons-in-law refused to sign a letter from the council approving the February indulgence, and the latter two had to be sacked (James never felt strong enough to take on the duke of Hamilton); three other privy councilors—the marquis of Tweeddale, Lord Yester, and William Hay of Drummelzier—opted for semiretirement rather than incriminate themselves further with James's policies.[30] Although James could count on the support of the archbishop of St. Andrews and the bishop of Edinburgh (the latter now promoted to the archbishopric of Glasgow), most of the clergy of the established church resented the indulgence. According to the earl of Balcarres, writing after the Revolution, the Episcopalian clergy condemned it in their private discourses and their sermons, being fearful that "by giving a general Liberty of Conscience," the king designed "to ruin the Religion then established."[31] One contemporary correspondent observed that it was "above all the episcopal party" who were "most opposite to this liberty and its establishment."[32] There was considerable opposition in some areas to the indulgence of Presbyterians, especially where there was a strong Episcopalian interest confronting a significant but minority Presbyterian presence. Thus, we have reports of Presbyterian ministers being arrested on the (false) pretext that their names were not on the list of approved preachers given to the magistrates, of people who hired out their barns or other buildings for Presbyterian worship being harassed, and of burgh freedoms being bestowed only upon condition of a promise not to frequent meetinghouses. One of the most troubled spots was Dundee, where the fanatical anti-Presbyterian crusader the earl of Claverhouse, soon to be created viscount Dundee, held the chief influence in the town.[33] In the summer of 1688 the Masters of the University of Aberdeen got into trouble "for presuming to take an oath from the Students, when graduated, to profess the Protestant religion," even though the king had recently "discharged the exacting of any oaths." Their defense was that they were required to do so by their foundation and statutes, to which they had sworn, so that they could not omit this oath without committing perjury—a defense similar to that used by the Fellows of Magdalen College, Oxford, in their dispute with James over the election of a new president.[34]

Although most Presbyterians (with the exception of the radical Cameronian faction) availed themselves of the toleration, and even delivered addresses thanking the king for the indulgence, they remained staunch in their opposition to popery and frequently took occasion to express their "dislike of the Tolleration given to the Papists for their Heresies and Idolatries."[35] In a sermon delivered at Gordon, Berwickshire, on 18 October 1687, the Presbyterian preacher John Hardy "thanked his Majesty for his toleration," but added, "if they behoved to take away the laws against Popery, it were better to want it." Summoned before the Privy Council, Hardy refused to retract, and at his trial on 1 December he not only boldly admitted what he had already said, but added, "it is the Presbyterian principle, that idolatry, even under the Gospel, is punishable by death, and that Popery is such; and so they can never think but laws against Popery are both just, lawful and necessary." Hardy persisted in maintaining, however, that he had said nothing seditious; the judges eventually agreed and set him free.[36]

III

There are grounds for believing, then, that the antecedents to the Revolution in England (if by *antecedents* we understand the opposition shown to James's policy of catholicization) found strong parallels in Scotland. Were the Scots more hesitant, however, to follow through on the implications of their stance than the English? Were they reluctant to conspire with William of Orange or support measures that would result in the downfall of James's Catholic regime? In England the campaign of noncompliance with the policies of James II reached a climax with the stance taken by the Seven Bishops against the second Declaration of Indulgence of 1688. Henceforth the regime gradually began to disintegrate. People took to the streets to show their dissatisfaction with James's policies. There were enthusiastic celebrations for the release of the bishops in late June, while in the autumn months of 1688 there was widespread anti-Catholic rioting in London and various other parts of the country (mainly in the form of attacks on mass-houses), reaching a crescendo in the second week of December following James's flight from the capital.[37] Various political dissidents, both at home and in exile in the Low Countries, conspired to bring over William of Orange to rescue English liberties. When Orange finally did invade, he met very little resistance since so many people—at all levels of society—deserted to his cause. Yet we see much the same in Scotland: noncompliance with James, active conspiracy with William, and collective agitation out-of-doors. The details are, of course, different in the two kingdoms, but the impression that the Scots were more passive than the English is illusory. Indeed, once political authority finally did collapse north of the border, we see a much more radical form of political activism out-of-doors than we do in England, as some seized on the opportunity provided by the revolutionary crisis to push forward their own agenda with a vengeance.

Although the invitation to William of Orange came from England, a number of Scots played an active part in the Williamite conspiracy that developed in the summer and autumn of 1688. Several exiled Scots were influential in William's entourage at The Hague and joined with William's invasion force in November. Among them were Gilbert Burnet and Robert Ferguson, although arguably their political preoccupations were centered on England rather than their native land. Yet there were others whose focus was clearly Scotland, such as Sir James Dalrymple of Stair, who had been in exile in Holland since 1681, and William's chaplain, the Reverend William Carstares, who together were responsible for Scottish intelligence. They sent over a number of agents both to gather news and to distribute propaganda, among them William Cleland and Dr. William Blackadder, the latter a veteran of the rebellions of 1679 and 1685. The earl of Argyll, also in Holland, pledged William the support of his own clan to fight against the family which had put both his father and grandfather to death. There, too, were leading Presbyterian politicians such as the earl of Melville (William's first Scottish secretary of state), the earl of Sutherland, and Sir Patrick Hume.[38] William's spies reported in the late summer of 1688 that there was considerable support "for the interest of the Protestant successors" among "the body of the Nobility, Gentry and Commons of the South and West parts of Scotland" and that the Nonconformist ministers were also "much devoted to their Highnesses."[39] When James withdrew his standing forces from Scotland into England at the end of September to deal with the threat of Orange's invasion, he created a power vacuum north of the border that gave his political opponents there the opportunity to organize. "The Presbyterians and discontented Party" from all over the kingdom, Balcarres informs us, descended upon Edinburgh and started meeting "publicly in several clubs, where they deliberated . . . what was fit for them to do in that Juncture." Among them were the earl of Glencairn and Lord Ross, former privy councilors who had been removed by James for their opposition in the Parliament of 1686; the Presbyterian earl of Dundonald, the duke of Hamilton's son-in-law, who had been brought on to the council and subsequently ejected by James; Sir James Montgomery of Skelmorlie, a Presbyterian and radical who was to play a crucial part in the events of 1689; Lord Shaw of Greenock, whose people had been responsible for the capture of Argyll in 1685; and various other figures, many of them sons or relatives of leading politicians of the day. Well connected, they were able to play a significant role in destabilizing the Scottish government in Edinburgh; among other things, they managed to intercept correspondence between the king and his Scottish Council.[40] Stair's son, Sir John Dalrymple, emerged as a leading Williamite on the Scottish Privy Council and played a major part, along with the marquis of Atholl and Viscount Tarbat, in persuading Chancellor Perth to resign and flee the capital.[41] Having in effect secured control of the Scottish government, they then persuaded the council to vote in favor of a free Parliament in accordance with William's invasion manifesto.[42] Other Scots were quick to join with William as he marched from the West Country to London. A battalion of the Scotch regiment under the command of General Douglas deserted to William as he reached the outskirts of Maidenhead on his march to London.[43] Lord Drumlanrig (the duke of Queensberry's son) and the duke of Hamilton, who were already in London, joined with the prince. Others made the long journey south. By Christmas there were a large number of Scots in London waiting on the prince over and above those who had been part of the invasion force. Among them were Hamilton, his sons-in-law the earl of Dundonald and Lord Murray (Atholl's son), the earl of Crawford (a former Scottish treasurer who had been put out for refusing to take the oaths), and Lords Drumlanrig, Ross, and Yester. On Christmas Day, Hamilton and the rest of the Scots who were then in London had a meeting with the prince, where they gave him their "great acknowledgements for his glorious enterprize," offered "their service to him to the utmost of their power," and requested that he "take upon him the administration of that kingdome in matters civill and military."[44]

As in England, there was an outbreak of anti-Catholic demonstrations in Scotland in the autumn 1688. The first disturbances, occurring in mid-October, were directed against "the masse houses there."[45] On 30 November, St. Andrew's Day, Glasgow University students burned effigies of the pope and the archbishops of St. Andrews and Glasgow, apparently "without any opposition."[46] In early December the students of Edinburgh University conducted their own pope burning at the Edinburgh town cross and on another occasion, a mock trial of "his Holiness" at the Parliament house, which they had entered by force in order to carry out their ritual.[47] Serious unrest broke out in the Scottish capital in the second week of December. On Sunday the ninth, rumors spread through Edinburgh that "a great number of Papists had got into the Town and designed to burn it that Night." The students of the college together with the apprentices sounded the alarm by beating drums throughout the city and running through the streets crying, "No Pope, No Papist, No Popish Chancellor, No Melfort, No Father Petres." On this occasion the magistrates prevented an anticipated attack on the Catholic chapel at Holyrood House by shutting the gates of the city and confining the crowds within the city walls. The following evening crowds gathered again and descended upon Holyrood House, where after overcoming the resistance of the palace guards, they proceeded to deface the Catholic chapel and the abbey church, tearing down any "monuments to idolatry" and burning their prizes in a huge bonfire in the abbey close. They also fell upon the house where the Jesuits lived, ransacked the lodgings of the earl of Perth and the residences of a number of other leading Catholics, and destroyed the Catholic printing office run by Peter Bruce. The next day the youths went to all the houses of known Catholics in the city, seized their books, beads, crosses, and images, and solemnly burned them in the street.[48]

There were similar attacks on the houses of Catholics elsewhere in Scotland. The earl of Traquair's house in Peeblesshire was besieged by a crowd who seized a variety of "Romish wares" (an altar, crucifixes, Eucharist cup, wafers, a box of relics, images, candles, and a large number of popish books) and who then carried them seven miles to the town of Peebles, where they burned them at the market cross. An identical incident happened at the Maxwell mansion in Dumfriesshire, where the spoils were likewise carried away and burned at the cross in the nearby town of Dumfries.[49] The anti-Catholic agitation continued through December and into the new year. On Christmas Day the students of

Edinburgh University held another pope burning at the town cross before thousands of spectators, among whom were a number of privy councilors and local magistrates.⁵⁰ There was a particularly elaborate pope-burning ritual at Aberdeen on 11 January 1689, organized by the students of the university. After a long procession of Catholic clergy through the town center and a short play depicting the downfall of the Scarlet Whore and the kingdom of Babylon, the students held a mock trial of the pope for committing "High Treason against . . . God" and for being "an enemy to Religion, Monarchy and Government, and an open and avowed Murderer of Mankind." They sentenced him to be burned to ashes at the market cross.⁵¹

The pattern of anti-Catholic agitation described here is very similar to what took place in England in late 1688. In both countries we see people celebrating the demise of James's catholicizing ambitions and attempting to take advantage of the collapse of royal authority to suppress what they still regarded as illegal forms of worship. The only difference was, as one English newspaper put it, that "the Rabble" in Scotland were "much more violent against the Papists than in England," for they "not only defaced the Popish Chappels, but . . . pulled down the Papists Houses, and destroyed whatever they found belonging to them."⁵² Yet we also see in Scotland a more radical type of crowd activity that did not have a counterpart in England. Starting on Christmas Day 1688 and continuing through the first half of 1689, there was a series of crowd attacks on conformist Protestant clergy in Scotland as local Presbyterians attempted forcibly to eject their Episcopalian ministers from their livings. The "rabblings," as they have come to be called, followed a common, ritualized pattern. The crowd would "carry the Ministers out of his House to the Churchyard, or some publick place of the Town, or Village, and there expose him to the People as a Condemned Malefactor," give him "strict charge never to Preach any more in that Place," and cause "his Gown to be torn over his head in a hundred pieces." Sometimes the Book of Common Prayer would be wrapped up in the minister's gown and both committed to the flames. The crowd would then seize the keys to the church, locking the doors, and forcibly eject the minister and his family from the manse, often destroying their books, furniture, and other possessions.⁵³ These were self-consciously revolutionary crowds, protesting here not against the indulgence of religious practices proscribed by law, but against the existing legal establishment in the church. Believing that the government had been dissolved as a result of James's flight to France on 23 December, they seized the opportunity to promote their own agenda for reform.⁵⁴ As one group who rabbled a minister at Cumnock in Ayrshire put it, "this they did not as States-Men, nor as Church-Men, but by violence and in a Military way of Reformation."⁵⁵ Most of the forcible dispossessions took place in the Presbyterian strongholds of the south and west, the area which had suffered most under the "Episcopal yoke" in the 1660s, 1670s, and 1680s and which had twice risen in rebellion (in 1666 and 1679) in protest against the cruel persecutions of the Episcopalian regime.⁵⁶ The rabblings, in other words, were born out of deep-seated religious tensions in this particular part of Scotland. By and large, they achieved their aim. Although precise totals are unknown, most accounts agree that somewhere between two and three hundred ministers were driven from their livings in the winter and spring of 1688–89.[57] Furthermore, following the settlement of the crown, the Scottish Parliament decreed that those who were "in possessione and exercise of their ministrie" and "behaveing themselves dutiefuly under the present government" as of 13 April 1689, when William and Mary were proclaimed king and queen, should be immune from "any injurie," thus in effect sanctioning any deprivations that had occurred during the interregnum.[58] In short, not only were these crowds more radical than anything we see in England, but they also had a significant impact on the nature of the eventual Revolution settlement north of the border.

IV

The evidence presented here should make us hesitate before describing the Scots as reluctant revolutionaries. Some Scots remained passive, to be sure. Others stayed loyal to James. Yet there were also many Scots who actively demonstrated their disapproval of James VII's style of kingship or support for William of Orange, and some even seized the opportunity to promote their own agenda for reform. Let us turn now to the question, then, of whether the Scots simply imported a ready-made revolution from England.

The Glorious Revolution in England, most historians would agree, was a compromise. The English were able to sustain a political consensus over the crucial months of 1688–89, but only at the expense of abandoning the more radical demands that many Whigs, or at least the "true Whigs," would have liked to have seen implemented. In the end, the Declaration of Rights eschewed any notion that the king had been deposed for breaking his contract with the people, but instead asserted that James had "abdicated the Government" and the throne was "thereby vacant." The framers of the Declaration of Rights claimed that they were doing no more than "vindicating and asserting their antient rights and Liberties."[59] There has been considerable debate among historians as to whether these claims should be accepted at face value. Some believe that the Declaration of Rights undoubtedly did break new constitutional ground, especially with regard to its condemnation of the suspending and dispensing powers, the peacetime standing army, and the Ecclesiastical Commission.[60] Yet while the Declaration of Rights clarified a number of ambiguities concerning the extent of the royal prerogative, contemporaries appear to have genuinely believed—and with good reason—that the suspending power, the dispensing power (as exercised of late), a peacetime standing army without parliamentary consent, and the Ecclesiastical Commission were illegal. Indeed, the makers of the Revolution made a conscious effort to avoid legal innovation in 1689;[61] it was James II who had acted illegally, and the members of the Convention could not rectify an illegal situation by acting unconstitutionally themselves. Since the Convention was not a legal Parliament, it could not legislate or make new law; a future king or queen would be able to declare null and void all legislation which had been passed by an assembly which had not been called by the king and which had not received the royal assent. The makers of the settlement in 1689 recognized that further changes were needed, but these would have to be legislated for in the normal constitutional way by a legally constituted Parliament once the succession had been settled. One of the first such measures was the Toleration Act, passed in the spring of 1689 after William and Mary had been declared king and queen and the Convention turned into a Parliament. In other words, the makers of the Revolution in England sought first to return to what they understood to be the existing legal constitution, as reestablished at the Restoration, before turning to a consideration of how they might want to change that establishment through further legislation.[62]

What happened in Scotland was very different in fundamental respects. Some people north of the border would indeed have liked to adopt the type of settlement reached in England. There was a minority within the Scottish Convention, which assembled in mid-March (after the succession had already been settled in England), who wanted to offer the crown to William and Mary with no conditions attached and leave it for subsequent parliaments to address constitutional and religious grievances. They got nowhere. Another group proposed political union with England: England and Scotland should be represented by one parliament, though Scotland should retain its own municipal laws and keep the existing polity and government of the church, which could later be modified by the Convention or an ensuing Parliament.[63] The proposal met fierce opposition precisely because it meant importing the English Revolution into Scotland. Jacobite sympathizers realized that a union would inevitably work to the advantage of the prince of Orange; political self-seekers recognized that their own ambitions for political dominance north of the border would be frustrated if Scotland were incorporated within a Greater Britain; while political and religious reformers, who formed the majority within the Scottish Convention, were worried that pursuing a union at this stage would deny them the opportunity "of distinguishing any rights or priviledges that belonged" to the Scots "as a people."[64]

It proved impossible north of the border to construct a moderate Revolution settlement built around compromise, because political and religious tensions in Scotland ran too deep. It would be misleading to suggest, however, that there was never any hope of coopting more conservative forces in the way that the Tory-Anglican interest had been brought into the Revolution in England. As we have seen, there was a legal constitutional opposition in Scotland to James VII's policy of catholicization, spearheaded by people who had a stake in the existing Restoration establishment in church and state, including leading Episcopalian nobility and gentry and many of the bishops and clergy. Moreover, it is not true to say that an ideological commitment to the theories of indefeasible hereditary succession, divine right, and passive obedience made it next to impossible for Scottish Episcopalians to jettison their support for James.[65] The way forward was shown by James Canaries in a sermon preached at Edinburgh on 30 January 1689 and later published in extended form, where he articulated a theory of limited resistance—one that condemned both popish and Presbyterian principles, and which sought to make the religious duty of subjection compatible with the secular right of people to hold their sovereign accountable if he violated the law.[66] Although the Scottish bishops made it clear that their consciences would not allow them to transfer their allegiance to William and Mary, many of the lesser clergy were prepared to make such an adjustment, while leading Episcopalian politicians such as the duke of Queensberry, viscount Tarbat, and the marquis of Atholl (although their precise motives are not always easy to penetrate) appear to have been looking to the possibility of a Williamite solution that would preserve episcopacy and the existing powers of the monarchy in Scotland.[67] In the end they were outmaneuvered; the Presbyterians and Whigs came to dominate the Convention, in large part because they were able to secure control over the elections to that assembly, and the solution they worked out was a highly partisan one which eschewed compromise.

The Scottish Convention rejected the notion that James VII had abdicated. The Scots could hardly follow the English, who had held that James's flight to France was tantamount to an abdication; Scottish kings had not resided in their native land since James VI inherited the English crown in 1603, and the same form of government existed in Scotland whether the king was in England or France.[68] The Scots could have followed the path advocated by the English Whigs and adopted by the House of Commons in a resolution of 28 January, that the throne had become vacant as a result of James having broken the "original Contract between king and people."[69] One pamphleteer maintained that "by the Constitution of the Government" of Scotland, "there was an Original Contract betwixt the King and the People, by which their Kings were obliged to Rule by Law"; this author sought to show that on a number of occasions in the past, "when the Kings made Invasion upon Religion, and the Law and Liberties of the Subject, tending to the Subversion of the Government," the Estates had convened "by their own Authority, and called their Kings in question for it."[70] Instead of taking this path, however, the Convention reached back into Scottish feudal law and declared that James, by his misgovernment, had "forefaulted the right to the Crown." It has been suggested that the use of the term *forfault* reveals the conservative and backward-looking nature of the Scottish Revolution.[71] This is questionable. The term seems to have been adopted because a mere deposition would have left James's recently born son as the new king, whereas a forfaulture also comprehended the heirs.[72] The renowned lawyer Sir James Dalrymple of Stair thought that the Convention had opted for a more radical solution than necessary by choosing the term *forfault*, since it implied that "the Conventione had a superiority of jurisdictione." Stair would have preferred the Convention to have settled for a straightforward breach of contract, declaring that since James "had violat his pairt of the mutuall engagments, they wer frie of ther part."[73]

The terms on which the Scottish crown was offered to William and Mary were laid out in the Claim of Right of 11 April. In structure it was similar to the English Declaration of Rights. The first half outlined the various illegal acts committed by James VII, while the second half established guidelines for future royal behavior by declaring certain things illegal or laying down prescriptions for what ought to be done. Moreover, like the English Declaration of Rights, it purported to be doing no more than "vindicating and asserting . . . antient rights and liberties."[74] In a number of significant respects, however, the Scottish Claim of Right did redefine the legal powers of the Scottish monarchy. The second half of the document began by asserting, "By the law of this Kingdome no papist can be King or Queen of this realme, nor bear any Office whatsoever therin." Yet the Succession Act of 1681 had explicitly stated that the heir to the throne could not be debarred from the succession on the grounds of his religion.[75] The Claim of Right condemned James for invading Scotland's "fundamentall constitution" and altering it "from a legall limited monarchy, to ane Arbitrary Despotick power," complaining that James had "asserted ane absolute power, to cass, annul and disable all the lawes, particularly arraigning all the lawes Establishing the protestant Religion." It also charged James with allowing Mass to be said in public and converting Protestant chapels and churches into public mass-houses, "contrary to the express lawes against saying and hearing of Mass." It is true that there were laws dating back to James VI's reign against the saying and hearing of Mass. Yet the Scottish Act of Supremacy of 1669 had invested the Scottish king with "Supream Authority and Supremacie over all persons and in all causes ecclesiasticall within this Kingdom," which allowed the king and his successors to "setle, enact, and emit such constitutions, acts and orders, concerning the administration of the externall government of the Church, and the persons imployed in the same . . . As they in their Royall wisdome shall think fit."[76] Under the terms of the Supremacy, as royal apologists had argued back in 1686, the Scottish king possessed the right, through his prerogative, to redefine the constitution of the church establishment by, for example, dispensing with or suspending penal statutes against Catholics or Protestant Nonconformists, or turning over Protestant churches to Catholic worship.[77] Indeed, the Act of Supremacy of 1669 had gone a long way toward establishing the Scottish monarchy as legally absolute. Shortly after its passage, the earl of Lauderdale had boasted to Charles II that "never was [a] King soe absolute as you are in poore old Scotland."[78] Moreover, as we have seen, the Parliament which James called at his accession confirmed that the Scottish monarchy was absolute.

Further legal innovations were introduced by the Claim of Right. The declaration that "the fyneing husbands for their wives withdrawing from the church was Contrary to law" flew directly in the face of an act of 1685 which confirmed that it was legal to fine husbands for their wives' withdrawing from church and ordained that this practice should be observed in all time coming.[79] The most remarkable clause inserted into the Claim of Right was the declaration that "Prelacy" was "a great and insupportable greivance and trouble to this Nation, and contrary to the Inclinationes of the generality of the people . . . and therfor ought to be abolished." Gilbert Burnet thought "it was an absurd thing to put this in a claim of rights; for which not only they had no law, but which was contrary to many laws then in being; so that, though they might have offered it as a grievance, there was no colour for pretending it was a national right." The demand was included here and not in a statement of grievances, where it more properly belonged, as a deliberate strategy to ensure that the new monarchs would be required to abolish the institution of episcopacy and make "presbytery a foundation ston of the government."[80]

The Claim of Right was accompanied by several Articles of Grievance, drawn up two days later, which sought to address a number of problems associated with the nature of the Restoration establishment in church and state. Among other things, the Articles of Grievance demanded the abolition of the Lords of the Articles (which managed parliamentary proceedings on behalf of the Crown) and the repeal of the 1669 Supremacy Act, the act of 1663 giving the king power to impose customs at pleasure, and most of the laws of the 1685 Parliament.[81] Moreover, the offer of the Scottish crown to William and Mary was made conditional upon their acceptance of the Claim of Right and the Articles of Grievance,[82] and all the demands of the Claim of Right and Articles of Grievance were met in a series of laws enacted over the next couple of years.[83] In short, unlike England, where the makers of the Revolution sought to restore what they understood to be the legal establishment, in Scotland the Revolution amounted to a deliberate attempt to undo the existing legal settlement as reestablished at the Restoration. The Scottish Revolution was an attempt to resolve Scottish problems, to deal with issues that had been a cause of concern as a result of the way the monarchy and the church had been reconstructed north of the border after 1660. In that sense the Scottish Revolution was very much one made in Scotland; it confronted issues that simply were not on the agenda in England.

V

The purpose of this essay has been more to raise questions than to provide definitive answers, in the hope of suggesting fresh areas of inquiry and stimulating much-needed research into a neglected area of Scottish history. I have covered a lot of ground in a short space, so my examination has necessarily been brief. Enough has been said, I trust, to call into question some commonplace but unexamined assumptions about the Revolution of 1688–89 in Scotland. The way the Scots responded to the policies of James VII was remarkably similar to the way the English responded to the policies of James II; there were in many respects the same antecedents to the Revolution in both kingdoms. Nor does it seem helpful to designate the Scots as reluctant revolutionaries. In fact, there were many Scots who very much wanted a revolution in 1688–89, and in the end they were able to achieve a settlement that was much more revolutionary than the one which the English had brought about. My main challenge, however, has been to those who want to see the Revolution of 1688–89 as essentially an English affair which the Scots simply imported into their own country. Such a view does a serious disservice to the Scottish achievement. We need to give the Scots back their agency and recognize that they were fighting their own battles and addressing issues and concerns that were rooted in the Scottish past. The Scots found themselves with William and Mary as their new sovereigns, it is true, but they did not simply take on the new English king and queen; they tried to forge a monarchy very different from that established in England in 1689.

This inquiry began with some reflections on the value of writing British history. It might appear that the conclusion is leaning toward the need for separate national histories; there seem to be discrete stories that have to be told to explain how and why Scotland and England went their own ways in 1689. Yet in a paradoxical way this divergence reaffirms the need to be sensitive to the British dimension. Perhaps the most significant thing about 1689, with respect to England and Scotland, is that it marked an abandonment of the policy of convergence pursued by every Stuart monarch since 1603. James I, Charles I, Charles II, and James II had all, in their own ways, tried to promote a greater degree of harmonization among their three kingdoms, particularly in the area of religion. The first three kings all saw their strength as resting on episcopacy, but even James II and VII, who abandoned this alliance, was consistent in the way in which he tried to promote religious and political freedoms for Catholics and Protestant Nonconformist groups in Ireland, Scotland, and England. Although William III would have liked to pursue a policy of convergence and maintain compatible religious establishments with an appropriate measure of toleration, his desires were frustrated as a result of the Revolution that was made in Scotland. The intrinsically Scottish Revolution that occurred north of the border created a British problem: the postrevolutionary regime had to face the daunting task of managing multiple kingdoms when the establishments in church and state in each were so very different. It was a problem that required a British solution, one which was eventually provided (for better or for worse, depending on one's point of view) by the incorporating Union of 1707.[84]

Notes

I am grateful for the assistance of the John Simon Guggenheim Memorial Foundation for a fellowship in support of the research for this paper.

1. Conrad Russell, *The Causes of the English Civil War* (Oxford, 1990); Conrad Russell, *The Fall of the British Monarchies 1637–1642* (Oxford, 1991); J. S. Morrill, "The Scottish National Covenant of 1638 in its British Context" and "The Causes of Britain's Civil Wars," in his *The Nature of the English Revolution* (London, 1993), 91–117, 252–72; J. S. Morrill, "The Fashioning of Britain," in *Conquest and Union: Fashioning a British State, 1485–1725*, ed. Steven G. Ellis and Sarah Barber (London, 1995), 8–39; Jane Ohlmeyer, *Civil War and Restoration in the Three Stuart Kingdoms: The Career of Randal MacDonnell, Marquis of Antrim, 1609–1683* (Cambridge, 1993).

2. Ronald Hutton, *Charles the Second: King of England, Scotland, and Ireland* (Oxford, 1989).

3. Richard L. Greaves, *Deliver Us from Evil: The Radical Underground in Britain, 1660–1663* (Oxford, 1986); Richard L. Greaves, *Enemies under his Feet: Radicals and Nonconformists in Britain, 1664–1677* (Stanford, 1990); Richard L. Greaves, *Secrets of the Kingdom: British Radicals from the Popish Plot to the Revolution of 1688–1689* (Stanford, 1992).

4. Mark Goldie, "Divergence and Union: Scotland and England, 1660–1707," in *The British Problem, c. 1534–1707: State Formation in the Atlantic Archipelago*, ed. Brendan Bradshaw and J. S. Morrill (Basingstoke, 1996), 220–45.

5. Cf. J. S. Morrill, "The British Problem, c. 1534–1707," in *The British Problem*, ed. Bradshaw and Morrill, 38.

6. Sir John Dalrymple, *Memoirs of Great Britain and Ireland: From the Dissolution of the last Parliament of Charles II till the Capture of the French and Spanish Fleets at Vigo*, 3 vols. (London, 1790), 2, pt. 1, bk. 5, app., 176.

7. Sir Richard Coxe, "Letter Containing Transactions since 1653," in *Hibernia Anglicana; or, The Second Part of the History of Ireland, From the Conquest thereof by the English, To this Present Time*, 2nd ed. (London, 1692), 18–19.

8. W. A. Speck, *Reluctant Revolutionaries: Englishmen and the Revolution of 1688* (Oxford, 1988), 15 n.25.

9. Lois G. Schwoerer, *The Declaration of Rights, 1689* (Baltimore, 1981).

10. Ian B. Cowan, "The Reluctant Revolutionaries: Scotland in 1688," in *By Force or By Default? The Revolution of 1688–89*, ed. Eveline Cruickshanks (Edinburgh, 1989), 65.

11. Gordon Donaldson, *Scotland: James V to James VII* (Edinburgh, 1965), 383.

12. Rosalind Mitchison, *Lordship to Patronage: Scotland, 1603–1745* (London, 1983), 116.

13. *An Account of What His Majesty Said at His First Coming to Council* (London, 1684/5).

14. For the most succinct summary of these years, see Tim Harris, *Politics under the Later Stuarts: Party Conflict in a Divided Society, 1660–1715* (London, 1993), 123–32.

15. *London Gazette*, nos. 2009, 16–19 February 1684/5; 2025, 13–16 April 1685; Historical Manuscripts Commission, *Laing*, 1:427; Narcissus Luttrell, *A Brief Historical Relation of State Affairs from September, 1678, to April, 1714*, 6 vols. (Oxford, 1857), 1:330.

16. *London Gazette*, nos. 2013, 2–5 March 1685; 2020, 26–30 March 1685; 2025, 13–16 April 1685; 2030, 30 April-4 May 1685.

17. *Acts of the Parliaments of Scotland* (hereafter cited as *APS*, 8:459–71 (quote on 459).

18. *Historical Selections from the Manuscripts of Sir John Lauder of Fountainhall*, vol. 1, *Historical Observations, 1680–1686* (Edinburgh, 1837) (hereafter cited as Fountainhall, *Historical Observations*), 176; HMC, *Athole*, 16, 18, 19, 20; Greaves, *Secrets of the Kingdom*, 65, 281–82; Ian B. Cowan, *The Scottish Covenanters, 1660–1688* (London, 1976), 98.

19. *APS* 8:455; James II, *His Majesties Gracious Letter to the Parliament of Scotland* (Edinburgh, 1685), 3.

20. Sir John Lauder of Fountainhall, *The Decisions of the Lords of the Council and Session from June 6th, 1678, to July 30th, 1713*, 2 vols (Edinburgh, 1759–61), 1:374; Fountainhall, *Historical Observations*, 227; Paul Hopkins, *Glencoe and the End of the Highland War* (Edinburgh, 1986), 97; F. C. Turner, *James II* (London, 1948), 369–71.

21. Dr. Williams's Library, London, Roger Morrice, Entring Book, P, 516.

22. *APS* 2:535, 3:36; Gordon Donaldson, comp., *Scottish Historical Documents* (Edinburgh, 1970), 124–26.

23. HMC, *Laing*, 1:'443.

24. Fountainhall, *Decisions of the Lords of the Council*, 1:371, 412.

25. James Canaries, *Rome's Additions to Christianity* (Edinburgh, 1686), sigs. b1, A5, 19–20.

26. Henry Paton, ed., *The Register of the Privy Council of Scotland* (hereafter cited as *RPCS*) (1685–86), 541–45; *RPCS* (1686), 7–16, 22–23, 30–34, 41–44, 69–71, 76; T. B. Howell, ed., *A Complete Collection of State Trials and Proceedings for High Treason and Other Crimes and Misdemeanors from the Earliest Period to the Year 1783*, 21 vols. (London, 1811–26), 11, cols. 1003–24; Fountainhall, *Historical Observations*, 1:243–44; Fountainhall, *Decisions of the Lords of the Council*, 1:399, 406, 407; Morrice, Entring Book, P, 525; Luttrell, *Brief Historical Relation*, 1:372; R. A. Houston, *Social Change in the Age of Enlightenment: Edinburgh, 1660–1760* (Oxford, 1994), 305.

27. James VII, *His Majesties Most Gracious Letter to the Parliament of Scotland* (Edinburgh, 1686), 2.

28. Morrice, Entring Book, P, 534–50 passim, 565–66; HMC, *Mar and Kellie*, 218–19; Fountainhall, *Decisions of the Lords of the Council*, 1:415–16; Robert Wodrow, *History of the Sufferings of the Church of Scotland, From the Restoration to the Revolution*, 2 vols. (Edinburgh, 1721–22), 2, app. 116, 160–61; HMC, *Laing*, 1:446–47; HMC, *Hamilton*, 173.

29. *London Gazette*, no. 2221, 28 February-3 March 1686/7; William Croft Dickinson and Gordon Donaldson, eds., *A Source Book of Scottish History*, 3 vols. (London, 1952–54), 3:195–97.

30. Fountainhall, *Decisions of the Lords of the Council*, 1:449–50.

31. Colin Lindsay, third earl of Balcarres, *An Account of the Affairs of Scotland, relating to the Revolution of 1688* (1714), 7–9.

32. *Calendar of State Papers, Domestic* (1687–89), no. 333, p. 68.

33. Wodrow, *History of the Sufferings of the Church*, 2:638–39.

34. Fountainhall, *Decisions of the Lords of the Council*, 1:513.

35. [Gilbert Rule], *A Vindication of the Church of Scotland; Being an Answer to Five Pamphlets* (Edinburgh, 1691), 5. Cf. [Gilbert Rule], *A Vindication of the Church of Scotland; Being an Answer to a Paper, Intituled, Some Questions Concerning Episcopal and Presbyterial Government in Scotland* (London, 1691), 31–32; Wodrow, *History of the Sufferings of the Church*, 2:623.

36. Fountainhall, *Decisions of the Lords of the Council*, 1:474; *RPCS* (1686–89), xix; Wodrow, *History of the Sufferings of the Church*, 2:626–27.

37. Tim Harris, "London Crowds and the Revolution of 1688," in *By Force or by Default?*, ed. Cruickshanks, 49–55; William L. Sachse, "The Mob and the Revolution of 1688," *Journal of British Studies* 4 (1964): 23–40; Robert Beddard, "Anti-Popery and the London Mob, 1688," *History Today* 38 (1988): 36–39.

38. Morrice, Entring Book, Q, 367; Fountainhall, *Decisions of the Lords of the Council*, 1:511; Dalrymple, *Memoirs of Great Britain and Ireland*, 2, pt. 1, bk.5, 21–22; Greaves, *Secrets of the Kingdom*, 323–24.

39. *Cal.S.P.Dom.* (1687–89), no. 2128, 388–89.

40. Balcarres, *Account of the Affairs of Scotland*, 30–31; Andrew Lang, *Sir George Mackenzie, King's Advocate, of Rosehaugh, his Life and Times, 1636(?)-1691* (London, 1909), 296; Dalrymple, *Memoirs of Great Britain and Ireland*, 2, pt.1, bk. 6, 210.

41. Balcarres, *Account of the Affairs of Scotland*, 36–37; *RPCS* (1686–89), liv; J. S. Clarke, *The Life of James the Second*, 2 vols. (1816), 2:336, 338.

42. *Five Letters from a Gentleman in Scotland to His Friend in London* (London, 1689), 2; *The Declaration of His Highness William . . . Prince of Orange, etc. of the Reasons Inducing Him, To Appear in Armes for Preserving of the Protestant Religion, and for Restoring the Lawes and Liberties of the Ancient Kingdome of Scotland* (The Hague, 1688); Edinburgh University Library, MS. La. III. 350, no. 238.

43. Dalrymple, *Memoirs of Great Britain and Ireland*, 2, pt. 1, bk. 6, 210.

44. Morrice, Entring Book, Q, 368–69, 395.

45. Luttrell, *Brief Historical Relation*, 1:469.

46. Wodrow, *History of the Sufferings of the Church*, 2:649.

47. *Five Letters from a Gentleman in Scotland*, 1; Houston, *Social Change in the Age of Enlightenment*, 306.

48. National Library of Scotland (hereafter cited as NLS), MS. 7026, fols. 81–82, 87; Balcarres,

Account of the Affairs of Scotland, 34–35, 38, 39–42; Luttrell, *Brief Historical Relation*, 1:488; British Library, Add. MSS 28850, fol. 93; Robert Chambers, *Domestic Annals of Scotland*, 2nd ed., 3 vols. (Edinburgh, 1859–61), 3:12; *Scotland Against Popery* (London, 1689); *Five Letters from a Gentleman in Scotland*, 1–4; [Thomas Morer], *An Account of the Present Persecution of the Church in Scotland, in Several Letters* (London, 1690), 15; [Charles Leslie], *An Answer to a Book, Intituled, The State of the Protestants in Ireland Under the Late King James's Government* (London, 1692), sig. b2v; [Alexander Monro], *An Apology for the Clergy of Scotland* (London, 1693), 8; *RPCS* (1686–89), lv; Wodrow, *History of the Sufferings of the Church*, 2:650–52; Clarke, *Life of James the Second*, 2:338; Gilbert Burnet, *History of his Own Time* (London, 1850), 510; Houston, *Social Change in the Age of Enlightenment*, 306–8.

49. Chambers, *Domestic Annals of Scotland*, 2:499–501; HMC, *Laing*, 1:460–62.

50. *Five Letters from a Gentleman in Scotland*, 4; Monro, *Apology for the Clergy*, 8.

51. [Robert Reid], *The Account of the Popes Procession at Aberdeene, The 11th of January, 1689* ([Aberdeen], 1689).

52. *London Courant*, no. 4, 18–22 December 1688.

53. [John Sage], *The Case of the Present Afflicted Clergy in Scotland Truly Represented* (London, 1690), 5–6; [Sir George Mackenzie], *A Memorial for His Highness the Prince of Orange, in Relation to the Affairs of Scotland* (London, 1689), 20; *The Present State and Condition of the Clergy and Church of Scotland* (London, 1690), 1–2; [Leslie], *Answer to . . . The State of the Protestants in Ireland*, sig. b2; Burnet, *History of his Own Time*, 510.

54. NLS, MS. 7026, fol. 119.

55. [Sage], *Case of the Present Afflicted Clergy*, "First Collection," 1.

56. [Rule], *Vindication of the Church of Scotland*, 22.

57. [Sage], *Case of the Present Afflicted Clergy*, 6; [Morer], *Account of the Present Persecution*, 41; [Leslie], *Answer to . . . The State of the Protestants in Ireland*, sig. c; HMC, *Laing*, 1:467.

58. Ian B. Cowan, "Church and State Reformed? The Revolution of 1688–9 in Scotland," in *The Anglo-Dutch Moment: Essays on the Glorious Revolution and its World Impact*, ed. Jonathan I. Israel (Cambridge, 1991), 176; *RPCS* (1689), xvii-xxi, 19–20, 77–78.

59. Schwoerer, *Declaration of Rights*, app. 1; quotes on 295–96.

60. For the debate see in particular Schwoerer, *Declaration of Rights*; Lois G. Schwoerer, "The Bill of Rights, 1689, Revisited," in *The World of William and Mary: Anglo-Dutch Perspectives on the Revolution of 1688–89*, ed. Dale Hoak and Mordechai Feingold (Stanford, 1996), 42–58; W. A. Speck, "Some Consequences of the Glorious Revolution," in ibid., 29–41; W. A. Speck, *Reluctant Revolutionaries*; J. R. Jones, ed., *Liberty Secured? Britain Before and After 1688* (Stanford, 1992); Harris, *Politics under the Later Stuarts*, chap. 5.

61. HMC, *12th Report*, app., pt. 6, 29.

62. I have offered my own thoughts on this subject in "The People, the Law and the Constitution in Scotland and England: A Comparative Approach to the Glorious Revolution," a paper presented at Professor Peter Lake's seminar at Princeton University, 3 May 1996.

63. NLS, MS. 7035, fol. 157.

64. *Culloden Papers: Comprising an Extensive and Interesting Correspondence from the Year 1625 to 1748* (London, 1815), 318; Balcarres, *Account of the Affairs of Scotland*, 75–76; NLS, MS. 7026, fol. 209.

65. Valuable insights into the ideology of the Scottish nobility and the Episcopal clergy can be found in two articles by Bruce P. Lenman: "The Scottish Nobility and the Revolution of 1688–1690," in *The Revolutions of 1688*, ed. Robert Beddard (Oxford, 1991), 137–62; Bruce P. Lenman, "The Scottish Episcopal Clergy and the Ideology of Jacobitism," in *Ideology and Conspiracy: Aspects of Jacobitism, 1689–1759*, ed. Eveline Cruickshanks (Edinburgh, 1982), 36–47.

66. James Canaries, *A Sermon Preached at Edinburgh, In the East-Church of St. Giles, upon the 30th of January, 1689* (Edinburgh, 1689).

67. Morrice, Entring Book, Q, 422, 426, 486; *Leven and Melville Papers. Letters and State Papers Chiefly Addressed to George Earl of Melville, Secretary of State for Scotland 1689–1691. From the*

Originals in the Possession of the Earl of Leven and Melville, ed. William Leslie Melville (Edinburgh, 1843), 12, 125–27; Tristram Clarke, "The Williamite Episcopalians and the Glorious Revolution in Scotland," *Records of the Scottish Church History Society* 24 (1990), 33–51.

68. Richard Butler, earl of Arran, *A Speech . . . to the Scots Nobility and Gentry, Met together at the Council Chamber in Whitehall, on the Eighth of January 1689* (Edinburgh, 1689); Clarke, *Life of James the Second*, 2:345.

69. William Cobbett, ed., *Parliamentary History of England*, 36 vols. (London, 1808–20), 5, col. 50; Morrice, Entring Book, Q, 444; J. P. Kenyon, *Revolution Principles: The Politics of Party, 1689–1720* (Cambridge, 1977), 7–11.

70. *A Short Historical Account Concerning the Succession to the Crown of Scotland, And the Estates Disposing of it, upon Occasion, as They Thought Fit* (London, 1689).

71. Bruce P. Lenman, "The Poverty of Political Theory in the Scottish Revolution of 1688–1690," in *The Revolution of 1688–1689: Changing Perspectives*, ed. Lois G. Schwoerer (Cambridge, 1992), 255.

72. Balcarres, *Account of the Affairs of Scotland*, 82. Unfortunately, a forfaulture also comprehended James's other children, including the Princess Mary, wife of William of Orange. The Convention therefore determined that the word "forfault should imply no other alteration in the succession to the crown, than the seclusion of King James, the pretended Prince of Wales, and the children that shall be procreated of either of their bodies." Dalrymple, *Memoirs*, 2, pt. 1, bk. 8, 308.

73. *Leven and Melville Papers*, 9.

74. All citations from the Claim of Right are taken from *APS* 9:37–40. The Claim of Right can also be found in Dickinson and Donaldson, *Source Book of Scottish History*, 3:200–207

75. *APS* 8:238–39; Dickinson and Donaldson, *Source Book of Scottish History*, 3:185–86.

76. *APS* 7:554; Dickinson and Donaldson, *Source Book of Scottish History*, 3:160.

77. "Reasons for Abrogating the Penal Statutes," in Wodrow, *History of the Sufferings of the Church*, 2, app. 118, 163–67.

78. Centre for Kentish Studies, Maidstone, Kent, U1015/043/2; Osmund Airy, ed., *The Lauderdale Papers*, Camden Society, n.s. 34, 36, 38, 3 vols. (Westminster, 1884–85), 2:164.

79. *APS* 8:461.

80. Burnet, *History of his Own Time*, 538; NLS, MS. 7026, fols. 173, 190.

81. *APS* 9:45; Dickinson and Donaldson, *Source Book of Scottish History*, 3:207–208.

82. *An Account of the Proceedings of the Estates in Scotland*, ed. E. W. M. Balfour-Melville, 2 vols. (Edinburgh, 1955), 1:85–89; *London Gazette*, no. 2453, 13–16 May 1689; HMC, *Hamilton*, 181–82; Luttrell, *Brief Historical Relation*, 1:533; *Culloden Papers* (London, 1815), 320–21.

83. *A Collection of All the Acts of Parliament* (London, 1693).

84. Cf. Goldie, "Divergence and Union."

Part II
The Play of Political Imagination

Politics and Memory: Sharnborn's Case and the Role of the Norman Conquest in Stuart Political Thought

Janelle Greenberg and Laura Marin

I

"Memory," opined Michel Foucault, "is actually a very important factor in struggle... If one controls people's memory, one controls their dynamism... It is vital to have possession of this memory, to control it, administer it, tell it what it must contain."[1] Yet despite a ring of truth, Foucault's statement is only partially correct: it omits the very important consideration that memory, being notoriously unstable and malleable, easily evades control, whether by individuals, groups, or governments. Consider, for example, the contemporary monument to the Warsaw Ghetto uprising, which has been appropriated for purposes that have nothing at all to do with the Holocaust. First, a largely non-Jewish population commandeered the monument as a reminder of Polish resistance, and then the Palestinians appropriated it as a symbol of the *intifada*. In other words, even memories physically enshrined in stone and steel defy exclusive ownership.[2]

It is all the more remarkable, then, that certain Stuart dissidents managed to corner the market on the memories and monuments of the English past. Indeed, few groups in the early modern Western world proved more adept at monopolizing revered symbols of their nation's collective history. And few proved as adroit in deploying their past against God's anointed on earth and his lawfully constituted government.

Stuart dissidents accomplished this rather remarkable feat by hijacking a historical construction called the ancient constitution and transforming it into a thoroughly radical and (what we now define as) Whiggish version of history and political thought.[3] This paper will deal with one particular aspect of that hijacking: the appropriation by seventeenth-century dissidents of a law case involving the Saxon Edwin of Sharnborn and William the Conqueror. As the story went, shortly after the Norman invasion William confiscated Edwin's lands in Norfolk, bestowing them upon his favorite the earl of Warenne. Sometime later Edwin petitioned the Conqueror for the recovery of this land on the ground that Edwin himself had not opposed William. In open court the Conqueror agreed, ordering Warenne to return the land and acknowledging the Saxon's right to hold by the tenure he knew under Edward the Confessor.[4]

Although not in the same league with other ancient constitutionalist sources such as the *Leges Edwardi Confessoris*, the *Mirror of Justices*, and the *Modus Tenendi Parliamentum*, Sharnborn's case nevertheless played a crucial role in Stuart political ideology. Indeed, its very brevity probably gave it an advantage over these other lengthier and weightier treatises. Pithy and involving recognizable and even sympathetic actors, Sharnborn's case condensed into a single anecdote the historical point on which much radical theorizing hinged, namely, that William did not rule as a conqueror, but as the legitimate heir to Edward the Confessor and by compact with the English people. The vignette functioned as a *tableau vivant*, portraying William the king as actually knuckling under to Saxon laws and institutions. Put differently, Sharnborn's case provided a script that Stuart dissidents could evoke at crucial periods in their history. It served as an ideal template that they could impose on their past in order to explain the present in ways that suited them and, equally important, that they themselves believed to be valid.[5]

The radical potential of Sharnborn's case lay in the interpretations it invited. Briefly referred to in Domesday Book and embroidered by medieval chroniclers and leading scholars of the early modern period, the case served the ideological purposes of dissidents such as Nathaniel Bacon, William Petyt, Edward Cooke, James Tyrrell, Henry Neville, William Atwood, and White Kennett.[6] From the late 1670s to 1700, writers deployed the tale to justify excluding James, duke of York from the throne and then sending him packing at the Glorious Revolution. The story's value lay in the fact that if "properly" interpreted, it supported assertions near and dear to rebel hearts. First and most basically, Sharnborn's case demonstrated to dissidents that William did not entirely dispossess the defeated Saxons. Although he undoubtedly rewarded his French followers with lands confiscated from some of the vanquished, he permitted those Saxons who early gave him allegiance to keep their lands as they had enjoyed them in the reign of the Confessor.

To reiterate, this meant that William governed his new kingdom according to Saxon customs, in particular the laws of Edward the Confessor, under whom the Sharnborn family held its Norfolk estates. As Petyt wrote in an enormously influential Exclusionist tract (1680), "William I gave away the estates of several of those who were in arms against him, to his adventurers and followers, but the rest of the English (as well by his coronation oath, as by a solemn ratification of St. Edward's laws in a parliament in his fourth year) were to enjoy their estates and the benefit of those laws."[7] William's policy, Henry Neville added, "made in this kingdom a mixture between Normans and Saxons, yet produced no change or innovation in the government."[8]

Once late-seventeenth-century dissidents had established that William reigned not as an absolute conqueror but by governmental contract, some enemies of the Stuarts moved nimbly to the contention that a ruler who violated the terms of his contract automatically freed his subjects from their allegiance to him. The conclusion then became obvious: a right to rebel followed from William's refusal to dispossess the conquered Saxons and impose feudal tenures wholesale upon England. Thus did radical ancient constitutionalists transform a rather minor historical event into a dagger aimed at the heart of the Stuart kingship.[9]

That the weapon had struck its mark appeared from the reaction of the high Tory historian Dr. Robert Brady, who found Sharnborn's case sufficiently threatening to merit a seething response. Complaining that the case pleased "all such as would have William to have possessed England by pact and bargain with the people, and not by right of war, or the sword," he condemned it as a "trite" and "old threadbare, over-worn fable." And he denied that Domesday even mentioned such a case.[10]

But Brady fought a losing battle, for throughout the mid- and late seventeenth century Sharnborn's case enjoyed a place of high esteem in radical political ideology, its polemical power stemming in large measure from the wide acceptance accorded the Whiggish version of history. This interpretation assumed the existence of an ancient constitution in which an immemorial Parliament and common law guaranteed individual liberties and rode herd on overmighty sovereigns. The ancient constitution which Stuart radicals commandeered, but did not create, boasted a long and eminently respectable pedigree. Perhaps in existence as early as the twelfth century and fully articulated by the sixteenth, the ancient constitution was deeply rooted in English culture and revered by centuries of clergymen, lawyers, scholars, and even the occasional king.[11]

The historical construction itself consisted of a series of beliefs about the relationship between past and present, in particular the assumption that a study of the way things used to be provided a reliable guide to the way things are and ought to be. Put differently, for ancient constitutionalists the essence of history was not the pastness of the past, but rather its presence. Indeed, the very term *ancient constitution* referred to a set of laws and political institutions which, while originating at some distant point in time, existed very much in the present.[12]

This assumption of continuity between past and present led sixteenth- and early seventeenth-century ancient constitutionalists to affirm the very premise at the heart of the more radical Whiggish view of English history, namely, that their kingship, their Parliament, and their common law predated Duke William's invasion and weathered his onslaught. This is not to say that ancient constitutionalists, or their more radical heirs, believed that nothing of importance had happened in 1066. On the contrary, throughout the sixteenth and seventeenth centuries, Englishmen of all political persuasions and callings readily admitted that Duke William defeated the English army and King Harold Godwinson and then savaged large areas of the country. Further, it was common knowledge that sometime in the eleventh century a decidedly French influence had entered England—though scholars debated whether Edward the Confessor or William the Conqueror had introduced the French language and French customs, including those of a feudal nature.[13]

However, many Tudor and Stuart writers agreed that the only kind of conquest that mattered was one that obliterated laws and institutions and imposed on the vanquished a set of foreign customs. If William had conquered Saxon laws as well as the Saxon king and army, then he and his successors had reigned as absolute sovereigns whose will constituted the basis of their legitimacy. But if he had not done so, then he ruled by contract and not as an absolute monarch. This point was politically critical.[14]

While many medieval and early modern authors depicted William as introducing alterations in both law and government, most allowed for significant elements of legal continuity after 1066. Thus, in respected medieval tracts such as the *Leges Edwardi Confessoris* and the *Leis Willelme* and in the medieval chronicles of such writers as Matthew Paris, Roger Hoveden, and Henry Knyghton, readers could find descriptions of Saxon parliaments and Saxon laws continuing to function after the Norman invasion. At worst, or so these sources alleged, the Conquest inflicted only a temporary and transient eclipse of these institutions. In no way did it seriously affect the fundamental continuity of English constitutional history. So suggested writers as diverse as the authors of Holinshed's *Chronicles*, Peter Heylyn, John Speed, Richard Rowlands (alias Verstegan), John Cowell, and Sir Richard Baker.[15]

Members of the Society of Antiquaries also addressed this issue. In a series of papers on the origins of Parliament, the common law, and other legal institutions, some of the best scholars of the age, including William Camden, William Lambarde, and Sir Henry Spelman, found in medieval treatises proof that Saxon laws and institutions survived and thrived after 1066.[16] Their friend John Selden, universally renowned for his legal and historical learning, concurred.[17] Buttressed by such scholarly dissertations, a Whiggish interpretation of the past took on credibility.

In sum, for most early modern historians and antiquaries, continuity as well as ancientness characterized the ancient constitution, which Stuart rebels hijacked and upon which they based their challenge to the Crown. From their point of view, no deep and lasting fissure such as that of a Norman Conquest permanently separated Stuart Englishmen from their ancient ancestors. Indeed, the trauma of 1066 appeared as little more than a blip on the seamless screen of English history.

Modern scholarship has, of course, given the lie to much of this version of history. Indeed, today we possess ample evidence proving that medieval and early modern English government was thoroughly king-centered. Moreover, we understand that Parliament and the common law, far from being immemorial, originated in the High and Late Middle Ages, initiated, in fact, by powerful monarchs who often manipulated them for their own purposes.

Some modern scholars posit that Stuart rebels would have known this, too, if the truths of English history had been more to their liking. As it was, these historians assert, the rebels' political agendas and ideological needs drove them to create a "bogus" and "propagandist" version of history whose contagion lasted well into the twentieth century.[18] Their responsibility for befouling the pure historical waters seems all the greater in light of the fact that Brady, writing in the late seventeenth century, not only spotted some of the weak points in the Whiggish version of the past, but managed to put forward a remarkably accurate account of the way things used to be.[19]

However, we suggest that Stuart dissidents deserve less castigation and more credit for their historical views. Modern scholars too easily overlook the fact that seventeenth-century views of the English past originated in a particular reading of respected medieval texts that passed into Stuart England through the writings of sixteenth- and early seventeenth-century historians and antiquaries. Admittedly, scholars now know that some of these medieval works carried unreliable and even spurious tales. But we must keep in mind that many Stuart Englishmen accepted both the sources and their stories as genuine. The truth is, they had no reason not to do so. After all, what was good enough for the likes of Camden, Lambarde, Spelman, and Selden was good enough for them. Small wonder, then, that the ancient constitution and its more radical variant the Whig interpretation carried such clout in the century of revolution.

II

Sharnborn's case proved persuasive in seventeenth-century political discourse because of its association with the ancient constitutionalist view of English history and its inclusion in several highly respected medieval and early modern sources. First, there was Domesday Book itself. The product of a nationwide inquiry ordered by William I in 1085 or 1086, the survey served several ends. In addition to giving William a reasonably accurate account of the wealth of his new kingdom, the inquest provided the king with an opportunity to exploit and refine the administrative machinery he had inherited from the Saxons. It also allowed him to define his and his vassals' relationship with the English.[20] Finally, the Domesday survey functioned as a judicial inquiry aimed at settling land disputes between Saxons and Normans, many of which had raged continuously since 1066.[21] The survey took the form of three questions, which the commissioners put to representatives assembled in each county court. One question asked them to describe, in great detail, the holdings of Saxons in the time of Edward the Confessor. The second asked the same question of the period immediately after the Norman invasion; and the third asked the question with regard to 1086, the date of the survey itself.

Two volumes resulted from William's inquest. The first, Great Domesday, contained findings from most of England, while the second, Little Domesday, covered Norfolk, Suffolk, and Essex. It was Little Domesday that carried a reference to the Sharnborn story, Sharnborn being a village in western Norfolk in Docking hundred. Today it lies several miles due east of Ingoldisthorpe. According to Little Domesday, William I himself ordered that a Saxon landowner, presumably Edwin of Sharnborn, be put back in possession of land the family lost in 1066 to the king's favorite, William of Warenne.[22]

If Stuart dissidents had possessed only this terse reference from Little Domesday, they might well have overlooked the polemical potential of Sharnborn's case. As luck had it, however, the story descended to them embellished and reinforced by a panoply of the most respected scholars in early seventeenth-century England: Camden, Spelman, Sir John Davies, and Sir Roger Owen, with Sir Roger Twysden, Sir Richard Baker, and Sir Matthew Hale weighing in later in the period. Not only did these eminent writers tell the tale in greater detail, but in the telling they imbued it with an ideological as well as a historical dimension.

More than this, Camden, Spelman, Davies, and Owen made it abundantly clear that early seventeenth-century Englishmen argued over the ideological meaning of the Norman Conquest. This assertion runs counter to the views of some modern scholars who suggest that the nature of the Norman Conquest did not arouse intense political interest in the early seventeenth century because most historians and antiquaries readily admitted that William I had conquered England, obliterated Saxon laws, and replaced them with those of Normandy.[23]

Although this is not the place to debate in great detail whether early Stuart writers saw William as a conqueror of Saxon laws and therefore as an absolute monarch—most of them emphatically did not—the history of Sharnborn's case makes it plain that the nature of the Conquest mattered earlier than the 1620s and the 1640s. What is more, the issue at stake for early seventeenth-century Englishmen was the same as for the enemies of the Stuarts throughout the century: Did William I, and therefore his Stuart successors, reign by compact or by conquest?

Camden appears to have been the first to publish a reasonably full account of Sharnborn's case. In his 1607 edition of *Britannia*, he added the story for the first time, having excluded it from the 1586, 1590, 1594, and 1600 versions. Writing of western Norfolk, Camden remarked,

> Sharnborn in this coast is not to be omitted both for Felix the Burgundian who brought these East Englishmen to the Christian faith and state of perpetual felicity . . . as also because it is verily thought and that by faithful testimony of the old deeds and evidences, that an old Englishman lord of this place before the coming of the Normans, by virtue of sentence given judicially in open court by William Conqueror himself, recovered his lordship against Warren, unto whom the Conqueror had given it.

Camden concluded his account of Sharnborn's case by noting that its "argument they enforce hard who would prove that the said William entered upon the possession of England by covenant and agreement, and not by right of war and conquest"—a clear intimation that the meaning of the Norman Conquest was now a matter of discussion.[24]

Although he cited no source for Sharnborn's case, Camden probably learned about it from his fellow antiquary Sir Henry Spelman, himself of Norfolk stock. Among Spelman's papers in the Bodleian Library is a history of the Sharnborn family that includes the story of Edwin of Sharnborn, the earl of Warenne, and William I. Further, Spelman expressly referred to it in his *Archaeologus*, published in 1626.[25]

In any event, within a decade of Camden's account in *Britannia*, the story was making the rounds in both scholarly and literary circles. Thus, Michael Drayton's versification of *Britannia* mentioned Sharnborn's case in a discussion of the nature of William I's title. "Our stories in every hand inform you," Drayton wrote, "of his lawful title enforced by a case reported of one English, who deriving his right from seisin before the Conquest, recovered by judgment of King William I the manor of Sharnborn in Norfolk against one Warren a Norman to whom the king had before granted it." Such an action "would have been unjust, if he had by right of war only gotten the kingdom."[26]

Camden's fellow antiquary Sir Roger Owen also included an account of Sharnborn's case in his tract "Of the Common Lawes of England," in which he presented a thoroughly ancient constitutionalist version of English history. Although never published, this work enjoyed a measure of renown throughout the seventeenth century, when writers such as Bulstrode Whitelocke, George Lawson, and James Tyrrell cited it.[27] Referring to Domesday Book as well as St. Edward's laws, Owen argued at length that William I "claimed England not *jure gladii*, but as the heir to the Confessor." As part of his proof he cited *Sharnborn v. Warenne* in order to "put an end to the modern argument that our laws were abolished by the Normans" and that William therefore reigned as a conqueror. Indeed, Englishmen, "by virtue of their English blood . . . did inherit land as if no conquest had been made."[28]

Neither Camden nor Owen provided any clues as to the authors of the "modern argument" that William, because he conquered England, governed not by compact but as an absolute ruler. But the answer probably lies in the timing of the 1607 edition of Camden's *Britannia*.[29] Talk of conquest theory in general and the Norman Conquest in particular then filled the air. Indeed, the issue loomed large in the debates over the proposed union with Scotland, and it also proved germane to the Irish question. Thus, the "modern authors" in question might well have been writers such as Sir Thomas Craig, Sir John Hayward, and Edward Ayscu, whose defenses of the union with Scotland included detailed accounts of how William I had conquered both the English and their laws.[30]

Ayscu, for example, wrote that William, in "taking upon him the part of a Conqueror . . . abrogated the ancient laws and customs of the land" and "established others, such as either he had brought out of Normandy, or that he thought more fit for the present government of the English nation." In addition, Ayscu continued, William also dispossessed the English of their lands and possessions, which he then bestowed upon "his followers and partakers in his conquest, at his own will and pleasure."[31]

James I's own propensity for describing the union in the language of conquest likely added fuel to the fire. In 1607 he encouraged the English Parliament to think of the union with Scotland "as if you had got it by conquest," and he also spoke of making Scotland "be as Wales was."[32] English anti-unionists also linked the project with conquest theory, warning that conquest constituted the only means by which a new British kingdom could be erected. From this a frightening conclusion necessarily followed. If England were "a kingdom conquered ... then may the king add and alter laws at his own pleasure." From this observation it was but a short step to the conclusion that the proposed union imperiled the most cherished of English institutions—Parliament and the common law.[33]

England's persistent difficulty in bringing about a definitive conquest of Ireland also provoked interest in the events of 1066. Sir John Davies, writing around 1612, found Sharnborn's case relevant to his discussion of why the English had never completely subdued Ireland. The explanation he discovered in England's failure successfully to implant its own legal system into its westernmost colony. Davies, a noted antiquary and common lawyer who served James I as solicitor general, attorney general, and speaker of the Irish House of Commons, readily acknowledged that the Normans had conquered England in some sense. After all, William the Conqueror made French the language of the law "as a mark and badge of conquest," and "he oppressed the English nobility very sore." Nevertheless, the Conqueror "governed all, both English and Normans, by one and the same law; which was the ancient common law of England, long before the Conquest." Davies's source for this statement may have been the *Leis Willelme*, in which the new king told the English, "I command and will, that all shall have and hold the law of King Edward in respect of their lands and all their possessions, with the additions of those decrees I have ordained for the welfare of the English people."[34]

In any event, Davies was convinced that William had not ruled as a conqueror. On the contrary, he had permitted "any Englishman (that submitted himself unto him)" to keep his lands. As specific proof, Davies cited "the notable controversy between Warren the Norman," a man "of the best rank, and in greatest favor," and Sharnborn, of Sharnborn Castle in Norfolk. Although William had given the castle to Warenne, "yet when the inheritor thereof, had alleged before the king, that he never bore arms against him; that he was his subject as well as the other, and that he did inherit and hold his lands, by the rules of that law, which the king had established among all his subjects; the king gave judgment against Warren, and commanded that Sherborn should hold his land in peace." By this means, Davies concluded, William had "obtained a peaceable possession of the kingdom within few years; whereas, if he had cast all the English out of his protection, and held them as aliens and enemies to the crown, the Normans (perhaps) might have spent as much time in the conquest of England, as the English have spent in the conquest of Ireland."[35]

The historian Sir Richard Baker also included the story of Sharnborn in his popular *Chronicle of the Kings of England*. First published in 1643, the work appeared in new, enlarged editions in 1653, 1660, 1665, 1679, 1684, 1696, and, finally, in 1730 and 1733. In words that warmed many a radical heart, Baker described how William had governed his new kingdom. Although "he hath had the name of Conqueror, yet he used not the kingdom as gotten by conquest, for he took no man's living from him, nor dispossessed any of their goods, but such only, whose demerit made unworthy to hold them." This conclusion Baker drew from Sharnborn's case. No isolated example, the case reflected in Baker's opinion the typical way that William treated both the English and the Normans, the latter receiving only the offices and lands of Saxons slain in battle or taking flight.[36]

This evidence also proved useful in Nathaniel Bacon's incendiary tract justifying the Long Parliament's war against Charles I. *An Historical Discourse of the Uniformity of the Government of England* appeared in two editions in 1647 and was secretly reprinted in 1672 and again in 1682 and 1689. Contemporaries therefore considered the tract relevant to the Civil Wars, the Exclusion controversy, and the Glorious Revolution. In making his case for Parliament's right to rebel against errant rulers, Bacon devoted extended space to the events of 1066. In a chapter entitled "A brief Survey of the sense of Writers concerning the point of conquest," he criticized the "story that the Conqueror altered and made laws at pleasure, brought in new customs, and took away estates." If true, these "clamors" led to the conclusion that William's "will [was] the only law." Fortunately for England, "William did never shake off the clog of Saxon law" or "raise the title of conquest" or take away Saxon estates. How did Bacon know this? Because of Edwin of Sharnborn's case.[37]

In spite of the fact that contemporaries associated Bacon's tract with 1649 and the spilling of the blood of the best of kings, the tale's significance and the esteem in which it was held actually grew. Its reputation in the scholarly and legal world was virtually guaranteed when Sir Roger Twysden included it in his new edition of Lambarde's *Archaionomia* (1644). Lambarde's work, which had first appeared in 1568, brought together the extant manuscripts of Saxon and early Norman laws, including those of Edward the Confessor and William I. Standing at the heart of the Saxonist revival associated with the Reformation, *Archaionomia* grounded the sixteenth- and early seventeenth-century ancient constitution by providing historical proof of the continuity of Saxon laws and institutions across the great divide of 1066.[38]

In his new edition Twysden, a noted Saxonist as well as a common lawyer, not only told the story of *Sharnborn v. Warenne*, he enshrined it by placing it among the laws of Edward the Confessor; the laws of William I, confirming the Confessor's laws; and Henry I's famous Charter of Liberties, in which he, too, promised to govern by those same laws. Then, with full understanding that he followed in the footsteps of King John's barons, Twysden linked Magna Carta to these Saxon and early Norman laws. Thus, in his reissue of Lambarde's much-admired treatise, Twysden figuratively and physically associated Sharnborn's case with precisely those legal works that seventeenth-century antiquaries and lawyers most revered. Here interested readers could find a full account of *Sharnborn v. Warenne* in company with the laws of ancient Saxon kings and early Norman rulers—indeed, with the Great Charter itself.[39]

Twysden repeated the story in his *Certaine Considerations upon the Government of England*, probably written in the late 1640s and early 1650s. Noting that Saxon kings enjoyed only a limited power, he described the Normans as governing upon the same conditions. Indeed, William's victory rested entirely upon his willingness to rule according to Saxon laws and his subsequent refusal to endow the Normans with lands seized from the English. This penchant he plainly demonstrated in "the memorable example" of the Sharnborn family of Norfolk, "whose estate the Conqueror having given to Warren, a Frenchman, yet sitting after himself in judgment, and finding it unjust in that the owner of it had never been against him, he brake what had been by him formerly done."[40]

Sharnborn's case also carried the imprimatur of the eminent common lawyer and royal justice Sir Matthew Hale. Writing after the Restoration, Hale noted of the Norman invasion "that those that were not engaged visibly in the assistance of Harold, were not, according to the rules of those times, disabled to enjoy their possessions, or make title of succession to their ancestors, or transmit to their posterity as formerly, though possibly some oppressions might be used to particular persons here and there to the contrary." However, Saxon titles generally rested secure, as "appears by that excellent monument of antiquity, the case of Edwin of Sharnborn and William the Conqueror."[41]

Thus, by the late seventeenth century Sharnborn's case enjoyed the blessings of generations of scholars and common lawyers of various political persuasions. But it was by no means the only case that described William as adhering to Saxon laws and legal tradition. Indeed, Sharnborn's polemical and ideological power was all the more potent because it often appeared in the company of similar tales found in Domesday and medieval chronicles. Particularly pertinent to seventeenth-century radicals was a trial held sometime in the 1070s at Pinenden Heath in Kent. Here an assembly consisting of both Norman and English suitors ruled that the liberty and land of the church at Canterbury belonged, by ancient Saxon custom, not to William I's brother Odo, bishop of Bayeux and now earl of Kent, but to archbishop Lanfranc. Present at the hearing was the Saxon Aethelric, formerly bishop of Selsey, "a man of great age and very wise in the law of the land, who by the king's command was brought to the trial in a waggon in order that he might declare and expound the ancient practice of the laws."[42]

Late-seventeenth-century Englishmen knew of the trial at Pinenden through Eadmerus and Selden's edition of his twelfth-century work[43] as well as through

Sir Edward Coke's *Ninth Reports*[44] and Hale's *History of the Common Law of England*. Here Hale once again assured his readers that William had not imposed Norman tenures upon the English. "It is . . . certain," he noted, "that no person simply, and *quatenus* an Englishman, was dispossessed of any of his possessions, and consequently their land was not pretended unto as acquired *Jure Belli*." This "appears most plainly" by the "many recoveries [that] were had shortly after this conquest, as well by heirs as successors of the seisin of their predecessors before the conquest . . . namely, that famous record *apud* Penendon." Thus, Hale concluded, "it is without contradiction, that the rights and inheritances of the English *qua Tales*, were not abrogated or impeached by this conquest, but continued notwithstanding the same; for, as is before observed, it was *Jure Belli quoad Regem, sed non quoad Populum*"—that is, by right of war William won the kingship but not the kingdom.[45]

Sharnborn's case also drew strength from its association with the story of the valiant men of Kent, who forced William I to allow them to continue to hold their lands by the ancient Saxon tenure of gavelkind. Exceedingly popular with Tudor and Stuart historians,[46] this particular tale described how after the battle of Hastings the men of Kent, led by Archbishop Stigand, surrounded William and his men at Swanscombe Down. In great fear the Normans "stood astounded, and he who thought he held the whole of England in the hollow of his hand was now anxious about his own life." At this point, however, the men of Kent offered to spare the lives of the Normans in return for retaining their "ancestral laws and customs." If William refused their offer, they stood ready "to die here rather than sink into slavery." Left with no choice, William, "more prudently than willingly," agreed, knowing that if he lost Kent he lost England.[47]

In addition to Sharnborn's case, the case of Pinenden Heath, and the story of the men of Kent, Domesday and medieval chroniclers told of less well known, though equally pertinent, instances in which William I had allowed the English to hold by ancient Saxon tenures. Thus, at a plea held at Kentford, Suffolk, in 1080 concerning the liberties of the abbey of Ely, William ordered that Ely should possess those rights "as it held them on the day on which King Edward was alive and dead."[48] Moreover, Little Domesday described occasions on which "the English redeemed their lands" from the Conqueror, as, for example, at Stonham and Ixworth Thorpe.[49] Then there were the cases of Ansgar the Staller, who preserved his holdings after 1066, and Ulf, who initially maintained both his lands and his political power by paying a heavy fine to William.[50] Further, Orderic Vitalis described how William allowed members of the pre-Conquest nobility who submitted to him after Hastings not only to retain their land, but to continue to serve as sheriffs and in other offices.[51] Such stories even found their way into the proceedings in the Ship-Money Case. In 1636, for example, the king's solicitor general, Sir Edward Littleton, noted that "William was no conqueror; for after he came in, men did recover the lands which were their ancestors."[52]

III

The long and respectable lineage of Sharnborn's case and its satellite tales came in particularly handy in the political atmosphere of the late seventeenth century, when enemies of the Stuarts launched two blatant assaults upon the monarchy. First, they attempted to exclude the Catholic duke of York from the throne, and, failing that, they replaced him altogether, altering the kingship into the bargain. The case proved indispensable at these times, because political discourse brought to the fore once again the matter of the Norman Conquest. Indeed, the Conquest now entered the polemical arena with a vengeance. On the one hand, some influential Tory writers supported Charles II and James II by arguing that William had ruled as an absolute conqueror whose will was law. On the other, many Whigs defended both Exclusion and the Glorious Revolution on the ground that William, and therefore his heirs and successors, had governed by a contract, which the Stuart kings had violated.[53] In these circumstances nothing better suited their polemical needs than a well-documented, heavily pedigreed law case that had earned the endorsement of generations of scholars. Moreover, unlike the *Leges Edwardi Confessoris*, the *Modus Tenendi Parliamentum*, and the *Mirror of Justices*, it told a rather simple story that required little interpretation; and unlike these other esteemed sources, it appeared conveniently in numerous Englished versions.

During the Exclusion controversy of the late 1670s and early 1680s, both sides rushed into print with works designed to prove either the indefeasible right of heirs to inherit the crown or, conversely, the right of "the people" or their representatives to alter the succession. The events of 1066 often appeared front and center in the Exclusionist literature, as many Whigs justified altering the succession on the ground that William I (and therefore his heir Charles II) reigned by a compact which bound monarchs to govern in accordance with the law. Furthermore, Whigs now insisted that the law that bound kings was not only the common law that had descended from the Saxons, but also statute law made by a sovereign Parliament in which three coordinate and equally ancient estates—king, Lords, and Commons—shared authority. The claim of the two houses to a coordinate share in government rested on their coevality, and any attack upon the ancientness of the Lords and Commons imperiled the new constitutional arrangement that the Civil Wars had bequeathed to Restoration England. Put differently, if no coevality marked the relationship between king, Lords, and Commons, the two houses relinquished all claim to share sovereignty equally with kings. And without this coordination, they possessed no right to alter the succession.[54]

As it happened, the Exclusionists had every reason to rue the vulnerability of their position, for Tories, led by the formidable Dr. Brady, would soon attack them on precisely this issue of coevality. Enjoying the patronage of Charles II himself, Brady launched a devastating assault on the ancient constitution. Because in his view the king constituted the earthly source of human authority, the two houses possessed only those rights which kings deigned to grant them. As for the House of Commons, Brady claimed that it had come into existence only in the late thirteenth century, summoned in 1265 by the usurper Simon de Montfort. For proof of his theorizing Brady turned to early English history, which in his opinion depicted William as conquering not only the English king and the English army, but the English laws as well. Moreover, not content to strip the vanquished of their estates, which he then bestowed upon his Norman followers, the Conqueror had imposed upon Saxons the foreign customs of Normandy, including feudal tenures. Such actions, Brady smirked, characterized the behavior of an absolute monarch, not a mere invader who graciously governed by a contract with his new neighbors. In other words, William, as well as his successors, had reigned as an absolute conqueror whose will was law and whose heirs therefore enjoyed an indefeasible right to the crown.[55]

In these endeavors Brady received support from the appearance of two powerful royalist Civil War tracts. The first was Sir Robert Filmer's *Patriarcha*, published for the first time in 1680, and the second, *The Free-holders Grand Inquest*, first printed in 1648 and republished in 1679. Both argued for a royal sovereignty in which the king shared his authority with no earthly agency, and both attacked the immemorial nature of the ancient constitution in general and the House of Commons in particular.[56] Brady also made use of William Prynne's later writings, in which he, too, presented evidence that the Commons had existed no earlier than 1265.[57]

The persuasiveness of the Tories' historical assault on the ancientness of the ancient constitution raised the stakes for Exclusionist writers. Among the first to defend Parliament's right to alter the succession were William Petyt and his friend and pupil William Atwood. Both argued for Exclusion on the ground that Parliament, in which the two houses possessed the lion's share of sovereignty, had existed prior to William I's arrival and had survived the invasion fully intact. That is, the two houses enjoyed coevality with Norman kings, which meant in turn that as coordinate estates they possessed the power to alter the succession. This conclusion could only follow if William had reigned by compact, not conquest. Fortunately, such was the case. As Petyt argued, although William defeated King Harold, he governed as the rightful heir to Edward the Confessor and according to his laws.[58]

This much Petyt knew from numerous medieval records, including the *Leges Edwardi Confessoris*, the *Modus Tenendi Parliamentum*, the *Mirror of Justices*, and the case of Pineden Heath.[59] Also pertinent was Domesday Book, "where the title and claim of many common persons to their own and ancestors possessions, both in his [William's] time and in the time of Saxon kings, are clearly allowed." However, "if King William had made an absolute and universal conquest of the realm in the modern sense . . . would he not have seized all into his own hands, and granted the conquered lands to others?" Yet William had obviously refrained from such practices, as *Sharnborn v. Warenne* plainly demonstrated. When Edwin of Sharnborn, "being an Englishman, and true owner of the estate, demands his right in open court, before the king, upon this reason of law, that he never was against the king, either before or after he came in," the king "gave judgment of right against the Norman, and Sharnborn recovered the lordship."[60]

Atwood deployed the same reasoning in his two Exclusionist tracts, citing Sharnborn's case and Domesday as proof that William allowed many Saxons to hold their lands under the titles they had enjoyed in the reign of Edward the Confessor.[61] Atwood also found the story of the men of Kent apt, since it showed how they had succeeded in keeping their gavelkind tenure exempt from feudal law. Here, surely, was ample evidence that manifestly contradicted Brady's "legendary tales, about King William's governing the nation as a conqueror."[62]

In *Argumentum Anti-Normannicum* (1682) Edward Cooke pleaded Sharnborn's case in the same cause, throwing in for good measure the story of Pinenden Heath and similar Domesday tales of Saxons holding their lands by ancient title. To Cooke, who wrote persuasively enough to engage Brady and to merit republication in 1689, all this evidence pointed ineluctably to one conclusion: so far had William been from being a conqueror of the English that "he suffered himself to be . . . conquered by them, that instead of giving to, he took the law from them, and contentedly bound himself up by those, which they called St. Edward's laws." Importantly, these very laws mandated that sovereign power resided in a king and the immemorial houses of Parliament.[63]

Petyt, Atwood, and Cooke all drew Brady's attention, indeed, his severest condemnation. Although he attacked them on numerous grounds, he singled out for special reproach their use of Sharnborn's case to prove that William had "disowned his conquest, or rather submitted his government and sceptre to the Saxon law." On this faulty premise antimonarchical writers based their claim that the commons were "an essential part of the great council." Petyt came in for special censure, Brady noting that "his huge argument is the famous legend, and trite fable of Edwin of Sharnborn, told . . . by all such as would have William to have possessed England by pact and bargain with the people, and not by right of war, or the sword."[64]

Brady then told the story as it appeared in Camden, Coke, Davies, and the Sharnborn family manuscript, warning, however, that the tale should not be taken at face value. For one thing, his royalist friend and fellow scholar Sir William Dugdale gave it differently. According to Dugdale, all Edwin had received from his audience with King William was to become tenant to Warenne, "notwithstanding the king's mandate." In other words, Edwin enjoyed no proprietary right in his land. Indeed, had Sharnborn's plea been good, then any number of others would have come and asked for the return of their land on the same ground.[65] More to Brady's point, "there is no such plea as this in all *Domesday Book* . . . nor is there any such person as Edwin to be found in *Domesday* that held any lands in Sharnborn."[66]

Here Brady was partly correct. Little Domesday, indeed, contained no reference to an Edwin of Sharnborn. It did, however, describe the case in other respects. This point Atwood argued at length in his answer to Brady, explaining that Domesday was not an entirely complete record of landholdings. After all, it sometimes omitted whole counties. All that mattered was that Domesday carried the story itself, which sufficed to prove that William had reigned by compact and not by conquest and that Saxon laws and institutions, including Parliament, had continued to function.[67]

Although the move to exclude the duke of York from the throne failed, Sharnborn's case survived to do good service at the Glorious Revolution. Now the major bone of contention was the power of Parliament to alter the kingship as well as the succession. Once again James's religion proved the catalyst, in particular his catholicizing policies, which he pursued by means of the controversial dispensing power. And once again Brady entered the lists. The first volume of his *Complete History* appeared in 1685 with a dedication to the new king, and his enthronement in the Tower records followed as a matter of course. Understandably, James II appreciated Brady's anticoordination views, since his enemies argued against the dispensing power on the ground that a statute must be dispensed with by the same authority that made it, namely, the three coordinate and coeval estates of king, Lords, and Commons.[68]

Brady's like-minded friend Dr. Nathaniel Johnston also found favor with the king, whose secretary of state, Lord Sunderland, commissioned Johnston's *Excellency of Monarchical Government*. Published in 1686, this tract turned to the Norman Conquest for proof of the legality of the royal dispensing power. Because William had conquered both England and its laws, he reigned as an absolute conqueror from whose will flowed the merely derivative powers of Parliament and the law. Railing against "the serpent of co-ordinate power," Johnston concluded that James II, as sovereign legislator, could dispense with statutes at his will and pleasure.[69]

Tory theorizing thus once again placed a premium on all historical sources that refuted the facts of a Norman Conquest. Many defenders of the Glorious Revolution and its settlement rushed into print with works that did just that, aiming to prove that the king could not dispense because he was not now, nor had he ever been, a sovereign legislator. Theirs was a daunting task, since for centuries lawyers had acknowledged the dispensing power (and its identical twin, the suspending power) as essential and inseparable parts of kingship. Their abolition in the Bill of Rights therefore constituted a revolution in the government as established by law.[70] How convenient, then, that James II's enemies had at their disposal respected sources such as the *Leges Edwardi Confessoris*, the *Modus Tenendi Parliamentum*, and the *Mirror of Justices*. All proved, or so the king's opponents claimed, that since Saxon times kings had shared authority with the Lords and Commons, an arrangement that the duke of Normandy and subsequent monarchs had ratified. Moreover, the Confessor's laws taught that a king like James II, who broke the terms of the governmental contract by ruling illegally, freed his subjects from allegiance. In so doing he in effect deposed himself, leaving the political nation free to replace him with another more to their liking and alter the kingship as they pleased.[71]

One of the most convincing Whig polemicists was James Tyrrell, who published a massive justification for the Glorious Revolution. This work, *Bibliotheca Politica*, consisted of thirteen dialogues between one Mr. Meanwell, who represented the royalist view, and a Mr. Freeman, who spoke for Tyrrell himself. For proof that William ruled by compact and not conquest, Freeman turned to the usual medieval sources—the Confessor's laws, the *Modus Tenendi Parliamentum*, the *Mirror of Justices*, and, of course, Sharnborn's case, all of which pointed unmistakably to the fact that William had governed according to Saxon law. Sharnborn's case in particular proved that royalists like Brady erred when they spoke of William as conquering English law and seizing English estates. As Spelman's manuscript and Domesday made clear, William dispossessed only those Saxons who fought against him. The others he left to hold by their ancient Saxon tenures.[72]

White Kennett, too, defended the Glorious Revolution by reference to the Confessor's laws and Sharnborn's case. These told him that whatever else had happened in 1066, no conquest had occurred. Throwing in the story of the men of Kent for good measure, he wrote that even though William had defeated Harold and slaughtered many English, "yet the crown was obtained by bargain and compact, as is plainly evident from those grants made to Stigand . . . and the men of Kent."[73]

Finally, there was the republication in 1689 of Bacon's *Historical Uniformity of the Government* and Cooke's *Argumentum Anti-Normannicum*. This time the latter appeared under the title *A Seasonable Treatise; Wherein is proved, That King William (commonly call'd The Conqueror) Did not get the Imperial Crown of England by the Sword, but by the Election and Consent of the People. To whom he swore to observe the Original Contract between King and People*. Both works, of course, deployed Sharnborn's case as well as the other usual ancient constitutionalist sources. And many supporters of the Glorious Revolution obviously considered both helpful in proving beyond doubt that because William I had reigned by compact, the political nation and its representatives in Parliament possessed the right to change kings as well as the kingship.

By the end of the century, Sharnborn's case had earned a place in the pantheon of medieval sources essential to the radical ancient constitution. Indeed, it helped make the Whiggish interpretation of 1066 and the political thought associated with it readily understandable and easily accessible. More than mere historical texts, Sharnborn's case, as well as the Confessor's laws, the *Modus Tenendi Parliamentum*, and the *Mirror of Justices*, deserved to be ranked with what Keith Michael Baker refers to as "documentary monuments," that is, works which many Englishmen "celebrated as a shared national possession."[74] The supreme value of such monuments lay in their power to evoke a collective and public past characterized by political stability and legal continuity.[75] In monopolizing these national treasures, radical ancient constitutionalists succeeded in forging a history and an ideology that resonated throughout much of the political nation. But we must keep in mind that they did not create their vision of the nation's history out of whole cloth. On the contrary, they merely put a certain radical spin on a particular view of the past as shaped by the leading scholars, historians, and antiquaries of the medieval and early modern period. It was this heritage that imparted credibility and persuasive force to the radical ancient constitution. To it generations of Englishmen gladly gave obeisance.

Notes

The authors wish to thank Hugh F. Kearney and Amy G. Remensnyder for favors along the way. We are also indebted to the entire Kearney family—Peter, Kate, and Hugh—who, on a perfect Sunday afternoon in July of 1996, drove J. G. around the graceful Norfolk countryside, and eventually to the village of Sharnborn.

1. Quoted in Keith Michael Baker, "Memory and Practice: Politics and the Representation of the Past in Eighteenth-Century France," *Representations* 11 (1985): 134. Baker's article is highly relevant to a study of ancient constitutionalism in Stuart England.

2. See Amy G. Remensnyder, "Legendary Treasure and Conques: Reliquaries and Imaginative Memory," *Speculum* 71 (1996): 884–906; and James E. Young, "The Biography of a Memorial Icon: Nathan Rapoport's Warsaw Ghetto Monument," *Representations* 26 (1989): 90–98.

3. There were, of course, other justifications for rebellion, in particular, theories of natural law and natural right. For these theories, and for the interplay between appeals to history and appeals to natural law and reason, see Johann P. Sommerville, "History and Theory: The Norman Conquest in Early Stuart Political Thought," *Political Studies* 24 (1986): 249–61; Richard Tuck, *Natural Rights Theories: Their Origin and Development* (Cambridge, 1979); Martyn P. Thompson, "A Note on 'Reason' and 'History' in Late Seventeenth-Century Political Thought," *Political Theory* 4 (1976): 491–503; Thompson, "The History of Fundamental Law," *American Historical Review* 91 (1986): 1103–28; Richard Ashcraft, *Revolutionary Politics and Locke's "Two Treatises of Government"* (Princeton, 1986), 208–9, 210–11, 572.

4. Sixteenth- and seventeenth-century Englishmen probably read of the story in Sir Henry Spelman's manuscript history of the Sharnborn family, which is now in the Bodleian Library, Ashmolean MSS 1141. V. 7362:1–16v. The story became more easily accessible when Spelman included it in his *Archaeologus. In Modum Glossarii ad rem antiquam posteriorem* (London, 1626), under "Drenges."

5. For a discussion of the anecdote and its uses, see Annabel Patterson, *Reading Holinshed's Chronicles* (Chicago, 1994), 42–47.

6. Sharnborn's case even made it into the debates over the Petition of Right, where the common lawyer Richard [Creswell] used it to argue the illegality of imprisonment without cause shown. He told the House of Commons that "the kings of England have had a 'monarchy royal,' not a 'monarchy seignoral.' If a monarch make a new conquest and receive the natives under his protection, they and their children must enjoy their ancient liberties. W. Conqueror in Norfolk gave away Sherborne's land to a Norman. Sherborne called it in question, the king judged against himself." *Commons Debates, 1628*, ed. Robert C. Johnson et al., 6 vols. (New Haven, 1977–83), 2:158, 154.

7. William Petyt, *The Antient Right of the Commons of England Asserted* (London, 1680), 35–36.

8. Henry Neville, "Plato Redivivus; or, A Dialogue Concerning Government c. 1681," in *Two English Republican Tracts*, ed. Caroline Robbins (Cambridge, 1969), 121.

9. Just as some modern scholars underestimate the radical nature of late-seventeenth-century politics, so do they underestimate the radical potential in appeals to history. In the view of many historians, this sort of ideology was inherently conservative, especially when compared with argumentation from natural law and natural rights. See, for example, Mark Goldie, "The Roots of True Whiggism," *History of Political Thought* 1 (1980): 209–10; Martyn P. Thompson, "Significant

Silences in Locke's *Two Treatises of Government,*" *Historical Journal* 31 (1988): 275–94; Ashcraft, *Revolutionary Politics*, 208–9, 210–11, 572. Not all scholars agree. J. G. A. Pocock, for one, suggests that "there can be no greater error than to suppose that the argument from natural rights by its nature tended towards radicalism, the appeal to history towards conservatism," in his *Virtue, Commerce, and History: Essays on Political Thought and History, Chiefly in the Eighteenth Century* (Cambridge, 1985), 226; see also Pocock's *The Ancient Constitution and the Feudal Law: A Study of English Historical Thought in the Seventeenth Century*, (Cambridge, 1957, reissued with a retrospect, 1987), 57–58, 360–61. See also Janelle Greenberg, "The Confessor's Laws and the Radical Face of the Ancient Constitution," *English Historical Review* 104 (1989): 611–37.

10. Robert Brady, *An Introduction to the Old English History* (London, 1684), 11–12, 170. *A Speech, According to the Answerer's Principle, Made for the Parliament at Oxford* (London, 1681), 4.

11. The classic account of the ancient constitution is, of course, Pocock's *Ancient Constitution and the Feudal Law*. For later research that both confirms and modifies some of his conclusions, see Paul C. Christianson, "Ancient Constitutions in the Age of Sir Edward Coke and John Selden," in *The Roots of Liberty: Magna Carta, Ancient Constitution, and the Anglo-American Tradition of Rule of Law*, ed. Ellis Sandoz (Columbia, Mo., 1993), 89–146; Corinne C. Weston, "England: Ancient Constitution and Common Law," in *The Cambridge History of Political Thought*, ed. J. H. Burns and Mark Goldie (Cambridge, 1991), 374–411; Glenn Burgess, *The Politics of the Ancient Constitution* (University Park, Pa., 1992); William Klein, "The Ancient Constitution Revisited," in *Political Discourse in Early Modern Britain*, ed. Nicholas Phillipson and Quentin Skinner (Cambridge, 1993), 23–44. For the view that an ancient constitution of sorts was present in the eleventh and twelfth centuries, see R. W. Southern, "Aspects of the European Tradition of Historical Writing: 4. The Sense of the Past," in *Transactions of the Royal Historical Society*, 5th ser. 23 (1973), 243–63, especially 246–56; J. C. Holt, "The Origins of the Constitutional Tradition in England," in *Magna Carta and Medieval Government: Studies Presented to the International Commission for the Study of Parliamentary Estates* (London, 1985), 1–21; Holt, "The Ancient Constitution in Medieval England," in *Roots of Liberty*, ed. Sandoz, 22–56.

12. Burgess, *Politics of the Ancient Constitution*, 7–11.

13. William Camden, for example, wrote, "Many approved customs, laws, manners, fashions, and phrases the English have always borrowed of their neighbors the French, especially since the time of Edward the Confessor, who resided long in France, and is charged by some historians of his time, to have returned from thence wholly Frenchified; than by the Norman conquest which immediately ensued." William Camden, *Remains Concerning Britain*, ed. R. D. Dunn (Toronto, 1984), 139. His fellow antiquary Sir Henry Spelman even reversed the flow of influence, insisting early in his career that the Normans borrowed from Saxon laws and customs, which they learned about when Edward the Confessor lived at the court of the duke of Normandy. Thomas Hearne, ed., *A Collection of Curious Discourses Written By Eminent Antiquaries upon several Heads in Our English Antiquaries*, 2 vols. (London, 1775), 2:344 (see also Arthur Agarde's remarks, 309); John Stow, *The Annales of England* (London, 1606), 122–23; William Lambarde, *A Perambulation of Kent* (London, 1576), 318. Medieval chroniclers also credited the Confessor with introducing Norman ways. See, for example, *The Historical Works of Gervase of Canterbury*, ed. William Stubbs (London, Rolls Series, 1880), 2:58. William Harrison, in the 1587 edition of Holinshed's *Chronicles* (222–23), suggested that Edward's mother, Emma, had brought in the Norman influence. For the view that Edward the Confessor introduced feuds, reliefs, and wardship, see Edmund Gibson's introduction to *Reliquiae Spelmannianae: The Posthumous Works of Sir Henry Spelman Kt. Relating to the Laws and Antiquities of England* (Oxford, 1698) 2–A3v; Lambarde, *Archaionomia* (London, 1568), 135, 137.

14. See Pocock, *Ancient Constitution*, 53, 189. In a work first published in 1612, Sir John Davies explained that the Romans "knew by experience, the best and readiest way of making a perfect conquest" lay in imposing their laws upon those whom they had conquered. John Davies, *A Discovery of the True Causes why Ireland was never Entirely Subdued . . .* (Shannon, 1969), 124–26. For the same view of conquest see the writings of antiroyalists such as Nathaniel Bacon, *An Historical Discourse of the Uniformity of the Government of England* (London, 1647), 160 and passim;

Edward Cooke, *Argumentum Anti-Normannicum; or, An Argument Proving from Ancient Histories and Records, That William, duke of Normandy, Made no Absolute Conquest of England by the Sword; in the sense of our Modern Writers* (London, 1682), xlix-l, lxvii, and passim; Neville, "Plato Redivivus," 121; Algernon Sidney, *Discourses Concerning Government* (London, 1698), 327–28 and passim.

15. See, for example, Raphael Holinshed, *Chronicles of England, Scotland, and Ireland*, 2 vols. (London, 1577), 1:206 and 2:291–92, 304, 306, 337; Holinshed, *Chronicles*, ed. Sir Henry Ellis et al., 6 vols. (London, 1807–8), 1:298 and 2:preface, 3–4, 16; Peter Heylyn, *A Little Description of the World* (Oxford, 1625), 457, 478, 480, 483, 486; John Speed, *History of Great Britaine*, 2 vols. (London, 1611), 1:398–99, 409, 411, 415–18, 434–35, 446, 501; Richard Rowlands (alias Verstegan), *A Restitution of Decayed Intelligence* (Antwerp, 1605), 155, 178–79, 182–87, 203; John Cowell, *The Interpreter; or, Booke Containing the Signification of Words* (Cambridge, 1607), under "Law," "Merchenlage," "Gavelkind," and "Parliament"; Richard Baker, *A Chronicle of the Kings of England* (London, 1643), 31ff.

16. The views of Camden and Spelman, as well as their fellow members Sir John Doddridge, Francis Tate, and Arthur Agarde, can be found in *The Antiquity and Power of Parliaments in England. Written by Mr. Justice Doddridge and several other Learned Antiquaries* (London, 1679); Hearne, ed., *Collection of Curious Discourses*; British Library, Add. MSS 48102A; BL, Cotton MSS, Faustina E.V. For Lambarde's views see *Archaionomia* and his *Archeion; or, A Discourse upon the High Court of Justice in England*, ed. Charles H. McIlwain and Paul L. Ward (Cambridge, Ma., 1957), 17, 124–25.

17. See, for example, John Selden, *Jani Anglorum Facies Altera, rendered into English, with large Notes thereupon by Redman Westcott* (London, 1683), 38, 47–50. See also Paul C. Christianson, "Young John Selden and the Ancient Constitution," *Proceedings of the American Philosophical Society* 128 (1984):271–315.

18. See, for example, Quentin Skinner's justly influential "History and Ideology in the English Revolution," *Historical Journal* 8 (1965): 151–78.

19. Robert Brady's views are contained in his *A Complete History of England* (London, 1685), I, passim; Brady, *Introduction to the Old English History* (London, 1684). Arthur Hall, writing in the reign of Elizabeth, also got the story right when he insisted that the House of Commons was a relative newcomer on the political scene, being called into existence only in the High Middle Ages. *A letter sent by F. A. touchying the proceedings in a private quarell and unkindnesse, betweene Arthur Hall, and Melchisedech Mallerie Gentlemen* (1579), pages unnumbered. See also G. R. Elton, *Studies in Tudor and Stuart Politics and Government*, 4 vols. (Cambridge, 1974–92), 2:563–64.

20. See F. W. Maitland, *Domesday and Beyond*, ed. J. C. Holt (Cambridge, 1987), including Holt's new forward; Sally P. J. Harvey, "Domesday Book and Anglo-Norman Governance," *Transactions of the Royal Historical Society*, 5th ser. 25 (1975), 175–93; J. C. Holt, "1086," in *Domesday Studies*, ed. J. C. Holt (Woodbridge, Suffolk, 1987), 41–63; V. H. Galbraith, *The Making of Domesday Book* (Oxford, 1961); H. R. Loyn, "Domesday Book," in *Proceedings of the Battle Abbey Conference* 1 (1978): 120–30.

21. David C. Douglas, *William the Conqueror* (Berkeley and Los Angeles, 1964), 352–53; "The Domesday Survey," in *Time and the Hour: Some Collected Papers of David C. Douglas*, (London, 1977), 229–31.

22. *Domesday-Book, seu Liber Censualis Willelmi Primi Regis Angliae, Inter Archivos Regni In Domo Capitulari Westmonasterii Asservatus*, 2 vols. (London, 1783), 2:213a. See also Welldon Finn, *An Introduction to Domesday Book* (London, 1962), 22n.; C. Warren Hollister, "The Greater Domesday Tenants-in-Chief," in *Domesday Studies*, ed. Holt, 220, 229, 242.

23. Skinner, "History and Ideology in the English Revolution," 151–78; D. R. Woolf, *The Idea of History in Early Stuart England* (Toronto, 1990), 26, 29. See also Christopher Brooks and Kevin Sharpe, "History, English Law, and the Renaissance," *Past and Present* 72 (1972): 133–42.

24. William Camden, *Britannia* (London, 1607), 350. Philemon Holland's translation is used here: *Britain* (London, 1610), 480.

25. Bodleian Library, Ashmolean MSS 1141. V. 7362:1–16v. Spelman, *Archaeologus*, under "Drenges." Spelman's history of the Sharnborn family was printed in *Reliquiae Spelmannianae* and in *The English Works of Sir Henry Spelman* (London, 1723).

26. Michael Drayton, *Poly-Olbion*, vol. 4 of *Works*, ed. J. William Hebel (Oxford, 1933), 343. *Poly-Olbion* was first published in 1612 and reappeared in 1622.

27. See, for example, Bulstrode Whitelocke, *Whitelockes Notes Upon the Kings Writt for choosing Members of Parliament*, 2 vols. (London, 1766), 1:412; George Lawson, *Politica Sacra et Civilis* (London, 1660), 76, 151, 161; James Tyrrell, *Bibliotheca Politica; or, An Enquiry into the Ancient Constitution of the English Government* (London, 1694), 739.

28. Roger Owen, Of the Common Lawes of England, BL, Lansdowne MS. 646:229–33.

29. Camden and Owen might even have had in mind Selden, who included these words in his discussion of Sharnborn's case: "But, (admit this case as you please, or any cause of right beside . . . [William's] sword) it is plain that his will and imperious affection (moved by their rebellions which had stood for the sworn Harold) disposed all things as a conqueror," including the lands of the Saxons. *Poly-Olbion*, 4:343. Or the Catholic writer Robert Parsons, who described William as conquering England and its laws when he criticized Coke for using English law and history to justify the persecution of Catholics. *An Answere to the Fifth Part of Reportes Lately Set Forth by Syr Edward Cooke* (1606).

30. See, for example, John Hayward, *A Treatise of Union of the Two Realmes of England and Scotland* (London, 1604); Thomas Craig, *De Unione Regnorum Britanniae Tractatus*, ed. C. Sanford Terry (Edinburgh, 1909); Edward Ayscu, *A Historie Contayning the Warres, Treaties, Marriages, and other occurents betweene England and Scotland, from King William the Conqueror, untill the happy Union of them both in our gratious King James* (London, 1606).

31. Ayscu, *Historie Contayning the Warres, Treaties, Marriages . . .*, 45, 47.

32. *Political Works of James I*, ed. C. H. McIlwain, Harvard Political Classics, vol. 1 (Cambridge, Mass., 1918), 202, 292, 294.

33. Quoted in Brian P. Levack, *The Formation of the British State: England, Scotland, and the Union* (Oxford, 1987), 38.

34. D. C. Douglas and G. W. Greenaway, eds., *English Historical Documents*, 2nd ed., 2 vols. (London, 1979–81), 2:432.

35. John Davies, *Discovery of the True Causes why Ireland was never Entirely Subdued* (London, 1612), 127–28.

[36]Baker, *Chronicle of the Kings of England*, 31.

37. Nathaniel Bacon, *An Historical Discourse of the Uniformity of the Government of England* (London, 1647), 155–61.

38. Lambarde, *Archaionomia*. See also John Guy, "Thomas Cromwell and the Intellectual Origins of the Henrician Reformation," in *Reassessing the Henrician Age: Humanism, Politics, and Reform, 1500–1550*, ed. Alistair Fox and John Guy (Oxford, 1986); John Guy, *Tudor England* (Oxford, 1990), especially chaps. 5 and 13; F. J. Levy, *Tudor Historical Thought* (San Marino, 1967); May McKisack, *Medieval History in the Tudor Age* (Oxford, 1971).

39. Lambarde, *Archaionomia* (Cambridge, 1644), 154–56. See 138–51 for the Confessor's laws, and 156–58 for Henry I's Charter of Liberties and Magna Carta.

40. Roger Twysden, *Certaine Considerations upon the Government of England*, ed. John Mitchell Kemble, Camden Society Publications, no. 45 (London, 1849), 37–39.

41. Matthew Hale, *The History of the Common Law of England*, ed. Charles M. Gray (Chicago, 1971), 47–71, especially 61–64.

42. Douglas and Greenaway, *English Historical Documents*, 2:308.

43. *Eadmer's History of Recent Events in England*, trans. Geoffrey Bosanquet (Philadelphia, 1965), 17–18; John Selden, *Eadmeri Monachi Cantuariensis Historia Novorum* (London, 1623), 197–200. Selden's source was the *Textus Roffensis*, a remarkably full collection of laws and legal texts dating from the seventh to the early twelfth century.

44. Edward Coke, *La neuf^{me} part des reports* (London, 1613), "To the Reader," unnumbered.

45. Hale, *History of the Common Law*, 62–63.

46. See, for example, Samuel Daniel, *The Collection of the Historie of England* (London, 1612), 39; Richard Grafton, *A Chronicle at Large and Meere History of the Affayres of Englande and the*

Kinges of the Same, 2 vols. (London, 1568), 2:2–3; Holinshed, *Chronicles* (1577), 2:292–93; Baker, *Chronicle of the Kings of England*, 35–36.

47. *William Thorne's Chronicle of Saint Augustine's Abbey Canterbury*, trans. A. H. Davis (Oxford, 1934), introduction and 47–49. The tale of the men of Kent was false, despite its widespread, indeed, universal acceptance in the early modern period. For a discussion of the story itself as well as its historiography, see Holt, "The Ancient Constitution in Medieval England," 53–55; Holt, "The Origins of the Constitutional Tradition in England," 9–11. We have used Holt's translation here.

48. Douglas and Greenaway, *English Historical Documents*, 484–85.

49. *Domesday-Book*, 2:360b, 367b. See also Finn, *Introduction to Domesday Book*, 22.

50. *Domesday-Book*, 2:376b, cited in Robin Fleming, "Domesday Book and the Tenurial Revolution," in *Anglo-Norman Studies 9: Proceedings of the Battle Abbey Conference, 1986*, ed. R. Allen Brown (Woodbridge, Suffolk, 1987), 100–101. Fleming writes with regard to Nottinghamshire, "It was only after England was shaken again and again by serious native rebellions that the Conqueror undertook a massive dispossession of lesser thegns" and granted their lands to his vassals (100). See also Peter Sawyer, "1066–1086: A Tenurial Revolution?" in *Domesday Book: A Reassessment*, ed. Peter Sawyer (London, 1985), 71–85.

51. *The Ecclesiastical History of Orderic Vitalis*, ed. and trans. Marjorie Chibnall, 6 vols. (Oxford, 1969–80), 2:183, 195. R. Allen Brown, *The Normans and the Norman Conquest* (New York, 1968), 184, 206.

52. T. B. Howell, ed., *A Complete Collection of State Trials and Proceedings for High Treason and Other Crimes and Misdemeanors from the Earliest Period to the Year 1783*, 21 vols. (London, 1811–26), 3:944. His point was that William confirmed the Confessor's laws, which supported the king's right to collect ship-money.

53. For the attempts to exclude James, duke of York from the throne see Howard Nenner, *The Right to be King: The Succession to the Crown of England, 1603–1714* (Chapel Hill, 1995), chaps. 5 and 6; Nenner, *By Colour of Law: Legal Culture and Constitutional Politics in England, 1660–1689* (Chicago, 1977).

54. Corinne C. Weston and Janelle R. Greenberg, *Subjects and Sovereigns: The Grand Controversy over Legal Sovereignty in Stuart England*, (Cambridge, 1981), chaps. 6 and 7.

55. Robert Brady, *A Full and Clear Answer to a Book lately written by Mr. Petyt*, published in 1681 and reprinted in *Introduction to the Old English History*, a collection of Brady's tracts. For Brady's career and views, see Pocock, *Ancient Constitution*, chap. 8 and 343ff.; Weston and Greenberg, *Subjects and Sovereigns*, chap. 7 passim.

56. Robert Filmer, *Patriarcha and Other Writings*, ed. Johann P. Sommerville (Cambridge, 1991) includes *The Free-holders Grand Inquest*. It is generally held that Filmer wrote this work. See Gordon J. Schochet, *Patriarchalism in Political Thought* (Oxford, 1975); Filmer, *Patriarcha*, xxxii–xxxvii. Corinne Weston, however, has forcefully argued that Sir Robert Holborne was its author. See Weston and Greenberg, *Subjects and Sovereigns*, 67, 80, 98, 119, 227, 268–69 n.5, 279 n.71, 313–14 n.72, 314–16 n.80; Corinne Weston, "The Authorship of the *Free-holders Grand Inquest*," *English Historical Review* 95 (1980): 74–98; Weston, "The Case for Sir Robert Holbourne Reasserted," *History of Political Thought* 8 (1987): 435–60.

57. Pocock, *Ancient Constitution*, 204–6. Weston and Greenberg, *Subjects and Sovereigns*, chap. 5.

58. Petyt, *Antient Right of the Commons*, 17–19, 22, 29–34, 62–63, 66–73, and passim. See also Pocock, *The Ancient Constitution*, 188–93, 345–48; Weston and Greenberg, *Subjects and Sovereigns*, 183–92.

59. Petyt, *Antient Right of the Commons*, 45. The author of the *Free-holders Grand Inquest* used the case of Pinenden Heath to prove that only the earls and barons were present at this assembly. "The Free-holders Grand Inquest," in Filmer, *Patriarcha*, 76–77.

60. Petyt, *Antient Right of the Commons*, 18–26, especially 22–24. In addition to Domesday, Petyt cited as his sources for Sharnborn's case Camden, Spelman, Davies, and Twysden. Petyt also mentioned Pinenden Heath as proof that William allowed Saxon laws to govern tenurial situations. In addition, he described this case between Odo and Lanfranc as decided by a Parliament

which represented the whole realm, thereby turning it into a proof that the Commons existed long before 1265 (45–46).

61. William Atwood, *Jus Anglorum ab Antiquo* (London, 1681), 100–105.

62. Ibid., 111. William Atwood, *Jani Anglorum Facies Nova* (London, 1680), 31–67.

63. Cooke, *Argumentum Anti-Normannicum*, lx-lxi, lxiii-iv, lxvii, lxix, lxxii, xcix, appendix, clx.

64. Brady, *Full and Clear Answer*, 11.

65. Ibid., 11–13, 261–62, 269–70. William Dugdale, *The Baronage of England* (London, 1675), 73ff. Dugdale apparently had Spelman's manuscript of the Sharnborn family history in his possession. William Hamper, ed., *The Life, Diary, and Correspondence of Sir William Dugdale*, (London, 1827), 455–56. In 1685 Dugdale wrote to Brady, thanking him for correcting the view of the Conquest put forward by Petyt "and his antimonarchical companions," who had tried to convince the world "that the people are the supreme power, as our late bloody regicides and their abettors, declared them to be" (459–60).

66. Brady, *Introduction to the Old English History*, 270.

67. Atwood, *Jus Anglorum ab Antiquo*, preface, 21, 32–39, 44–47, 100–104, 114–16, and passim.

68. Pocock, *Ancient Constitution*, 212ff; Weston and Greenberg, *Subjects and Sovereigns*, chap. 8.

69. Nathaniel Johnston, *The Excellency of Monarchical Government* (London, 1685), introduction, 127–28, 139, 145, 151–53, 155, 157, 301–307. See also Pocock, *Ancient Constitution*, 212–15; Weston and Greenberg, *Subjects and Sovereigns*, 223–30 and passim.

70. See Lois G. Schwoerer, *The Declaration of Rights, 1689* (Baltimore, 1981).

71. Weston and Greenberg, *Subjects and Sovereigns*, chap. 8; Greenberg, "The Confessor's Laws and the Radical Face of the Ancient Constitution," 631–37.

72. Tyrrell, *Bibliotheca Politica*, 734–38.

73. White Kennett, *A Dialogue between Two Friends, a Jacobite and a Williamite*, in *A Collection of State Tracts Publish'd on the occasion of the late Revolution in 1688 and during the Reign of King William III*, 3 vols. (London, 1705–7), 1:288–89.

74. Baker, "Memory and Practice," 134–35, 144–45.

75. See Holt, "Ancient Constitution in Medieval England," 51, 55; Gordon Schochet, "Why Should History Matter? Political Theory and the History of Discourse," in *The Varieties of British Political Thought, 1500–1800*, ed. J. G. A. Pocock (Cambridge, 1993), 323. Here Schochet writes that the goal of public discourse "is to create, and even sanctify, a tradition that tells a people who they have been and are and allows them to ponder who they might become."

"A General War amongst the Men... but None amongst the Women": Political Differences between Margaret and William Cavendish

Hilda L. Smith

A great deal of attention has been directed to Margaret Cavendish, duchess of Newcastle, by feminist scholars over the last two decades. This scholarship can be divided fairly evenly between those interested primarily in her as a writer of fantasy and those works concerned with her as an iconoclastic early female author of scientific treatises. This scholarship has consistently carried with it a special interest in her views about women. Did such views constitute what some have termed seventeenth-century feminism? Or were they either too inconsistent or too often harsh against her own sex to constitute a feminist outlook? No clear consensus has arisen in answer to the latter question.[1]

This chapter will focus on her unique political and social views and the manner in which they agreed with and differed from the views of her husband and the royalist circle connected to their household at Welbeck Abbey. In so doing I hope to highlight a series of questions and initial analyses that might provide fresh insights into Cavendish's intellectual career and her place within the Cavendish family. In looking at her place within the family of the first duke of Newcastle, I offer a somewhat more negative assessment of her private life than is normally put forward. Further, the chapter emphasizes a greater divide between the values and writings of the duke and duchess than has recently been presented. Both of these areas contribute to a portrait of her peculiarly problematic and radical place within feminist and royalist rhetoric of the mid-seventeenth century. In so many ways Margaret Cavendish was a unique and remarkable figure: a woman who raised questions about women's status not articulated earlier and seldom matched later; an individual who supported royalist rule and social hierarchy, but combined those views with statements that undercut the monarchy and questioned artificial or social differences among human beings; an individual for whom little was sacred.

Margaret Cavendish within the Family and Intellectual Circle of William Cavendish, First Duke of Newcastle

It has generally been taken for granted that Margaret Cavendish lived a charmed life as the wife of William Cavendish, duke of Newcastle. An ill-educated, overly verbose, and little-disciplined thinker, she had an indulgent older husband to assume the costs of publishing her many works and to write elaborate, indefensibly fawning introductions to those works making inflated claims for their wisdom and the greatness of their author. As the duke's wife, she had an opportunity to meet individuals such as Thomas Hobbes and René Descartes and to learn from her husband the principles of their thought, to be a part of an intellectual circle in Paris during the late 1640s, when the recently married couple was in exile, and to continue to participate in intellectual discussions upon their return to England. Apart from her husband's intellectual interests, she gained even more from her association with his brother Charles Cavendish, a scholar interested in a range of philosophical topics, but especially in the nature of mathematics, and a friend and correspondent of both Hobbes and Descartes. He encouraged Cavendish's scholarship and, unlike many others, did not ridicule her unlettered scientific interests. His early death in 1654 surely undercut Margaret Cavendish's opportunity for connections with serious intellectuals after 1660.[2]

Margaret and William's was clearly a love match, as their courtship letters demonstrate, and there is little reason to doubt the duchess's claim that "he was the only person I ever was in love with." There is certainly strong evidence to confirm the duke's assistance and his defense of his wife's learning and publications, but there is also evidence that not all was well for her either abroad or, after 1660, at Welbeck, their isolated estate. The duke appears to have been a consistently unfaithful husband and one much concerned with her inability to produce another son for him (he had six sons from his previous marriage, although only one survived the Interregnum). He wrote regularly to the physician Sir Theodore Mayerne about the duchess's illness and infertility, prompting Mayerne to ask of Newcastle after learning of his melancholy whether "in the state she's in, you ought earnestly to desire it. It is hard to get children with good corage, when one is melancholy, and after they are gott & come into the world, they bring a great deal of paine with them, and after that, very often one looses them."[3] Such pressure on the duchess found expression in her glorification of passionless love and her defensive writings concerning a second wife incapable of producing children.

The duke further revealed himself to be a particularly self-indulgent and profligate husband in his determination to keep up his aristocratic way of life abroad while confronting clearly reduced circumstances. He insisted on keeping horses while they lived in Antwerp, forcing her to return to England to raise money; she pawned her gown for food so the duke could keep his favorite pair of horses. Eventually, he returned to England on the first available ship (an unseaworthy vessel that sank on its next channel voyage), leaving the duchess behind as collateral for their debts. There is thus some question as to whether the marriage was quite as idyllic as it is customarily portrayed.[4]

Yet more serious problems for Margaret Cavendish came from other members of the family, especially from the duke's children, who resented her. Thus far we have only clues that require more detailed follow-up, but they point to efforts to undercut her authority within the household and to engender dissension between herself and William Cavendish. Henry Cavendish, who ultimately became the second duke of Newcastle upon his father's death in 1676, clearly resented his stepmother and the influence she wielded over his father. In a letter written not long before her death, Henry told the earl of Danby, "I am very mallencholly, finding my Father more perswaded by his Wife then I could thinke it possible." A document among the Portland Papers refers to the confession in 1671 of John Booth, a household servant who confessed to libeling the duchess "for the purpose of making dissensions between the Duke and Duchess." More research needs to be done on the context of this confession to determine whether he was paid or encouraged by other family members to create tension between William and Margaret Cavendish. Whether or not one can term the family "dysfunctional," there is at least a serious dissonance between Henry Cavendish's comment to Danby and a letter of about the same time sent by the duke to his son. On 20 January 1670 the old duke wrote, "All your children are well, but Harry loves my wife better than any body, and she him." One can hardly help wondering how William could send this affectionate domestic news with such apparent disregard of his son's strong dislike of his stepmother.

Lady Jane Cheyne, the duke's eldest daughter, was an author herself, although she did not identify with her stepmother's intellectual interests. She predeceased both Margaret and William Cavendish, and in her funeral sermon, which focuses on the need for an equal respect for women's and men's abilities, there is no mention of Margaret Cavendish; the minister does speak of "a learned Woman of Utrecht," Anna van Schurman, who has in a "Printed Discourse fairly in this behalf vindicated the Reputation of her Sex." This judgment follows a passage that could easily have come from Margaret Cavendish's own "Female Orations": "[Woman is] no less fitted in her natural Ingeny [ingenuity] for all kind of Studies and Imployments: though Custom, like a Salique Law, hath excluded them from Public Offices and Professions; and confin'd them mostly to the narrow Territories of Home." Most likely this failure to identify with Margaret Cavendish as a woman intellectual was tied to familial opposition to the duke's remarriage, the greater social conformity of Lady Jane and her sister Lady Elizabeth Brackley than that displayed by their unorthodox stepmother, and, finally, the daughters' strong attachment to their father, exemplified in a manuscript compilation of "Poems, Songs, a Pastorall & a Play."[5]

Documents concerning the deaths and burials of both Margaret and William Cavendish contain other hints. In a manuscript held at the British Library, Edward Walker, a royal official whose duties included arranging funerals, left a description of the duchess's funeral which raises doubts about how highly she was regarded by other family members. It reveals that army officers were paid to march in her funeral procession and that the chief mourners were two of her sisters, not the duke, who was ill, or any of her stepchildren. The posthumous treatment of the duke seems even more surprising. He was given no funeral at all; in the words of his heir, the duke's body was "privately interred without any Funerall Solemnity in a Vault under a magnificent Stone prepared in his life times neath a Chapel upon ye North side of ye Abby Church at Westmin'st." Henry goes on to state that "his Grave married 2 wives." This official notification of death to Charles II gives much space to Henry's mother and her children, but little to Margaret Cavendish. In contrast, the inscription on the tomb mentions only William and Margaret Cavendish. It was composed by the duke at the time of Margaret's death; almost all of its text is devoted to her. Thus, Henry had his mother's body exhumed and placed in the grave with his father and second wife—against the duke's stated desire and under an epitaph acknowledging only Margaret.[6]

While Henry states in his letter to King Charles that there was no funeral in accordance with his father's personal wishes, no such orders are confirmed in Newcastle's will. The will states, "I will and appoint that my Body shall be interred in the Abey at Westminster where my late dear wife Magt Dutchess of Newcastle lies buried in the vault there by me procured." He does name Henry "my well-beloved son sole and only executor," but despite a diminished estate, he bequeaths £2,000 per annum for improvements to Nottingham Castle: "I earnestly desire [construction] may be finished" based on "the form and modell thereat by me laid and designed." According to the account of his burial by Edward Walker, only four coaches were allowed to accompany the party to the burial site. The second duke of Newcastle seemed most concerned that his father be hurriedly buried. He clearly resented the attention given to his stepmother. Thus, while the duke's private requests remain undetermined, his son's actions, including the removal of his mother's remains to the Westminster crypt, at least suggest an economizing act that could serve as partial revenge against a father who too greatly honored his second wife while giving insufficient attention to the needs of his heirs.[7]

Before a definitive judgment can be made concerning these documents, a thorough study of the second duke's correspondence needs to be completed and investigations undertaken into the views of other household members or friends of the couple. Yet they do raise some doubt about the accuracy of the image of the happy, isolated intellectual partnership that is usually offered in accounts of the duchess's private life. Clearly it was not simply the contemporary public assessment of her as "Mad Madge" that put in question her intellectual capacity and the relationship she had with her husband.

Intellectual and Value Differences between Margaret and William Cavendish

While many have assumed that the duchess's views and the intellectual context for her writings were linked to William Cavendish, I would argue that this is an area that needs rethinking. The duke was a classic conservative, while the duchess veered from offering opinions similar to her husband's to others diametrically opposed. Again, while more research is necessary before any final judgment can be rendered on the intellectual relationship between the Newcastles, there is at least evidence that William and Margaret may have had more fundamental differences than has traditionally been recognized. Clear contrasts exist between the duke of Newcastle's sixty-page letter to Prince Charles, written as Charles prepared to assume the throne in 1660, and the political views his wife offered in *Orations of Divers Sorts* (1662) and *Sociable Letters* (1664).

The duke's work, which was originally attributed to Clarendon, is mostly a Machiavellian statement encouraging Charles to overturn any political or religious policies that might encourage independent thinking or action on the part of his subjects. It attacks the growth in the numbers of university students during the 1620s and 1630s, the distribution of Bibles to a broader segment of the population, freedom of conscience and freedom of the press, the pretensions of merchants, and breaches of the sumptuary laws. It posits a tough, uncompromising set of social and political controls with portions strongly reminiscent of *The Prince*. Yet a range of arguments offered by the duchess opposes such views.[8]

In assessing William Cavendish's political views, we are fortunate in having two recent transcriptions of his lengthy letter of advice to Charles II. In this work he offers the king counsel which focuses on the establishment of religion, the maintenance of military authority in the king's hands, the mistakes monarchs make in allowing too much diversity of opinion, and the special problems inherent in relationships with Scotland, Ireland, and foreign nations. The work focuses continually on the mistakes of the Civil War era. It is the work of a man who believes that trust and tolerance, while perhaps good in principle, in reality lead only to religious dissidence and political upheaval. He opposes giving one's potential enemies the benefit of the doubt, nor, he contends, can a monarch allow institutions to thrive which can legitimate or empower opponents. Finally, one must be extraordinarily cautious and deliberate in determining who such opponents are.

The duke's advice contains a number of revealing points. First, he displays real skill as an armchair historian. He notes that the manuscript was written from memory, his "haveing no notes by mee, att All." His comments reflect both remembrance of what happened to Charles I and a disdain for book learning—a trait he shares with Thomas Hobbes as well as Margaret Cavendish, who are echoed in such passages as, "There is no oratory in it, or any thing stollen out of Bookes, for I seldome or Ever reade any, but these Discourses are out of my long Experience." It is experience, tied to the insights of a perceptive mind, that should most govern a prince. But with the recent memory of the 1640s, Cavendish relies on a dark experience grounded in perfidy and betrayal.[9]

While he begins with a discussion of the militia and the navy, the greatest space is given to the possibility that subjects might pursue evil under the cloak of religion and to the resulting need for a state church which enforces uniform beliefs. Newcastle does not trust a military beyond the monarch's sure control. Such authority is the king's "undoubted perogative," and if he lacks such control, he is "but a king upon a Curtesy of others." Although the monarch is the "Supreame Judg" of the law, military dominance alone can protect him against "the factious, & vaine Disputes of Sophesterall Devines, & Lawyers, & other Philosophicall Booke men, [who] will Raise Rebellions" (5–6).

Taken as a whole, it is a fascinating work, preponderantly Machiavellian, but also reflective of his old-fashioned chivalric interests and values. As William Cavendish's oft-used phrase "in my time" indicates, he wrote as an older man offering a younger one advice based on what he feared were outmoded standards. In only one area does William Cavendish seem more advanced than his contemporaries, and, as perhaps could be expected, that is in his characterization of women. He continually includes women in his analysis of precedents and appropriate policies for Charles to pursue; also uniquely, his analysis encompasses all classes. He has unlimited respect for Elizabeth's abilities to govern; but it is likely that his continual reminder of what a superb monarch she was in contrast with the mistakes he consistently points to on the part of James I and Charles I did not sit well with the young king. He includes both men and women when outlining appropriate subjects for royal policy. Finally, his meshing of chivalric deference to women with the inclusion of both sexes in practical political and economic goals is a strikingly unusual blend for seventeenth-century authors.

In advising the king always to appear regal before his subjects and to avoid overmuch familiarity, he recommends Elizabeth's model; if Charles follows it, the people "will Downe of their knees, which is worshipp, & pray for you with trembling Feare, & Love, as they did to Queen Elizabeth, whose Goverment Is the beste presedent for Englandes Govermente, absolutly." In advice that emphasizes the need for a direct tie between a monarch and the people unmediated by courtiers or other royal officials, he continues his praise of Elizabeth and includes an unusual reference to female subjects identifying with the queen: "And the Queen would say God bless you my good people,—& though this Saying was no great matter, in it selfe, yet I assure your Majestie, itt went very farr with the people,—nay of a Sunday when shee opend the window, the people would Cry, oh Lord I saw her hand, I saw her hand, & a woman, cryed out oh Lord Sayd shee, the Queens a woman" (45).

Newcastle again includes women in a passage elaborating his warning that the king not allow his officers to rob the people in ways that bring no gain to the monarch, but elicit opposition to royal rule. A ruler has most to be concerned with the lord treasurer, for this post can easily enrich its holder, as it did when "old Burgley raysed two Earles, & a viscounte, of great and vaste Estates, besides many more of his famelly, both Male & female"(28). And in his discussion of trade, he is again gender inclusive when he suggests the need for domestic cloth production, "butt if itt were for nothing Else, butt to sett your subiects a worke, both male, & female, not only to busie them, but that by their labor they might live, & many grow rich without being a Burthen to the Comon wealth" (41). Dealing with the poor, he encourages deforestation of the king's most distant and least useful woodlands, for "itt will sett all the Beggers a worke, Male, & female, for Corne hath always somethinge, to be Done aboute itt, Even from the Sowing, to the Reaping" (44).

Explicit inclusion of women in discussions of economic policy was rare until the late seventeenth century, but perhaps most unusual was the duke's mixing of chivalric ideals with historical precedent and public policy. Chapters such as "For Seremoney, & Order" make clear that the duke's real love was heraldry and the social interaction between the monarch and his nobility and gentry. He goes into great detail as to appropriate dress for each rank, the types of parties and social gatherings the king should sponsor, and who should be invited to which event. He encourages old-fashioned jousting, suggesting to Charles that in commemoration of his coronation day, he should "have a Tilting by your young Lordes, & other Great persons, which I assure your Majestie is the most Glorious Sight That can bee seen, & the manlyeste." The tie of such efforts to the honoring of women is made explicit in his advice to Charles to go to Newmarket for riding and hunting with the best people of England. At first he suggests that the meat of a killed stag or buck should be sent to important local lords, but then amends his advice: "Nay rather if your Majestie Send that venison to their Ladyes, Itt will bee taken much better, for as Sir Edward Cooke Sayd, which knew itt to well, that the night Crowe was powerfull, & Indeed For the most parte in England, the Gray mare is the better horse,— which I profess & acknowledg, for my perticular, for truly I am Not pleased Excepte itt bee so,—& when your Majestie Is happy In a vertious Queen, I beleeve wee muste flatter her to, & good Reson" (60–63).

Other than this unusual gender treatment, the work as a whole is a conservative document, integrating a call for prohibitions against political, religious, or intellectual independence with advice to the king to develop a good rapport with his subjects. It argues against the expansion of grammar schools and universities, against any toleration of religious differences, and against social mobility and presumption on the part of the middle class and those living in cities. (There is some deviation from this pattern in the chapter on trade, in which the merchant is considered a hero, and Newcastle strongly advocates the value of free trade.) He encourages the king to build up a strong military for use at home and abroad and to maintain a strict social and political hierarchy through harsh measures. To pursue such a program the king should first master London, and he will then "master your whole kingdome." He should do so through the "DisArming of them totally," including local watches. He needs to construct two additional forts to govern the City. Newcastle believes that all of these terms can be gained through a new charter, noting that the City "will bee glad to take a newe one Uppon your Majesties Termes."

Next, the king should institute the Church of England "wholy & totally Depending uppon your Majestie"; and the church will instill "active obedience, to all . . . lawfull Comands [and] passive obedience, even to those commands that are not Lawfull." Within the church there must be "no Lectorers, att all, in no place," and both grammar schools and universities must employ only those who are "orthodoxe according to the Church of England." Emphasis should be on the catechism; ministers should preach only with the approval of their bishop and only once a day. The basic message is to limit instruction and to control the rank of those who attend universities. "The Bible In English under Every weavers, & Chamber maids Armes hath Done us much hurte, that which made it one way is the universitys Abounds with to many Scollers." He urges the value of illiteracy, "for when Moste was Unletterd, it was a much better world, both for Peace & Warr." Finally, censorship is crucial; any works that "make the Leaste rente In Church, or state, [are] presently to bee condemnd, & burnte by the hands of the Hangman, & the Authors severly punisht, Even to Death, if the Crime requier itt" (6–21 passim).

The Machiavellian aspects of the work are most evident when Newcastle proposes a particular policy first for its palliative effects and then for its usefulness to the Crown. He believes, for example, that reducing the number of lawyers would be good for the people, but would also undercut a threat against the king, for lawyers became "no smale meanes to fomente & continue this late & unfortunate Rebellion." Their numbers can be reduced by first reducing the number of grammar schools, "for if you Cutt of much reading, & writing, their muste bee fewer Lawyers." Similarly, in a discussion of wards he asks the king to "have such Comiseration of your poore subjects, that wards May not bee baughte, & sold like Horses in Smithfield," but to devise rules in a way "that your Majestie may have the Benefitt." Charles should also direct judges to ensure that juries be dominated by the gentry, which "hath a neerer dependance of your Majestie, then the free holders have, & so att your Comand." Finally, in arguing that appointing a recorder of deeds for each county would undercut the multiple lawsuits encouraged by lawyers, Newcastle claims the institution of such an office "would bee a great Ease to the subiecte, & add something To your Majesties Revenues" (23–32 passim). The letter contains a number of examples of useful advice to Charles and often exhibits genuine concern for the people suffering at the hands of unscrupulous officials and courtiers. Still, the duke's advice so values loyalty and conformity—and sanctions a range of such coercive measures to ensure them—that it is an essentially conservative document, displaying little trust in either the king's subjects or other political entities in England.

Like her husband, Margaret Cavendish ridicules the overly lavish habits of social upstarts and opposes any actions which could return the country to civil war. She does not, however, display the same Machiavellian streak as her husband, and she allows for greater diversity of personal opinions and religious viewpoints. Whether as an outsider to intellectual and political circles or as a woman not capable of being a political player, she does not display the immediate loyalty to the Crown that her husband does or identify with policies that would protect the king's authority.

There is evidence that when the duchess offers conservative views similar to her husband's, she is apt to be adopting William's persona, for example, in the large number of orations or letters in which she speaks as a general to his troops or as a retired military officer offering advice to his country.[10] She sometimes undercuts her own arguments, too, at points where she is defending herself against attacks on her unseemly or unlearned statements. The introductions to *Sociable Letters*, which are strongly defensive, are directed to critics of her earlier writings. Here she is trying to make herself more acceptable to a public which clearly has not always appreciated what she has had to say. Thus, her differing positions may not simply be random or represent an effort to present both sides of an argument; at some points they may easily be representing her husband's views more than her own or be attempting to gain acceptance following earlier criticism.[11]

While she clearly was critical of social and political upheaval, she often offered startlingly radical statements sounding closer to Winstanley than to Charles I, her husband, or even Clarendon. Is it possible, then, to make distinctions among her views, selecting the genuine ones and ignoring those stated purely for literary or argumentative effect? While I think there is no clear answer to this query, it does seem important to note where she speaks outside the range of acceptable royalist and Anglican viewpoints. It is perhaps less significant and remarkable when she repeats the positions of her husband and his circle than when she offers opposing views. Thus, her statements on behalf of social equality or freedom of conscience, while inconsistent, set her apart from those whose ideas she has been assumed to follow. Further, one needs, I think, to give greater significance to her raising topics that others avoided and not to judge her solely on the basis of intellectual consistency.[12]

Some of her more remarkable views are offered in an oration defending a man who had stolen to support his family. Interestingly, she appeals not to God, but to Nature, allowing her not simply to avoid traditional Christian phraseology, but to employ gender inversion as well. She invokes a personified Nature, "who made all things in Common. She made not some men to be Rich, and other men Poor, some to Surfeit with overmuch Plenty, and others to be Starved for Want: for when she made the World and the Creatures in it, She did not divide the Earth, nor the rest of the Elements, but gave the use generally amongst them all." She then appears to attack men like Thomas Hobbes (who is normally credited as a significant influence on her):

> But when Governmental Laws were devised by some Usurping Men, who were the greatest Thieves and Robbers, (for they Robbed the rest of Mankind of their Natural Liberties and Inheritances, which is to be Equal Possessors of the World;) these grand and original Thieves and Robbers, which are call'd Moral Philosophers,

or Common-wealth makers, were not only Thieves and Tyrants to the Generality of Mankind, but they were Rebels against Nature, Imprisoning Nature within the Jail of Restraint, Keeping her to the spare Diet of Temperance, Binding her with Laws, and Inslaving her with Propriety, whereas all is in Common with Nature.[13]

While William Cavendish feared freedom of conscience above all things as encouraging political upheaval, the duchess in her "Oration for Liberty of Conscience" argues that "since that Freedome hath been given, the Inconveniency cannot be Avoided." The best solution, she believes, is to "let them have Liberty of Conscience" so long as they do not use such right to "meddle with Civil government." She ties such policies to clear revolutionary rhetoric: "no Governour or Magistrate shall in any kind Infringe our Just Rights, or Civil or Common Laws, nor our Ancient Customs." The oration that follows argues against liberty of conscience, but on grounds of utility, not principle; such policy will lead to "such a confusion, as the Kingdome will be like a Chaos, which the Gods keep us from." (Her final sentence reflects another peculiar quality: she was one of few seventeenth-century writers who used the plural "gods" consistently rather than God; she even placed the names and identities of classical gods and goddesses in Judeo-Christian narratives.) And, significantly, a third essay that she terms a compromise leans decidedly toward the one favoring freedom of conscience: "If those Sects or Separatists . . . Disturb not the publick weal, why should you Disturb their Private Devotions?"[14]

Much of her writing reflects the perspective of the outsider, even though we have trouble grappling with this self-assessment by a duchess in a prominent family (and the most prolific author among mid-seventeenth-century women to boot). Yet how can we explain her identification with the peasantry, her severe portrayal of women's powerlessness, and her unexpected deviations from royalist and religious orthodoxy? There is so much of the unexpected in Margaret Cavendish's writings that it is hard not to believe that she rejected at least some of what others of her circle thought it appropriate to think or say. For instance, she begins "A Widdows Funeral Oration" by castigating the dead woman for her "Very Intemperate and Irregular Life all the time of her Widdowhood"; not merely Nature, but "the Gods might be Angry with her." Yet while seeming to imitate so many pious works before her, the duchess surprises. The widow's failing was not that she "did waste her Wealth in Vanities, but she did waste her Life in Sorrow; She Sate not on the Knees of Amorous Lovers, but Kneeled on her Knees to God." Such behavior led her to end her life decorated only in tears. In a series of essays on the nature of heaven and hell, the duchess questions their very existence. Heaven and hell or devils and angels are mere imaginings, "for Man cannot Know what is not in his Portion of Reason and Sense to Know"; even so, men continue to believe, "which is Ridiculous even to Human Sense and Reason." Finally, in a series of orations from peasants representing their lives, she identifies with them and with rural life. One peasant notes that "we are all Fellows in Labour, Profit, and Pleasure," though not in "spoils." They "live in the Fields of Peace [and] our Commanders are our Landlords who often Deceive us of the Increase of our Labours," as do officers deceive "Common Souldiers of the Profit of their Spoils." Peasants are superior to soldiers, for the latter "be crule to Men, they Thrive by Blood, we by Milk." One peasant oration attacking women of his own station as unattractive and unsophisticated is followed by a reply maintaining that peasant women "Waste not their time in Vanity . . . their Faces are their Own . . . and as for their Garments, they are Plain, yet Commodious, Easie, and Decent, they are not Ribb'd up with Whale bones, nor Incumbred with Heavy Silver and Gold Laces, nor Troubled with New Fashions." In her own life, while the duchess clearly did not dress as a peasant, she refused to conform to the fashions of her class, designing her own clothes and exhibiting eccentric social as well as intellectual habits. While we may never grasp the essential qualities of this iconoclastic woman, we can recognize that she clearly lived and wrote like no other representative of her class and political circle.[15]

Assessing the Social and Political Views of Margaret Cavendish

Margaret Cavendish's published work yields a self-portrait of a woman who never conformed to social, political, or intellectual norms. Just when the reader seems to have a handle on her political and cultural loyalties, Cavendish shifts her standpoint and adopts the identity and viewpoints of her opponents. She most consistently identifies with women, but even here, such identification leads her both to praise and criticize, to defend and reprimand her sex. In seeking her essence, there seems little hope—or, probably, point—in attempting to define a consistent core of political values. Strongly royalist (she once refused to take an oath abjuring antiparliamentary efforts, a condition of her returning to Antwerp to visit her ailing husband), Cavendish nevertheless did not feel obligated to follow the royalist position on a wide range of social, religious, and political issues.[16]

Iconoclastic views appear throughout her works, but political heterodoxy is most prominent in her *Orations* and *Sociable Letters*. The phrase used as the title of this chapter appears in Letter Sixteen of *Sociable Letters*: "But howsoever, Madam, the disturbance in this Countrey hath made no breach of Friendship betwixt us, for though there hath been a Civil War in the Kingdom, and a general War amongst the Men, yet there hath been none amongst the Women, they have not fought pitch'd battels; and if they had, there hath been no particular quarrel betwixt her and me." This passage comes near the end of the letter, which is written to an acquaintance expressing hope that no difference will arise between a mutual friend and Cavendish. It begins, "I Hope I have given the Lady D. A. no cause to believe I am not her Friend; for though she hath been of Ps. and I of Ks. side, yet I know no reason why that should make a difference betwixt us, as to make us Enemies, no more than cases of Conscience in Religion, for one may be my very good Friend, and not of my opinion, every one's Conscience in Religion is betwixt God and themselves, and it belongs to none other."[17]

This letter is one of the more remarkable political statements penned by a woman in the seventeenth century. Not merely does it relegate military disputes to men and offer strong advocacy for religious toleration, but it includes her now-famous remarks on women's relationship to the state. While seeming to separate women from governments (because "we Women understand them not" and are not "bound to State or Crown" through either oaths of loyalty or allegiance), she ends by coming close to treason: "if we be not Citizens in the Commonwealth, I know no reason we should be Subjects to the Commonwealth." Women are "no Subjects, unless it be to our Husbands." Yet after this extraordinary set of arguments, she goes on to insist that while women are politically powerless, they are actually supremely powerful, because nature has so shaped men's affections that women "oftener inslave men, than men inslave us; they seem to govern the world, but we really govern the world, in that we govern men." Yet men "will not believe this," which is all to the good, for it prevents them from seeing "how they are Led, Guided, and Rul'd by the Feminine Sex." It is following this claim that she includes the sentence about war dividing only men.[18]

Analyzing this statement in conjunction with those of her works claiming that because of common law realities and patriarchal customs, children fulfill only men's needs, it is clear that Margaret Cavendish was most apt to break with royalist orthodoxy over the standing of women within the state and family. Perhaps the clearest breach was her continual reminder that women needed to be fitted somewhere into the assumptions regarding seventeenth-century social and political hierarchy, something seldom done. It is true that her husband, most often in a chivalric mode, wanted women treated with kindness and respect and that his friend Thomas Hobbes postulated women's natural equality, but for the most part, even they envisioned politics as a male affair seldom requiring reference to women. While Hobbes's greatest attention to women's equal standing was in his formulation of the state of nature, still, he did point to their ancient military prowess and more recent successes at governing. Yet he offered his views defensively in both *De Cive* and *Leviathan*, recognizing the broad acceptance of patriarchal justifications for sovereignty. Even so, late in life, in a theological dispute with the mathematician John Wallis, Hobbes included the following irascible reminder about "his Attributing to the Civil Sovreign all Power Sacerdotal. But this perhaps may seem hard, when the Soverignty is in a Queen: But it is because you are not subtle enough to perceive, that though Man may be male and female, Authority is not."[19]

While Cavendish was most apt to dispute seventeenth-century political truisms in her published model letters and orations, she also managed to get in digs at current English government and manners in her fantasy *The Blazing World*, where she made a place for a female emperor as well as female scholars, and in her plays, where wives lead military campaigns and offer speeches that outshine the wisdom and skill of their soldier husbands.[20] On the whole, she indulged in works and ideas that were apt to shock. While there is much to admire in this iconoclastic approach, she sometimes appears to be a privileged, sheltered individual escaping the reproach others would face for espousing such views.

The impulse to shock did not stop with politics; it encompassed cultural and sexual topics as well. Not only did she write plays with obvious lesbian themes, but she even included a defense of incest by one character in *The Unnatural Tragedy*. Her explanation for the social controls society exerts against incest are similar to later anthropological explanations for the development of taboos. The following dialogue begins with a young virgin explaining by way of background that Monsieur Frere is fatally attracted to his sister, Madam Soeur, whom he was parted from because of long years at boarding school and university and, ultimately, traveling.

> Soeur. Why how would you have me love? . . .
> Frere. And will you lie with me?
> Soeur. How! would you have me commit Incest?
> Frere. Sister, follow not those foolish binding Laws which frozen men have made.[21]

After a discussion as to whether restrictions against incest are held by educated men or only by primitive peoples, he explains why learned men cling to such beliefs. "They do not know it, but they believe as they are taught, for what is taught men in their Childhood, grows strong in the Manhood; and as they grow in years, so grow they up in Superstitions. Thus wise men are deceiv'd and cozen'd by length of time, taking an old forgotten deed to be a true Seal'd bond: wherefore, dear Sister, your Principles are false, and therefore your Doctrine cannot be true." While Frere is pleased that she is not aghast at his love and defense of incest, still she refuses to submit, and the play ends with her rape and the death of both. Along with so much else she wrote, this play clearly broke with acceptable topics and opinions for a woman of the duchess's time and rank.[22]

Interspersed throughout her works are judgments that the monarch and church should be supreme and not subject to question, that women are unworthy partners to men intellectually or socially, that social and political hierarchy are preferable to change and questioning. But unlike her husband and others around her, she criticized the abuse of animals, of the peasantry, and of women, and at points in virtually all that she wrote, she broke from a social vision that saw some individuals as more worthy than others. Surely those moments define her independent voice more so than those statements where she reiterated the views and language of others.

Deciphering motives behind such views is not easy. It may have been simply to shock, as was likely the case in her discussion of a thinker surely meant to represent Francis Bacon. She calls him "Lord B." and portrays him as "fit for State Counsel and Advice, to Plead Causes, Decide Controversies, and the like, And his Works or Writings have been very Propagating and Manuring other mens Brains; the truth is, his Works have proved like as some sorts of Meats, which through Time, or moisture of some Flatuous or Human Substance, Corrupt, and Breed Maggots or Worms; so his Writings have produced several other Books."[23]

But she also consistently rejected acceptable behavior for a woman of her rank. In an introductory note addressed to William Cavendish, after thanking him because "your Lordship never bid me to Work," she continues, "I cannot Work . . . as Ladies use to pass their Time withall," and contends that "such works would cost more than the Work would be worth" (she means "Needleworks, Spinning-works, Preserving-works," cooking, and so on). But it is not this well-known rejection of a lady's regimen, but the following paragraph that reveals even more her distance from her cohort: "I understand the Keeping of Sheep, and Ordering of a Grange, indifferently well, although I do not Busie my self much with it, by reason my Scribling takes away the most part of my Time."[24]

Her nature seems to be stamped with a lack of knowledge of, and an unwillingness to conform to, social and cultural mores. While her writings generally set her apart, it is still her views concerning the lives of women that created her unique vision among seventeenth-century writers and within her intellectual circle. No one else claimed that women had no reason for their own sake to have children, given that children take their father's name and inherit his property and that daughters are lost to another family as adults; no one else claimed that women's separation from the Commonwealth as non-officeholders and oath-takers meant they were not subjects of the Crown; no one else satirized women's gaining special favors during childbirth as emblematic of their fulfilling their most important role; and no one else called women to unite as a group to fight against the tyranny of men. At the same time, she had a husband who supported her efforts as well as many of her views, she sometimes adopted the views of Hobbes and other important thinkers in the Cavendish circle, and she often echoed the most severe critics of her sex.

Taken as a whole, she remained an independent spirit. While clearly a royalist, she seems unfairly characterized by that label alone. For Margaret Cavendish, politics was not restricted to court and Parliament, and women were not regarded as nonpolitical beings incapable of judging their own status and that of their male counterparts in political terms. For a woman to whom little was sacred, the range of human relationships was open to scrutiny, and this led her to contemplate power and political relationships wherever she discovered them.

Notes

I would like to thank the Taft Memorial Fund at the University of Cincinnati for support for a brief research trip during spring 1996 to read manuscripts and printed materials concerning Margaret Cavendish at the British Library, and the Huntington Library for a Mayers Fellowship to use their collection in 1996.

1. My own scholarship on the duchess appears in *Reason's Disciples: Seventeenth-Century English Feminists* (Urbana, 1982) and in a more recent essay, "'Though it be the Part of Every Good Wife': Margaret Cavendish, Duchess of Newcastle," *Women and History: Voices of Early Modern England*, ed. Valerie Frith (Toronto, 1995). Other studies of her and editions of her works include Sara H. Mendelson, *The Mental World of Stuart Women: Three Studies* (Amherst, Mass., 1987); Margaret Cavendish, *The Blazing World and Other Writings*, ed. Kate Lilley (London, 1994); Margaret Cavendish, *Sociable Letters*, ed. James Fitzmaurice (New York, 1997).

2. There is only limited information about the relationship between Margaret Cavendish and her brother-in-law Charles, but what does exist suggests a close intellectual bond in which he was both teacher and supporter of the younger woman's interests and writings. For discussions of their shared concerns see Douglas Grant, *Margaret the First: A Biography of Margaret Cavendish, Duchess of Newcastle, 1623–1673* (Toronto, 1957), 91–92, 131–32, 142; and Geoffrey Trease, *Portrait of a Cavalier: William Cavendish, First Duke of Newcastle* (New York, 1979), 153–54, 169–72. She included an epistle in verse to her recently deceased brother-in-law in introducing *The Worlds Olio* (1655) that highlighted both his scholarship and his kindness.

3. Margaret Cavendish authored a number of defenses of women, particularly second wives who chose not to bear children, and she expressed especially severe satire against women who used pregnancy to enhance their standing. See especially *Sociable Letters*, 123–28 for her attack on the pretensions of "breeding women." In her autobiography she claimed not to indulge in "passion," and described her love for the duke in more elevated, often Platonic terms. "I love extraordinarily and constantly, yet not fondly." See especially *The True Relation of my Birth, Breeding, and Life* attached to her *Life of William Cavendish, Duke of Newcastle* . . . , ed. C. H. Firth (London, 1886), 311–13. A series of letters in the Portland Literary Collection treats the duke's concern over Margaret's health. Pw V 90, fols. 6v-8r, 14r-21r, 25r-28v, 78v-81r, and 114–16, Department of Manuscripts and Special Collections, University of Nottingham Library. (Relevant folios were identified and excerpted by Dr. H. C. Johnston and Caroline Kelly, keeper and assistant keeper of the collection.) I plan to pursue this collection more systematically during research in Nottingham.

4. For discussion of the duke's personal life, see the introduction to William Cavendish, *Ideology and Politics on the Eve of Restoration: Newcastle's Advice to Charles II*, trans. and intro. by Thomas Slaughter (Philadelphia, 1984), xxix; Slaughter notes similarities in personality between Newcastle and Charles II, each being given to sexual indulgence and only irregular spurts of directed energy, as well as Newcastle's fiscal irresponsibility. Turberville also discusses the latter: "The Marquess had difficulty in borrowing the money necessary to redeem his Margaret out of pawn . . . too little by £400, so that she had to do some borrowing herself." Arthur Stanley Turberville, *A History of Welbeck Abbey and its Owners*, 2 vols. (London, 1938–39), 1:143. The reference to the duchess's having to pawn her clothes for dinner is in Turberville, 1:127. I am not portraying the duke as a bad husband, or as a man insensitive to women. He affirmed that "I have an Extreordinarye opinion of both male & female," something not disputed here. William Cavendish to John Bramhall, 20 March 1648/9, Huntington Library.

5. Adam Littleton, *A Sermon at the Funeral of the Right Honourable the Lady Jane Eldest Daughter to his Grace William Duke of Newcastle* . . . (London, 1669), 20–21. For a fuller analysis of the manuscript work by the duke's daughters, see Margaret J. M. Ezell, "'To Be Your Daughter in Your Pen': The Social Functions of Literature in the Writing of Lady Elizabeth Brackley and Lady Jane Cavendish," *Huntington Library Quarterly* 51 (1988): 281–96. Ezell notes that Elizabeth Brackley, "the perfect and pious wife of the second earl of Bridgewater," and Jane Cheyne were more

independent, but still distant from "the notoriety of their abrasive stepmother" (282–83). Their manuscript play has a character, the Lady Tranquility, who chases after the father of two sisters and who is thought by some to be a portrayal of Margaret Lucas (289). The sisters write verse to their father about missing him extraordinarily during his exile; the poems are more reminiscent of those directed to a lover than a father. One passage ends, "Once more I beg this of you; Prithee come / Then joy is my companion's total sum" (290–93).

6. The earl of Ogle (later second duke of Newcastle) to the earl of Danby, 10 August 1671, S. Arthur Strong, comp., *A Catalogue of Letters and Other Historical Documents Exhibited in the Library at Welbeck* (London, 1903), 61–63. For reference to the confession of John Booth, see Historical Manuscripts Commission, *Portland*, 2:149: "1671, July 14.—Confession by John Booth before James Chadwick, a justice of the peace for Nottinghamshire, that he had written a libel against the Duchess of Newcastle for the purpose of making dissensions between the Duke and Duchess." For a discussion of a conspiracy spearheaded by Andrew Clayton, the duke's steward, to misuse rents and other financial resources, witnessed by the servant John Booth and making accusations against Margaret (who was seen as too closely scrutinizing the books and looking to feather her own nest), consult Grant, *Margaret the First*, 228–39; and Trease, *Portrait of a Cavalier*, 200–203.

7. William Cavendish's will, Public Record Office, 1677–22. PROB 11–353; 11/Hale/22, 11/353/22; Henry, duke of Newcastle to Charles II, 6 February 1676/7, British Library, Add. MSS 12514. In the same BL volume appears Edward Walker's account of the expenses of Margaret Cavendish's funeral, including £130 for the costs of suits of armor, payment for mourning, food, etc. for "four officers of [the] Army" (fol. 290).

8. Other than Thomas Slaughter's edition of Newcastle's letter, see Gloria Italiano Anzilotti, *An English Prince: Newcastle's Machiavellian Political Guide to Charles II* (Pisa, 1988); and Conal Condren, "Casuistry to Newcastle: *The Prince* in the World of the Book," in *Political Discourse in Early Modern Britain*, ed. Nicholas Phillipson and Quentin Skinner (Cambridge, 1993), 164–86.

9. William Cavendish, *Ideology and Politics*, 5. Subsequent page references to this work will be included parenthetically in the text.

10. Her *Orations of Divers Sorts, Accommodated to Divers Places* (London, 1662) opens with orations directed to issues of war and peace (3–16). The majority espouse peace; the "Oration to Prevent Civil War," for instance, speaks of the great harm civil war can bring to a people. These are followed by fourteen essays focusing on the lot of the common soldier, loyalty and disloyalty on the battlefield, proper treatment of people within an army's path, and similar issues (16–40). This group concludes with the "General's Oration to Mutinous Soldiers" (37–40), which clearly represents the views and experience of William Cavendish. While there is some understanding of the state of the enlistee (especially in the earlier set of orations on war and peace, for example: "though Covetness and Revenge is their hire, yet loss and Slavery is many times their reward" [9–11]), those essays representing the general's perspective are generally harsh.

11. In the six introductory pieces to *CCXI Sociable Letters written by the thrice Noble, Illustrious, and Excellent Princess, the Lady Marchioness of Newcastle* (London, 1664), Margaret Cavendish veers between apologizing for her failings and defending the worth of her works. While this is a common format for her works, here she especially is defending earlier works from unfair attack.

12. Margaret Cavendish is shoehorned with more difficulty into a single aesthetic or political camp than virtually any other seventeenth-century woman writer. While often critical of women, she virtually never distanced herself from them. In the "Praefatory Oration" to *Orations of Divers Sorts*, she combined her identification with her sex with her acceptance of its failings: "But by reason I have not been bred, being a Woman, to publick Affaires, Associations, or Negotiations, it is not to be expected I should speak or write wisely, the truth is, it were more easie and more proper for one of my Sex, to speak or write wittily than wisely."

13. In "A Case Concerning Theft," she argues on behalf of the defense, if they "be Judges of the most Ancient Laws, and not Usurping Tyrants, you will not only [ac]quit this Poor man . . . but you will cause his Accusers, who are Rich, to Divide their Wealth Equally with Him and all his Family." She then offers the plaintiff's view, which paints a Hobbesian picture of nature and undercuts the ability of individuals to rule themselves: "If it were not for Civil Government, Ordained from

an Higher Power as from the Creator of Nature her self, all her Works would be in a Confusion." (Margaret Cavendish, *Orations*, 85–88).

14. One sequence of orations includes "Oration for Liberty of Conscience," "Oration against Liberty of Conscience," and "Oration proposing a Compromise between Last Two" (Margaret Cavendish, *Orations*, 69–71). They reveal a variety of viewpoints concerning religious toleration, concluding in the compromise oration, "Wherefore, give them leave to follow their Several Opinions, in their Particular Families, otherwise if you Force them, you will make them factious" (71). For the duke's stringent controls see William Cavendish, *Ideology and Politics*, 12–23.

15. Margaret Cavendish, *Orations*, 170–72, 191–93, 243–50.

16. *Calendar of State Papers, Domestic* (1652–53), 467, 69, quoted in Grant, *Margaret the First*, 132.

17. Margaret Cavendish, *Sociable Letters*, 26–28.

18. Ibid.

19. Ibid., 185–86. For Hobbes's discussion of women in the state of nature, see *De Cive*, chap. 9 and *Leviathan*, chap. 20. While others have noted the examples of the reign of Elizabeth I and the Stuart inheritance through the female line, I would stress Hobbes's early life (in which a supposedly drunken father was banished from his living as a cleric and forced to flee, leaving the household in the management of Hobbes's mother) as instilling him with a view of the equal competence of the sexes. His father's fate is discussed in Noel Malcolm, "A Summary Biography of Hobbes," in *The Cambridge Companion to Hobbes* (Cambridge, 1996), 1–13; Arnold A. Rogow, *Thomas Hobbes: A Radical in the Service of Reaction* (New York, 1986), 17–41; Thomas Hobbes, *Considerations upon the Reputation, Loyalty, Manners, & Religion, of Thomas Hobbes of Malmesbury . . .* (London, 1680), 40.

20. The most accessible edition of *The Blazing World* is Kate Lilley's (see n.1). In Cavendish's play "First Part of Bell in Campo," a woman described as "the Generals Lady" is incensed that the women had been separated from the men at the time of battle. She reminds her followers that they did not come to enjoy their husbands or to share in "their troublesome and tedious marches," but to take part in their battles. They have now been deprived, perhaps from their husbands' "desire of preserving our lives and liberties," but more likely "out of jealousy we should Eclipse the fame of their valours with the splendour of our constancy." *Playes Written by the Thrice Noble, Illustrious and Excellent Princess, the Lady Marchioness of Newcastle* (London, 1662), 586–88.

21. Margaret Cavendish, "The Unnatural Tragedy," in *Playes*, 348–65. While a number of the plays of Margaret Cavendish have lesbian themes (often tied to cross-dressed characters), love between members of the same sex is probably described most openly in "The Convent of Pleasure." The agony of the convent's mistress over being attracted to a female character is typical: "My name is Happy, and so was my Condition, before I saw this Princess; but now I am like to be the most unhappy Maid alive: But why may not I love a Woman with the same affection I could a Man?" This exchange occurs between the women:

Princess: Then let us please ourselves, as harmless Lovers use to do;
Lady Happy: How can harmless Lovers please themselves?
Princess: Why very well, as, to discourse, embrace and kiss, so mingle souls together;
Lady Happy: But innocent Lovers do not use to kiss . . .
(They imbrace and kiss, and hold each other in their Arms.)
Princess: These my Embraces though of Female kind, May be as fervent as a Masculine mind. (act 4, sc. 1)

The Convent of Pleasure. A Comedy, ed. Jennifer Roswell (Oxford, 1995), 25–26. The princess is later discovered as a prince, but the play is filled with discussion of passions raised between women.

22. For a recent discussion of the literary and political significance of Margaret Cavendish's drama, see Marta Straznicky, "Reading the Stage: Margaret Cavendish and Commonwealth Closet Drama," *Criticism* 38 (Summer 1995): 355–90.

23. Letter 69, Margaret Cavendish, *Sociable Letters*, 146.

24. Margaret Cavendish, "To His Excellency the Lord Marquis of Newcastle," Ibid., n.p. The epitaph the duke authored for his and Margaret's tomb reads:

Here lyes the Loyall Duke of Newcastle and his Dutches, his second wife, by whome he had noe issue; her name was Margarett Lucas, youngest sister to the Lord Lucas of Colchester; a noble familie, for all the Brothers were Valiant and all the Sisters virtuous. This Dutches was a wise, wittie and learned Lady, which her many Bookes do well testifie; she was a most Virtuous and a Loving and carefull wife, and was with her Lord all the time of his banishment and miseries, and when he came home never parted from him in his solitary retirements.

Constructing a New Context for Hobbes Studies

Linda Levy Peck

On 14 January 1611 Edward Bruce, Lord Kinlosse, Master of the Rolls to James VI and I, died unexpectedly in London.[1] A month later, on 17 February 1611, a large funeral procession, heraldic banners and standards unfurled, wound its way toward Chancery Lane, where Bruce was buried in the Rolls Chapel. The funeral procession was elaborate, as befitted this major Jacobean figure: Nicholas Charles, Lancaster Herald, who helped to organize the funeral, recorded the procession, the banners, the helm and crest, the coat of arms, that marked the passing of this notable Jacobean.[2] Sixty-two poor men led the procession, followed by Bruce's friends and their servants. Members of his household such as Robert the Embroiderer and Frank the Barber were followed by a group of Jacobean court officials in cloaks and gowns that marked their professions as doctors, civil and common lawyers, and even one historian. Three heralds took part, including Garter King of Arms, who bore Bruce's coat of arms. Bruce's eldest son, Edward, the new Lord Kinlosse, was the chief mourner, assisted by his brother Thomas Bruce, his brother-in-law Sir William Cavendish, and Cavendish's brother-in-law Sir William Maynard. Among a group described as "freinds servants with cloaks"[3] was Sir William Cavendish's secretary, Thomas Hobbes.

As a political philosopher Hobbes is, of course, associated with the period of Civil War and Restoration, with the publication of his works on politics, law, and natural philosophy, including *Elements of Law, De Cive, Leviathan,* and *Behemoth*. Hobbes's reading and writing must be situated, however, in the political debates of the early seventeenth century. Yet how is that context to be recovered? Hobbes scholars have long been frustrated by how little contemporary evidence exists for the period when, after graduating from university in 1608, Hobbes was appointed by Lord Cavendish as tutor to his son Sir William Cavendish, only two years his junior.[4] There is no correspondence before 1622; no acknowledged works until Hobbes's translation of Thucydides, published in 1629 with a laudatory dedication to Cavendish, who had just died.[5] Noel Malcolm, who published the Oxford edition of Hobbes's correspondence in 1994, writes that "we know frustratingly little, we do know that he had contacts with Bacon, that he pondered the appearance of a comet in 1618, that he had experience of public affairs in the Virginia and Summer Island Companies, and that he translated Thucydides."[6]

Two new books draw attention to the writings of the early Hobbes. The first, by Noel Reynolds and Arlene Saxonhouse, argues that three discourses in the collection of essays entitled *Horae Subsecivae* and published in 1620 were written by Hobbes. The rest are acknowledged to be by Cavendish. In her analysis of these early writings, Saxonhouse emphasizes, as did Leo Strauss, the debt that Hobbes owed to Machiavelli.[7] In the second work, *Reason and Rhetoric in the Philosophy of Hobbes*, Quentin Skinner says that his intention "is to situate Hobbes's theory and practice of civil science within the intellectual context in which it was formed."[8] But what was that intellectual context? Skinner suggests that it was the rhetorical tradition of the humanists. Both Leo Strauss in 1936 and Keith Thomas in 1965 addressed what they described as the "aristocratic" influence in Hobbes's writings by examining his works from the translation of Thucydides to *Leviathan*.[9] Based on evidence at Chatsworth and elsewhere, we can be more specific. In his manuscript dedication to his father of several of the essays later expanded and published as *Horae Subsecivae*, Cavendish wrote that he addressed topics (Arrogance, Ambition, Affectation, Detraction, Selfwill, Masters and Servants, Expenses, Visitations, Death and Readings of Histories) "because I desired to shew your Lordship . . . rather what impression I receive from those thinges that be continually before my eyes then what I can say of such as be more removed from use."[10] What was before Cavendish's eyes? Hobbes scholars might say Bacon's essays. My argument is that, in addition, before his eyes was the life of the Jacobean court and the political and intellectual elite of which he, his family, and his secretary, Hobbes, were a part.

In the first essay to try to map Hobbes's connections with members of the Virginia Company in the 1620s, Noel Malcolm writes, "Hobbes's introduction to the world of politics took place among politicians such as Sandys, Digges and Danvers, whose sympathies lay, in general terms, with Country against Court, Common Law against Chancery and parliamentary privilege against royal prerogative."[11] Quentin Skinner notes that Hobbes encountered Dr. Theodore Goulston at meetings of the Virginia Company in the 1620s and wonders whether they discussed Goulston's new book, the first English translation of Aristotle's *Art of Rhetoric*.[12] The Bruce funeral ten years earlier, I would argue, tells a different story, the moral of which is that Hobbes scholars need to look more closely at the court networks in which the Cavendishes, and therefore Hobbes, were situated.

It has long been thought that Hobbes and Cavendish embarked on the Grand Tour—a very long Grand Tour—from 1610 to 1615. The Chatsworth accounts, with a few exceptions, offer little support for such a trip. Cavendish had been granted a license to travel on 6 February 1609/10,[13] and the accounts for early February 1609/10 record £2 "Delivered to John Rose at his going with Sir William into France." But if the two did go to France, Rose was back by March, when he claimed charges for a trip "by water to Southwarke and back again." Sometime after 8 May, Lord William Cavendish gave ten shillings "to my Lord of Cranborne's that brought a letter from Sir William Cavendish."[14] Cranborne, heir to Robert Cecil, earl of Salisbury, was in Paris in the winter of 1609/10 but returned home right after the assassination of Henry IV in May.[15] But even if Cavendish had joined Cranborne in Paris between February and May, the account books show Hobbes in the country in April 1610.[16]

Moreover, the Lancaster Herald's book of Jacobean funerals demonstrates that in February 1610/11 Hobbes was neither in Venice nor in Paris, as is often suggested, but in London at Bruce's funeral. Moreover, most Hobbes scholars have not noticed that Sir William Cavendish sat in two parliamentary sessions, in October 1610 and April-June 1614, while he was ostensibly on the continent.[17] While Hobbes scholarship, then, has focused on the philosopher's first trip to the continent and the contacts he established with French and Italian political theorists, it now seems likely that the trip with Cavendish was both later (1614–1615) and shorter (perhaps six months) than previously thought.[18]

But if Hobbes and Cavendish were not in France and Italy, where precisely were they? Commentators have routinely assumed that when they were not on the Grand Tour, Hobbes and Cavendish were at "the country estate in Derbyshire where Hobbes spent most of his life as a tutor and family retainer to the Cavendish family."[19] Moreover, if we physically resituate Hobbes and Cavendish, what impact will that have on resituating the work and the mentality of the early Hobbes?

The very detailed Chatsworth accounts enable us to establish the whereabouts of the Cavendishes and of Hobbes. They show that in 1608 Lord Cavendish, who had rented a house in Holborn, purchased the house on Aldersgate Street near Charterhouse that belonged to Chief Justice Popham.[20] The accounts track Lord Cavendish back and forth from Derbyshire to London, to Doctors' Commons (home to the civil lawyers), to Parliament, and to the court. In addition, his son, Sir William Cavendish, and Thomas Hobbes received their allowance at times in London.[21]

Quentin Skinner quotes Hobbes's verse autobiography on the first year of his employment: "During the year that followed I spent almost the whole of my time with my master in the city, as a result of which I forgot most of the Latin and Greek I had ever known."[22] The earliest product of Hobbes's work with Cavendish, *A Discourse on Flatterie*, was published in 1611 before they went abroad. Upon their return from their travels in 1615, they began a correspondence with Fulgenzio Micanzio. On 30 October that year, Micanzio thanked Cavendish, "by your most welcome letter from Paris, this of mine will arrive to doe you humble reverence, about the time of your being backe at Court."[23] I will argue that by situating Cavendish and Hobbes in the context of London and the court, we can create an additional intellectual context in which to consider their early work, and in particular, its connections to the court of James VI and I, who called himself "Emperor of Great Britain."

The Bruce funeral demonstrates Hobbes's introduction to the world of politics a decade before his participation in the Virginia Company. It reorients the setting for Hobbes's early work to the intellectual concerns of the Jacobean court, which are reflected in both Hobbes's and Cavendish's reading and writing. Using as texts the funeral, A *Discourse on Flatterie* published by Cavendish in 1611, the *Horae Subsecivae* of 1620, and the catalog of books that Hobbes collected for Cavendish at Chatsworth in the 1620s, I hope to document the existence of a Bruce-Cavendish circle and to demonstrate its members' concern with contemporary issues such as the union of England and Scotland, the polemics generated by King James against the papacy, including the oath of allegiance and the Venetian interdict, the critical contemporary issue of dueling, and the Tacitean criticism of courts, generated within courtly discourse itself.

The Bruce-Cavendish Circle

The Bruce funeral provides tantalizing clues to the makeup of what I am calling the Bruce-Cavendish circle. Bruce, whose funeral the Cavendish household attended,[24] was a Scottish judge and King James's close ally. He had been one of the principal Scottish negotiators who, in the waning days of Queen Elizabeth's reign, engaged in secret correspondence to assure the succession of James VI of Scotland to the English throne in 1603. In gratitude James had given Bruce, who was abbot of Kinlosse, first the English title of earl of Kinlosse, then the office of master of the Rolls, and finally a position on the English Privy Council in 1603. One of the leading Jacobean Scots who surrounded the new king, Bruce's influence went beyond the Bedchamber, where many of the Jacobean Scots became political brokers. At his death an account of "Gifts from King James to Sir Edward Bruce, Lord Bruce, and Profits made by him out of his office in 8 years. Mastership of the Rolls" showed that most of his profits came from the sale of offices in the Rolls Office; they amounted to £33,000.[25]

William Cavendish was created baron Cavendish of Hardwicke in 1605 and earl of Devonshire in 1618. Son of Bess of Hardwick, Lord Cavendish carefully positioned his family within the new Jacobean elite of Jacobean Scots, the Cecils, and the Howards. His sister Mary, countess of Shrewsbury, was aunt to Arabella Stuart, and her daughter married Thomas Howard, earl of Arundel. Cavendish married his daughter to William Maynard, who had close ties to Robert Cecil, and he married his son Sir William to Christian Bruce, Kinlosse's twelve-year-old daughter. James I, following the uxorious pattern he established at the beginning of his reign, took a personal interest in the marriage, ensuring that the couple were given appropriate maintenance by the wealthy Cavendish, as befitted the marriage of his "kinswoman," as he described Christian Bruce.[26] Arabella Stuart, cousin to both King James and Sir William Cavendish, with whom she had been brought up,[27] was one of those who expressed concern that Cavendish was contracted to another.[28] Despite such concerns, Sir William Cavendish and Christian Bruce were married at the Rolls Chapel in Chancery Lane in 1608. In the same year Hobbes entered Sir William's service.

Other members of the Bruce-Cavendish circle who participated in Lord Bruce's funeral at the Rolls Chapel in 1611 included Jacobean officials from both England and Scotland, civil and common lawyers, and doctors. John Wylde was chief baron of the Exchequer.[29] James Primrose, who carried the great banner with Bruce's arms, had been appointed clerk of the Scottish Privy Council for life in 1599.[30] Dr. John Craig, third son of Sir Thomas Craig, the famous Scottish feudalist, received his M.D. at Basle and became physician to James VI, whom he accompanied to England.[31] Craig corresponded with Tycho Brahe, the Danish astronomer.[32] Gideon Delaune, inventor of Delaune's pills, was apothecary to Anne of Denmark. Francis Nicolls of the Middle Temple, kinsman to Cavendish and to Bruce, was a nephew of the noted Jacobean judge Sir Augustine Nicolls. Richard Martin was a well-known lawyer of the Middle Temple who later, briefly, became recorder of London.[33] Alongside this group of London lawyers and physicians was one Mr. Hayward, probably John Hayward the historian, author of the politically sensitive *Henry IV* published in 1599.

What message did this funeral send? Most notably, the creation of a unified state of Great Britain and of a new elite that was simultaneously English and Scottish. Bruce's impressive tomb with the figures of his widow, Magdalen, his daughter, Christian Bruce, his heir, Edward, and his younger son Thomas is a visual contribution to the debate over the Union and reflects King James's attempt to create a unitary state with an Anglo-Scottish elite over which he was emperor. The tomb's inscription stresses that Bruce was both Scottish and English.[34] Furthermore, the brothers-in-law Sir William Maynard and Sir William Cavendish supported the king's attempts to create a British elite. Both were knighted on 7 March 1608/9;[35] both sat in Parliament in 1610 and 1614. There Maynard supported Cavendish's speech in 1614 on behalf of the naturalization of two Scots, Sir Francis Stewart, the son of a Scottish earl, and William Ramsay, a Scottish member of the king's Bedchamber.[36]

The Anglo-Scottish connection of the Bruces with the Cavendishes and the court outlasted the death of Lord Kinlosse. Magdalen Bruce, the widow, married Sir James Fullerton in 1616. Fullerton was surveyor general to Prince Charles, duke of York, and was later keeper of the Privy Purse to the prince. With the death of Prince Henry, Charles's Household officials took on greater importance. Sir William Cavendish maintained close connections with Fullerton.[37] Thomas Bruce, who became a gentleman of the king's Bedchamber, was made earl of Elgin by Charles I in 1633. Together, Thomas, Lord Bruce and Sir William Cavendish held the reversion of the mastership of the game and keeping of the house and parks at Ampthill, Bedfordshire. William Ramsay was granted the reversion after them shortly after Cavendish had spoken for his naturalization in Parliament.[38] Christian Bruce, Cavendish's young bride, was an ardent royalist and supporter of Charles I and at the Restoration a supporter of Charles II. According to the biography published after her death in 1685, she took great pleasure in the close friendship of her son, William Cavendish, earl of Devonshire, and her Bruce nephew, Robert Bruce, earl of Ailesbury.

The Bruce-Sackville Duel

Two members of this procession, Cavendish's two brothers-in-law, Edward Bruce, second lord Kinlosse, and Sir William Maynard, help shed more light on what was continually before the eyes of Cavendish and Hobbes. First, in 1613 Bruce (having been made a knight of the Bath in 1610 and then a gentleman of the Bedchamber) repeatedly challenged Richard Sackville, later fourth earl of Dorset, another member of the Household, to a duel.[39] Before leaving for the Low Countries in late 1613, Bruce wrote his will in terms that show the continuation of the Bruce-Cavendish connection. He left his sister Christian, Lady Cavendish £200 in gold; his brother-in-law, Sir William Cavendish, a ring worth £100; £200 to his kinsman Francis Nicolls of the Middle Temple and his wife. Bruce appointed Cavendish one of the overseers of the will with his uncle George Bruce and Nicolls one of his executors, along with his mother. He left lands to his mother so long as she remained unmarried and at her death, or should she remarry, to his younger brother Thomas.[40] Ominously, Bruce left £200 to his second, William Cranford.

Despite the intervention of the king, Bruce continued to challenge Sackville from abroad.

> I that am in France heare how much you attribute to your self in this time that I have given the world leave to sing your praises . . . And if you call to memory when I gave you my hand last I told you . . . if you be the noble gentleman, then . . . come . . . you owe your birth and country . . . your honor gives you the same courage to do me right, that it did to do me wrong. Be master of your own weapon and time the place wheresoever . . . by doing this you shall shorten revenge, and cleere the jealous opinions the world hath of both our worths.[41]

In arranging the duel, held on the border of the Netherlands and the archduke's dominions to allow escape, Bruce insisted that they be attended by none but their physicians. According to Sackville, who wrote an apologia, Bruce had said that "a little of my blood would not serve his turn; And therefore he was resolved to have me alone, because he knew (for I will use his own words) that so worthie a gentleman and my friend could not endure to stand by and see him do that which he must to satisfy himself and his honor."[42]

King James's Scottish advisor, the earl of Mar, described the outcome. "If Kinlosse had been wise or God content with him, he might with great honor and no harm to himself have satisfied himself, for when he had hurt the other . . . Kinlosse was not hurt at all . . . There was none present but two surgeons for Kinlosse would not have a second, least upon only small hurt they might have been parted. They did both come in together carried upon one cart and did forgive one another."[43]

Dueling figured in Hobbes's *Leviathan*, a point Keith Thomas noticed thirty years ago. Hobbes wrote that it was "a custom not many years since begun" and one that "a gallant man, and one that is assured of his own courage, cannot take notice of." Thomas points out that Hobbes developed his attack on dueling at greater length in the Latin version of *Leviathan*.[44] Neither he nor anyone else, I think, has observed that dueling was a personal issue for the Bruce and Cavendish families. The library that Hobbes had put together by the 1620s contained "King James touching Duels," King James's February 1614 proclamation against dueling. The library also included a tract commissioned by the king from Henry Howard, earl of Northampton, lord privy seal, prepared in November 1613 after a spate of duels, including that of Bruce and Sackville.[45] In his tract Northampton called for the most stringent measures against dueling, including the punishment of family members who supported the dueler. The Chatsworth account books show that in November 1613, Cavendish gave "my Lord Privy Seal's man 2–6" and in December gave another six shillings. The coincidence of dates may indicate that Cavendish was cementing his relationship with Northampton and the king's new favorite, Robert Carr, earl of Somerset, in the wake of the duel, and perhaps that he received the tract on dueling from the earl himself.[46]

Sir William Maynard's Logic Lecture

The second member of the procession who helps illuminate the new context for Hobbes studies is Cavendish's other brother-in-law, Sir William Maynard. Maynard was the son of Sir Henry Maynard of Easton, Essex, secretary to Lord Burghley. Shortly after the death of Burghley in 1598, John Chamberlain reported that "Master Maynard is become the Quene's man and that with such high favor that in goode earnest he is thought to be neerest in election to be Secretarie, and the rather for that Master Secretarie is altogether for him."[47] Maynard traveled to France with the son of Robert Bowyer, clerk of the Parliament, carrying a letter of recommendation to Sir George Carew from Robert Cecil, earl of Salisbury.[48] On the point of returning from France on 25 January 1608, Maynard wrote to Salisbury of the news of the French court and recalled "the honour I have in being known as a servant of your house, and particularly of yourself."[49] He was in close touch with Michael Hickes, who had been the linchpin of the Cecils' secretariat. Maynard's brother Henry wrote in 1610 to ask for the second reversion of clerk of the Parliament after Robert Bowyer, "my father's ancient and affectionate friend and the present Clerk of the Parliament House." Recalling Hicks's affection for his father, Sir Henry Maynard, he asked him to intercede with Salisbury, now lord treasurer: "If I may obtain his Lordship's honorable approbation, I am in good hope of meanes to proceed in my suit to the king."[50] William Maynard referred to "his uncle Bowyer" and wrote that his brother was going up to London to attend "my Lord Treasurer and both my brother Harry and hee would be glade to intreate your favour in procuring them a license to goe over into France."[51] He sought to arrange a visit by Hickes to Easton followed by a trip to Cambridge.[52]

Upon his return from France in 1608, Maynard became a gentleman of the Privy Chamber. In 1609 he was knighted by King James at the same time as Sir William Cavendish, received an M.A. from St. John's College, Cambridge, and in 1611 was admitted to study law at the Inner Temple. Only slightly older than Cavendish, Maynard married his sister Frances, and the Chatsworth accounts record the families' exchanges of deer and New Year's gifts.[53] Maynard was made a baronet in 1611, an Irish baron in 1620, and in 1628 an English lord. Although his wife, Frances, died young, Maynard appears to have continued to have links to Cavendish. Both he and Lord Bruce were admitted to the council of the Virginia Company in 1624.[54]

But Maynard aspired to more than just favor at court. The 1610s saw a flurry of endowments at Oxford and Cambridge by figures prominent in Jacobean political culture. Sir Henry Savile founded professorships in geometry and astronomy. At St. John's College, Cambridge, Sir Edwin Sandys left £1,000 in his will to found a lecture in metaphysics, Fulke Greville, Lord Brooke founded a history lecture with a stipend of £100, and Sir Henry Spelman founded a Saxon lecture. In 1618 Maynard endowed a logic lecture based at St. John's.[55] The foundation documents for the logic lecture survive, as does the correspondence about the lecture between Maynard and the master of the college, Dr. Owen Gwynn, beginning in 1618.[56] At first Maynard planned to set up the lecture with John Argall, a relation, perhaps, of the logician John Argall, whose 1605 work on logic attacked medieval scholasticism and urged a return to Aristotle.[57] The overseers of the lecture were a group of university dons, including Robert Scott, vice-chancellor of the university, Valentine Cary, John Richardson, John Davenant, Samuel Ward, Owen Gwynn, Samuel Collins, and John Gostlin. Although Maynard originally wanted the lecturer appointed for life and to lecture three times a week, he had to settle for twice-weekly lectures in term.[58] He insisted that lodgings at St. John's be made available in case the lecturer came from outside the college.[59] While Robert Lane balked at three lectures a week, Thomas Thornton, who received his B.A. in 1611 and M.A. in 1615, became the university reader of Lord Maynard's logic lecture, acknowledging in 1624 receipt of £25 to give the lecture.[60] Thornton was ejected from his fellowship in 1644 as a royalist by the earl of Manchester. At the time he was also president of the college.[61]

Maynard's lecture is part of the Aristotelian revival of the early seventeenth century at both Oxford and Cambridge, perhaps part of an anti-Ramist agenda.[62] Maynard specified commentary on Aristotle's *Organon*, Porphyry's *Isagoge* (a third-century commentary on Aristotle), and Cicero's *Topica*.[63] The lecturer's notes were to be transcribed and deposited in the university library. In 1636 Archbishop Laud's statutes followed sixteenth-century practice in placing Aristotle at the center of the study of logic.[64] Indeed, as part of his studies at Oxford, Hobbes had studied Aristotle's logic.[65] In short, if Hobbes wanted to talk about Aristotle, he did not have to wait to run into Dr. Goulston at Virginia Company meetings. He could have done so with his own contacts at

Oxford and Cambridge, more particularly his contacts with Maynard and St. John's.

Maynard wrote frequently to the master of the college, Dr. Gwynn, to invite him to Essex and to lobby for fellowships for his kinsmen, his mother's and his wife's relatives, and his neighbors in the 1620s. In these letters he repeatedly stressed that the candidate was not inclined to Puritanism.[66] One of those for whom he wrote was named Mason; he may have been related to Robert Mason, a fellow of St. John's, Cambridge, the earliest of Hobbes's correspondents whose letters have survived.

Hobbes and Cavendish themselves also had strong connections to St. John's. Cavendish matriculated there and received his M.A. in 1608; Hobbes was incorporated at St. John's in 1608. Hobbes maintained connections with their mutual friend Robert Mason, who had entered St. John's in 1606 and received his B.A. in 1610 and his M.A. in 1613. As Malcolm points out, Mason was a fellow of the college from 1610 to 1632 and senior proctor in 1620. Mason, too, had court connections: in 1625 he took a leave of absence from St. John's in order to become secretary to the duke of Buckingham, who left him £500 in his will.

The earliest surviving letter in the Hobbes correspondence is one from Mason in response to an earlier letter from Hobbes. While discussing the war in the Palatinate, the return of the archbishop of Spalato (De Dominis) to Rome, and his reconversion to Catholicism after spending six years in England as a Protestant, Mason also requested further news.

> I trust we shall neither of us be thought immodestly to abuse the libertie of true and loyall subjects, for mine own part as I am not of their curiositie who would seem to be ignorant of nothing that shall occurre remarkable; for there are many things, as your letter discreetly intimates, whereof it becomes us to be ignorant, so I would be loath to be thought so great a stranger to the Commonwealth I live in as not to know what the greater sort of men do, that wish a prosperous successe to the designes both of their Prince and Country, which I hope henceforth to have from you, tis no matter though it be at the sixt, seventh, or 50th hand . . . Arcana imperii nihil moror. periculum intelligere. My ambition reaches no furder then the Exchange, W. Barret's shop, or the middle Isle in Pauls, where when old Wymarkes mint goes, I would desire you would but send me now and then of his coyne, it wil passe for currant here amongst the Clerks in Cambridge.

Mason sent Hobbes a picture for Cavendish, probably a portrait; "if the painter had time he should have written upon it, those few liness which I have sent you inclosed, which might briefly express the quality of the person whom it represents, which if you can gett done before my Lord see it, you shall knitt one knot more upon the tye of his affection who is Your true and loving friend."[67] Mason's letter confirms the portrait of Hobbes at home in London, a figure whom Mason wished would function like the great Jacobean letter-writer John Chamberlain, one who frequented the newsmongers in St. Paul's and the Royal Exchange.[68]

It should by now be clear that the Bruce-Cavendish circle was strongly attached to the court. Hobbes himself had important connections to other Jacobean officials. Sir Francis Bacon, for whom Hobbes served as secretary and who lived near Cavendish in London, is the best known.[69] But Hobbes was also friendly with Sir Robert Ayton, kin to Christian Bruce, Cavendish's wife.[70] A Scot who studied civil law in Paris, wrote Latin poetry, and was good friends with Ben Jonson as well as Hobbes, Ayton was, according to Aubrey, "acquainted with all the wits of his time in England." He became a gentleman of James's Bedchamber as well as personal secretary and Master of Requests to Queen Anne. His poetry lauded the king and commemorated the duke of Buckingham. Ayton offered to forgo his £500–a-year pension in exchange for the provostship of Eton in a letter to Buckingham. "Now my Lord, it is in your power as I hear to strike the stroke." As of 1639, Ayton had three pensions granted by King James totaling £840.[71] The Bruce-Cavendish circle brought together the new British elite of English and Scots. They shared intellectual interests in humanism, law, medicine, and the Aristotelian revival and practical experience of the way in which the Jacobean court worked.

Hobbes and Cavendish: Early Writings

Their web of connections at the Jacobean court and beyond provides a new and additional context in which to analyze the writings of Hobbes and Cavendish. The first work produced by Cavendish, as we have seen, was *A Discourse on Flatterie*, dedicated to Lord Bruce, baron of Kinlosse, whom he claimed had asked him to write it.[72] Cavendish tells us why he chose the topic in the dedication: "Sir it is ones proper right to challenge that for his due, for whose sake, and at whose commandment is [sic] was first undertaken . . . this can rightly belong to none but yourself . . . This good office at the least it will performe, eyther put you in mind of that you knew before, or else confirme you in that opinion, wherein I assure myselfe you are already setled." Why would *A Discourse on Flatterie* confirm his opinion? The topic of flattery was one generated by court life and literature. Kinlosse had now had long-term experience of the frantic favor-seeking at the Jacobean court.

Cavendish also presented a group of essays to his father, the earl of Devonshire, as a New Year's gift sometime before 1620.[73] Hobbes scholars have emphasized the influence of Sir Francis Bacon, whose essays were first published in 1597 and for whom Hobbes appears to have acted as secretary after Bacon's disgrace in the 1620s. F. J. Levy has located Bacon's essays in the context of the politics of the late Elizabethan court.[74] Similarly, the essays and discourses published in the *Horae Subsecivae* tell us about the discourse and practice of the Jacobean court in the early seventeenth century, particularly Cavendish's essay "Of Ambition" and Hobbes's "A Discourse upon the Beginning of Tacitus" and "A Discourse of Laws."[75] (Whether one accepts the specific attribution of the three discourses to Hobbes or not, it seems clear from the manuscripts at Chatsworth that these writings were produced by Hobbes and Cavendish between 1611 and 1620.)

The essay on ambition combines a humanist and baronial attack on favorites. A staple of court political discourse since classical antiquity, the critique of favorites was widespread at the Jacobean court. Similar language can be found in tracts generated by the Overbury murder trial as well as the letters of that disappointed office-seeker Sir John Holles. Thus, a traditional trope was appropriated to fit the contemporary politics of the Jacobean court. Cavendish wrote:

> An Ambitious man is in a kinde of continuall perambulation, or perpetuall courting of advancement, not respecting the meanes, Bribery, Flattery, Humility, Popularitie, seeming Severitie or Austerenesse. Any of which, so they either conferre, or conduce to his owne ends, whether for Titles, or Preheminence, or Estimation, shall bee disguises good enough for the present occasion . . . infected, with this Leprosie . . . If the current of their Ambition be once stopped, like an impetuous torrent, it beates and breakes the bankes, growes dangerous, and manie times causes inundations. Therefore Princes respects, if they be fixed upon such natures, are tyed not only to a continuation, but an addition of favors; for the least surcease makes declination in service.

Cavendish went on to warn of the danger of favorites to

> all well ordred Commonwealths. For when every one seeks to be principall, or to engrosse all within his owne Circumference, and to compasse the rest with subjection, or affects to make himselfe the encreasing figure, whilst the rest serve but for supplyes, faction in business, confusion in directions do necessarily follow. And what be these men that so extremely affect Superiority, and primacy in all affaires? Do they good to the Publike,[76] or is their service equivalent to their preferment? . . . No. For an Ambitious man, so soone as he is advanced, remembers no more the duty, but the precedency of his place.

Nonetheless, Cavendish left room for the good courtier.

> If a man seeke or labour to attaine favour, and preferment, with this onely intention, that by that way, he may have better meanes to do good, to reduce ill Custome, to the most ancient, and commendable forme . . . without the least tincture of vaineglory, or any other selfe-desire, this kinde of ambition I admit as a Vertue, and in this case, I allow it to be generous . . . men that have good aymes and ends . . . are not . . . secluded . . . to raise or encrease their Fortunes, to honor and advance their Posteritie, so it be done with moderation, and modestie.[77]

Let me compare Cavendish's essay with "A Discourse upon the Beginning of Tacitus," now attributed to Hobbes by Saxonhouse and Reynolds. Tacitism was, of course, an important part of the neo-Stoic revival in the late sixteenth century fostered by Justus Lipsius. It became, especially in England, an anticourt literature usually written by those (such as the followers of Essex) who wished for court favor but were frustrated.[78]

Hobbes addressed the issues of favor and corruption in this discourse on Tacitus in language similar to that of other Jacobean writers. Thus, he takes up the issue of the exchange of benefits, a staple of sixteenth- and seventeenth-century discourse.[79] Contemporaries drew on Seneca's *De Beneficiis*, translated into English in 1578 by Arthur Golding and again in 1614 and 1620 by Thomas Lodge. Hobbes analyzes Tacitus's statement that Augustus made Marcus Agrippa his son-in-law in a way that suggests the Senecan view. "The greatness of this benefit bestowed on one that could no ways exact, or extort it from Augustus gives here an occasion to enquire into the minds of all men in the matter of giving and receiving benefits." Hobbes's distinction between benefits and extortion resembles Lodge's 1614 translation of Seneca: "These things which either are extorted from the giver, or seeme to fall from his hands that giveth them: although they seeme highly prized and of great appearance, yet, as I said, they are unworthy of thankes, because a gift is much more gratefully accepted and reckoned of that come from a free and liberall hand, than from a full and rich-fisted penny-father."[80] But after citing Tacitus's contention "that benefits received are pleasing so long as they be requitable," Hobbes goes on to suggest that giving benefits the giver more than the receiver. Moreover,

> when men can, without lessening of themselves, reward those to whom they have been beholden, so as to satisfy them according to their own estimate, they will then overdo it, and heap one favor upon another, thinking by showing their affection to them, to gain theirs in the same proportion: but it falls not so out in human nature: for benefits increase the love of the bestower, more than of him that receives them.[81]

This was not the Senecan view of exchange, but the Machiavellian view of liberality.

So, Hobbes wrote, "It is both justice, and good policy, to reward with preferments those that yield their obedience readily, and willingly; for it stirs emulation in men, to exceed each other in diligence. And on the contrary, to heap benefits on the sullen and averse, out of hope to win their affection, is unjust and prejudicial." Speaking of the Augustan Age, he continued, "But the rich, and such as were in love with titles of honor, found more ease and contentment here, than they could expect in the Civil War, and did accept the present with security, rather than strive for the old with danger" (46). Hobbes might well be describing Jacobean patronage policy in the wake of the turbulence of the last years of Elizabeth.[82] For the Jacobeans, too, were in love with titles of honor. Lord William Cavendish bought his barony, and Sir William Maynard bought his baronetcy. In fact, Maynard also bought an Irish barony and later an English barony.

In his analysis of Tacitus's comment about "the contention of great men and covetousness of the Magistrates," Hobbes went on to analyze corruption. "That purse that was heaviest, that bribe that was greatest carried the cause. Justice was not seen, but felt; a good bribe was their best Advocate. Such in those times were the Magistrates, and Judges. Everything was carried by might, ambition and corruption. He that was not ambitious, was neglected: and he that was not corrupt was esteemed indiscreet" (48). Hobbes argued that corruption was less likely in a monarchy and more likely in a "factious and divided Commonwealth." The remedy was to strengthen the laws with authority. "For force, friends, and money overthrew their validity" (49). While Hobbes provided a singular view of Tacitus, he adopted a contemporary vocabulary with which to describe favor and corruption.

Similarly, dominating Hobbes's "Discourse of Laws" was an image that was particularly resonant in the Jacobean period.[83] Hobbes wrote, "the King, who being reputed to be as the fountain of Justice, so Justice keeps the fountain free from corruption, infection, or danger, prescribing rules for fear it corrupt, ascribing Antidotes for fear of infection, and preserving his person, and reputation both from sensible, and insensitive danger" (108–9).[84] Arlene Saxonhouse suggests that the image may be borrowed from Francis Bacon's *Advancement of Learning* of 1605, where in the dedication to the king, James is compared to a fountain of learning. In fact, the trope of the monarch as fountain was common in the Elizabethan and early Stuart period, whether as the fountain of favor or the fountain of justice. John Stoughton preached that "the ancients were wont to place the Statues of their Kings by fountains, intimating they were the Fountaines of good or ill in the common-wealth." In 1613, within a few years of the composition of the "Discourse of Laws," John Webster wrote in *The Duchess of Malfi*,

> A Prince's Court
> is like a common Fountaine, whence should flowe
> Pure silver-droppes in general. But if't chance
> Some curs'd example poyson't neere the head,
> Death and diseases through the whole land spread.[85]

This is, of course, only one way to read these early works of Cavendish and Hobbes, one that shows familiarity not only with the humanist discourse of courts, but equally with what, in Cavendish's phrase, was before their eyes—the specific practice of patronage and politics at the Jacobean court.

The catalog of the library that Hobbes put together for Cavendish is part of the archive at Chatsworth. It points to the political issues that animated the Jacobean court.[86] James Jay Hamilton analyzed these catalogs, but that analysis has significant omissions since, as he puts it, "I have chosen only books of most interest to the students of political and moral thought."[87] In the manuscript catalog, "Chatsworth E 1a," as Hobbes recorded it, the largest number of books are not by Machiavelli—not by a long shot.[88] Rather, they reflect the Jacobean propaganda battles with the papacy over the Venetian interdict and the oath of allegiance, as well as the creation of what Peter Lake has called advanced conformist thought—what we might call pre-Arminian thought—of the Jacobean bishops and clerics. While Hamilton lists ten works by Bacon and two works by

Machiavelli, the greatest number of works in the library are actually by James I and by Cardinal Bellarmine, represented by twelve items each. Johann Sommerville points out how central to Hobbes's argument in *Leviathan* is his attack on Cardinal Bellarmine, and the presence of twelve books by the cardinal testifies to the interest taken by Cavendish and Hobbes in the controversy over the oath of allegiance.

The works of James I include the editions of his works in English, Latin, and French and his earlier writings, such as his *Apologie for the Oath of Allegiance* (1608). I have already drawn attention to the king's 1614 edict against dueling. Another significant work is "King James his edict touching his Bownty." This was an attempt to restrain the king's liberality, drafted by Cecil and Northampton in 1608 and published in 1610. It was a work that laid out the limits on royal bounty, a matter of great interest to the Bruce-Cavendish circle. The Chatsworth account books show that it was purchased early in 1611, just after Bruce's funeral, for seven pence.[89]

Conclusion

Let me return to my earlier question: What does this new context contribute to our understanding of Hobbes's early writings? We need not decide whether to label Hobbes a Machiavellian, a Baconian, a humanist. But we do need to situate Hobbes and Cavendish at court and in the city. Describing the "generosities" of Cavendish's mind, his wife's biographer wrote carefully about his debt: "even when Earl of Devonshire, he rather increased it by the Magnificence of his living both in Town and Country (his House appearing rather like a Princes Court than a Subjects) for nothing but the greatest Actions could answer the Heights of his nobler thoughts."[90]

Let Hobbes have the last word. More than fifty years after Sir William Cavendish's death, Hobbes recalled his patron fondly, lauding both patron and library in the shaping of Hobbes's own career.

> Then Oxford left; served Ca'ndish known to be
> A noble and Conspicuous Family . . .
> Thus Youth Tutor'd a Youth . . .
> Serv'd him full twenty years, who prov'd to be
> Not a Lord only but a Friend to Me
> That my Life's sweetest Comfort was, and made
> My Slumbers pleasant in Nights darkest shade.
> Thus I at Ease did live, of Books, whilst he
> Did with all sorts supply my Library.[91]

In addition to the Venetian Micanzio, the French Descartes, Francis Bacon, and the Great Tew Circle,[92] I would argue that we need to connect the young Hobbes to the urban, court-centered group of Jacobean Scots, gentlemen of the Bedchamber, English clients of the earl of Salisbury, lawyers, physicians, and historians with close and continuing connections to the court of James VI and I. This is not to argue for an insular culture. The issues with which the Jacobean court was caught up were European in scope, including the contest of papal and monarchical power, the aristocratic code of dueling, and anticourt rhetoric. Prior to going on the Grand Tour, Hobbes and Cavendish were immersed in Jacobean court life and a new court culture increasingly oriented toward the continent. When "Youth Tutor'd a Youth," Hobbes and Cavendish were part of a learned court circle whose influence on the great philosopher, I would argue, has only begun to be charted.

Notes

I am grateful to His Grace the duke of Devonshire and the Trustees of the Chatsworth Settlement for permission to work in the Chatsworth archives. I also thank Peter Day for his help there. I am grateful to Elizabeth Leedham-Green for advice on Sir William Maynard's logic lecture.

1. His will dated 9 August 1610 was proved 14 January 1610/11. The inquest was held 6 April 1611. *Calendar of State Papers, Domestic* (1611–18), 268.

2. British Library, Add. MSS 14417, fols. 20v-21. While Bruce's funeral was elaborate, it was not as large as that of Sir Henry Lee, the great Elizabethan courtier.

3. BL, Add. MSS 14417, fols. 20v-21. The group of "freinds servants with cloaks" was made up of "Sir William Maynards 2 men / Tho Hobbes and one of my Lord Cavendishes men / 2 More of my lo. Cavendishes men." That the herald Charles noted Hobbes's name (but none of the other servants) suggests that he knew him.

4. Manuscript letters between Micanzio, the Venetian humanist, and Sir William Cavendish that Hobbes transcribed begin in 1615. Hobbes's earliest letters date from 1622.

5. Hobbes to Christian Bruce, widow of William Cavendish, second earl of Devonshire, in Thomas Hobbes, *The Correspondence*, ed. Noel Malcolm, 2 vols. (Oxford, 1994), 1:6–7. Hobbes wrote from Devonshire House in Bishopsgate, London. "I have made an Epistle dedicatorie to my Lord, according to the forme which your Ladyship gave me leave to use. Wherein I have intended to do his Lordship honor, as far as my discretion and the nature of an epistle will permitte." He asked her to correct or alter it and then return it "because the Presse will shortly be ready for it."

6. Hobbes, *Correspondence*, 1:xxi.

7. Thomas Hobbes, *Three Discourses*, ed. Noel B. Reynolds and Arlene W. Saxonhouse (Chicago, 1995).

8. Quentin Skinner, *Reason and Rhetoric in the Philosophy of Hobbes*, (Cambridge, 1996), 6.

9. See Leo Strauss, *The Political Philosophy of Hobbes*, trans. Elsa M. Sinclair (Chicago, 1952), 44–58; Keith Thomas, "Social Origins of Hobbes's Political Thought," in *Hobbes Studies*, ed. K. C. Brown (Cambridge, Mass., 1965), 185–236.

10. Chatsworth, Hobbes MS. D3.

11. Noel Malcolm, "Hobbes, Sandys, and the Virginia Company," *Historical Journal* 24 (1981): 301.

12. Skinner, *Reason and Rhetoric*, 223. Skinner points out that the records of the Virginia Company suggest that at one meeting Hobbes and Goulston sat next to one another.

13. Public Record Office, SO 3/4, 6. I am grateful to the History of Parliament Trust for this reference, which appears in its draft biography of Cavendish. In 1610 Cavendish was licensed to travel "for three years with three servants three nags and £50 in money, 6 February, 1610." He received another license in 1614.

14. Chatsworth, Hardwick MS. 29, pp. 150, 152, 157, 159. Note also the entry of 20 July 1610 "to sundry of Sir William Cavendish creditors according to a particular thereof for my Lord first of £2000 allowed by his Lordship towards the discharge of Sir William's debts." After 25 May the accounts record the purchase of "three pamphlets of the French king's death."

15. John Stoye, *English Travellers Abroad, 1604–1667: Their Influence in English Society and Politics* (New Haven, 1989), 30.

16. "Rose and Hobbes for their charges down 1–0–0," Chatsworth, Hardwick MS. 29, p. 157.

17. Linda Levy Peck, "Hobbes on the Grand Tour: Paris, Venice or London?" *Journal of the History of Ideas* 57 (1996): 177–83.

18. On the dating of the trip see ibid.; see also Skinner, *Reason and Rhetoric*; Noel Malcolm, *De Dominis, 1560–1624: Venetian, Anglican, Ecumenist, and Relapsed Heretic* (London, 1984).

19. Hobbes, *Three Discourses*, 4.

20. April 1608, 2 May 1608, Chatsworth, Hardwick MS. 29. Cavendish paid £850 for Popham's house and in April 1614 paid "watchmen to watch in Armor all next night at Aldersgate for my Lord," p. 368.

21. Skinner, *Reason and Rhetoric*, 219 n.39; see Chatsworth, Hardwick MS. 29 for evidence of payment of Cavendish's quarterly allowance. The Chatsworth account books show in detail the connections of the Bruce and Cavendish circles, for example five shillings to "my Lord Kinloos cook," p. 11 [April 1608].

22. Quoted in Skinner, *Reason and Rhetoric*, 231.

23. Ibid., 219 n.41. Skinner notes only that Hobbes was back in London.

24. "Delivered to my Lord at my Lord Bruce's funerall" £10. Chatsworth, Hardwick MS. 29, p. 222.

25. BL, Lansdowne MS. 163, fol. 353. These sales included six clerkships of the Hanaper, 3 clerkships of the petty bag, and one examiner in addition to eight years' profit from office of £1,800 a year.

26. See Thomas Pomfret, *The Life of the Countess of Devonshire* (London, 1685), 23–25.

27. Arabella was the only child of Charles Stewart, earl of Lennox by Elizabeth, second daughter of Sir William Cavendish. Arabella was brought up by her aunt, the countess of Shrewsbury, daughter of Bess of Hardwick and Lord William Cavendish's sister.

28. Arabella to Charles Gossing, "From the court at Whitehall this 28th of March 1609," about the contract of marriage with Mary Chatterton. BL, Stowe MS. 142, fol. 30.

29. Wylde took his M.A. from Balliol in 1610 and was called to the bar at the Inner Temple in 1612. He was later an M.P.

30. Another Scot, Mr. Dalyell, was a member of a family of baronets of Linlithgow.

31. Craig also received an M.D. from Oxford in 1605; he died in 1620.

32. Tycho Brahe's works are part of the Cavendish Library. Chatsworth, Hobbes MS. E 1a.

33. See *The Letters of John Chamberlain*, ed. Norman Egbert McClure, 2 vols. (Philadelphia, 1939). See also Chatsworth, Hardwick MS. 29, p. 218: "given by my Lord to Doctor Trevor and Mr. Doctor Martyn for Sir William £4," 1610. Dr. Martyn was possibly William Martyn, (1562–1617), lawyer and historian; he became a barrister of the Middle Temple in 1589.

34. The tomb is at the Public Record Office, Chancery Lane, into which the Rolls Chapel was later incorporated.

35. W. A. Shaw, *The Knights of England*, 2 vols. (London, 1906), 2:147.

36. 23 May 1614. Maija Jansson, *Proceedings in Parliament 1614* (Philadelphia, 1988), 320–21. Cavendish was reprimanded by another M.P. "that Mr. Speaker should have found fault with a gentleman which read out of his book what he should have spoken. Sir Jerome Horsey replied that divers of the House have usually helped their memories with their notes."

37. I am grateful to the History of Parliament Trust for permission to consult and to cite their unpublished biography of Sir William Cavendish.

38. July 27, 1614. *Cal.S.P.Dom.* (1611–1618), 249.

39. May and September 1613. See Chamberlain, *Letters*, 1:450, 453, 474.

40. 15 August, 1613. PRO, PROB 11/123, 22 Lowe, fols. 179–179v. Bruce remembered others who had taken part in his father's funeral, including Mr. Parkinson, Mr Dayalle, and Alexander Dunsyn.

41. "Mr Edward Sackville, (now Earle of Dorset) his relation of the manner of the combat and death of the Lord Bruse Baron of Kinlosse sent to his Freinds in England. 1613." BL, Add. MSS 48848, fols. 177–179v. A similar exculpatory manuscript is Add. MSS 18644.

42. BL, Add. MSS 18644, fol. 4.

43. Historical Manuscripts Commission, *Mar and Kellie*, 2:53–54, 119.

44. Thomas, "Social Origins of Hobbes's Political Thought," 194–96.

45. Chatsworth, Hardwick MS. 29, pp. 357–59. Chamberlain describes the series of threatened duels, 9 September 1613.

46. Ibid.: "To my Earl of Northampton's man that brought a doe and to his waterman, 1s2d; to one that brought my Lord gloves from my Lord of Somerset, 1s." Noel Malcolm points out that Cavendish challenged the earl of Warwick to a duel in the 1620s over a disagreement within the Virginia Company. See Malcolm, "Hobbes, Sandys, and the Virginia Company," 300.

47. Chamberlain to Carleton, 30 August 1598, in Chamberlain, *Letters*, 2:42.

48. 18 February 1607/8. HMC, *Salisbury*, 20:75.

49. Maynard to Robert Cecil, earl of Salisbury. Ibid., 28.

50. Henry Maynard to Michael Hickes, June 1610. BL, Lansdowne MS. 91, no.77, fol. 155.

51. Sir William Maynard to his "loving friend" Sir Michael Hickes, 14 August 1610, BL, Lansdowne MS. 91, no. 87, fol. 172; Strand, 27 March 1611, Lansdowne MS. 92, no. 36, fol. 66; 16 March 1611/12, Lansdowne MS. 92, no. 88, fol. 152.

52. 16 March 1611/12, BL, Lansdowne MS. 92, no. 88, fol. 152; Maynard to Hickes "at his lodging on the Strand," 8 April 1612, Lansdowne MS. 92, no. 109, fol. 193; 14 April 1610, Lansdowne MS. 92, no. 110.

53. Payments are recorded to "Sir William Maynard's man that brought half a doe," 1610; and £20 "To Sir William Maynard and my Lady for New Years gift." Chatsworth, Hardwick MS. 29, pp. 219, 220.

54. *Records of the Virginia Company of London*, ed. Susan Myra Kingsbury, 3 vols. (Washington, 1906). Noel Malcolm notes that one brother-in-law was named to the council in May 1623 but does not name him. He does not note that Maynard was admitted on 5 February 1623/4; Malcolm, "Hobbes, Sandys, and the Virginia Company," 299 n.

55. *Cal.S.P.Dom.* (1619–23), 9 July 1620: "License to William, Lord Maynard, of Wicklow, to found a Logic Lecture in Cambridge and to give lands in mortmain to the value of £50 per annum." Thomas Baker, *History of St. John's College, Cambridge*, 2 vols. (Cambridge, 1869), 1:211–12; A. F. Torrey, *Founders and Benefactors of St. John's College, Cambridge* (Cambridge, 1888), 19.

56. Cambridge University Library, University Archives, O.XIV.2 (i. ii. iii); O.XIV.3: Lord Maynard's Logic Lecture, no. 3 (Transcript of Patent and Foundation Documents). The 1570 statutes had said that the logic lecturer was to lecture on Aristotle and Cicero.

57. See *The Eagle: A Magazine supported by Members of St. John's College*; extracts are published in Robert Forsyth Scott, *Notes from the Records of St. John's College, Cambridge* (Cambridge, 1889–1913), 4:127–32, 150–58. I. Thomas, "Medieval Aftermath: Oxford Logic and Logicians of the Seventeenth Century," *Oxford Studies Presented to Daniel Collins*, Oxford Historical Society, n.s. 16 (Oxford, 1964), 297–311.

58. *Notes from the Records of St. John's College*, 4:131.

59. Ibid., 155–56.

60. Baker, *History of St. John's College*, 1:211, suggests that he was university reader of Lord Maynard's logic lecture from 1628/9 to 1640, but the receipt of £25 in 1624 demonstrates that the lecture was being delivered from an earlier date. CUL, Archives U. ac.2 (1).

61. Torrey, *Founders and Benefactors of St. John's College*, 19.

62. See Maynard to vice-chancellor of Cambridge upon the subject of his gift to the University (the founding of a logic lectureship), 25 November 1618. BL, Sloane MS. 3562, fol. 25. See also Thomas, "Medieval Aftermath."

63. For a discussion of sixteenth- and seventeenth-century approaches to logic, see Charles B. Schmitt, ed., *The Cambridge History of Renaissance Philosophy* (Cambridge, 1988), 143–98.

64. Ibid., 146.

65. Strauss, *Political Philosophy of Hobbes*, 30.

66. *Notes from the Records of St. John's College*, 4:127–32, 150–58.

67. Robert Mason to Hobbes, 10 December 1622, in Hobbes, *Correspondence*, 1:1–6.

68. On the circulation of news see Richard Cust, "News and Politics in Early Seventeenth-Century England," *Past and Present*, 112 (1986): 60–90; F. J. Levy, "How Information Spread Amongst the Gentry," *Journal of British Studies*, 21 (1982): 11–34.

69. Hobbes, *Correspondence*, 2:628 n.13. John Aubrey, in his life of Hobbes, points out the philosopher's connection to Bacon. *Brief Lives*, ed. Oliver Lawson Dick (London, 1958), 149–50.

70. Skinner, *Reason and Rhetoric*, 233–34. Ayton replaced Fowler as the queen's secretary.

71. Linda Levy Peck, *Court Patronage and Corruption in Early Stuart England*, (London, 1990), 64–65.

72. Because Kinlosse died in January 1611, it is possible that the dedicatee is his brother-in law, although it seems more likely that it was written for his father-in-law.

73. Chatsworth, Hobbes MS. D3. These essays were first identified as in Hobbes's hand by Leo Strauss, *The Political Philosophy of Hobbes*, trans. Elsa M. Sinclair (Oxford, 1936), xvi.

74. F. J. Levy, "Francis Bacon and the Style of Politics," *English Literary Renaissance* 16 (1986): 101–22.

75. See "A Discourse upon the Beginning of Tacitus" and "A Discourse of Laws," in Hobbes, *Three Discourses*, 31–67, 105–19.

76. The manuscript reads "republique." See Chatsworth, Hobbes MS. D3, fols. 8–16.

77. *Horae Subsecivae*, (London, 1620), 11–30.

78. See J. H. M. Salmon, "Seneca and Tacitus in Jacobean England," in *The Mental World of the Jacobean Court*, ed. Linda Levy Peck (Cambridge, 1991), 169–88; Peter Burke, "Tacitism, Skepticism, and Reason of State," in *The Cambridge History of Political Thought*, ed. J. H. Burns and Mark Goldie (Cambridge, 1991), 479–98.

79. Linda Levy Peck, "Benefits, Brokers, and Beneficiaries: The Culture of Exchange in Seventeenth-Century England," in *Court, Country, and Culture: Essays on Early Modern British History in Honor of Perez Zagorin*, ed. Bonnelyn Young Kunze and Dwight D. Brautigam (Rochester, N.Y., 1992), 109–27.

80. "On Benefits," in *The Workes of Lucius Anneas Seneca, Both Morrall and Natural*, trans. Thomas Lodge (London, 1614), bk. 1, chap. 7, 80.

81. Hobbes, *Three Discourses*, 51. Subsequent quotations from the discourses will refer to page numbers in this edition and be included parenthetically in my text.

82. See Peck, "Peers, Patronage and the Politics of History," in *The Age of Elizabeth I*, ed. J. A. Guy (Cambridge, 1995), 87–108.

83. In the "Discourse of Laws," Hobbes writes that "law is nothing but reason dilated" and sets out the categories of natural law theory, the law of nature, of nations, and the civil law of the individual country. Differences in laws depend on those who first established them, "as may be observed in the different Constitutions and Laws, in our two late Plantations, of Virginia, and the Bermudas." He concludes by showing the similarities of the Roman law and English common law (116). For the dating of this tract see Noel Malcolm, "Hobbes, Sandys, and the Virginia Company," 321.

84. And again, "there are certain fountains of natural justice and equity . . . so these laws and the virtue of them, which be fetched from an original fountain, receive a new kind of application, and tincture, in respect of the situation of the Country, the genius and nature of the people" (112).

85. See Peck, *Court Patronage and Corruption*, 1–2 and 222 nn.1–3.

86. Chatsworth, Hobbes MS. E 1a.

87. James Jay Hamilton, "Hobbes Study and the Hardwick Library," *Journal of the History of Philosophy* 16 (1978): 448.

88. For a list of books purchased at the end of 1611 see Chatsworth, Hardwick MS. 29, p. 220.

89. Chatsworth, Hardwick MS. 29, fol. 223.
90. Pomfret, *Life of the Countess of Devonshire*, 24–25.
91. *The Life of Mr Thomas Hobbes of Malmesbury Written by himself in a Latine Poem and Now Translated into English* (London, 1680), 4–5.
92. See Malcolm, "Hobbes, Sandys, and the Virginia Company," 312.

Irony, Modernity, and Miscellany: Politics and Aesthetics in the Stuart Restoration

Steven N. Zwicker

I

The subject of my inquiry, indeed celebration, is the Stuart Restoration: its rule of irony and obscenity, its qualities of cultural miscellany and miscegenation. Pieties marked the decade preceding this Restoration, and reformation the decade that followed its inglorious flight. The years between are distinguished by an insistent mixture of ranks and forms, of literary genres and social modes, and by an aesthetic of mockery, miscellany, and transposition. In his preface to *Samson Agonistes*, Milton denounced, and with his play he aimed to correct, the now common "error of intermixing comic stuff with tragic sadness and gravity."[1] But Milton must have understood, and only too well by 1671, that the idioms and energies of the culture at large, and, more specifically, of its theatrical and its literary practices, derived from the very proximity of high and low, of epic and burlesque. Where once the Stuart court had been articulated through the codes and conduct of a rarefied Neoplatonism, pornography now inhabited its center.[2] And if Van Dyck had supplied an earlier age with the visual idioms of aristocratic culture, now the postures of Aretine held sway.[3] This was a world where distinctions between the sacred and the profane, between fecundity and fornication, had blurred and even threatened to disappear. It had not always been so, and it was not to be for very long, but the years between the return of Charles II and the invitation to William III can be defined by an instability and opportunism, at once political and literary, in which irony and miscellany were the rule.

This is not to say that the intimacy of high and low was a sudden apparition in 1660. Stuart kings had early promoted the Book of Sports,[4] and the royalist cultivation of folk culture and folk customs in the midst of the Civil War has been well documented.[5] But strategic alignment is one thing, and the elision, indeed violation, of distinctions quite another. Strategy no doubt guided Charles I in his preservation of folk rhythms and rituals,[6] but the abandon to bawdry and vice in the rites of Charles II's court cannot be understood as strategy in any familiar sense of that word. No one could have missed the social and political meaning of pleasure in 1660, its reconstructive, even retributive, force. But those early idioms of softness and ceremony were soon transmuted into a blunt and transgressive vocabulary. The commingling of high and low in the Restoration may have begun, and surely was glossed by contemporaries, as a memory of older royal ways,[7] but their conjunctions and abrasions came to define and to dominate court culture and literary practices to an extent that could have been neither imagined nor intended in the, shall we say, innocence of 1660.

How, and to what effect, had irony and the instability of pleasures come to rule? The central event in this dynamic was the Restoration itself, and central to that Restoration was Charles II. And surely biography has its place within this narrative: the wit, the lassitude, the theatricality of this king, the commingling of secrecy and ease of access, of candor and masquerade, and, of course, the dominion of priapic pleasures, the whoring, scandal, and license of the person and the court.[8] But I want to argue that Restoration ironies and instabilities are situated more deeply than biography can allow. Charles II is more symptom than cause; the scandal of his person and court are emblematic, but the fault lines in this culture were structural features rather than personality traits.

The Restoration of Charles II was the fixing of old forms atop new facts. From that uncertain and unsteady arrangement, and from the willed and even unwilling complicities in its practices and fictions, its indemnities and oblivions, flowed the turmoil of Restoration politics and the instability of Restoration culture: its theater of wonder and bathos; its inversions, mockeries, and transpositions; the brilliant variety of its satiric genres; the dominance of masquerade; and, above all, the triumph and the pervasiveness of irony. Irony was at once a psychology and a set of rhetorical practices that allowed and even honored the necessity of familiar political and spiritual and cultural formations while compromising their authority and denaturing their integrity. Irony was the distinctive voice of Restoration poetry and the solvent of its new, might we say modern, politics.

Modern and, of course, not so modern. The politics of the restored monarchy was harbinger of the new and remnant of the old. This was an age aspiring to the Augustan rationalization of politics, yet haunted by the past. And the historiography corroborates both themes. J. H. Plumb has given us the classic account of the new politics: the growth of party, an ascendant oligarchy, and progressive political stability.[9] But more recent study insists on the sustained relevance of the past: the religious dimension of this political world,[10] the significance of deference and obligation in the structure of its political institutions and relations,[11] and the continuity of its radicalism with programs at midcentury—a recognition that figures like Shaftesbury, Locke, and Sidney are more revealingly associated with the practical and ideological programs of the 1640s and 1650s than with the commercial projects of Georgian England.[12] Those who managed the practical side of Restoration politics became adept at new techniques—at patronage and corruption, at electioneering, bribery, and scandal—but even as such practices grew in authority and refinement, we must allow that religion still haunted this world, and that the structures of patriarchalism and the binding ties of gratitude were experienced, and not wholly as irony or nostalgia.

The acceptance of partisanship was a crucial feature of Restoration politics, but what I would call the modernity of those politics derived neither from the fact of partisanship nor from its accommodation—even triumph—but rather from the cohabitation of party with the conventions of the Jacobean and Caroline commonweal. The authority of older idioms had not disappeared; the conjugal embrace of king and nation, the sacred character of English history, the antiquity of the ancient constitution, the perfection of the mixed monarchy—all might be urged in 1660. But no one using such language, however wishful, however naive, could have sustained a belief in the integrity of those conventions through the decades following the return of Stuart monarchy. The Restoration comprised a world where older ways were situated alongside the new, and where both were held in suspension over civil divisions that might be denied or camouflaged but would not disappear. What emerged was a self-consciousness about politics, an anxiety over its stability, an ironic take on the efficacy of its conventions, cynicism and disaffection, and perhaps even a willingness to entertain the idea that the very structure of politics, and not simply the form of the state, was merely a convenience and a construction.

In 1660 the political world understood that the present had been abruptly layered onto the past; over the next two decades it came to appreciate not only the fragility consequent on this arrangement, but what we might call the *constructedness* of the whole. We associate that concept with nineteenth- and twentieth-century attacks on foundationalism in ethics or ontology; but I want to use the term to suggest a new and insistent concession to the arbitrary character of the state, to the politics not of prophecy or Providence, but of fear and prudence. It may not have taken much, even in 1660, to acknowledge the fragility of the state; by 1680 the state must have seemed not only fragile and patchwork, but a loose, perhaps arbitrary and surely unstable, collective which might be returned with dangerous ease to that condition where "all have Right to all."[13]

The phrase comes not from Hobbes or Locke, but from one of the most self-conscious and celebrated passages on political theory in Restoration literature, the little treatise on governance embedded in *Absalom and Achitophel*, Dryden's Exclusion Crisis masterpiece. I want to spend some time with this text because of its exemplarity and expressiveness. The poem exposes the temper of Restoration politics as it implicates an aesthetic of irony and miscellany in that politics. And while Dryden is supremely confident of his aesthetic, he seems at points anxious over his poem's sentiments and over its formal as well as ideological instabilities.

II

"Oh foolish Israel! never warn'd by ill" (753); late in *Absalom and Achitophel*, Dryden sketched a theory of the state, or rather several theories of the state, discarding one after another in favor of a kind of patchwork quietism. In assessing the political temper of Dryden's poem, as well as his self-conscious theorizing, we ought to note how carefully Dryden guarded his account of the politics of Stuart monarchy (the politics, that is, of patriarchalism) from charges of tyranny and slavery.[14] Indeed, so guarded is Dryden's patriarchalism in *Absalom and Achitophel* that we might think he had taken careful note (as surely he could not have) of John Locke and John Tyrrell on Sir Robert Filmer's *Patriarcha*.[15] There is, of course, plenty of antiquity, custom, and sanctity displayed in Dryden's poem; there are the familiar and comforting idioms of obligation and gratitude—those key words in Jacobean and Caroline politics—but there is as well a surprisingly wide scope given to political prudence, a willingness to put aside claims of divinity, sanctity, and custom for a position of least exposure, a minimalism and an argumentative latitude that allowed, at the very least, a rhetorical authority for prudentialism while revealing a nervous and indeterminate sovereignty:

> Oh foolish *Israel*! never warn'd by ill,
> Still the same baite, and circumvented still!
> Did ever men forsake their present ease,
> In midst of health Imagine a disease,
> Take pains Contingent mischiefs to foresee,
> Make Heirs for Monarks, and for God decree?
> What shall we think! can People give away
> Both for themselves and Sons, their Native sway?
> Then they are left Defensless, to the Sword
> Of each unbounded Arbitrary Lord:
> And Laws are vain, by which we Right enjoy,
> If Kings unquestioned can those laws destroy.
> (753–64)

It did not take a lot of courage to dismiss Hobbesian tyranny from the defense of Stuart sovereignty; but the tyranny that loomed on the horizon in the fall of 1681 derived more from the example of France (and from the religion of the king's brother and heir presumptive) than from the widely repudiated theorizing of Hobbes. Nor is it difficult to see why Dryden is quick to dismiss notions of the Crown as power in revocable trusteeship, a contractual pact in which kings are mere "Tenants to their Peoples pleasure" (776).

What is more surprising is the pending series of moves: the poet's willingness to concede the force, almost the right by power, of a people to fashion the state:

> Yet, grant our Lords the People Kings can make,
> What Prudent men a setled Throne woud shake?
> For whatsoe'r their Sufferings were before,
> That Change they Covet makes them suffer more.
> All other Errors but disturb a State;

> But Innovation is the Blow of Fate.
> If ancient Fabricks nod, and threat to fall,
> To Patch the Flaws, and Buttress up the Wall,
> Thus far 'tis Duty; but here fix the Mark:
> For all beyond it is to touch our Ark.
> To change Foundations, cast the Frame anew,
> Is work for Rebels who base Ends pursue:
> At once Divine and Humane Laws controul;
> And mend the Parts by ruine of the Whole.
> The Tampering World is subject to this Curse,
> To Physick their Disease into a worse.
> (795–810)

It is not difficult to detect condescension and irony, and surely a sense of grievance, at the opening of the argument ("Yet, grant our Lords the People Kings can make") or even to allow the rhetorical force of conceding a position that the speaker will quickly refute. What does surprise is the cover Dryden so quickly seeks in prudentialism, and the flight to metaphor with which he brings the whole passage to a close. At the end of the passage, sovereignty is no longer a matter of covenant, custom, or even prudence, but a mere cover, a tattered fabric to be sewed and patched, a frame to be buttressed and mended. Dryden's work as a theorist of the state ends in a startling abnegation of theory, though Dryden would hardly have been alone in displaying some anxiety over the handling of political theory. But the flight toward metaphor is more than a case of conventional nerves. For the hallmark of the passage is Dryden's willingness to concede the prudential basis of politics and in turn to allow, through shifting metaphors and figures of speech, the arbitrary and constructed character of the whole. It is one thing to concede, for rhetorical purposes, the force of prudentialism, even to allow under pressure of Civil War memory (a memory, after all, assiduously cultivated in the efforts to defeat Exclusion) the fragility of the state, the ease with which the "crumbling pagent" might fail. But the flight toward metaphor and the apparent eagerness to seek closure in this mixture of figures—statecraft as patching, sewing, buttressing, and framing—seem to concede not only the arbitrary character of political language, but the constructed nature of the subject. How different is this representation of Stuart monarchy from those mounted in the Jacobean and Caroline past, even from that imagined in 1660. The Exclusion Crisis excited a flood of polemical activity; we can find in its midst more ardent defenses of the Crown, but I suspect we cannot find a more knowing expression of the anxiety that attended those charged with a defense of the divinity and sanctity of a state that teetered once again on the edge of civil war. It would not, after all, be so long until the political nation would effect, by a judicious deployment of the language of Providence and a careful juggling of such terms as demise and vacancy, a convenient and hasty exchange of monarchs in a palace coup called the Glorious Revolution.

Perhaps Dryden's shyness with theory and his retreat into the familiar materials of metaphor and homily might be a way of defending the politics of his patron against those charges of absolutism so potent in the polemics of Exclusion. It may be that a defense against absolutism is being made by way of concession: Look, the poet might be saying, so far are we from tyranny and absolutism that the best a laureate might do is to offer his attempts at theory and his cautious prudentialism in defense of a monarchy that is itself prudent, judicious, and partial in its claims of privilege. Here is no high hand of divine politics, but an anxious and hesitant defense of current practice. Nor need we choose between the political temper of the passage and its rhetorical efficacy. As well as anyone writing of politics late in the seventeenth century, Dryden was aware of the past, of the chasms that might reveal a state where "all have Right to all" (794). The baffled and witty invocation of patriarchalism at the poem's opening, the halfhearted protest against party politics in the preface, like the cautious and metaphoric concession to the prudential basis of the state in the passage on sovereignty—all these moves, like so much of the layering of past onto present, of scripturalism yoked to lewdness, argue a poem and world keenly alert to dissonance and irony.

III

For those who chose to play at this board, the game may have seemed familiar, but it was not clear if the old rules still applied, or if new rules were needed to play the same game, or if new rules were needed for a new game. Some may have wondered if there were any rules at all. The reign of Charles II was dated from 1649, and the laws passed during his stay at Whitehall were named as if he had taken up residence the day after his father's demise. But few in the mid-1660s, and surely no one by 1681, could have thought that the politics of the Restoration had proved an easy recovery of ancient ways. Restoring the past meant the return of familiar languages and a knowingness in their use, but it also demanded an awareness of how fragile was the ark that had been recovered and how likely—despite its name, and appearances to the contrary—it would prove no ark at all. In that skepticism, that irony and self-consciousness, the particular character of Restoration modernity and instability is to be found.

But if irony and instability were the rule, how then might we explain the appearance and the surprising force in 1680 of that tract of ancient ways, that utter denial of skepticism and irony, Sir Robert Filmer's *Patriarcha*? The Popish Plot and Exclusion occasioned a vast literature of controversy, a flood of broadsides, pamphlets, tracts, and treatises; of sermons, libels, and satires; of elegies and anatomies; and the months following the disclosure of the plot and the lapse of the licensing laws in May 1679 seemed, even to contemporaries steeped in the habits of late-seventeenth-century accusation and animadversion, a riot of publication. But *Patriarcha* was not simply one more pamphlet issued in a circus of publication, and its simultaneity and the nature of its coexistence, indeed congruence, with *Absalom and Achitophel* need to be explored within the context of the problems we have been surveying. For it is Dryden's handling of patriarchalism that most exactly explicates Restoration ironies and modernity; the poet depends on the aura of sanctity that surrounds Filmer's patriarchalism, yet he is daring, casual, and at moments lewdly comic, even brutal, in his scripting of patriarchal themes. The poem evokes the power of old modes of political thought, but the evocation is calibrated against the changes that had come over both the structure and the language of politics in the years between the Civil Wars and the Exclusion Crisis.

Filmer's treatise was, of course, composed not in the midst of Exclusion, but in the crisis of the early years of Charles I's rule;[16] through publication in 1680, it came to live a strong polemical life during Exclusion.[17] In a quite obvious way, Filmer's exposition of patriarchalism is fitted to the topics, if not the temper, of Exclusion, that crisis of executive office and inheritance. Filmer provided a rationale for the immutability of kingly rule by tracing it to the model of God's original donation of familial sovereignty to Adam. Unfolding the structure of political sovereignty within a frame of sacred history and domestic sanctity, *Patriarcha* proved a strong text for framing defenses of the Crown. Yet the very foundationalism of Filmer's text was a burden for publicists of the Crown, suggesting not only anachronism, but the yet more unwelcome specter of tyranny, popery, and slavery. And that threat loomed on the horizon in 1680 in the form of French absolutism and Roman Catholicism abroad as well as in the person and religion of the English king's brother and presumptive heir.

At the time of the crisis, and in the midst of heated sloganeering, Whig theorists sensed the cogency of Filmer's case. Yet if we read Filmer according to John Locke, it is difficult to discover exactly what in the conduct of his argument would have engaged such theoreticians of liberty and property as Locke, Tyrrell, and Algernon Sidney.[18] Indeed, there are moments near the opening of the *First Treatise* when Locke seems puzzled by Filmer's sway over the political nation, perhaps over Locke himself, for he goes out of his way after acknowledging the success of the pamphlet to ridicule the rhetorical and intellectual thinness of Filmer's argument and to deride Filmer's simpering manner. We would expect such abuse, and worse, in the charged atmosphere of seventeenth-century polemics. And yet if Filmer's exposition of patriarchalism is dated and burdensome (and *Patriarcha* would not be republished between 1685 and 1889), the more sustained relevance of patriarchalism to Restoration political culture cannot so easily be dismissed.

Here *Absalom and Achitophel* as master code of the language and psychology of Restoration politics might best explain the anachronism of *Patriarcha* and the endurance of Restoration patriarchalism. My argument is not simply that this poem, or works like it, were responsible for the distribution of Filmer's ideas in ways more accessible and attractive than his tract (though that may well be true), but rather that Dryden's poem allows us to listen to the Restoration inflections of these ideas, to their erotic energy, their domestic sentiment, their affirmation of nature, their celebration of gratitude, as well as to the ironic deflation of the rhetoric of absolute rule in the wit and subtle and soothing pragmatism of Restoration irony. Dryden's poem is a window on the life of patriarchalism in the Restoration body politic and a brilliant demonstration of how the principles of patriarchal authority could be simultaneously stripped of their overbearing, even anachronistic, overtones and reasserted with a sardonic edge that struck some of the poet's contemporaries as fashionably atheistic. To readers in the 1680s, early Stuart patriarchalism might have seemed a hodge-podge of antiquated ideas, a stale and desperate rehearsal of Civil War royalism. But in Dryden's text patriarchalism emerged in a sleek and ironic dress that had the capacity to remind its audience of the force of such concepts as patriarchal rule and paternal authority, while rewriting those concepts in a brilliantly contemporary light which the poem suggests was antiquity itself:

> In pious times, e'r Priest-craft did begin,
> Before *Polygamy* was made a sin;
> When man, on many, multiply'd his kind,
> E'r one to one was, cursedly, confind:
> When Nature prompted, and no law deny'd
> Promiscuous use of Concubine and Bride;
> Then, *Israel*'s Monarch, after Heaven's own heart,
> His vigorous warmth did, variously, impart
> To Wives and Slaves: And, wide as his Command,
> Scatter'd his Maker's Image through the Land.
> *Michal*, of Royal blood, the Crown did wear,
> A Soyl ungratefull to the Tiller's care:
> Not so the rest; for several Mothers bore
> To Godlike *David*, several Sons before.
> (1–14)

The poet blurs the force of patriarchalism as a theory of absolute and unconditional obedience by underscoring the gratitude, the patience, and the indulgence of Charles II's paternal care. More daringly, Dryden charges the figure of the king as patriarch with the more than affectionate sexual appetite of what must have been recognized by 1681 as the king's fading libido. There is surely more nostalgia than realism or admiration in the image of the king's seraglio sketched at the opening of the poem; contemporary satires on Charles II's sexual performance rather stressed luxury and effeminacy than masculine authority. But the image of the dedicated agriculturist of these lines is not the only place in the poem where Dryden conjures the erotic energies of patriarchal politics. The body politic is given a powerfully erotic force both in the initial disclosure of the procreative within the political and in the blighting of Shaftesbury's production within this metaphoric field. For Dryden's Shaftesbury, sexual labor is huddled toil (a brilliant figure that just allows us to glimpse the physical within the sexual), and the product of that labor, "born a shapless Lump, like

Anarchy" (172). The verse hovers between allegory and libel, superbly balancing pathos against contempt, harshly particular in its sketch of the hunchback, grandly figurative in its conjuring of the productive and the anarchic capacities of the political libido. What Shaftesbury *fathers* is not only a "lumpish heir,"[19] but also a political program that would replace patriarchal harmony—a state tempered and regulated by eros and affection, by loyalty, generosity, and gratitude—with the ruthless disorder of a political economy in which trade and property are the ruling passions. It is crucial to the sway of metaphor in this poem that the erotic energy of politics be acknowledged not only in the ironic warmth of the poem's opening lines on Charles II, but as well in the suggestions of the lewd and libidinous anarchy and frigid appetites that crowd the sketches of the rebels, and not only Achitophel, but also Balaam, Caleb, and Corah.

What Dryden does in the fictions and figurative play of his verse is to endow the field of patriarchalism with a range of affect that takes us far beyond the Jacobean world of Filmer's tract. Patriarchalism was a potent thing in 1680, not because of the force of Filmer's exposition of *jus paternum*, but because the concept proffered, in a flexible and compact package, a broad rationale for executive authority outfitted with spiritual, domestic, and natural concepts and institutions. Dryden's exposition allowed a superb range of affect and irony to work on its behalf. And just as abundance, gratitude, and pleasure are part of the affective life of the poem's politics, so, too, is erotic suggestiveness and wit. It had been a standard claim of literary royalism that the restoration of monarchy signaled the revival of wit. In this poem Dryden's wit allowed the polemical anachronism of Filmer's patriarchy to live a subtle and brilliant life in the politics of the Exclusion Crisis and well beyond those years. The poem provoked translations, imitations, responses, keys, and anatomies that charged the figure of Stuart kingship as patriarchy with a broad imaginative life, not the polemical life of the English civil Wars, but that of the play and the ironies and instabilities of Charles II's rule.

Dryden's essay on Charles's paternal capacities rewrites the luxury, effeminacy, and indifference, perhaps even the corruption, of the personal politics of Charles's court as a fully contemporary, a witty and ironic, patriarchy. But if irony refurbishes the political figure, we must also acknowledge that it destabilizes and endangers, and not only the language, but also the dignity of the form. For the tow of irony in Dryden's poem brings us dangerously close to the very disorder and instability that it conjures to excoriate.

In that complex work, *Absalom and Achitophel* is emblematic of both Restoration political and sexual instabilities and the instability of form itself, the threatening miscellany and dissolution of Restoration writing and of Restoration politics. One of the most remarkable properties of Dryden's poem is its cultivation and denial of so many genres and modes: epic and lampoon, history and satire, Scripture and libel, panegyric and cartoon. At some moments the poem cultivates Virgilian piety, at others the manners of sexual comedy. Dr. Johnson long ago observed the poem's fractured allegory, its desperateness of effect.[20] Indeed, splintered forms and brilliant images are everywhere licensed by this verse, yet the poem seems intent not simply on cultivating but on combating disjunction, on making a case for coherence and stability while toying with the very disintegration it warns against. The poem may be the work of a singular master of literary miscellany—and the poet had by 1681 practiced all of the literary forms—but I would urge that it be situated within the broader culture of Restoration miscellany, of political and social as well as aesthetic practice. Literary miscellany has its local aesthetic circumstances, but it was as well a response to broader issues: to a general failure to renaturalize the body politic, with its hierarchies, obligations, and endowments, in the restoration of old ways (c. 1660) as well as to the perception and the presence, the satires and the send-ups, of social fluidity and mixture in those crucial sites of Restoration sociability: the coffeehouse, the theater, the parks and fairs and spas.

IV

Of course, neither the literary miscellany nor the coffeehouse was wholly innovation. The origins of coffeehouses in the turmoil of the 1650s and their associations with riot and Dissent have been mapped.[21] And the miscellany of the manuscript commonplace book had long performed the private work of anthologizing verse forms.[22] Print miscellanies were an important feature of the late-sixteenth-century literary landscape,[23] but the project of Elizabethan anthology was far different from that of Restoration miscellany. The early anthology aimed to stabilize a vernacular literary canon; a century later, the collecting, printing, and distributing of aesthetic mixture had become a way of marketing literary modernity,[24] that heady mixture of satire and solicitation, of piety and scandal, that *Absalom and Achitophel* so brilliantly enacts. The effect of the commercial market, of repeated editions, and of the rapid expansion, indeed explosion, of the miscellany in the Restoration, both reflects and participates in the formation of a new taste for fragment and juxtaposition, for ode and epitaph read against satire and theatrical prologue, for ballads and characters, catches and songs, read together with anacreontics and pindarics, for adaptations of Virgil read against translations of Fracastoro's *Syphilis*.

In those very terms we might read, as did the Restoration itself, the contemporary sites of sociability. In prologues and epilogues as in plays themselves, in panegyric elaboration as in satiric inversion, the social ensemble of the Restoration was an object often of scorn and always of comment. The earl of Rochester brilliantly cartoons the social miscegenation of religious, theatrical, popular, and commercial culture:

> But ne're cou'd Conventickle, Play, or Fair,
> For a true Medley, with this Herd compare.
> Here Lords, Knights, Squires, Ladys, and Countesses,

Chandlers, Mum-Bacon-Women, Sempstresses,
Were mixt together, nor did they agree,
More in their Humours, than their Quality.²⁵

And Rochester's "A Ramble in St. James's Parke" excoriates the royal demesne, newly refashioned by Charles II, as a scene of sexual, but more shockingly of social, promiscuity. By that term Rochester would scandalize not swiving but social mixture, not the whoring but the proximity of carmen and divines:

Unto this all-sin-sheltering Grove
Whores of the Bulk, and the Alcove,
Great Ladies, Chamber Mayds, and Drudges,
The Ragg picker, and Heiress Trudges;
Carrmen, Divines, Great Lords, and Taylors,
Prentices, Poets, Pimps, and Gaolers,
Footmen, Fine Fopps, doe here arrive,
And here promiscuously they swive.²⁶

Part of the effect derives from conventional and abrasive juxtapositions, the catalog as well of Juvenal and Persius as of Rochester, Dorset, and Mulgrave. But miscellany is the peculiar and particular aesthetic and social program of Restoration culture. Marvell's "race of Drunkards, Pimps, and Fools,"²⁷ like Dryden's send-up of Buckingham as a mere anthology of mankind ("Chymist, Fidler, States-Man, and Buffoon" *Absalom and Achitophel* l. 550), suggests unmistakably the rhythms and energies of Restoration political and social culture. And that mixture of ranks and offices, of the vulgar and the sublime, of pornography and portraiture, is to be discovered at the very center of the restless energy of Restoration politics and aesthetics, social practices and literary satire. Are there words more exact in their knowing embrace of miscellany and miscegenation than Rochester's invocation of nothingness:

The great mans Gratitude to his best friend
Kings promises, Whors vowes towards thee they bend
fflow Swiftly into thee, and in thee ever end.²⁸

The force of the verse lies partly in its spareness, its punishing exactitude, its careful rhythms and bold rhymes. But part of the authority comes as well from Rochester's juxtaposition of gossip and philosophical reflection. We know, as did Rochester's audience, that the poet conjoins not merely social abstractions, but the quite contemporary practices of a court that had through the 1660s and 1670s insistently joined, indeed flouted, the intimacy and bad faith—political, spiritual, and diplomatic—of kings, their creatures, and their whores.

Such conjunction and publicity is not peculiar to the years of Charles II's rule, but it is emblematic of institutions and tonalities that we can discern across a broad spectrum of Restoration practices: social and political, theatrical and literary. What had provoked Milton in the 1660s to denounce the miscellany and modernity of Restoration theater might just be thought, all due respect to his politics and taste, to constitute the particular genius (in our own and in the early modern senses of that word) of the Restoration—its embrace of contingency and arrangements; its irony and immodesty; the failure of heroic schemes, military as well as literary; its skepticism and reluctance, perhaps incapacity, to totalize in politics, in spirituality, or in aesthetics.

We began with Milton's reproof of the vulgarity of Restoration theater; I want to conclude with some reflections on the complex position of *Paradise Lost* within this culture. We have become quite skilled at reading the poem's traffic with the Stuart Restoration, its overt and covert engagements, the poet's allusions, and the poem's surprising topicality.[29] But we should not now lose sight of what was once honored as the poem's manifest altitude over circumstance, the ways in which the poem's themes and formal practices, its copia, complexity, and totalizing impulses, seem at once to deny miscellany and to yearn for a wholeness more idiomatic than could be imagined in the years of Stuart rule. The poem traffics with and repudiates empire and imperial sway;[30] it polemicizes by implicating barbaric splendor in kingly form and rule. At the same time it displays a pervasive nostalgia for integrity of imagination. The psychology and rhetorical practices of Restoration irony, those it repudiates as false consciousness. It is not simply, or at least not only, that the poem would repudiate wit, but rather that irony in this poem is the language and psychology of the damned. Of course, the poem's powerful dramatic irony allows us to embrace its central paradox, our sense of the tragic yet happy fate of humanity. But irony as wit, as soothing contingency, as compromise and masquerade—that it consigns to hell.

For all of Marvell's nervous appreciation, or Dryden's cagey admiring, of *Paradise Lost*, the epic did not begin to hold sway until after the Protestant redemption of 1688. In the midst of projects of politeness and reform, and when the poet's life had been spiritualized by Toland,[31] Milton's epic began its move, through edition and annotation, to an iconic status as poetry of the sublime, eventually to its position as the very emblem of Romantic integrity of the imagination. In that ascent the poem as contravening memory of the Stuart Restoration began to fade. Nor is it surprising that the 1690s would so quickly construe the former Stuart laureate or that court's most aristocratic wit, the earl of Rochester, as disturbing reminders of another age. We might be surprised that Rochester's stunningly pornographic *Farce of Sodom* was first published in 1689,[32] but its representation of the sexual and spiritual tyranny of Stuart kingship surely rescued for the 1690s, if not the pleasures, the ideological force of the text. And though the veiled Jacobitism of Dryden's lyrics and translations had limited appeal, their melancholy and sense of abandon would have seemed a broadly welcome valediction to Stuart irony and misrule:

> All, all, of a piece throughout;
> Thy Chase had a Beast in View;
> Thy Wars brought nothing about;

Thy Lovers were all untrue.
'Tis well an Old Age is out,
And time to begin a New.[33]

Whatever our own sense of the indelicacy of its politics and pleasures, this age of slippage and irony and masquerade proved a remarkably productive literary culture. We may not equally admire all of its affect, but of its abundance and energy and invention, and of the deep engagement of its cultural forms with civic facts and institutions, there can be no doubt or gainsaying. Indeed, so continuous are Restoration civics and aesthetics that we might even think that it was the very form of politics in the rule of Charles II that structured its pleasures, its poetry, even its imagination.

Notes

1. John Milton, "Of That Sort of Dramatic Poem Called Tragedy," in *Complete English Poems*, ed. Gordon Campbell (London, 1993), 507.

2. On Neoplatonism at the court of Charles I, see Kevin Sharpe, *Criticism and Compliment: The Politics of Literature in the England of Charles I* (Cambridge, 1987); on Restoration libertinism see Warren Chernaik, *Sexual Freedom in Restoration Literature* (Cambridge, 1995) and James Grantham Turner, "Pepys and the Private Parts of Monarchy," *Culture and Society in the Stuart Restoration: Literature, Drama, History*, ed. Gerald MacLean (Cambridge, 1995), 95–110. J. Douglas Stewart discusses the transmuted Neoplatonism of Lely's Restoration portraits of the Windsor Beauties; see his "Pin-ups or Virtues? The Concept of the 'Beauties' in Late Stuart Portraiture," in *English Portraits of the Seventeenth and Eighteenth Centuries: Papers Read at a Clark Library Seminar* (Los Angeles, 1974), 3–43.

3. The cultivation of Aretino at the court of Charles II is suggested by Pepys as early as 1663: "After dinner I went up to Sir Tho. Crew . . . and there I sat talking with him all the afternoon from one discourse to another. The most was upon the unhappy posture of things at this time; that the King doth mind nothing but pleasures and hates the very sight or thoughts of business. That my Lady Castlemayne rules him; who he says hath all the tricks of Aretin that are to be practised to give pleasure." [May 15, 1663], *The Diary of Samuel Pepys*, ed. R. C. Latham and W. C. Matthews, 11 vols. (Berkeley and Los Angeles, 1970–83), 4:136–37. See also the stage directions for Act 1 of Rochester's *Farce of Sodom*: "The Scene: an antechamber hung with Aretine's postures"; John Wilmot, earl of Rochester, *Complete Poems and Plays*, ed. Paddy Lyons (London, 1993), 129. On the proverbial status of "Aretine's Postures," see, late in the century, *The London Spy. For the Month of March, 1699* (London, 1699), 3: "In our Loitering Perambulation round the outside of Pauls, we come to a Picture-sellers Shop, where as many Smutty Prints were staring the Church in the Face, as a Learned Debauchee ever found in Aretine's Postures."

4. See Leah S. Marcus, *The Politics of Mirth: Jonson, Herrick, Milton, Marvell, and the Defense of Old Holiday Pastimes* (Chicago, 1986), chap. 1; and Kevin Sharpe, *The Personal Rule of Charles I* (New Haven, 1992), 354–55.

5. See, for example, David Underdown, *Revel, Riot, and Rebellion: Popular Politics and Culture in England, 1603–1660* (Oxford, 1985); Wallace Notestein's portrait of John Taylor in his *Four Worthies* (London, 1956), 169–208; and Jonathan Barry, "Literacy and Literature in Popular Culture: Reading and Writing in Historical Perspective," in *Popular Culture in England, c. 1500–1850*, ed. Tim Harris (New York, 1995), 69–94.

6. Sharpe, *Personal Rule of Charles I*, 359.

7. Early in the Restoration there were several conspicuously royalist publications featuring

Robin Hood. See, for example, *Robin Hood and his crew of souldiers* (London, 1661); and *Robin Hoods garland* (London, 1663).

8. On the king's character and habits, see Ronald Hutton, *Charles the Second: King of England, Scotland, and Ireland* (Oxford, 1989), 446–58.

9. J. H. Plumb, *The Growth of Political Stability in England, 1675–1725* (Harmondsworth, 1967).

10. See Tim Harris, Paul Seaward, and Mark Goldie, eds., *The Politics of Religion in Restoration England* (Oxford, 1990).

11. See J. C. D. Clark, *English Society, 1688–1832* (Cambridge, 1985), especially sect. 3, "The Survival of the Dynastic Idiom," 118–89.

12. See Richard Ashcraft, *Revolutionary Politics and Locke's "Two Treatises of Government"* (Princeton, 1986).

13. *The Poems of John Dryden*, ed. James Kinsley, 4 vols. (Oxford, 1958), 1:237, line 794; subsequent quotations from *Absalom and Achitophel* will refer to line numbers in this edition and be included parenthetically in my text.

14. On Restoration patriarchalism see Gordon Schochet, *Patriarchalism in Political Thought* (New York, 1975), 179–91.

15. On relations between *Two Treatises of Government* and *Absalom and Achitophel*, see Steven N. Zwicker, *Lines of Authority: Politics and English Literary Culture, 1649–1689* (Ithaca, 1993), 130–72.

16. On the dating of Patriarcha see *Sir Robert Filmer: Patriarcha and Other Writings*, ed. Johann P. Sommerville (Cambridge, 1991), xii, xxxii-xxxiv.

17. *Patriarcha* was issued twice in 1680. In 1685 Edmund Bohun, sometime Dissenter, sought preferment at James II's court by issuing a "corrected" edition of *Patriarcha*; Bohun dedicated this act of loyalty to "Regal Government" to Henry, duke of Beaufort. The book was not published again until 1889.

18. James Tyrrell, *Patriarcha Non Monarcha* (London, 1681); Algernon Sidney, *Discourses Concerning Government* (London, 1698).

19. The phrase belongs to Peter Laslett, who rather astonishingly borrows it from Dryden's abusive portrait of Shaftesbury as Achitophel; see John Locke, *Two Treatises of Government*, ed. Laslett (Cambridge, 1988), 28.

20. *The Works of Samuel Johnson*, 9 vols. (Oxford, 1825) 7:277–78: "[Absalom and Achitophel] is not, however, without faults; some lines are inelegant or improper, and too many are irreligiously licentious. The original structure of the poem was defective; allegories drawn to great length will always break; Charles could not run continually parallel with David."

21. See Bryant Lillywhite, *London Coffee Houses* (London, 1963); Steven Pincus, "'Coffee Politicians Does Create': Coffeehouses and Restoration Political Culture," *Journal of Modern History* 67, no. 4 (December 1995): 807–34; and Derek Hirst, "Locating the 1650s in England's Seventeenth Century," *History* 81, no. 3 (1996): 373, 383.

22. See Harold Love, *Scribal Publication in Seventeenth-Century England* (New York, 1993); Mary Thomas Crane, *Framing Authority: Sayings, Self, and Society in Sixteenth-Century England* (Princeton, 1994) on Elizabethan commonplace books, anthologies, and the dissemination of anthologies; Arthur F. Marotti, *Manuscript, Print, and the English Renaissance Lyric* (Ithaca, 1995), 212–28; and Jonathan Crewe, *Trials of Authorship: Anterior Forms and Poetic Reconstruction from Wyatt to Shakespeare* (Berkeley and Los Angeles, 1990), 118–39.

23. The standard bibliography is Arthur E. Case, *A Bibliography of English Poetical Miscellanies, 1521–1750* (Oxford, 1935).

24. See Jacob Tonson's proposal to collect the most contemporary literary contributions in order to form an annual literary miscellany, "The Bookseller to the Reader," prefatory to *Examen Poeticum: Being the Third Part of Miscellany Poems* (London, 1693).

25. "Tunbridge Wells," lines 92–97, in *The Poems of John Wilmot, Earl of Rochester*, ed. Keith Walker (Oxford, 1984), 71.

26. "A Ramble in Saint James's Parke," lines 25–32, in Ibid., 64.

27. "The Last Instructions," line 12, in *The Poems and Letters of Andrew Marvell*, ed. H. M. Margoliouth, 3rd ed., rev. Pierre Legouis with E. E. Duncan-Jones, 2 vols. (Oxford, 1971), 1:147.

28. "Upon Nothing," lines 49–51, in *Poems of John Wilmot, Earl of Rochester*, 64.

29. See, for example, Stevie Davies, *Images of Kingship in Paradise Lost: Milton's Politics and Christian Liberty* (Columbia, Mo., 1983); David Quint, *Epic and Empire: Politics and Generic Form from Virgil to Milton* (Princeton, 1993); Blair Worden, "Milton, Samson Agonistes, and the Restoration," in MacLean, ed., *Culture and Society in the Stuart Restoration*, 111–36; and Steven N. Zwicker, "Milton, Dryden, and the Politics of Literary Controversy," in ibid., 137–58.

30. See David Armitage, Armand Himy, and Quentin Skinner, eds., Milton and Republicanism (Cambridge, 1995).

31. Toland's life of Milton was first published as a preface to his *Complete Collection of the Historical, Political, and Miscellaneous Works of John Milton* (London, 1698).

32. On the manuscripts and the dating of Sodom, see Larry Carver, "The Texts and the Text of Sodom," *Publications of the Bibliographical Society of America* 73 (1979): 19–40; and Rochester, *Complete Poems and Plays*, 312–14.

33. "The Secular Masque" (1700), lines 92–97, in *Poems of John Dryden*, 4:1765.

THE SHAPE OF RESTORATION ENGLAND:
A RESPONSE

Lois Green Schwoerer

During my entire academic career, the most exciting era of study in English history has been Stuart England. For a long time the first half of the seventeenth century claimed the attention of some of the most accomplished historians in the business. They bent their minds to many fundamental questions: the causes of the Civil Wars, the nature and role of religion and religious institutions, the appearance of radical religious and political ideas, the shape and functioning of successive governments, and the interplay between politics and literature. They trained attention on society—and became obsessed with whether the gentry was rising, falling, or standing still—on the condition of the family, and on the role of women in both private and public spheres. Although fine work went on all during this time in Restoration/Revolution studies (for there has never been a dearth of accomplished historians!), none of that work (it is only fair to say) generated the same kind of intellectual excitement—excitement so intense that tears were not unknown and verbal fisticuffs a commonplace—as did work in the earlier period. Over the past twenty years or so, however, the focus has begun to shift, and late-Stuart England, which includes, of course, the early eighteenth century, now has a place in the scholarly limelight. Genuine revisionism, so long resisted, has taken hold in an era where it had been thought that the major issues were comfortably settled. New questions have been posed, some among them reflecting preoccupations of our own troubled late twentieth century, some drawing upon issues raised by early Stuart historians. The result has been to reshape understanding of the Restoration/Revolution era.

The essays gathered here testify as much. They give us snapshots, as essays do, of new or lately emerging concerns. But they differ from recent scholarship in that they are not *preoccupied* with questions of religion or gender or the Exclusion Crisis, although these matters have a place in them. There is nothing here, either, about the Irish or French or Dutch dimension of Restoration/Revolution England; one essay, however, does deal with the Scottish component. Rather, collected under the subtitles "The Politics of Violence and Revolution" and "The Play of Political Imagination," they stress English politics and political ideas and take up such diverse themes as violence, law, literature as a political barometer, Hobbes, a woman's political voice, imagination and memory in politics, and, from several perspectives, the Revolution of 1688–89. As one would expect and desire, they differ sometimes in their interpretations. Taken severally and as a whole, they contribute to the reconfiguration of the politics and what might be called the political "mental world" of the Restoration.

The authors represented here do me great honor in choosing to present their fine papers to me in this volume and, even more, in inviting me to respond to them. I am very grateful, and I thank them one and all. I am especially indebted to Howard Nenner for editing the volume; I hope my thanks and gratitude have eased the burden and will erase the memory of that heavy task!

I

One of the most striking features of this collection is the dark side of Restoration England that several papers expose. Restoration political culture emerges as more violent, more sharply divided, more absolutist, and at the same time more radical, than is usually thought. This vision of the society may well reflect the authors' sensitivity to the violence and division endemic in late-twentieth-century society and surely shows what may be achieved when a perspective embracing men and women from the middle and lower ranks of society is trained on neglected sources. It offers a sharp contrast to an earlier image of an era of the "Merry Monarch" King Charles II and his self-indulgent, amoral, lascivious court abounding in "wits," available women, and party-loving, theater-going people.

In no essay is vindictiveness and cruelty more explicit than in "The Hilton Gang" (chap. 3). Mark Goldie brings to center stage a particularly unsavory character, the informer, a figure heretofore virtually ignored in serious discussions of Restoration political culture. Here we meet Captain John Hilton, his brother George, and their gang of forty or more ruffians, including fifteen women, who actively and relentlessly persecuted Dissenters between 1682 and 1686. At the height of their influence, the Hilton brothers moved in multiple social and class circles spanning the ranks from near bottom to top. Politically self-conscious and not unintelligent, they perceived that they might advance their personal fortunes by offering their services as informers to the king to help him root out people, especially in London, who were defying the law regarding religious practices. George Hilton took the initiative in May 1682 in seeking an audience with Charles II to put the proposal to him; it was an especially fraught time during the Exclusion Crisis, when division and discord were intense and the Tories were intent upon dislodging the Whigs from positions of power in London.

The apparently easy access to the king, although not unique to Hilton during the Restoration era, still is to late-twentieth-century observers as astonishing as the king's go-ahead. The story shows that Charles drew ideas for trying to make the fragile late-Stuart bureaucracy work from many persons, including those far outside politically and socially elite circles.[1] Restoration society was hierarchical and self-conscious about rank and status, but Goldie's essay demonstrates that at times of controversy and disorder, the boundaries could be penetrated by bold and ambitious people from outside elite categories. In keeping with this perception is the thought, offered by Goldie, that the story of the Hilton brothers uncovers the presence of a kind of intrepid individualism in this society that flies in the face of some current preoccupations with community.

The "Hilton Gang" also shows how far persons at the topmost reaches of the established government and church were willing to go to implement laws against Dissenters, whom they feared as religious and political radicals more than they feared any other group, even papists. Goldie gives us a picture of a cruel and malicious central government and established church and, equally to the point, of subjects of the one and communicants of the other who were more than willing—because of some combination of conviction, prejudice, and greed— to make the lives of their fellow English men and women miserable. Interestingly, there was an important mitigating factor operating at the local level in the person of the constable. In showing how this lowly officer sometimes protected Dissenters from the predatory attentions of the Hiltons, Goldie also throws light on how late-Stuart government at the local and national levels operated.[2]

Informers and the political culture that countenanced them provide another reason why Restoration society was so deeply "fractured" (as Gary De Krey puts it).[3] The divisions go beyond those that underlay the emergence of Tory and Whig parties at the time of the Popish Plot and Exclusion Crisis. They go beyond the theological differences that separated Dissenters from the Church of England and dissenting groups from each other. The Reverend Gilbert Burnet offered a penetrating remark about the hostility and divisions between Dissenters and Anglicans in a sermon he preached on 26 November 1689. Doctrinal differences, he felt, were too "inconsiderable" to explain the discord. Rather, he asserted, "it is a secret dislike that we bear to one another"[4] that sharpens the animosity. Surely one thing that explains the antipathy and its intensity is the persecution of Dissenters carried out by the government and the church with the help of informers.

A political culture stained by violence is also a central theme in Melinda Zook's and Tim Harris's essays, both of which are directed to larger questions about the Revolution of 1688–89. Zook's essay (chap. 4) not only reminds us of the violence that characterized the 1680s, but also shows how ideologically extreme were radical Whigs in their writings and conversations. Restricting the term "radical" to those willing to use and justify violence for political ends, Zook has identified about one hundred such persons from across class lines; these were men and a handful of women who struggled against the establishment during the 1680s, from the time of the Popish Plot to the Revolution of 1688–89. Drawing upon these data and emphasizing in this paper the "lower circle of conspirators," she asserts that *all* Whigs between 1679 and 1685 were Exclusionists (thus contesting the position of Mark Knights, who sees Exclusion as a policy that came late and was reluctantly embraced).[5] She also contends that after 1685 *radical* Whigs had as their goal the removal of the Catholic James II, although it has to be said that some radical Whigs joined the king's side during part of that time.

It is unusual to find in earlier scholarship—Richard Greaves's trilogy is one important exception; William Sachse's early article is another[6]—contemporaries contemplating physical violence and voicing in theoretical terms political and religious radicalism. Zook brings forward men who did. Finding that "Whig politics truly began to radicalize" from late 1681, when it became clear that no peaceful resolution of Whiggish demands for a change in the royal succession was likely, Zook argues that Whigs, especially radical ones, created a political culture during that decade that assisted and justified the Revolution of 1688–89. She draws evidence for this point from the Rye House Plot and the trials associated with it; from Monmouth's Rebellion, Argyll's invasion of Scotland, and the brutal response to both by James II and Chief Justice George Jeffreys; and finally from the Glorious Revolution. Focusing mostly on individuals from the "lower cabal," she shows that their strategies took the form of plotting and implementing violence, legitimizing and sanctifying violence in trials and scaffold speeches later printed, and also creating a cult of Whig martyrs in published propaganda. The willingness of these men to consider brutal, unspeakable acts is demonstrated in little-known data that Zook has assembled. Members of the "lower cabal" in the Rye House Plot, for example, envisioned murdering former Tories, judges, ministers, and "rich old citizens [of London]." They suggested that judges' skins should be "stuft and hung up at Westminster hall" and "rich old citizens . . . hanged on sign-posts and their houses given as plunder to the mobile" to frighten the populace.

Zook traces theoretical radicalism by bringing together statements also connected to the major upheavals of the decade. Among the central and constant provisions in the radical Whig reform program were liberty of conscience for Nonconformists, annual Parliaments with limitations on royal power to dissolve, limits on the role of the king in legislation, shift of the militia to Parliament, popular election of sheriffs, and changes in tax policy. In setting out these terms of the radical Whig reform program, she argues that the demands would "have fundamentally altered the church and state in England."

For Zook the "radical Whigs" are the "real revolutionaries of the late Stuart era," and she is quite successful in demonstrating that point. Her essay significantly extends a portion of Robert Beddard's thesis, laid out in his lengthy introduction to the *The Revolutions of 1688*.[7] There he insists on the central part played by Whigs, including their radical wing, and the City of London, notes the presence of violence, and details the political miscalculations of James II and the Tories. But in this brief paper she perhaps overstates her position on the role of the radicals in the Revolution of 1688–89. First, she writes without qualification that the radicals' "insistence over the previous decade on the right of the people to restore the constitution provided the English with a justification for their actions in 1688–89." It has to be remembered that while that idea animated some left-wing Whigs, the "English" as a nation drew upon several other ideas to rationalize their deeds, including Providence, necessity, notions about the ancient constitution (as Greenberg's and Marin's essay explains), legal concepts (or sometimes concepts "coloured by law"),[8] and abdication theory. Second, Zook perhaps claims too much for Ferguson's tract *A Brief Justification of the Prince of Orange's Descent* when she writes that it was "probably the most influential tract published during the Revolution." While not denying its importance, one may debate whether it was the *most* influential of all the pamphlets printed during the months of revolution. For example, one may make the case for William of Orange's *Declaration of Reasons* as a tract of greater significance on grounds of its circulation, numbers, and place in debate.[9] Further, Tony Claydon has recently argued for the overriding importance of Gilbert Burnet's printed sermon preached before Prince William in St. James's Chapel on 23 December 1688.[10] Still, Zook's contention that the road to the Revolution of 1688–89 was "not nearly so bloodless, glorious, or tame" as it is often portrayed is well taken. The violence in action and language which she documents requires us to see the 1680s through a different lens.

Tim Harris presents his essay (chap. 5) as a fresh interpretation of the Revolution of 1688–89 in Scotland and places it in the service of "begin[ning] the process" of creating a "multiple-kingdoms approach" to the Glorious Revolution like that used by early Stuart historians in studying the Civil Wars. He is right to lament the myopic approach to the Revolution of 1688–89 that has characterized earlier scholarship.[11] But efforts have been underway for several years to change that approach to the Revolution and, beyond the point Harris makes, to broaden the perspective on early modern England in general so that the relationships with Scotland, Ireland, the continent, and the Americas are included.[12] Moroever, excellent work has recently focused on the Dutch role in the Revolution,[13] and done so with such persuasiveness as to convince the editor (not a late-seventeenth-century scholar) of another collection of essays that the Revolution of 1688–89 was not an English affair at all, but rather the result of dynastic and Dutch political and commercial interests.[14]

Harris, however, takes a different tack. Like Zook, he uncovers greater violence in the political process and the accompanying religious and political ideology than has heretofore been recognized. Arguing that the same kind of response to the catholicizing policies of James VII (James II in England) occurred in Scotland as in England, Harris presents an impressive array of new or little-known details showing "noncompliance with James, active conspiracy with William, and collective agitation out-of-doors." Among his most important points is that the violence was more "radical" than that found in England in that attacks by "self-consciously revolutionary crowds" were made against about three hundred Episcopalian ministers. Episcopal men of God were forcibly ejected from their churches, and manses and their possessions were destroyed. In other words, the object of attack was not Catholics, but Protestants who had offended other Protestants, namely, Presbyterians. These so-called "rabblings" were clearly against the "legal establishment in the church"; it is this that makes them so radical and sets them apart from what happened in England. Harris contends that men who perpetrated such acts of violence cannot reasonably be termed "reluctant revolutionaries." Their acts show the radical lengths to which they were willing to go to achieve changes in the political and religious establishment.

Harris's further purpose is to argue that the changes achieved in the settlement in Scotland were more radical than those won in England. It is a serious historical misinterpretation, he contends, to think that the Revolution was imported into Scotland from England, that the Scots did nothing more than react to signals from England. Although his interpretation of the nature of the English settlement is debatable, there is no doubt that the arrangement finally reached in Edinburgh accomplished significant changes in church and state that went beyond those achieved in the immediate aftermath of the Revolution in the Declaration/Bill of Rights and the Toleration Act. Seeing the changes as a whole, as Harris urges us to do, underscores their importance: the abolition of the Lords of the Articles, the denial of the king's right to impose customs at pleasure, and the effort to assure that the king would make presbytery the basis of government.

Harris's essay may well signal the start of further study of the 1680s and the Revolution of 1688–89 in Scotland and, it is to be hoped, inspire like work in Ireland. Further consideration of why it was that the Scots embraced advanced political views and were successful in achieving them are topics that deserve high priority. In that connection it seems to me that a fundamental question lies essentially—and silently—at the heart of Harris's essay, namely, the emergence in Scotland of a sense of national identity that assisted in the independent response to the Revolution that Harris insists upon. Broad interest in the creation and nature of a *British* sense of identity has recently enjoyed a revival. How and when a people develop a feeling that they are set apart by shared characteristics are questions intrinsic to the evolution of the early modern state. Linda Colley's *Britons: Forging the Nation, 1707–1837* is perhaps the best known of several studies of these matters. For Colley, Britain became an *"invented* nation" as a result principally of wars in the eighteenth century.[15] For Scotland, it is possible that the "invention" of an integrated nation resulted from the experience in fending off England and constructing its own response to the Revolution of 1688–89. Identity arguably develops from one's perception of the "other" as much as from the discovery of self. Colley and others (like Benedict Anderson)[16] have promoted the idea that a nation is best defined as "an *imagined* political community," that is to say, national identity is a collective intellectual construct. These insights could be usefully adapted in pursuing the theme of national identity for Scotland.

Offering still more to the point about the dark side of late-Stuart England is John Pocock's multilayered and subtle essay (chap. 1). His central theme is that cynicism pervades what Sir William Blackstone called a "wicked and turbulent" Restoration society. Responding to Blackstone's comment, Pocock sets out to discover the sources of that wickedness and violence and the nature of their relation to the constitution; he finds them in the cynicism of the era. By dissecting the nature of cynicism, he sheds bright light on the political culture—or the political mental world—of the period. If stretched, his remarks may also inspire readers to uncover their own interesting parallels between Restoration cynicism and present-day cynicism in the United States and Great Britain.

Cynicism, of course, is characterized by an inclination to find fault, disbelieve in human goodness, and sarcastically dismiss political or religious principles. As Pocock reads it, Restoration cynicism was rooted in the experience and/or memory of the the horror of the Civil Wars, the trauma of regicide, and the failure of the Cromwellian interlude to provide intellectual and physical security. Fueled by disillusionment with the person and court of Charles II, it was, above all, advanced by an acute self-awareness of an inability to discover—and, more to the point, believe in—principles that would explain the events of the midcentury. "A principal cause of Restoration cynicism," writes Pocock, was the inability to make sense of what had happened between 1640 and 1660. Lacking spiritual and intellectual confidence and convinced that political discourse was blemished by hypocrisy, contemporaries suffered from disbelief and guilt over that disbelief, the latter cast of mind, one might add, more disabling and discomforting than the former.

Hobbes is an important element in Pocock's depiction of Restoration cynicism on several grounds. First is Hobbes's view of God. In necessarily elliptical remarks (obviously this brief essay is no forum for exploring the big question of the nature of Hobbes's religious thought), Pocock implies that Hobbes believed in and feared God, but that his fear was not that found in a conventional reading of Judeo-Christian theology. Rather, Hobbes feared God on grounds of his dread that God might abandon man and not bother to judge and correct his ways, leaving him to stew in a "perpetual exile." Pocock muses that contemporaries who, not understanding the intricacies of Hobbesian theology (the intricacies continue to challenge and baffle historians), denounced him not so much because of his presumed atheism, but because they feared that they themselves did not fear God as much as they knew they should. This subtle interpretation puts a different spin not only on Hobbes, but also on how one might understand Restoration religious thought and cynicism.

Second, Pocock focuses on the implications of Hobbes's ideas about civic religion: his dismissal of the notion that the king needed to be head of an established church and his belief that people should worship as they pleased as long as they did so in private. The consequences would be to change the character of the English monarchy, since one of the king's two heads—the traditional (since the sixteenth century) head of the established church—would be lopped off. Pocock glosses this obvious point about the consequences in most interesting ways, first intimating that this view of the monarchy lay *au fond* of the Anglican fury at him and that it explains on a different level why the polemic against him was "overwhelmingly" driven by spokesmen for the Church of England. He is suggesting that Hobbes's point really changed the way people saw the world. Further, underscoring that the role of the king as head of the church had sacralized the monarchy, Pocock argues that were that head removed, the monarchy would be essentially changed not only in structure, but also in its very nature, for it could be perceived as "imperfectly legitimate because imperfectly sacralized." This idea was profoundly unsettling to people who were searching for legitimacy, for it plainly implied that the monarchy would have to be reinvented. What kind of monarchy would result from this Hobbesian view? One possibility was a secularized king ruling over a society of multiple religious confessions, to some degree what developed after the Revolution of 1688–89. Another possibility, and not unlikely in the circumstances of Restoration England, was a Catholic ruler who exploited the religious diversity to achieve the imposition of a Gallican/Catholic monarchy. If the latter occurred, the monarchy would obviously be resacralized and relegitimated on very different terms. This possibility appalled the majority of English people, but as Pocock observes, intellectuals such as John Dryden who were well read in European ideas, history, and theology found that solution preferable to a secular kingship or to one sacralized, as before, by the Anglican church.

Pocock's abbreviated comments provoke the question, How did Hobbes himself view these alternatives? There is a bare intimation in this essay that Hobbes himself, who detested sectarianism and had lost his fondness for the Church of England, would have preferred the Gallican/Catholic solution. The idea that Hobbes was a Gallican is intriguing, and it comports very well with what we now know about Hobbes's personal life, his travels abroad, the influence of humanism and Machiavelli on his thought, and, as Linda Levy Peck's essay in this volume shows, his connections with the Jacobean court. When we see him as a man well experienced in continental affairs and knowledgeable about Europe's intellectual heritage, it is not surprising that Hobbes should conceive of the authority of the English king in continental terms and prefer a Gallican to an Anglican solution.

The idea of a Hobbesian desacralized kingship in a nation of multiple religious persuasions, the response to it, and Pocock's reading of cynicism open the delicate question of whether or not in fact contemporaries really believed that a *true* sacral monarchy continued to exist. There is evidence that many did not during the Restoration, although they may have shifted back to belief in a sacral monarchy during the reign of Queen Anne.[17] The thought only intensifies the cynicism of the era. Pocock does not pursue this difficult question, but we are invited to do so.

The vindictiveness of the Anglican community against those they blamed for upending them in the Civil Wars, writes Pocock, "did much to create the wickedness and turbulence of Restoration politics." His point reinforces Goldie's essay. But cynicism remained at the heart of the era's sense of insecurity. In a nice turn of phrase, Pocock links the two: "The turbulence might come of sheer vindictiveness; it was the cynicism that made it wicked." Lacking the guidance and security offered by political and religious principles, people viewed with profound horror the possibility of renewed civil war during the Popish Plot and Exclusion Crisis and, animated by a cynical attitude, turned with special ruthlessness on their enemies. This bent of mind and spirit, Pocock suggests, may help explain the nation's willingness to accept any power which made civil war unlikely, including that of William of Orange. Pocock agrees with those historians who see the royal brothers as responsible for acts of absolute government and concurs that men in 1688–89 sought to counter such measures and protect the nation against them in the future. In these terms the carefully spelled-out settlement that put William and Mary on the throne in 1689 can be seen as legitimating politics and thereby addressing one of the fundamental problems of the Restoration.

The notion of Restoration England as violent and vindictive requires us to reshape our understanding of that society, obliging us to ask, What does all this do for our understanding of the power of religion in people's lives, so much insisted upon in recent scholarship? What does it do for unquestioning belief in divine-right monarchy? In sacral kingship? Further, we might consider that brutality, skepticism, satire, and corruption may well assist in creating a context that is not incompatible with the interest in the scientific inquiries of the era, inquiries that are ignored in the present collection but, of course, take center stage in other recent work. Moreover, this vision of the Restoration creates new circumstances for the writing of poetry, as shown in Zwicker's paper.

No one is suggesting that a description of the Restoration as violent, cynical, and skeptical can alone give us an accurate and adequate understanding of the era. Blackstone himself, as we saw, used his unflattering depiction in a concessive manner, pointing to the substantial legal achievements of the period. Howard Nenner's essay on "The Trial of the Regicides" (chap. 2) carries that thought about law further in addressing the nature of retribution and treason in the opening years of the era. Again, there is an interesting parallel between the late seventeenth century and the late twentieth century, in this case between the trials of the regicides in the one and the Nuremberg, Bosnian, and South African trials in the other; all these societies have faced the problem of how victors should handle the defeated.

Nenner tracks the evolution of the king's attitude toward retribution versus clemency, showing him intent upon only one thing—returning to or enhancing his position on the English throne. Over eleven years he shifted with the political needs of the moment from "unalterable vengeance to near-total forgiveness." As Nenner puts it, the king's "vengeance, like most of his principles, was negotiable." With respect to handling this issue, as was true in many other matters, Charles II showed his political acumen when, for example, in the Declaration of Breda in April 1660, he promised a general pardon and passed on to Parliament the final decision about who would be excepted from that pardon and therefore suffer. Incidentally, Nenner's less than flattering assessment of Charles conforms with the unenthusiastic appraisal of the king expressed in Ronald Hutton's recent biography[18] and with the picture of the monarch that emerges from Goldie's article in this collection. Charles II has always had a much better press than he deserved, in my opinion, and these correctives are long overdue.

Parliament itself made decisions about the exceptions not so much by carefully weighing the guilt of Charles I's enemies, but rather by pondering personal and political considerations, the whole process being complicated by the "tendency" of the two houses to "reject each other's victims." Clearly at issue in 1660 were the same passions as those animating governments and societies in the late twentieth century: the thirst for vengeance, the "kingdom's need to expiate its sin," and the degree of political wisdom in a policy of clemency. In 1660 the new establishment was looking to punish and make example of those guilty of rebellion, republicanism, and regicide. Yet the desire for vengeance was seemingly less strong in the early years of the Restoration than it was later on. The political need for conciliation operated to restrain the bloodletting to the execution of ten persons (an inconsequential number to all but those who suffered!) out of the twenty-seven men tried.

Nenner joins literature to legal and constitutional history in a fine illustration of the benefits of their union to show that the blood ritual was an important, indeed, an integral, part of England's political culture. Shakespeare's plays establish the point. The tragicomedies that draw upon the regicide trials, as Nancy Maguire has shown, could have carried the point further. So, too, might have a canvass of the relevant iconographical material.

Nenner's announcement that "regicide was not a crime" may well astonish some readers. He explains why this is so by stating the laws governing treason and quoting generously from remarks the prosecution, especially the lord chief baron, Sir Orlando Bridgeman, made before and at the regicide trials. According to English law, treason lay "solely" in the "compassing and imagining" the king's death; overt acts of various kinds—including regicide—were only proofs of the mind-set of the individual. Thus, the intention of the person is enough to convict him of treason.

The trials (as is true of all treason trials, I think) were marvelous theatrical stage pieces that reveal through the dialogue between prosecutor and accused not only treason law, but political theory. On the one hand, the prosecution stressed the theory of divine-right monarchy, reiterating the point that there is nothing on earth that has authority over the king of England, for the monarch, who in his person can do no wrong, is beyond temporal judgment. At the same time, an absolute king is under the law, a condition that secures the rights, liberties, and property of his subjects. On the other hand, the accused erected their defense largely on the argument of obedience to de facto authority, on the face of it a compelling argument used with good effect in 1649 and 1689, but dismissed out of hand in 1660. Further points to buttress the defense included that the person was innocent of malice and guilty only of "ignorance or misguided conscience," doing his duty or protected by privilege of Parliament against a charge for words spoken in debate.

Although a guilty verdict was virtually certain, the trial process was based on the law. The terms of treason law, as that law existed in 1660, were rigorously observed. This has been proved to be so in other treason trials of the era, which earlier Whig historians painted as kangaroo courts.[19] Nenner's essay makes clear that while vengeance and the need of the kingdom to take steps to purge itself of sin and guilt found satisfaction in the regicide trials and executions, respect for the law was a central element in the political culture of Restoration England.

II

Janelle Greenberg's and Laura Marin's sophisticated essay (chap. 6) illuminates Stuart political thought by exploring the role of memory and myth in its construction, an approach to history that would have astonished many earlier historians of Stuart England. Indeed, the very title of this subsection—"The Play of Political Imagination"—might well have confounded them. Today, however, these two authors are not alone in understanding that early modern European political ideas may be more profoundly discerned by asking such delicate questions as how memory of the past and myths that may be constructed from memory contribute to their development.

Focusing on the terms and legacy of a law case dating from the time of the Norman Conquest, Greenberg and Marin show how the case was shaped into a component of the ancient constitution and radical Whig political ideology from 1679 to 1700 as Whig lawyers, clergymen, and intellectuals remembered and applied the past to present political problems. Preserved in medieval and early modern sources, the case was available to early Stuart antiquaries, historians, and lawyers. They and others interpreted it to show that King William was no conqueror, but rather a law-abiding monarch who honored Saxon laws and institutions. Contrary to some historians, Greenberg and Marin contend that the nature of the Norman Conquest was an ideological issue as early as the first decade of seventeenth-century England.

Sharnborn's Case fortified the widely accepted assumptions about the ancient constitution, including an emphasis on continuity, the existence of an immemorial Parliament, and the power of past history to teach the present. A simple story easy to understand, it could be further construed to offer additional evidence of the ancientness of common law and individual rights and the idea that there had been no destruction of earlier laws and institutions in 1066. In fact, Sharnborn's Case was no myth, but the memory of it reinforced myths about the ancient constitution. In their impressively researched paper, Greenberg and Marin show that Sharnborn's Case was only one of several sources (such as the *Leges Edwardi Confessoris*) and several stories (such as those of the men of Kent, who also contended with William I over their lands, and of the struggle with William to keep the liberties of the abbey of Ely) that critics of the established government remembered and employed for political reasons. At no time did the enemies of the establishment do this more effectively than at the time of the Exclusion Crisis in 1679–83 and the Revolution of 1688–89.

It was at these two points of crisis when political tensions were high that the radical implications of Sharnborn's Case were drawn out. Late-seventeenth-century lawyers, theorists, and historians like William Petyt, William Atwood, Edward Cooke, and Henry Neville maintained that Sharnborn's Case showed that William ruled "by compact with the English people," and therefore, so should all subsequent monarchs. More, if kings violated the compact, their subjects were freed from allegiance and thus free to rebel. On another tack, James Tyrrell and White Kennett, citing numerous medieval sources, argued that the king had no authority to dispense with or suspend the laws. Denying the king this authority in the Bill of Rights in 1689 was a significant achievement for Whig critics of James II.

Greenberg and Marin very successfully illustrate how memory of the past operated in politics, showing how a law case was brought into play by partisan participants to help achieve a political goal in a "present" political arena. They add an important piece to Greenberg's earlier work in which she identified a radicalism in the medieval sources of the ancient constitution and showed how the ancient constitution itself could serve radical reform.[20] Enlarging significantly the intellectual context within which the Revolution of 1688–89 took place, they are emphatic in asserting that at that moment not only the king but the kingship was changed.

Peck's essay on "Constructing a New Context for Hobbes Studies" (chap. 8) is the only one in this collection set in the early seventeenth century—which should remind us that the century is not bifurcated at 1660, and neither should be the study of it. Since Hobbes's thought is important to the entire seventeenth century and beyond, a fresh account of the intellectual influences operating on him as a young man is of real significance. Peck maintains that those influences included a learned circle of aristocrats of intellectual bent—the "Bruce-Cavendish circle," she dubs it—at the court of James I as well as a cluster of public issues to which the youthful Hobbes would have been exposed. Those issues reflected the questions that animated this circle and included the union of England and Scotland, polemics against the pope, the oath of allegiance, and the Venetian interdict, dueling, and favor and corruption in the context of Tacitus. Peck's present essay, when added to her earlier note in the *Journal of the History of Ideas*,[21] is weighty enough to require amendment to the recent work on the early Hobbes by Quentin Skinner, Noel Malcolm, and Arlene Saxonhouse. Peck, while not denying the influence of the humanist rhetorical tradition, Machiavelli, the Virginia Company, or Hobbes's connections with Parliament, contends that the men and ideas of the English royal court must be added.

Peck's arguments are erected on two methodological approaches. First, in a tour de force of scholarly detective work, Peck uses what may be called old-fashioned positivist scholarship, a piling up of details until the conclusion is inescapable. Her essay illustrates what can happen when a historian with a well-filled mind comes across a tiny piece of evidence, in this case a list of persons participating in a funeral in London in February 1611. In support of her thesis, Peck surrounds this one datum with a mass of details drawn from contemporary archival materials, especially family account books at Chatsworth. She names persons in the circle who touched Hobbes and Cavendish, shows their movements and family connections, and identifies their ideas and writings. Her second strategy is to discuss the ideas and events that were in the writings and "before the eyes" of the early Hobbes and Cavendish as a historian of discourse might do.

Of great interest is Peck's uncovering of a "Bruce-Cavendish circle." Patient research enabled Peck to work out the connections between the families of Edward Bruce, Lord Kinlosse, master of the Rolls to James VI and I, and William Cavendish, baron Cavendish of Hardwicke and earl of Devonshire. The details certify the presence of a new British elite around King James I promoted by him and composed of Scottish and English individuals drawn closely together by marriage, friendship, and coinciding interest in governmental posts and issues. The very existence of this circle of men puts a different light on James's efforts to advance an Anglo-Scottish union and on the way in which individuals cooperated to that end.

Another matter that Peck opens is Cavendish's attention to the questions of ambition and favorites and Hobbes's reflections on favor, corruption, and court patronage. Hobbes's thoughts are contained in an essay, "A Discourse upon the Beginning of Tacitus," now attributed to him. Peck contends that Hobbes's description shows the influence of multiple sources: Tacitus, Seneca, Machiavelli, and specific examples in the lives of Cavendish and many others about the king whom Hobbes himself had observed. She notes that Hobbes distinguishes benefits and extortion in ways that draw upon but modify the Senecan view of exchange (for example, Hobbes declares that giving benefits the giver more than the receiver) and show his awareness of actual Jacobean patronage policy. In sum, by linking social, intellectual, and cultural history, Peck redefines the influences operating on the early Hobbes and situates him in a court culture. Her focus on the early Stuart court may, it is hoped, provoke interest in studying the late Stuart courts. Work is badly needed, especially on the royal courts of James II and Mary of Modena and of William and Mary. If approached from multiple perspectives, including the structural, political, social, cultural, intellectual, and biographical, this subject is almost inexhaustible in its possibilities. Models of different kinds of approaches are already at hand, as, for example, the recent study of Queen Anne's court by Robert O. Bucholz or Malcolm Smuts's book on the earlier Caroline court.[22] Linda Peck adds a stimulating and suggestive guide to studies of the royal court as well as of The Great Philosopher.

Hilda Smith's is the sole essay in this collection to address directly the question of women in society (chap. 7), although Goldie's chapter includes a discussion of the women who had a part in the Hilton Gang. Significantly, both portray women as more independent and more involved with matters outside the private sphere than commonly held patriarchal assumptions would allow. The small role for women's history in these essays does not reflect accurately the tremendous interest it has generated both generally and among early modern English historians and literary scholars. For a long time it was said that the history of Tudor-Stuart women was not doable because of the dearth of primary materials. Today it is clear that although often difficult, it is possible for the well-trained scholar with innovative questions at the ready to discover ample archival data about women and to use primary printed sources in ways to force them to yield answers and insights about sex and gender. The quantity of publications in book and article form and of conference papers testifies to this success. The recent appearance of reference guides also underscores burgeoning interest in the field.[23] Equally to the point, scholars now go far beyond studying women as victims or "women worthies" to focus on women as intellectuals, activists in politics and religion, early feminists, and figures in families and households and deal with basic methodological questions in reconstructing the lives and ideas of women. Smith has pioneered in the field and contributed to some of these questions.

Smith uses this present essay, which was inspired by her ongoing, book-length study of Margaret Cavendish, duchess of Newcastle, an eccentric and prolific writer in many genres, to offer what she insists are tentative conclusions and suggestive insights about the duchess and her social and political views. She treats Margaret's husband William, the duke of Newcastle, along with the duchess without shifting the spotlight from the duchess herself. This approach has several positive consequences. First, Smith not only deepens our understanding of these two individuals, but she also offers persuasive evidence that confutes the generally accepted picture of their marriage as well as of the relationship between Margaret and other members of the Newcastle family. By a fresh reading of old sources added to newly recovered ones, Smith identifies the areas of emotional conflict between husband and wife (his infidelities and unconscionable extravagance, her inability to conceive a child and her avowed support of women of second marriages who tried to avoid pregnancy) that invite fundamental amendment to the traditional picture of idyllic harmony. Moreover, the duchess was the target of her stepchildren's jealousy, apparent disapproval, and evident dislike. This personal animosity took several forms, including deliberate slights by her stepdaughter and intrigues concocted against her, but none was more bizarre than her stepson's dumping his own mother's body into the grave marked as holding only the bodies of his father and stepmother, William and Margaret. The figure of the stepparent was common in early modern English society and has attracted scholarly attention. Smith contributes fascinating data to this ongoing analysis.

Smith amends traditional understanding of the political and social thought of both the duke and duchess. By comparing the duke's *Advice to Charles II* with the duchess's *Orations of Divers Subjects* and the *Sociable Letters*, she discovers, contrary to some historians, some sharp differences. Without denying the now well-documented Machiavellian component in Newcastle's *Advice*,[24] Smith complicates his thought by insisting that it reflects the duke's "old-fashioned chivalric interests and values." Categorizing the duke as a "classic conservative" (which conforms generally to the interpretation of Thomas Slaughter),[25] Smith goes to lengths to illustrate the point, detailing, for example, the duke's attitude toward the militia, the press, education, and religion. The duke, an Erastian, was especially adamant against any toleration of religious differences, regarding them as the root of dissension in society.

Yet in effect Smith qualifies her designation of Newcastle as a conservative by underscoring what she regards as his rather advanced attitude toward women. Her close reading of the *Advice* from a feminist viewpoint (a perspective not employed by previous commentators) stresses Newcastle's adulation of Queen Elizabeth and uncovers his inclusion of women in discussions of several governmental policies, including trade, treatment of the poor, and the need for vigilance respecting the office of lord treasurer, as well as advice on sending gifts of meat following a hunt to the local lady rather than the local lord. It must be said, however, that to some readers (this one included), Newcastle's remarks may seem casual and parenthetical rather than indicative of genuine sympathy for or interest in women. But Smith is surely right in maintaining that Newcastle's "meshing" of the chivalric code with practical governmental policies respecting women was "strikingly unusual" in the seventeenth century.

The major thrust of this paper, however, is on the duchess's work as a political and social theorist. Anyone who knows Margaret Cavendish's works will doubtless agree that in large part because of their prolix style they are, at least at a first reading, difficult to understand and analyze. Smith is particularly helpful in identifying the multiple topics treated by the duchess and in sorting out the contradictions in the duchess's thought. On the one hand, Margaret Cavendish wrote in terms that echoed her husband's ideas and those of his wider circle. On the other hand, she articulated sentiments that were radical in theory, outrageous in their suspension of social restraints, entirely independent of the duke, and in violation of accepted norms of behavior and beliefs for a woman of her class in Stuart England. Thus, for example, it is astonishing that Margaret should write at all about lesbianism and incest, deeply taboo topics until the late twentieth century, even more that she should do so in a nonjudgmental manner. Equally surprising are her comments on a widow whom she criticizes for excessive mourning and failure to get on with a useful life. It is also astonishing that the duchess of Newcastle should write so sympathetically and understandingly about peasants and their work, attitudes, and family life. Her concern for a thief who had stolen to support his family and for the poor in general is expressed in dramatically radical terms. Invoking Nature rather than

God and conceiving of it as a female figure, Newcastle asserts that in the beginning Nature "made all things in Common," without distinctions of status and wealth. In language that Smith perceives as an attack on Thomas Hobbes (said to have been a great influence on her), she excoriates "Usurping Men" as the "greatest Thieves and Robbers" and "Rebels against Nature" for violently destroying the commonalty that Nature had created and tyrannizing over the "Generality of Mankind." Smith offers the fascinating suggestion that the duchess sounds a lot like Gerard Winstanley! In another place she will no doubt explore the social and intellectual relationship between Lady Newcastle and Hobbes.

Of even greater interest are Newcastle's views on rights and freedom of religious conscience. Worthy of special note is the duchess's assertion that governmental authorities shall not "Infringe our Just Rights, or Civil or Common Laws, nor our Ancient Customs." It is remarkable for an aristocratic English woman to voice such sentiments. Further, although stained by some inconsistency, her basic position seems plain enough: in sharp contrast to her husband, Margaret advocates freedom of religious conscience.

In this essay Smith, although noting that Newcastle's views about women were "unique," devotes only a little space to highlighting them. As she says at the outset, scholars have argued over the degree to which the duchess's ideas about women were feminist. Smith, who writes about Newcastle in her book *Reason's Disciples*, intimates that they truly are, although she holds out the possibility that the desire to shock had a part in the duchess's reluctance to conform both socially and intellectually. One will have to await the completion of her Newcastle project for a fuller exposition of that and other points.

An assumption long held by Steven Zwicker, the lone literary scholar in this group, is that an era's politics and political ideas are embedded in its literature and that literature is a particularly powerful and effective mode for illuminating a political moment, person, or idea. In his present essay (chap. 9) he uses a literary/critical approach focusing primarily on John Dryden's great political poem *Absalom and Achitophel*. On the basis of it and other literary evidence, he offers an especially sensitive reading (as is always the case with his work) of the era's political and literary culture. Dedicating his essay to "celebrating" the Restoration because of its "rule of irony and obscenity, its qualities of cultural miscellany and miscegenation," Zwicker uncovers these attributes (which he regards as unique to the era) in both political and literary culture, thereby, presumably, justifying the celebration. Describing the period further as one of political instability, social fluidity, and rank opportunism, Zwicker explains that these features resulted from Charles II's moral failings, the juxtaposition of high and low literary forms (epic consorting with burlesque, pornography with portraiture, comedy with tragedy), the mingling of persons from high and low social ranks, and the very design of government and society "constructed" (as he puts it) by the Restoration settlement, which "fix[ed] old forms atop new facts." This admixture of the new and old[26] had dire consequences—

"turmoil" in politics and "instability" in culture—and was evidenced especially by the "pervasiveness of irony." The suggestion that political unsteadiness results from the conjoining of old and new forms is, I think, enlightening; it conforms well with Pocock's insistence that the main reason for instability was the "unlegitimated state of politics." Further, the idea that irony was the "distinctive voice of Restoration poetry and the solvent of its new . . . modern politics" is also compatible with John Pocock's emphasis on cynicism. Indeed, irony and cynicism may be regarded as mutually reinforcing characteristics: the cynic points to the irony perceived in literature as further reason for his cynicism, while the writer of irony sees in the era's cynicism further reason for the employment of irony. But to see these characteristics all across the culture on the basis mostly of literary evidence, while intellectually exciting, is not entirely convincing to this historian.

Zwicker's interpretation of *Absalom and Achitophel* holds special interest and invites brief comment. He makes large claims for the poem, declaring that it "exposes the temper of Restoration politics as it implicates an aesthetic of irony and miscellany in that politics," serves as the "master code of the language and psychology of Restoration politics," and is "emblematic of . . . Restoration political and sexual instabilities." With several other literary scholars, Zwicker rejects the older view of the poem as a heroic epic, defining its genre (as he has in earlier work) as a mixture of forms that parallel miscellany in politics and society.[27] According to Zwicker, the confusion of genres underlines the anxiety in Dryden's mind "over his poem's sentiments and . . . ideological instabilities." As poet laureate, Dryden, of course, faced the responsibility of justifying the government's arbitrary steps and winning over moderates. To that end he released *Absalom and Achitophel* early in November 1681, a time of intense warfare in the press conducted by some of the most skilled polemicists England has ever produced. Thus, the poem appeared eight months after Charles II had dissolved the Third Exclusion Parliament, declaring that he drew strength from the conviction that he had the church as well as "law and reason and all right-thinking men on [his] side," and vowing not to be "bullied" any longer. The king ruled thereafter without calling Parliament, implementing, as essays in the present collection remind us, policies that were harsh and vindictive. Largely successful, his moves left the Whigs in great disarray. As Dryden put it in *Absalom and Achitophel*, "For Lawfull Power is still Superiour found / When long driven back, at length it stands the ground" (lines 1024–25). With their popularity, prospects, and standing beginning to fade, in the absence of Parliament in the fall of 1681, the Whigs began to contemplate violent actions. The immediate political context of the poem, then, was full of danger and instability, and the stakes for winning the minds of the people through the contest in the press were very high.

Within this setting, Zwicker holds, the poet offers only an "anxious and hesitant defense of current practice" rather than a robust justification of the divine right theory of monarchy, and he does so by employing irony generously throughout. I would like to suggest, however, that Dryden, however subtly and ironically he expresses himself, is ultimately firm and uncompromising in his defense of Charles. Announcing in his prefatory remarks that he is drawing "his Pen for one Party," he flags his subtlety by saying that he is deliberately practicing restraint ("I can write Severely, with more ease, than I can Gently") and that he has committed the fault of "Extenuat[ing], Palliat[ing] and Indulg[ing]." One may also infer from this preface a tactical move designed to quiet the political scene and appeal to moderates to support the king. His hopes for reconciliation are emphatically expressed. Within that context Dryden subtly chastises the king. The important opening lines of *Absalom and Achitophel* poke fun at early patriarchalism and its polygamous habits and imply a comparison with Charles and his royal court. But far from condoning such behavior, as used to be said, these lines and the poem can be read, as Howard Weinbrot does, as respectfully instructing the king to mend his ways and become a better father and monarch. David himself (symbol of Charles) was, after all, a "fallible paragon."[28] But that Dryden did *not* intend to assail Charles—to provide an "anxious and hesitant" defense—is suggested, I think, by the charges of hostile contemporary Whigs that he had done so. Henry Care, a Whig polemicist almost without peer, lashed out at Dryden as a "Bull-Dog" biting the king; such also was the theme of a poem by another advanced Whig, Elkanah Settle.[29] Dryden was too skilled deliberately to open himself to that charge.

Another possible subtext of the opening lines of *Absalom and Achitophel* also supports my point: that is, they can be read as a dismissal of the idea that the personal qualifications of the heir to the throne affect his/her right to the succession.[30] Dryden is saying at the very outset that Charles is unquestionably the legitimate ruler and implying that whoever his rightful successor is, never mind his qualifications, must succeed to the throne. This is not a hesitant endorsement of the theory of direct hereditary succession.

Further to my point, Dryden clearly says that Charles has the authority and power to deal forcefully with the crisis. On the one hand, Dryden certainly rejects the thought of a people having the right to fashion the state; his dismissal of anything more than the duty to repair is emphatic. On the other hand, toward the end of the poem, David/Charles asserts that "'Tis to Rule . . . that's a Monarch's End" (line 946). Reflecting what had indeed happened— the poet says in his preface that he is "only the Historian"—Dryden presents Charles as a long-suffering, patient king who, tired of bearing "these loads of Injuries," was "inspir'd" by God and spoke God's will: "His Train their Maker in their Master hear" (line 938). Charles is almost God, never mind being God's representative, in these lines. Haughtily Charles dismisses "Those heap'd Affronts that haughty Subjects bring / [They] Are burthens for a Camel, not a King" (!) (lines 951–52) and expresses his entire impatience with the "petitioners," a reference, surely, to the petitioning campaign orchestrated by the Shaftesburian camp. They are "Unsatiate as the barren Womb or Grave; / God cannot Grant so much as they can Crave" (lines 987–89). Dryden continues, asserting that "Kings are the publick Pillars of the State, / Born to sustain and prop the Nations weight" (lines 953–54). Charles prefers to rule by law ("The Law shall still direct my peacefull Sway, / And the same Law teach Rebels to Obey" [lines 991–92]), but Dryden portrays him as prepared to use force: "Must I at length the Sword of Justice draw?" (line 1003). Dryden ends by adverting to "Godlike David [who] was Restor'd / And willing Nations [should one read, "no choice in the matter"?] knew their Lawfull Lord." In sum, Zwicker's belief that Dryden is anxious and unsure in his support of Charles is problematic in my view.

For me the most exciting and persuasive part of Zwicker's reading of the poem is his contention that Dryden assisted in making palatable to contemporaries Sir Robert Filmer's *Patriarcha* (reissued in 1680), and that he did so in ways that "modernized" the text to reflect contemporary idioms and practices. This thought sharpens the ironic thrust of the opening stanzas, connecting it with the era's eroticism and immoral court culture, but it does not necessarily deny the point I have made. Zwicker's essay exemplifies the intellectual excitement that may come from a multidisciplinary approach to the past and the value that such an approach holds for a deeper understanding of an era.

III

As we have seen, several essays—those by Zook, Harris, Pocock, and Greenberg—deal directly or indirectly with the Revolution of 1688–89. They contribute to reshaping our understanding of it, but the fact is that the historiography of the Revolution has long been in revision. Even before the tercentenary celebrations in 1988–89, scholars had begun to reevaluate aspects of this central event in late-Stuart-Britain. The celebrations, however, marked a historiographical turning point, resulting in an avalanche of books and articles, among them a commemorative volume and four major collections of essays.[31] The pertinent essays in the present collection continue variously to advance the process of revision. They insist upon the presence of violence and radicalism in politics and political ideas in the runup to and duration of the actual event; or demand the inclusion of the Scottish dimension, both for its own sake and as a comparison to the process and settlement in England; or offer a measured appraisal of the significance of the settlement.

All this interest and ongoing scholarship is persuasive proof of the complexity of an event that earlier historians had made to seem simple and obvious. It is now generally accepted, I think, that the "Revolution was a multilayered event, more complex and subtle in process, ideology, settlement and result than has been recognized."[32] As someone who was for a time captivated to the point of obsession with it, I can testify to how fascinating the Revolution may become.

How one views the Revolution may have something to do with one's national origins; it has been said that Americans incline to see it as providing liberal underpinnings to Anglo-American developments, whereas English scholars regard it as a conservative affair that accomplished very little. But I think one's attitude has more to do with whether one approaches the Revolution from the perspective of its past or of the eighteenth and nineteenth centuries looking back. If one slices into political time at points in the sixteenth and earlier seventeenth centuries and reflects on the powers and status of the Crown and the nature of the political discourse, one will find not "progress," but difference, and be inclined to appreciate the significant change that was accomplished in 1688–89. I am delighted that John Pocock has labeled me a "Whig" and added appropriate qualifications to that term. I am pleased to stand in some kind of lineal descent from Caroline Robbins, who years ago, long before it was fashionable, taught me (along with much else) the value of the tract literature that abounds in Stuart England and much later seemed to approve my use of iconographical material and my interest in ceremonies and the press. I employed such sources in studying the Revolution, and with the help of them and many other materials, came to conclusions that differed from the then-traditional view.

There are a few features of the Revolution that scholarship to date allows one to insist upon. First is the matter of who was responsible for the settlement. Sixteen years ago I claimed that the Whigs should receive the lion's share of credit for transferring the throne to the prince and princess of Orange and for linking the offer of the throne to a claim of rights in one document, the Declaration of Rights.[33] Ten years later that same conclusion emerged from Robert Beddard's very close analysis of the politics of the Revolution up to the end of 1688. Beddard wrote that the Whigs "played an essential and indispensable part in bringing about the unexpected Revolution of 1688." In his view, they were the "real revolutionaries." The "extraordinary resurgence of the Whigs . . . lay at the heart of the revolutionary process." The point to make is that in an effort to see the Revolution as a compromise, which it was, historians have tended to overplay the role of the Tories. Beddard concurs, writing that the Tories were "outpaced, outmaneuvered, and outclassed by their Whig adversaries, particularly in London."[34]

The second feature of the Revolution on which historians may find common ground is the requirement of placing greater emphasis than before on the dynastic and Dutch element. Essays collected by Jonathan Israel and Dale Hoak's introduction to another collection of essays leave no doubt of that fact. Dubbing the event "the Anglo-Dutch Revolution of 1688–89," Hoak describes it without qualification as a "dynastic putsch undertaken . . . by a Dutch prince in concert with powerful Dutch commercial interests" for "reasons of state, the security of the Protestant Netherlands."[35] This seems to me to be an overstatement that neglects both the domestic English context of deepening animosity toward James II and the English initiatives, including steps taken by the king's critics after 1686 and the letter of invitation signed by the Immortal Seven and sent in June 1688 to William of Orange asking his assistance in the crisis. Without the prince and the commercial and political ambitions of the Dutch, there would have been no revolution. But the dissatisfaction on the part of the English with the government of James II and Charles II and the overtures they undertook to enlist William of Orange were also essential to the Revolution.

Third is the nature of the settlement. The idea that political leaders in 1688–89 desired no change, but rather crafted the 1689 settlement simply to restore the status quo ante now sounds rather quaint. In my view it reflects a misreading of the debates in the Convention and the terms and nature of the Declaration of Rights and its statutory formulation, the Bill of Rights. Compromise defined the debates on "what powers . . . to give the Crown . . . and what not" and underlaid the conclusion. But the Declaration of Rights that resulted contained terms (made law by the Bill of Rights) that achieved a new kingship, especially with respect to military and legal authority. This Greenberg and Marin confirm in their essay and other scholars have come to accept. Whether uncertain or sure, the authors of the Declaration wrapped change in words that were deceptive, denying that they had done anything new. Their language and political imagination have long, I think, distorted understanding of the settlement.

Even with all this, study of the Revolution of 1688–89 is not yet exhausted. A comprehensive examination of the pamphlets that were reprinted in 1688–89 would go far toward answering questions about the relationship between early and later Stuart intellectual and political discourse. Further, the sermons preached at the time of the Revolution were numerous, and their message reached a lot of people. Their circulation, religious and political ideology, and influence need to be explored. John Hampden, the son of the great Hampden of ship-money fame, was a player in 1688–89; a biographical study of this troubled individual would surely be of interest. Finally, J. R. Jones's call to "municipalize" the research into the Revolution, issued years ago, still needs to be answered.[36]

III

A number of other promising topics bear mentioning. I do so with the hope of provoking others' interest. First is the need for further exploration of Restoration print culture, a subject of enormous popularity among French historians and of increasing concern to students of England. As historians address this topic they need to take on theoretical questions such as the nature of the text, authorial intention, rhetorical strategies and reader response, questions that have helped enormously to unlock the deeper meanings of an era's social and political culture as well as its writings. On a different level, what cries out for specific study is the role of women in the printing industry. The work done to date has uncovered an astonishingly large number of active women, and a systematic study is needed to reach a more accurate assessment of the true nature of that burgeoning industry. Another subject who would reveal a great deal about many things such as rhetoric, governmental policy, propaganda and administration, and the printing industry (to say nothing of a fascinating character) is Sir Roger L'Estrange, Charles II's chief censor and major polemicist, an intellectual with wide interests and specific talents as a translator. Of nearly equal interest and value would be an investigation of Henry Care, L'Estrange's chief sparring partner in the press, a man who matched him in intellectual acuity and rhetorical skills. The author of the well-known *Weekly Pacquet of Advice from Rome*, in which he excoriated Roman Catholics and blasted the Catholic duke of York, Care changed sides when the duke became King James II and with the same skill presented arguments in favor of religious toleration—for Roman Catholics, among others.

A second subject of great promise and importance is the nature and role of Roman Catholic thought throughout the century, but especially during the latter half, when Catholic thought, persons, and institutions became political lightning rods. Virtually ignored, this topic has wide dimensions. One thing it would do would be to complement the work of such historians as J. C. J. Aveline and John Bossy,[37] thereby building toward a comprehensive understanding of the Catholic community. Another dimension of this approach is biographical. Studies of Catholic spokesmen such as Thomas Blacklow (the pseudonym of Thomas White), Hugh Paulinus (or Serenus) Cressy, and John Gother hold great promise. Also needed is a modern biography of James II that would build and expand on John Miller's study[38] and attempt a definitive answer to basic questions about the king's religion, his political intentions, and the number and role of Catholics, as well as Anglicans and Dissenters, whom he drew about him.

The third and last subject that I will nominate for future research shifts the focus to Europe and European Catholic nations: it is a multiple-*nations* approach, which should be added to the multiple-kingdoms approach pursued by scholars of the earlier part of the century. By *multiple-nations approach* I mean a broad perspective that links England with nations in Europe in terms of intellectual, cultural, and religious connections. Work of this kind is already in train, and what needs to be done instanter is a study of the political, intellectual, and social connections and influences between Rome and England in the seventeenth century.

IV

The essays in this collection contribute substantially to the historiographical reshaping of Restoration England. They show not only the complexity of the era, but also the diversity and complexity of the scholarship that it has attracted. Their authors illustrate how apropos to history are old proverbs, for as their individual careers show, they have been "rolling stones" that "gather no moss"; they have not "let grass grow under their feet" (!). Their papers have been erected on new questions and freshly excavated materials—or materials already known but seen in a different light. Their fresh interpretations are solidly grounded. In the case of the papers that deal with violence, division, cynicism, the ironic mode, and the tug between amnesty and vindictiveness, the perspective seems peculiarly relevant to the twentieth century. The social viewpoint in this collection varies. Some authors focus on elite figures; others include men and women from the middle and lower ranks of society. By implication one essayist inspires us to recognize that although this volume spotlights late-Stuart England, it would be wrong to think that 1660 was a huge divide across which ideas, persons, issues, and political and religious structures were unable to cross or crossed with great difficulty. Indeed, one of the most promising lines of inquiry, already underway, is the connections between ideas first generated in the earlier part of the century and then exploited and amended for various reasons in the latter part.

Taken as a whole, these essays deal with political history, cultural history, literary studies, social history, and intellectual history or the history of discourse. They make a significant methodological contribution by demonstrating how porous and permeable the boundaries actually are between and among these sub-disciplines of history and literature. For all these reasons, they help inform the study of late-Stuart England with some of the intellectual excitement formerly associated with scholarship about early Stuart England, and in so doing reshape Restoration/Revolution England and help us to see it in a new light.

Notes

1. Another example of Charles's drawing upon the ideas of persons outside the loop of high political influence is that of Sir Roger L'Estrange, who in 1663 managed to persuade the king to set up an office of the Surveyor of the Imprimery and put him in charge of it. L'Estrange's apparatus for censoring the press and punishing persons who violated the law was designed to augment the mechanisms used since the mid-sixteenth century and reinforced by those created by the Licensing Act of 1662.

2. These data conform generally with the view of the constable in Cynthia Herrup, *The Common Peace: Participation and the Criminal Law in Seventeenth-Century England*, Cambridge Studies in Early Modern British History (Cambridge, 1987).

3. Gary De Krey, *A Fractured Society: The Politics of London in the First Age of Party, 1688–1715* (Oxford, 1985).

4. The Reverend Gilbert Burnet, *An Exhortation To Peace and Union, In A Sermon Preached At St. Lawrence-Jury* (London, 1689), 15. Cited in Dale Hoak and Mordechai Feingold, eds. *The World of William and Mary: Anglo-Dutch Perspectives on the Revolution of 1688–89* (Stanford, 1996), 10. Burnet addressed the same themes in a sermon of much the same title which he preached on 29 September 1681 at the election of the lord mayor of London.

5. Mark Knights, *Politics and Opinion in Crisis, 1678–81* (Cambridge, 1994) prefers the term *Succession* Crisis, argues that Exclusion was not central until October 1680, and contends that party divisions into Whig and Tory did not appear until early 1681.

6. Richard Greaves, *Deliver Us from Evil: The Radical Underground in Britain, 1660–1663* (New York, 1986); Greaves, *Enemies under his Feet: Radicals and Nonconformists in Britain, 1664–1677* (Stanford, 1990); Greaves, *Secrets of the Kingdom: British Radicals from the Popish Plot to the Revolution of 1688–89* (Stanford, 1992); William Sachse, "The Mob and the Revolution of 1688," *Journal of British Studies* 4 (November 1964): 23–40.

7. Robert Beddard, "The Unexpected Whig Revolution of 1688," in *The Revolutions of 1688: The Andrew Browning Lectures, 1988*, ed. Robert Beddard (Oxford, 1991), 11–101.

8. Howard Nenner, *By Colour of Law: Legal Culture and Constitutional Politics in England, 1660–1689* (Chicago, 1977).

9. *Declaration of His Highness William Henry, Prince of Orange, the Reasons Inducing Him to appear in Armes in the Kingdom of England for Preserving of the Protestant Religion and for Restoring the Laws and Liberties of England, Scotland, and Ireland*. See Lois G. Schwoerer, "Propaganda in the Revolution of 1688–89," *American Historical Review* 82 (1977): 843–74.

10. Tony Claydon, *William III and the Godly Revolution* (Cambridge, 1996).

11. Interestingly, early-eighteeenth-century historians included Scotland and Ireland in their accounts of the Revolution of 1688–89.

12. Essays on the connection between the Glorious Revolution and all those just named areas appeared in Lois G. Schwoerer, ed., *The Revolution of 1688–89: Changing Perspectives* (Cambridge, 1992). The Folger Institute Center for the History of British Political Thought, founded in 1984, has as its steering committee J. G. A. Pocock, Gordon J. Schochet, and Lois G. Schwoerer. Two volumes pertinent to the point have been published: Roger A. Mason, ed., *Scots and Britons: Scottish Political Thought and the Union of 1603* (Cambridge, 1994) and John Robertson, ed., *A Union for Empire: Political Thought and the Union of 1707* (Cambridge, 1995).

13. Jonathan I. Israel, ed., *The Anglo-Dutch Moment: Essays on the Glorious Revolution and its World Impact* (Cambridge, 1991).

14. Dale Hoak, "The Anglo-Dutch Revolution of 1688–89," in *The World of William and Mary*, ed. Hoak and Feingold, 1–28. See Pocock's comment above in chap. 1, n.10.

15. Linda Colley, *Britons Forging the Nation, 1707–1837* (New Haven, 1992).

16. Benedict Anderson, *Imagined Communities: Reflections on the Origin and Spread of Nationalism* (London, 1991).

17. Paul Kleber Monod, *Jacobitism and the English People, 1688–1788* (Cambridge, 1989).

18. Ronald Hutton, *Charles the Second: King of England, Scotland, and Ireland* (Oxford, 1989).

19. Lois G. Schwoerer, "The Trial of Lord William Russell (1683): Judicial Murder?" *Journal of Legal History* 9 (1988): 142–68.

20. Janelle Greenberg, "The Confessor's Laws and the Radical Face of the Ancient Constitution," *English Historical Review* 104 (1989): 611–37.

21. Linda Levy Peck, "Hobbes on the Grand Tour: Paris, Venice, or London?" *Journal of the History of Ideas* 57 (1996): 177–83. She shows that Hobbes and his pupil, William, Lord Cavendish, were at that funeral and not, as long thought, on the continent engaged in a lengthy Grand Tour lasting from 1610 to 1615. It has to be said that neither in the note nor in the present essay does Peck successfully prove that the Grand Tour lasted only for six months in 1614–15, as she says. What she does prove is that the two men were not on the continent in 1610 and 1611.

22. Robert O. Bucholz, *The Augustan Court: Queen Anne and the Decline of Court Culture* (Stanford, 1993); R. Malcolm Smuts, *Court Culture and the Origins of a Royalist Tradition in Early Stuart England* (Philadelphia, 1987).

23. Hilda Smith and Susan Cardinale, comps., *Women and the Literature of the Seventeenth Century: An Annotated Bibliography Based on Wing's Short-Title Catalogue* (New York, 1990).

24. Conal Condren, "Casuistry to Newcastle: *The Prince* in the World of the Book," in *Political Discourse in Early Modern Britain*, ed. Nicholas Phillipson and Quentin Skinner (Cambridge, 1993), 164–88.

25. Thomas P. Slaughter, *Ideology and Politics on the Eve of the Restoration: Newcastle's Advice to Charles II* (Philadelphia, 1984).

26. Zwicker's assignment of the techniques of "patronage and corruption, electioneering, bribery, and scandal" to the category of *new* features of the era is debatable in light of what we know about the uses of these techniques earlier in the century.

27. See Steven N. Zwicker, *Politics and Language in Dryden's Poetry: The Arts of Disguise* (Princeton, 1984).

28. Howard Weinbrot, "'Nature's Holy Bands' in *Absalom and Achitophel*: Fathers and Sons, Satire and Change," *Modern Philology* 85 (May 1988): 373–92 (quoted passage 378).

29. Henry Care, *Towser the Second: A Bull-Dog* (London, 1681); Elkanah Settle, *Absalom Senior; or, Achitophel Transpros'd* (London, 1682). Other responses are reported in Weinbrot, "Nature's Holy Bands," 378.

30. George deF. Lord, "*Absalom and Achitophel* and Dryden's Political Cosmos," in *Writers and their Background: John Dryden*, ed. Earl Roy Miner (Athens, Ohio, 1972), 171.

31. William Speck, *Reluctant Revolutionaries: Englishmen and the Revolution of 1688* (Oxford, 1988); and volumes edited respectively by Hoak and Feingold, Beddard, Israel, and myself (see nn.4, 7, 12, 13).

32. Schwoerer, Introduction, *Revolution of 1688–89*, 12.

33. Lois G. Schwoerer, *The Declaration of Rights, 1689* (Baltimore, 1981), 286 and passim.

34. Beddard, "Unexpected Whig Revolution of 1688"; see especially 18, 19, 21, 22, 42, 43.

35. Hoak, "Anglo-Dutch Revolution of 1688," 26.

36. J. R. Jones, *The Revolution of 1688* (London, 1972).

37. Several books by Aveling were published by the Catholic Record Society starting in 1963. John Bossy, *The English Catholic Community, 1570–1850* (London, 1976).

38. John Miller, *James II: A Study in Kingship* (Hove, East Sussex, 1978). Earlier still: F. C. Turner, *James II* (London, 1948).

Selected Publications of Lois Green Schwoerer

Books

The Varieties of British Political Thought, 1500–1800, ed. J. G. A. Pocock, with the assistance of Gordon J. Schochet and Lois G. Schwoerer (Cambridge, 1993).

The Revolution of 1688–89: Changing Perspectives, ed. Lois G. Schwoerer (Cambridge, 1992).

Lady Rachel Russell: "One of the Best of Women" (Baltimore, 1988).

The Declaration of Rights, 1689 (Baltimore, 1981).

"No Standing Armies!": The Antiarmy Ideology in Seventeenth-Century England (Baltimore, 1974).

Articles and Chapters in Books

"Women's Public Political Voice in England, 1640–1700," in *Women Writers and the Early Modern British Tradition*, ed. Hilda L. Smith (Cambridge, 1997), 56–74.

"British Lineages. American Choices," in *The Bill of Rights: Government Proscribed*, ed. Ronald Hoffman and Peter J. Albert (Charlottesville, Va., 1997), 1–41.

"The Bill of Rights Revisited, 1689–1989," in *The World of William and Mary: Anglo-Dutch Perspectives on the Revolution of 1688–89*, ed. Dale Hoak and Mordechai Feingold (Stanford, 1996), 42–58.

"The Attempted Impeachment of Sir William Scroggs, Lord Chief Justice of the Court of King's Bench, November 1680–March 1681," *Historical Journal* 38 (1995): 843–74.

"The English Bill of Rights, 1689: A Perspective on Liberty," in *Three Beginnings: Revolution, Rights, and the Liberal State: Comparative Perspectives on the English, American, and French Revolutions*, ed. Stephen F. Englehart and John Allphin Moore, Jr. (New York, 1994), 93–114.

"The Right to Resist: Whig Resistance Theory, 1688 to 1694," in *Political Discourse in Early Modern Britain*, ed. Nicholas Phillipson and Quentin Skinner (Cambridge, 1993), 232–52.

"Liberty of the Press and Public Opinion, 1660–1696," in *Liberty Secured? Britain Before and After 1688*, ed. J. R. Jones (Stanford, 1992), 199–230.

"Locke, Lockean Ideas, and the Glorious Revolution," *Journal of the History of Ideas* 51 (1990): 31–48.

"Celebrating the Glorious Revolution, 1688–1989," *Albion* 22 (1990): 1–20.

"Images of Queen Mary II, 1688–95," *Renaissance Quarterly* 42 (1989): 717–48.

"The Queen as Regent and Patron," in *The Age of William III and Mary II: Power, Politics, and Patronage, 1688–1702*, ed. Robert P. Maccubbin and Martha Hamilton-Phillips (Williamsburg, Va., 1989), 217–24.

"The Trial of Lord William Russell (1683): Judicial Murder?" *Journal of Legal History* 9 (1988): 142–68.

"The Role of Lawyers in the Revolution of 1688–89," in *Die Rolle der Juristen bei der Entstehung des modernen Staates*, ed. Roman Schnur (Berlin, 1986), 473–97.

"Women and the Glorious Revolution," *Albion* 18 (Summer 1986): 195–218.

"William, Lord Russell: The Making of a Martyr, 1683–1983," *Journal of British Studies* 24 (1985): 41–71.

"Seventeenth-Century English Women Engraved in Stone?" *Albion* 16 (1984): 389–403.

"The Transformation of the Convention into a Parliament, February 1689," *Parliamentary History* 3 (1984): 57–76.

"The Contributions of the Declaration of Rights to Anglo-American Radicalism," in *The Origins of Anglo-American Radicalism*, ed. Margaret Jacob and James Jacob (London, 1983), 105–24.

"The Glorious Revolution as Spectacle: A New Perspective," in *England's Rise to Greatness, 1660–1763*, ed. Stephen B. Baxter (Berkeley and Los Angeles, 1983), 109–50.

"The Bill of Rights: Epitome of the Revolution of 1688–89," in *Three British Revolutions, 1641, 1688, 1776*, ed. J. G. A. Pocock (Princeton, 1980), 224–43.

"Propaganda in the Revolution of 1688–89," *American Historical Review* 82 (1977): 843–74.

"Press and Parliament in the Revolution of 1689," *Historical Journal* 20 (1977): 545–68.

"A Jornall of the Convention at Westminster begun the 22 of January 1688/9," *Bulletin of the Institute of Historical Research* 49 (1976): 242–63; reprinted in *A Parliamentary History of the Glorious Revolution*, ed. David Lewis Jones (London, 1988), 232–47.

"The Fittest Subject for a King's Quarrel—An Essay on the Militia Controversy, 1641–42," *Journal of British Studies* 11 (1971): 45–76.

"Lord Halifax's Visit to Germany, November 1937," *The Historian* 32 (1970): 353–75.

"Chronology and Authorship of the Standing Army Tracts, 1697–1799," *Notes and Queries* 211, n.s. 13 (1966): 382–90.

"The Role of King William III of England in the Standing Army Controversy, 1697–1699," *Journal of British Studies* 5 (1966): 74–94.

"The Literature of the Standing Army Controversy, 1697–1699," *Huntington Library Quarterly* 28 (1965): 187–212.

"Roger North and his Notes on Legal Education," *Huntington Library Quarterly* 22 (1959): 323–43.

"The Chronology of Roger North's Major Works," *History of Ideas News Letter* 3 (1957): 73–78.

Index

Alsop, Vincent, 57
Anderson, Benedict, 202
Anne, Queen, 79, 204, 209
Annesley, Samuel, 61, 67
Antrobus, Benjamin, 53
Argall, John, 168
Armiger, Sir Clement, 55, 63
Armstrong, Sir Thomas, 77
Atwood, William, 122, 133, 134, 208
Austin, Charles, 65
Aveline, J. C. J., 218
Axtell, Daniel, 29, 33, 36, 37
Ayloffe, John, 77, 78
Ayscu, Edward, 127
Ayton, Sir Robert, 170

Bacon, Sir Francis, 156, 170, 174; *Advancement of Learning*, 173
Bacon, Nathaniel, 122, 129; *An Historical Discourse of the Uniformity of the Government of England*, 129, 136
Baker, Charles, 65
Baker, Keith Michael, 136
Baker, Sir Richard, 124, 126, 129; *Chronicle of the Kings of England*, 129
Bateman, Charles, 88
Bates, Robert, 59
Baxter, Richard, 53, 56, 57
Beare, John, 45
Beckford, Sir Thomas, 55, 65
Beddard, Robert, 200, 216
Behn, Aphra, 87
Bellamy, Anne, 46
Bellarmine, Cardinal, 174
Bethel, Slingsby, 49, 50
Blackadder, William, 105
Blacklow, Thomas, 218
Blackstone, Sir William, 11, 12, 17, 18, 202, 204, 205
Booth, Sir George, 22
Booth, George, Lord Delamere, 80
Booth, Henry, Lord Delamere, 80, 89
Booth, John, 145
Bossy, John, 218
Bowyer, Robert, 167
Brackley, Lady Elizabeth, 145
Braddon, Laurence, 81

Bradshaw, John, 22
Brady, Robert, 123, 125, 132, 133, 134, 135, 136; *Complete History*, 135
Brahe, Tycho, 165
Bridgeman, Orlando, 25-38, 206
Brown, Robert, 25
Brown, John, 47, 62, 64, 65
Bruce, Christian, Lady Cavendish, 164, 166, 170
Bruce, Edward, Lord Kinlosse, 161, 165, 166, 167, 168, 170, 209
Bruce, Magdalen, 165
Bruce, Peter, 106
Bruce, Robert, earl of Ailesbury, 165
Bruce, Thomas, 161, 165, 166
Bucholz, Robert O., 209
Burke, Edmund, 1
Burnet, Gilbert, 1, 64, 104, 112, 199, 201
Burton, Philip, 63, 64
Butler, James, duke of Ormonde, 14
Butler, Sir James, 55, 62
Butterfield, Herbert, 11

Camden, William, 124, 125, 126, 127, 134; *Britannia*, 126, 127
Campbell, Archibald, earl of Argyll, 86, 100, 105
Canaries, James, 101, 110
Capel, Arthur, earl of Essex, 80, 81, 82, 84
Care, Henry, 7, 214, 218; *Public Occurrences*, 65; *Weekly Pacquet of Advice from Rome*, 218
Carew, Sir George, 167
Carew, John, 32, 33
Carr, Robert, earl of Somerset, 167
Carstares, William, 105
Cary, Valentine, 168
Cavendish, Charles, 144
Cavendish, Henry, 145, 146
Cavendish, Margaret, duchess of Newcastle, 4, 143-56 passim, 210, 211, 212; *The Blazing World*, 155; *Orations of Divers Subjects*, 147, 152, 153, 211; *Sociable Letters*, 147, 151, 153, 154; *The Unnatural Tragedy*, 155
Cavendish, William (1617-84), 165
Cavendish, Sir William (1591-1628), 161-75 passim, 209; *Discourse on Flatterie*, 163, 164; *Horae Subsecivae*, 162, 164, 170-71

Cavendish, Lord William (1552-1626), 161, 162, 163, 164, 170, 172, 209
Cavendish, William, duke of Newcastle, 4, 143–56 passim, 210, 211, 212; *Advice to Charles II*, 147–50, 211
Cecil, Robert, earl of Salisbury, 163, 164, 167, 174
Cellier, Elizabeth, 49
Chamberlain, John, 167, 169
Charles I, 13, 17, 22, 23, 24, 25, 26, 27, 28, 29, 30, 31, 32, 33, 35, 37, 38, 113, 148, 151, 165, 181, 187, 206
Charles II, 2, 5, 14, 15, 18, 21, 22, 38, 43, 46, 48, 49, 55, 58, 67, 79, 81, 89, 111, 113, 132, 147, 148, 149, 150, 165, 181, 182, 186, 188, 189, 193, 198, 205, 206, 212, 213, 214, 215, 217, 218
Charles, Nicholas, 161
Cheyne, Lady Jane, 145
Churchill, John, 11
Clark, Jonathan, 11
Claydon, Tony, 201
Clayton, Arthur, 47, 65
Clayton, Sir Robert, 53, 57, 59, 61, 65, 79
Cleeve, William, 62
Cleland, William, 105
Clement, Gregory, 32, 33
College, Stephen, 49, 78, 81
Collingwood, Hester, 47, 55, 57, 63, 65
Collingwood, John, 47
Collins, Samuel, 168
Coke, Sir Edward, 131, 134
Colley, Linda, 202
Cook, John, 26, 33, 34, 35, 36
Cooke, Edward, 122, 134, 208; *Argumentum Anti-Normannicum*, 134, 136
Cooper, Anthony Ashley, earl of Shaftesbury, 77, 80, 82, 84, 182, 188, 189
Cornish, Henry, 49, 50, 53, 55, 78, 88
Cowan, Ian, 98
Coward, William, 59
Cowell, John, 124
Coxe, Thomas, 56
Craig, John, 165
Craig, Sir Thomas, 127, 165
Cranford, William, 166
Cressy, Hugh Paulinus, 218
Cromwell, Oliver, 14, 15, 22, 83
Cromwell, Thomas, 67

Dalrymple, James, 105, 110
Dalrymple, Sir John, 105
Danvers, Henry, *Murder Will Out*, 81

Davenant, John, 168
Davies, Sir John, 126, 128, 134
De Krey, Gary, 199
Deerham, Sir Richard, 55
Delaune, Gideon, 165
Descartes, René, 144, 174
Digby, George, earl of Bristol, 25
Donaldson, Gordon, 98
Doolittle, Thomas, 57
Douglas, Lord George, earl of Dumbarton, 100
Douglas, William, duke of Hamilton, 103, 105, 106
Douglas, William, duke of Queensberry, 110
Drayton, Michael, 127
Drummond, James, earl of Perth, 100, 101, 105, 106
Drummond, John, earl of Melfort, 100
Dryden, John, 15, 192, 204, 213, 214, 215; *Absalom and Achitophel*, 4, 183–90, 212–15
Dudley, Charles, 51, 52
Dugdale, Sir William, 134
Dunton, John, 58, 60, 67

Edward II, 26
Edward V, 26
Edward the Confessor, 122, 124, 125, 127, 129, 133, 134, 135
Edwards, Sir James, 65
Edwin of Sharnborn, 121, 122, 127, 128, 130, 133, 134
Elizabeth, Queen, 148, 211
Ellwood, Thomas, 52, 53, 61; *Caution to Constables*, 61
Emerson, Timothy, 53
Evelyn, John, 53

Ferguson, Robert, 16, 77, 78, 80, 82, 84, 85, 86, 89, 90, 91, 104; *A Brief Justification of the Prince of Orange's Descent*, 89, 90, 91, 201; *Enquiry into and Detection of the Barbarous Murder of the Late Earl of Essex*, 81
Filmer, Robert, 4; *Patriarcha*, 83, 133, 184, 186, 187, 189, 215
Finch, Heneage, 29, 30, 32, 33, 34
Fleetwood, Charles, 59
Fogg, Martha, 47
Foster, Sir Robert, 33
Foucault, Michel, 121
Fox, George, 13, 57, 61, 63
Fullerton, Sir James, 165

Gaunt, Elizabeth, 86, 87
Gilbert, John, 51

Godfrey, Sir Edmund Berry, 81, 82
Gold, Sir Thomas, 53
Goldie, Mark, 3, 97, 198, 199, 204, 210
Golding, Arthur, 172
Goodenough, Francis, 77, 84
Goodenough, Richard, 49, 77, 84, 88
Gordon, George, duke of Gordon, 100
Gordon, John, earl of Sutherland, 105
Gostlin, John, 168
Gother, John, 218
Goulston, Theodore, 162, 168
Graham, John, earl of Claverhouse, 103
Graham, Richard, 63, 64
Greaves, Richard, 97, 200
Greenberg, Janelle, 3, 4, 18, 201, 207, 208, 215, 217
Greville, Fulke, Lord Brooke, 168
Grey, Ford, Lord Grey of Werk, 77, 80, 84, 88
Grimstone, Sir Harbottle, 23, 24
Gwynn, Owen, 168, 169

Hacker, Francis, 33, 36, 37
Hale, Sir Matthew, 126, 130, 131; *History of the Common Law of England*, 131
Hamilton, James Jay, 173
Hampden, John, 80, 88, 89, 217
Harcourt, Simon, 58
Hardy, John, 104
Harold, King, 123, 133
Harris, Tim, 3, 76, 199, 201, 202, 215
Harrison, Thomas, 24, 29, 30, 31, 32, 33
Hartopp, Sir John, 59
Hay, John, marquis of Tweeddale, 103
Hay, William, 103
Hayward, Sir John, 127, 165
Henrietta Marie, 15
Henry I, 129
Henry IV, 25
Henry V, 25
Henry VI, 26
Henry VII, 35
Herrup, Cynthia, 48
Heveningham, William, 38
Heylyn, Peter, 124
Hickes, Michael, 167
Hilton, George, 43–68 passim, 198, 199
Hilton, John, 43-68 passim, 198, 199; *Conventicle Courant*, 44, 48, 49, 50, 51, 54, 56, 60
Hoak, Dale, 216
Hobbes, Thomas, 4,5, 12, 13, 14, 15, 144, 147, 151, 154, 161–75 passim, 183, 184, 197, 203, 204, 208, 209, 212; *De Cive*, 154; *Leviathan*, 14, 15, 154, 166–67, 174
Holinshed, Raphael, 124
Holles, Sir John, 171
Hollingworth, Richard, 56
Holloway, Sir Richard, 64
Holmes, Richard, 51
Holmes, Oliver Wendell, Jr., 4
Horle, Craig, 58
Hoveden, Roger, 124
Howard, Henry, earl of Northampton, 167, 174
Howard, Thomas, earl of Arundel, 164
Howard, William, Lord Howard of Escrick, 77, 88
Hume, David, 18
Hume, Sir Patrick, 105
Hutton, Ronald, 14, 22, 97, 206
Hyde, Edward, earl of Clarendon, 14, 15, 38, 151
Hyde, Henry, earl of Clarendon, 78
Hyde, Laurence, earl of Rochester, 78

Israel, Jonathan, 216

James I, 21, 75, 113, 128, 148, 163, 164, 165, 168, 173, 174, 209; *Apologie for the Oath of Allegiance*, 174
James II, 2, 5, 15, 17, 18, 62, 63, 65, 66, 68, 75, 82, 86, 88, 89, 90, 97–113 passim, 132, 135, 200, 201, 208, 209, 216–18
Jeffreys, George, 49, 50, 56, 58, 64, 86, 87, 88, 200
Jeffries, Sir Robert, 65
Jenkins, Sir Leoline, 50, 52, 56, 67
Jenner, Sir Thomas, 55, 56, 57, 58, 59, 62, 63, 65, 66
John, King, 130
Johnson, Samuel, 83, 88
Johnston, Nathaniel, *Excellency of Monarchical Government*, 135
Jones, J. R., 217
Jones, John, 32, 33

Keeling, Josiah, 51
Kennett, White, 122, 136, 208
Kindon, Henry, 63
Knights, Mark, 76, 199
Knyghton, Henry, 124

Lake, Peter, 173
Lambarde, William, 124, 125, 130; *Archaionomia*, 129

Lane, Robert, 168
Lawson, George, 127
L'Estrange, Roger, 16, 49, 56, 83, 218; *Observator*, 48, 54
Levy, F. J., 170
Lindsay, Colin, earl of Balcarres, 103
Lindsay, William, earl of Crawford, 106
Lisle, Alice, 87
Littleton, Sir Edward, 131
Lobb, Stephen, 47, 51, 53, 57, 61
Lock, Joshua, 85
Locke, John, 6, 66, 182, 183, 184, 187; *Two Treatises*, 76
Lodge, Thomas, 172

Macaulay, T. B., 1, 5,
Machiavelli, Niccolò, 162, 173, 174, 204, 209
Mackenzie, George, viscount Tarbat, 105, 110
Maguire, Nancy, 206
Maitland, John, earl of Lauderdale, 111
Malcolm, Noel, 161, 162, 208
Marin, Laura, 3, 4, 201, 207, 208, 217
Marten, Henry, 29
Martin, Richard, 165
Marvell, Andrew, 192
Mary II, 7
Mary of Modena, 209
Mason, Robert, 169
May, Thomas, 13, 17
Mayerne, Sir Theodore, 144
Maynard, Sir Henry, 167
Maynard, Sir William, 161, 164, 165, 166, 167, 168, 169, 172
Melville, George, earl of Melville, 105
Micanzio, Fulgenzio, 163, 174
Miller, John, 218
Millington, Gilbert, 38
Milton, John, 13, 191; *Paradise Lost*, 192; *Samson Agonistes*, 181
Mitchison, Rosalind, 98
Monck, George, 22
Montfort, Simon of, 133
Montgomery, Sir James, 105
Moore, Sir John, 52, 55, 78
Morrice, Roger, 62, 64
Murray, John, marquis of Atholl, 105, 110

Nenner, Howard, 18, 198, 205–7
Neville, Henry, 122, 208
Nicholas, Sir Edward, 14
Nicolls, Sir Augustine, 165
Nicolls, Francis, 165, 166
North, Sir Dudley, 49, 55, 66

North, Francis, 53, 55, 56
North, Roger, 57, 66
Norton, Edward, 77
Nutley, James, 34

Oates, Titus, 88
Orby, Sir Thomas, 55
Osborne, Thomas, earl of Danby, 145
Overton, Richard, 60
Owen, John, 59
Owen, Sir Roger, 126; "Of the Common Lawes of England," 127

Paley, Ruth, 66
Paris, Matthew, 124
Papillon, Thomas, 78
Partridge, Nathaniel, 59
Pearse, Edward, 52
Peck, Linda Levy, 5, 204, 208, 209
Penn, William, 57
Pepys, Samuel, 24, 25
Peters, Hugh, 26, 33, 37
Petyt, William, 122, 133, 134, 208
Pilkington, Sir Thomas, 50
Pinfold, Thomas, 56
Pitt, William, 67
Player, Sir Thomas, 50
Plumb, J. H., 182
Pocock, J. G. A., 4, 5, 6, 202–5, 213, 215, 216
Porter, Roy, 67
Pritchard, Sir William, 50, 55
Primrose, James, 165
Prynne, William, 133

Ramsay, William, 165
Rawlins, Edward, *Heraclitus Ridens*, 48
Raymond, Sir Jonathan, 55, 65
Reynolds, Noel, 162, 171
Rich, Peter, 49
Richard II, 25, 26
Richardson, John, 168
Robbins, Caroline, 11, 216
Rosewall, Thomas, 57, 58, 64
Ross, William, Lord Ross, 105, 106
Rowlands, Richard, 124
Rumbold, Richard, 77, 87
Rumsey, John, 77, 80, 88
Russell, Lady Rachel, 7
Russell, William, Lord Russell, 7, 77, 80, 81, 82, 83, 84, 86, 87

Sacheverell, Henry, 58
Sackville, Charles, earl of Dorset, 191

Index

Sackville, Richard, 165, 167
Sancroft, William, 43, 56, 68
Sandford, Sir Richard, 26
Sandys, Sir Edwin, 168
Saunders, Sir Edmund, 56
Savile, George, marquis of Halifax, 78
Savile, Sir Henry, 168
Sawyer, Sir Robert, 83
Saxonhouse, Arlene, 162, 171, 173, 208
Schwoerer, Lois, 2, 5, 6, 7, 11, 12, 17, 18, 98; *The Declaration of Rights*, 5; *No Standing Armies!*, 6; "Seventeenth-Century English Women Engraved in Stone?", 7
Scot, Thomas, 32, 33
Scott, James, duke of Monmouth, 77, 80, 82, 84, 85, 86, 87, 100
Scott, Jonathan, 16
Scott, Robert, 168
Scroop, Adrian, 32, 33
Sculthorpe, Frances, 47
Selden, John, 124, 125, 130
Settle, Elkanah, 214
Shadd, Gabriel, 47, 52, 55, 57, 61, 63, 65
Shafto, Eleanor, 47, 57, 58, 62, 65
Shakespeare, William, 24, 206; *Richard II*, 25
Sharples, John, 47
Sheffield, John, earl of Mulgrave, 191
Shiell, George, 101
Shorter, Sir John, 56
Shower, Bartholomew, 83
Sidney, Algernon, 16, 35, 55, 80, 83, 84, 86, 182, 187; *Discourses concerning Government*, 83
Skinner, Quentin, 163, 208; *Reason and Rhetoric in the Philosophy of Hobbes*, 162
Slaughter, Thomas, 211
Smith, Aaron, 77, 78
Smith, Anne, 65
Smith, Christopher, 47, 60, 62, 65
Smith, Elizabeth, 47, 57, 58
Smith, Hilda, 4, 5, 210, 211, 212; *Reason's Disciples*, 212
Smith, Sir James, 55, 65
Smith, Sir William, 52
Smuts, Malcolm, 209
Sommerville, Johann, 174
Speed, John, 124
Speke, George, 81
Speke, Hugh, 81
Spelman, Sir Henry, 124, 125, 126, 127, 136, 168; *Archaeologus*, 127
Spencer, Robert, earl of Sunderland, 58, 64, 135

Stephens, Robert, 54
Stewart, Sir Francis, 165
Stigand, archbishop of Canterbury, 131
Stone, Lawrence, 7
Storey, Samuel, 85
Stoughton, John, 173
Strauss, Leo, 162
Stuart, Arabella, 164
Sylvester, Ephraim, 47
Sylvester, Matthew, 57

Talbot, Sir John, 58
Talbot, Richard, earl of Tyrconnell, 98
Thomas, Keith, 162, 166, 167
Thompson, Nathaniel, 49, 56, 57; *True Domestic Intelligence*, 48, 54
Thornton, Thomas, 168
Toland, John, 192
Trenchard, John, 77, 80
Trevelyan, G.M., 1
Tulse, Sir Henry, 55
Turner, Sir Edward, 30, 34
Tutchin, John, 83
Twysden, Sir Roger, 126, 129, 130; *Certaine Considerations upon the Government of England*, 130
Tyrrell, James, 122, 127, 136, 184, 187, 208; *Bibliotheca Politica*, 136

Van Dyck, Sir Anthony, 181
van Schurman, Anna, 145
Vaughan, John, 52
Vitalis, Orderic, 131

Wade, Nathaniel, 77, 80, 84, 88
Walcot, Thomas, 77, 78
Walker, Edward, 146
Waller, Sir William, 51
Wallis, John, 154
Ward, John, 51
Ward, Sir Patience, 53, 59, 79
Ward, Samuel, 168
Waterman, Sir George, 55, 65
Webster, John, *Duchess of Malfi*, 173
Weinbrot, Howard, 214
West, Robert, 77
Whitehead, George, 43, 47, 55, 63, 64, 65
Whitelocke, Bulstrode, 127
Wild, Jonathan, 66
Wildman, John, 77
Wilmot, John, earl of Rochester, 13, 190, 191; *Farce of Sodom*, 192–3
William I, 121-137 passim, 207–8

William III, 11, 16, 17, 18, 66, 85, 89, 91, 98, 100, 104, 105, 181, 201, 205, 216–17,
William and Mary, joint monarchs, 75, 91, 108, 109, 110, 111, 112, 113, 205, 209
William, earl of Warenne, 121, 122, 126, 127, 128, 130, 134
Windham, Wadham, 34

Winstanley, Gerard, 151, 212
Wright, Sir Robert, 64
Wrightson, Keith, 50
Wylde, John, 165

Zook, Melinda, 3, 16, 199, 200, 201, 215
Zwicker, Steven, 3, 4, 5, 205, 212–13, 215